Birding Colorado

Help Us Keep This Guide Up to Date

Every effort has been made by the author and editors to make this guide as accurate and useful as possible. However, many things can change after a guide is published—trails are rerouted, roads close, regulations change, techniques evolve, facilities come under new management, etc.

We welcome your comments concerning your experiences with this guide and how you feel it could be improved and kept up to date. While we may not be able to respond to all comments and suggestions, we'll take them to heart, and we'll also make certain to share them with the author. Please send your comments and suggestions to the following address:

The Globe Pequot Press
Reader Response/Editorial Department
P.O. Box 480
Guilford, CT 06437

Or you may e-mail us at:

editorial@GlobePequot.com

Thanks for your input, and happy birding!

Birding Colorado

Over 180 Premier Birding Sites
at 93 Locations

**Hugh E. Kingery
Assisted by Urling C. Kingery**

GUILFORD, CONNECTICUT
HELENA, MONTANA
AN IMPRINT OF THE GLOBE PEQUOT PRESS

FALCONGUIDES®

Text design by Eileen Hine
Maps created by XNR Productions, Inc. © Morris Book Publishing, LLC
Photos by Hugh Kingery, unless otherwise credited.

Library of Congress Cataloging-in-Publication Data
Kingery, Hugh E.
  Birding Colorado : Over 180 premier birding sites
  at 93 locations/ Hugh E. Kingery ; assisted by
  Urling C. Kingery. — 1st ed.
    p. cm. — (A FalconGuide)
  Included bibliographical references.
  ISBN 978-0-7627-3960-8
  1. Bird watching—Colorado Guidebooks. 2.
  Birds—Colorado—Guidebooks. 3. Colorado—
  Guidebooks. I. Title.
  QL684.C6K56 2007
  598.072834788—dc22
2006035291

Manufactured in the United States of America
First Edition/First Printing

To buy books in quantity for corporate use
or incentives, call **(800) 962–0973**
or e-mail **premiums@GlobePequot.com.**

To the mentors who piloted my bird-watching experience:
Bob Niedrach, Dick Beidleman, Howard Cogswell, Bob Arbib,
Alex Cringan, Ron Ryder, and Lois Webster.

To birding companions in Audubon, DFO, CBAP, and CFO.

And to my feathered mentors—the dippers, nuthatches,
chickadees, and other birds of Colorado.

This Gray Jay—also known as a Camp Robber—has a bold demeanor!

Contents

Colorado's Premier Birding Locations

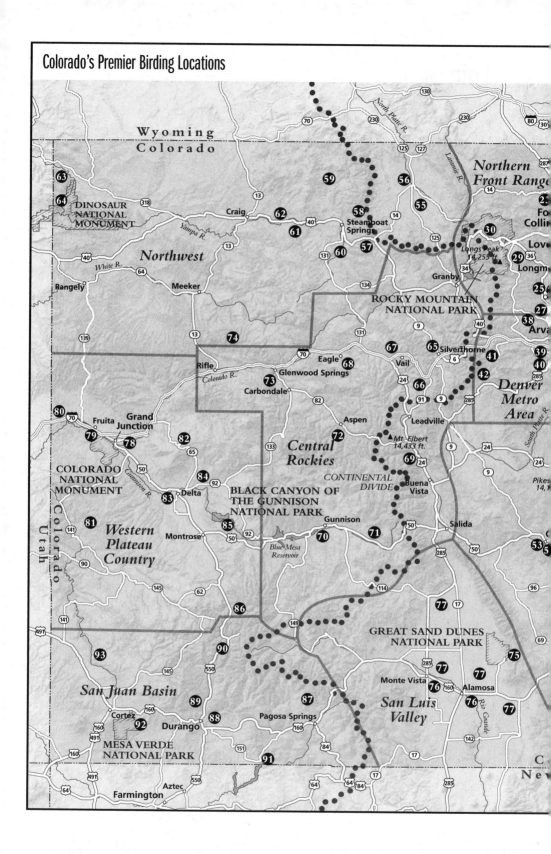

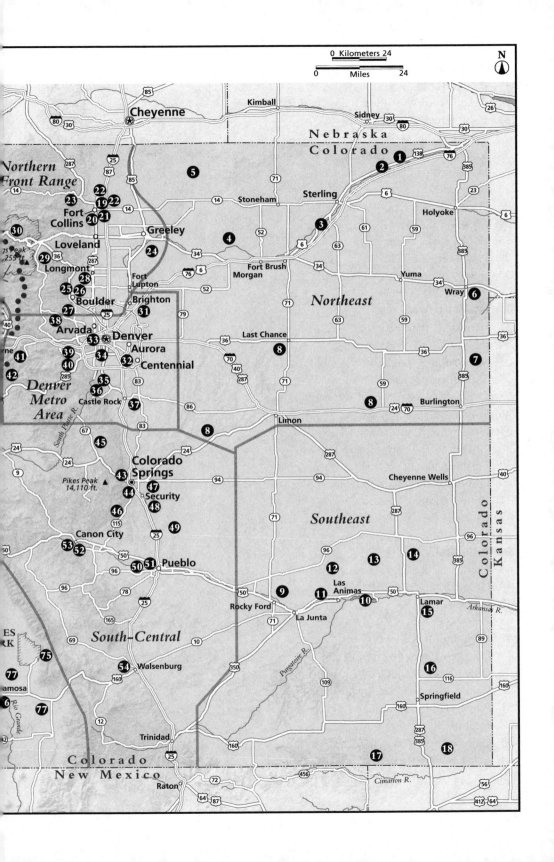

White-tailed Ptarmigan congregate on Guanella Pass year-round.

PHOTO © WILLIAM EDEN

Acknowledgments

A pageant of people helped Urling and me put together this tome, therefore we acknowledge:

Susan Allerton, protector of exotic hummingbirds and director to Durango hot spots;

David Elwonger, who, perched up at Skyway, drafted two Colorado Springs accounts and reviewed all of them;

Carolyn Gunn, who directed us to special places around Cortez;

Allison Hilf, who routed us around Routt (County);

Christy Honnen, who has a sharp editor's eye and an uncanny knack for picking out inconsistencies in style;

Nick Komar, who took us to half a dozen Fort Collins hot spots;

Tony Leukering, an information bank of knowledge of Colorado birds statewide;

Rich Levad, a walking encyclopedia on western Colorado birds and bird places, who reviewed parts of the manuscript with that background plus his eye as an English teacher;

Duane Nelson, who, during his labors to protect Piping Plovers and Least Terns, has amassed a huge amount of knowledge about birds and the places they like in the Arkansas Valley and who amiably shares his data bank;

Stan Oswald, specialist in Arkansas Valley birds around Rocky Ford;

David and Sherrill Pantle, who led us to four splendid sites around Cañon City;

Linda Vidal, who spent two days squiring us to gorgeous places around Aspen and Glenwood Springs;

Mark Yaeger, artist, conservationist, and bird-watcher, who wrote one and reviewed all Pueblo sites;

Jessica Young, who welcomed us to the Gunnison Sage-Grouse lek and filled us with scientific data about this special new species.

Bill Eden, Chris Schultz, and **Glenn Walbek** for contributing their first-rate photographs of birds.

Wendy Shattil and **Bob Rozinski** (www.dancingpelican.com) for yeoman efforts to produce suitable cover photos and for offering their incomparable images.

For directions and advice on specific sites, **Joey Kellner, John Koshak, Steve Larson,** and **Randy Lentz.**

And especially to **Cobirds,** which collects constant chatter about when who saw what where—it and its contributors constitute an invaluable resource for birders in Colorado.

Preface

It all started when my scoutmaster challenged me, at age thirteen, to earn Bird Study Merit Badge on my own. My family had a rustic stone cabin in the foothills west of Lyons, Colorado, in a secluded valley with a perfect trout stream, the North St. Vrain, running through it. (The valley is gone—inundated by Longmont to build Button Rock Dam—but my memories remain.) Armed with the first *Peterson Field Guide to Western Birds* and assisted by my mom and dad, I spent several weeks identifying birds out of the book.

Mom couldn't believe I'd never noticed a Steller's Jay, and Dad showed me a dipper nest on a 40-foot cliff above a special trout hole. Pygmy Nuthatches clamored through the ponderosa pines, and I took pride when I identified a Williamson's Sapsucker. But one bird I absolutely couldn't find in the field guide was an electric blue number with a pink blotch on its breast. Finally after a week, we figured it out: Lazuli Bunting.

That identification challenge stimulated me to a lifelong fascination with birds that I carried through mountain climbing during my high school years, hiking and canoeing during college, a short stint in the Air Force, and law practice in Denver. When my last employer quit business, I switched gears and volunteered to direct the *Colorado Breeding Bird Atlas*—a challenging project that enlisted 1,200 volunteers to survey the breeding birds of the state. We surveyed "blocks" 3 miles on a side, one in each topographic map—1,745 blocks in all. We met the challenge and produced a 636-page book that delineates Colorado's breeding birds.

Urling and I, and lots of companions, "atlased" in over 200 blocks and discovered parts of Colorado we'd never seen before. We drove, we hiked, we backpacked. We studied birds in all parts of Colorado and enjoyed it all (except getting stuck in a mud hole north of Cañon City). We enhanced our appreciation of Colorado birds of the mountains, the plains, the deserts, and the canyons.

We listened to singing Hermit Thrushes in many pockets of the Rockies and Lark Buntings larking across the plains. We watched a Long-billed Curlew frantic because of a bullsnake swallowing eggs in her nest, saw a Barrow's Goldeneye prospect for a nest-hole in the Flattops Wilderness, and confirmed the presence of ptarmigan by finding one white feather. We marooned (briefly) a baby snowshoe hare between us and its mother, and I met a bear face-to-face—we retreated in opposite directions.

Since 1979, Urling and I have taught a class for beginning bird-watchers twice a year, through Denver Audubon, and at Chatfield State Park we "Walk the Wetlands" with Audubon members monthly. We find fulfillment by sharing our Colorado and our Colorado birds with old and new bird-watchers. And frankly, visiting wild places delights me as much as seeing wild things.

We hope you enjoy your Colorado birding trips as much as we do.

Introduction

The varied landscapes of Colorado defy the popular image of a state that has mountains everywhere. Although we do indeed glory in our incomparable mountain scenery, we bird-watchers also glory in the wide-open prairie, pinyon-clad mesas, dazzling canyons, and even mundane reservoirs.

In the flamboyant language of the early twentieth century, Parsons (1911) opined that Colorado visitors "can revel in the magnificence of nature. The curious rock formations, the riot of color in trees and flowers, the flashing rivulets tumbling down the slopes, and the thundering waterfalls awe and exhilarate. . . . A Colorado summer with the eternal hills, beneath a turquoise sky is an unforgettable experience."

The plains have their charm, too. Summer ribbons of green along the streams turn to bands of yellow in fall and then in winter to gray and straw colors. Prairie grasslands undergo subtle changes with the seasons—each lovely in its own way.

With these varied habitats and splendid places and its location in the middle of the continent, Colorado has a bird list of 482 species, ranking it among the top-ten states nationwide. We welcome a mix of eastern and western birds, and we welcome birders from east and west to sample our birds and our scenery.

PHOTO © WILLIAM EDEN

During migration, ducks such as this American Wigeon flock abundantly at reservoirs and lakes all over Colorado.

This guide aims to direct budding Colorado bird-watchers and their congeners from other parts of the country and the world to the most birdy sites in the state. We address two types of enthusiasts: visitors vacationing in a particular place (families, hikers, skiers) and birders who want to design specific birding trips for a day, a weekend, or a week or two.

Mountaingoers find a stable collection of birds pretty well defined by habitat—Pygmy Nuthatches piping in ponderosa pines, Ruby-crowned Kinglets chirruping from spruce trees, and American Pipits larking above timberline. American Dippers patrol tumbling mountain streams and Gray Jays float silently into ski slope restaurants searching for handouts.

The short-grass prairie has its coterie of larking songsters (Horned Lark, Lark Bunting, longspurs, and meadowlarks) and a few specialists such as Mountain Plover. Southeastern Colorado's eclectic mix of species hails from the South and Southwest—Mississippi Kites glide gracefully on insect hunts, Greater Roadrunners and Curve-billed Thrashers sneak around cactus grasslands, Canyon Towhees and Rufous-crowned Sparrows titter from rocky hillsides.

Seven of the nine grouse species of the lower forty-eight states breed here—but a birder must travel to all four corners of Colorado to find them.

Colorado hot-shot birders don't spend much time in the mountains, where they can fairly well predict the birdlife they will find. With Colorado's avifauna primarily western, local listers head for the eastern third of the state to seek errant waterbirds and eastern vagrants. These rarity hunters aim for two habitats: woodlands and the hundreds of reservoirs that add water to a dry landscape. Along stream corridors, several eastern species breed (Red-eyed Vireo, Blue Jay, Eastern Bluebird, Brown Thrasher, and Orchard Oriole), and many more drop in during migration. Reservoirs, built for irrigators and municipalities, now double as recreation sites or wildlife areas. They attract an impressive influx of waterbirds, especially during migration. The state list includes 39 duck species, 42 shorebirds, 20 gulls, 24 flycatchers, 46 warblers, and 31 sparrows and longspurs. The list includes many rarities, most recorded in eastern Colorado.

The *Colorado Breeding Bird Atlas* reported 273 breeding species plus 14 other possible breeders. A few span the state, but many pick specific habitats or geographical regions. Site accounts refer to relevant *Atlas* data to convey an idea of site diversity. (The *Atlas* surveyed "blocks" that are 3 miles long on a side, one in each topographic map.) Birders can consistently find breeding birds in specific sites, and this guide emphasizes those places. Too bad a birder can't bird everywhere in the state in June!

Welcome to our birdlife and to our state.

How to Use This Guide

This book guides you to some of the best places in Colorado for rewarding bird-watching. It tells you how to get there and which birds you might find, and it offers a few facts about history, geology, and ecology. Use it to find tempting places and great birds.

First a few basics:

After each site name, a series of symbols tells you a little about the site:

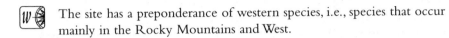 The site has a preponderance of western species, i.e., species that occur mainly in the Rocky Mountains and West.

The site charges an entry fee. Several different entrance fees apply. *National parks* sell passes for the specific park. *National forests* charge user fees in some places. *Colorado state parks* charge a daily or annual fee. You may buy these passes on-site. Some private sites also charge fees.

Colorado Habitat Stamp: As of January 1, 2006, *State Wildlife Areas* instituted a fee system. Everyone who enters a State Wildlife Area must have a Colorado State Habitat Stamp *on his or her person*. This is a *personal pass,* not a vehicle pass. People under eighteen or over sixty-five don't need one. Those with a hunting or fishing license automatically buy this stamp.

You must buy the $10 stamp *before entering* any State Wildlife Area. You can't get one on-site. Stores that sell hunting and fishing licenses sell them; many big twenty-four-hour box stores carry them. You can also buy them by telephone (800–244–5612) or online at http://wildlife.state.co.us/shopdow/appsandlicenses.

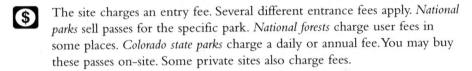 The site has at least one facility—a trail or pier—to accommodate people with physical disabilities.

You can obtain a bird list for this site, usually from an entrance station or visitor center.

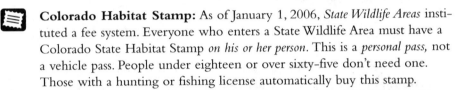 The National Audubon Society recognizes the site as an **Important Bird Area.** This international program identifies sites important to birdlife in one or more respects: breeding, migration, habitat, research. Designation indicates that the owner of the site concurs and has some commitment to management for birds and other wildlife.

The **Habitats** section lists site characteristics. Consult it, below, for birds in that habitat—you should find them at sites that list the particular habitat.

Specialty Birds suggests likely birds at the site. Up to four subheadings list species that you might find *in addition to* those typical of the habitat, by season (resident, summer, migrant, winter).

Best times to bird recommends the time of year to find the most birds at the site.

We next describe the site, first to give you general information about why you might like to visit. **Directions** describe road access: Some are in this special section; some in the text. **The birding** discusses target species and explains where, once you arrive, to look for them. In this section site names in *italics* indicate those within the geographic boundaries of the main entry name; those in **boldface** signify those outside the outline of the entry name.

Maps: You'll need a map to supplement this guidebook. The state of Colorado issues a highway map, as do various vendors, but these lack necessary detail about county and forest roads. Two detailed atlases map back roads: *Colorado Atlas and Gazetteer* published by DeLorme Mapping, P. O. Box 298, Freeport, ME 04032, and *The Roads of Colorado*, Shearer Publishing, 406 Post Oak Road, Fredericksburg, TX 78624. Service stations and other stores that cater to travelers carry one or both. In this guide we reference pages and subdivisions in the first one, the DeLorme guide, for site locations.

Elevation: Listed altitudes represent either the average elevation for relatively level sites or the range of altitudes when driving or hiking involves going up.

Hazards: Lists hazards that you might encounter.

Nearest food, gas, lodging: Lists the closest towns with these amenities.

Camping: Indicates if the *site* has camping facilities; national forests have multiple campgrounds and nearby towns usually have commercial sites. In many parts of the national forests and on Bureau of Land Management land, you may camp anywhere, as long as you place your tent or trailer 100 feet from any water, road, or trail.

For more information: Tells you where to obtain maps, brochures, and more information. We list post office locations, Web sites, and telephone numbers. *Caution:* Web sites and pages have a habit of changing their addresses and names. And sometimes they're not updated in a timely manner, which may limit the usefulness of a site.

Climate

Colorado has more than one climate. It spans an elevation differential of 11,000 feet, from the low point east of Holly where the Arkansas River leaves the state (3,350 feet) to Mount Elbert (14,443 feet). That span and the topography (from the rugged Continental Divide to the barely noticeable Palmer Divide between Colorado Springs and Denver) create local climates of varying temperature, precipitation, and winds. Coloradans use a rule of thumb: For each 300-foot climb in elevation, the temperature drops 1 degree. Average annual temperatures at Pikes Peak and Las Animas (115 miles east) differ by 35 degrees—comparable to the difference between Florida and Iceland. At Manitou Lake west of Colorado Springs, temperatures over sixteen months ranged from −22 degrees to 90 degrees.

A warm day may give way, as you go up, into quite a chilly one. You could start in Estes Park (7,500 feet) at 60 degrees and three hours later on Trail Ridge Road (12,183 feet) find the temperature at 30 degrees. Colorado's dry climate causes cool nights; temperatures routinely drop at night by 40 degrees. Precipitation varies similarly: from 7 inches annually in the San Luis Valley to 36 inches on the Continental Divide just 30 miles away.

Winter weather can change suddenly—so be prepared with extra clothing, food, and blankets to thwart the elements if you somehow get stranded.

> **FIRST GUIDELINE:** Dress in layers. If it warms up, you can shed your parka; if the temperature drops, you can put it back on. Take extra food and blankets just in case.

We have a dry climate. Rainfall varies from 10 inches in the east to 14 inches around Denver to 35 inches just below timberline. Relative humidity is low.

> **SECOND GUIDELINE:** Take along a couple of bottles of water to avoid dehydration. Drink water frequently in both winter and summer.

This is high country. The air is thin. You may find yourself breathless at 4,000 feet, 8,000 feet, or maybe not until 12,000 feet. Allow yourself a couple of days to get used to our oxygen-deprived air.

> **THIRD GUIDELINE:** If you come from sea level, take it easy the first day or two. Drink lots of water.

Another result of thin air: The sun shines more intensely. We do have lots of sunshine, and that means pleasant weather most of the year, but it also means that you can sunburn more readily, summer and winter. (Sun reflecting off the ski slope, the ptarmigan snow pile, or a summer snowbank does an especially good job of burning your skin.)

> **FOURTH GUIDELINE:** Slather sunscreen on all your exposed skin—face, arms, legs, even the backs of your hands. Wear a hat to keep the sun off your face and sunglasses to protect your eyes.

Lightning can strike unexpectedly, on both mountain and plain. During storms or if you hear thunder, retreat, stay off ridges, and avoid high points, caves, and isolated trees.

Bugs and Other Critters

Colorado harbors a few irritating insects and some bigger fauna that you might prefer to avoid. In spring and summer, ticks spring off bushes and, given four to eight hours, burrow into fleshy body parts. The result can be nothing or maybe Rocky Mountain spotted fever—not a healthy experience.

We also have mosquitoes. Some carry West Nile virus, though this threat receded somewhat after 2004. Reservoir shores may harbor other biting insects—from deer and horse flies (impervious to repellents) down to minute no-see-ums; their reigns are seasonally transitory. Squirrels, prairie dogs, and other rodents carry fleas that may carry plague; this kills their hosts and may (rarely) infect humans. A few deer mice carry a lethal disease called hantavirus. Despite these dire descriptions, we haven't heard of any bird-watchers being afflicted by these scary things.

Sad to say, that beautiful clear mountain stream may harbor cysts that cause a debilitating intestinal disease called giardia.

> **FIFTH GUIDELINE:** Take and use insect repellent. Check for ticks before you go to bed. Don't drink water from any stream or lake.

In dry and rocky country, the fauna includes rattlesnakes (active from April to September). Usually they warn before striking, but walk cautiously where you might encounter them. Other attack animals include brown bears (rarely seen), mountain lions (even rarer), moose and bull elk (don't get close), and porcupines (steer clear).

Only one plant poses a problem: Poison ivy grows in many stream bottoms and some hillsides. Recognize its leaves of three and let it be.

Driving

Many dirt roads suggested in this guidebook get muddy and slippery in wet weather. Even the occasional county road gets mucky; Baca County (southeastern corner) has a reputation during wet spells for sending vehicles into borrow pits (roadside ditches where construction "borrowed" dirt to build up the road). Winter driving requires special caution; sudden storms may crop up, or snowbanks may block the road. Don't try to get around them; turn around and go back.

> **SIXTH GUIDELINE:** Drive with care. Avoid muddy roads. Don't buck the snowbank blocking the road.

Roads with steep grades and exposure require extra-cautious driving. As well as brakes, use low gears to slow down. Any time you stop on a busy highway (or not-so-busy road), park well off the traffic lanes, look before you open the door, and don't plop your scope in the middle of the road.

> **SEVENTH GUIDELINE:** Use common sense and good road sense on backcountry roads as well as highways. Use low gears to temper downhill grades.

Other Resources

Colorado has eleven Audubon chapters, several local bird clubs, and a statewide ornithological organization. See **appendix C** for contact information. The Rocky

Mountain Bird Observatory (RMBO) conducts ornithological field activities such as banding stations, landowner incentive programs, and monitoring programs. An e-mail listserve, Cobirds, facilitates reports and discussion of Colorado birds.

Conditions can change drastically in the mountains with little notice. Even in the middle of July, snow may fall and winds may blow as strong as hurricanes. The Colorado Department of Transportation provides road and weather conditions: (303) 639–1111 (in-state toll-free: 877–315–ROAD); www.cotrip.org. You can obtain site-specific weather predictions at www.noaa.gov.

Habitats

Mountains, despite spectacular calendar pictures and the state's license-plate outline, cover only a third of Colorado. Plains in the east occupy 40 percent of the landmass, and in the west a mosaic of valleys, mesas, basins, and ridges introduces different topography and different ecosystems. In between, the famous Rockies burst up in dozens of ranges separated by valleys of the great rivers that rise in the high country: the Colorado, North and South Platte, Arkansas, Rio Grande, San Juan, Gunnison, White, and Yampa.

Colorado's large list of birds flows from a wealth of habitats (and from its middle-of-the-country geographical location). Rarities, especially from the eastern United States, buttress bird lists of parks and reservoirs. Chatfield and Barr Lake State Parks, near Denver, boast bird lists of over 360 species; Bent County claims 374 species; and Pueblo County almost 400, but many on these lists occur only rarely.

Plains

Several habitats spread over the plains: riparian woodlands, short-grass prairie, non-native grasslands, croplands, rural towns and farms with associated shelterbelts, and reservoirs. For the most part, eastern species populate the plains, especially riparian and human-altered sites. Easterners (i.e., anyone from east of Colorado) see more of these species at home.

Short-grass Prairie

Once upon a time, prairie grasses, mainly buffalo grass and blue grama, covered most of eastern Colorado. Agricultural development has left only remnants, except in the Pawnee and Comanche National Grasslands and on some large ranches. Wind and aridity (7 to 10 inches of rain annually) create conditions that cause the two prairie grasses to form a thick turf of short grass 3 to 8 inches tall. After a wet spring, colorful prairie flowers bloom in profusion in June.

Lacking perches from which to declare their territories, prairie songbirds sing on the wing. The dawn chorus on the prairie features larking songsters: Lark Bunting (Colorado's state bird), Horned Lark, Cassin's Sparrow, Chestnut-collared and McCown's Longspurs, and Western Meadowlark. The largely treeless short-grass landscape hosts only a few other breeding birds, each with its own allure.

Burrowing Owls find ready-made tunnel homes in prairie-dog towns, and Mountain Plovers gravitate to them, too, though they also use other parts of the prairie. Swainson's Hawks look for big cottonwoods and Loggerhead Shrikes for small clumps of little trees such as hackberries. Long-billed Curlew (mainly in southeastern Colorado), Ferruginous Hawk, Common Nighthawk, and Grasshopper and Lark Sparrows seek their special niches. Mid- and tall grasslands (there are not many of either) welcome breeding Upland Sandpipers.

In fall Swainson's Hawks mass in the hundreds to scour agricultural fields for grasshoppers before they migrate to South America. Undeterred by the terrain underneath, southbound Sandhill Cranes in flocks of 20 to 500 fly over most of eastern Colorado.

In winter thousands of Horned Lark flock together, often joined by Lapland Longspur, and a contingent of raptors descends on the prairies. Northern Harrier, Rough-legged Hawk, Golden Eagle, Prairie Falcon, and Merlin cruise the landscape seeking rodents, rabbits, and larks.

Prairie Woodlands and Wetlands

Gallery forests of cottonwoods line prairie streams and reservoir edges. These attract, at different times during the year, 75 percent of the species recorded in the state. Most of these birds simply pass along streams as transients. During May landbird migration peaks, and Colorado birders scour their favorite streamsides and reservoir woodlands for eastern flycatchers, vireos, thrushes, warblers, and other rarities. Cottonwood groves with a shrubby understory (more cover and more food) draw a richer variety than those with grassy floors. A breeding-bird census of a cottonwood forest in Chatfield State Park showed a bird density greater than any Colorado habitat except marshes. Many State Wildlife Areas protect islands of these fertile habitats. Plains groves host Northern Bobwhite, Yellow-billed Cuckoo, Red-headed Woodpecker, Eastern Bluebird, and Brown Thrasher. Near the eastern border, stands of trees attract eastern breeders such as Red-bellied Woodpecker, Great Crested Flycatcher, and Orchard and Baltimore Orioles. Dickcissels like weedy patches between shrubby shelterbelts. Cassin's Sparrows specialize in sand-sage and other expanses of low, scattered bushes; in the most easterly part, Bell's Vireos like plum thickets and Field Sparrows breed in grasslands with shrubs.

Small plains towns and rural farmsteads with shelterbelts transformed the high plains into hybridized riparian boroughs. Generalists among the riparian species tolerate the boroughs: Mourning Dove, Western Kingbird, American Robin, Northern Mockingbird, and House Sparrow, among others, and some species prefer rural habitats, for example, Say's Phoebe and Barn Swallow. Chimney Swifts colonized many plains towns, followed now by Eurasian Collared-Doves. Northern Cardinals reside in one place only: residential sections of Wray, 10 miles from Nebraska. (In the last five years, they have become regulars in two other places: at the South

Cottonwoods dominate eastern Colorado river bottoms.

Platte River within 30 miles of Nebraska and the Arkansas River within 30 miles of Kansas.)

Historically, plains rivers lacked the green ribbon of cottonwoods that today marches from the state line to the foothills; rampaging spring floods swept clean the river channels, and nibbling bison munched the remaining tender saplings. As settlement removed both factors, trees grew and the streams became corridors for expanding species. Blue Jay and Common Grackle advanced upstream to become common breeders in the cities of the Front Range, and Least Flycatcher and American Redstart timidly moved to the edge of the foothills.

Regular migrants include Swainson's Thrush (abundant in late May), Orange-crowned, Yellow-rumped, and Wilson's Warblers, flycatchers, and orioles. Lark Buntings, in flocks of hundreds, roll over the prairie in May. Shrubby thickets and grassy glades on the plains draw migrating sparrows: Chipping, Clay-colored, Brewer's, Vesper, Lark, and White-crowned. In winter White-throated and Harris's Sparrows sometimes accompany the abundant American Tree and White-crowned Sparrows.

Southeastern Colorado sports a mixture of southeastern and southwestern U.S. species. Riparian zones feature Mississippi Kite (in Arkansas Valley cities from Pueblo downstream), Yellow-billed Cuckoo, Greater Roadrunner, Ladder-backed Woodpecker, and Eastern Phoebe. They share some species with western riparian streamsides: Western Screech-Owl, Black-chinned Hummingbird, and Lewis's Woodpecker. On brushy, rocky hillsides, Scaled Quail scurry and Rufous-crowned Sparrows sneak around and sing a subdued trilling song. A few Curve-billed

Thrashers stay year-round where a cactus nicknamed "cholla" sprinkles the grassland, and Chihuahuan Ravens nest on power poles.

Lakes and Reservoirs

The plains lack any sizable natural bodies of water, but irrigation and municipal projects created hundreds of reservoirs of varying sizes and varying abilities to attract birds. Particularly productive reservoirs lie between Denver and Fort Collins, northeasterly along the South Platte River from Fort Morgan to the state line, and along the Arkansas River from Pueblo to the state line. A few isolated reservoirs function as oases amid deserts of grassland or wheat fields (for example, Two Buttes and Bonny). Their water and trees draw migrating waterbirds and land birds.

American White Pelican and California Gull breed in fewer than five sites, although nonbreeders populate many reservoirs. From July to October flocks of Franklin's Gulls spend the night on safe reservoirs and in daylight fan out to feed on flying insects above croplands, urban centers, and mountains (sometimes joined by Common Nighthawks). In late fall, birders search eastern Colorado reservoirs for straggling scoters, grebes, loons, jaegers, and gulls.

Water regimes of irrigation reservoirs directly impact bird distribution, especially shorebirds. Irrigators fill their reservoirs during the winter—October to April—and use the water during the summer months. By August drawdowns of reservoirs that brimmed with water in May create muddy and sandy shorelines that attract migrating shorebirds. The palette can vary from arctic migrants to oceanic vagrants—from Long-tailed Jaeger to White-winged Scoter, from Buff-

Prairie wetlands act as oases for migrating birds looking for relief from monotonous grasslands, desert shrubs, and croplands.

breasted Sandpiper to Long-billed Murrelet! Which reservoir pulls in the most shorebirds varies year to year among Chatfield, Cherry Creek, Barr, Jackson, Prewitt, Bonny, Blue, Great Plains, and others. In October 2000 Jackson Lake held 7,500 American White Pelicans; in October 2003 it had only 25 to 50.

Reservoirs often nourish marshes on their shores, inlets, or below leaking dams and create habitat for breeding and migrating marsh birds. Semivagrants nest in a few places: Great and Snowy Egret, Green Heron, Snowy and Piping Plovers, and Least Tern. Avid birders have found Black Rail—unknown in Colorado before 1991—in over a dozen marshes along the Arkansas River.

Mountain and Western Slope Reservoirs

The largest and deepest natural lake in Colorado, Grand Lake, covers a measly 600 acres; immediately downstream two larger reservoirs (Shadow Mountain and Granby) store water sent by tunnel under the Continental Divide to irrigate farmlands and provide municipal water supplies to the northern Front Range. Dams control the water flow of all the major rivers. Mountain reservoirs, for the most part, attract few waterbirds. IBA Fruitgrowers Reservoir east of Delta stands out as an excellent exception. North Park and the San Luis Valley also buck the norm, each supporting several wildlife refuges and impressive arrays of waterbirds and shorebirds.

Mountain and Plateau Country

Mountain scenery occupies the center of the state. The Colorado Rockies tumble up and down; peaks rise 7,000 feet above the plains (Pikes Peak) or merely 4,000 feet above the valley (Mounts Massive and Elbert). Coloradans contend that if you flattened it out, Colorado would be bigger than Texas.

Within the space of 5 miles, a peak with a bottom-to-top span of 5,000 feet may contain five ecological zones, with an accompanying span of birds. The 10-square-mile *Colorado Breeding Bird Atlas* block in Rocky Mountain National Park recorded ninety-three species in nine habitats.

The Colorado Rockies have a limited variety of trees (ten species of conifers plus aspen and narrow-leaf cottonwood) that tend to grow in pure stands, separated by altitude and latitude. Five main ones form distinct ecological niches. Elevation provides a clue to likely birds because it equates to tree species. By distinguishing tree species, birders can anticipate the birds they will find. Within a particular habitat, subniches exist so that, for example, a parklike ponderosa pine woodland attracts more species than ponderosas growing densely with no understory of grasses or shrubs.

Pinyon/Juniper ("P/J") (4,500 to 8,000 feet)

The "pygmy forest" of pinyon pine and juniper blankets the arid mesa and canyon country; the trees grow 20 feet tall and are usually widely spaced. This ecosystem dominates the Western Slope from Wyoming to New Mexico, Eastern Slope hills and mesas from Colorado Springs and Buena Vista south, and the fringe of the San Luis Valley. At higher elevations pinyon pines predominate, and in lower, hotter, drier situations, only junipers grow. Poor soil in many places supports only a sparse understory. Controlling runoff, a thin blackish crust of algae, fungi, lichen, and other micro-organisms creates "cryptogammic" soil that bonds the surface. A delicate organism, the crust, once disturbed or crunched (for example, by birders' feet) breaks down and erosion accelerates. The most accessible and productive pinyon/juniper stands occur in national park properties: Mesa Verde, Black Canyon, Colorado, and Dinosaur.

P/J has its special suite of bird specialists: Gray Flycatcher, Pinyon Jay, Juniper Titmouse, and Black-throated Gray Warbler. In low-elevation "juniper savannahs," Gray Vireo and a few Scott's Orioles nest; higher up in more mixed P/J, Plumbeous Vireo replaces Gray. Clark's Nutcrackers exhibit a fascinating adaptation to P/J. One bird can gather 120 pinyon seeds in a throat pouch and carry them to higher breeding grounds, bury them individually on south-facing slopes, and six months later remember where it stashed the seeds (sometimes 6,000 in a season) and retrieve them to feed to its young.

Ponderosa Pine (6,500 to 8,500 feet; 10,000 feet in South Park)
An ideal, mature ponderosa woodland features large-trunked trees, spaced wide apart, with grasses and forbs growing in between. Over 150 years of western settlement altered these woodlands; now many ponderosa stands consist of small to medium-size trees, often crowded together. Fire suppression, building, and logging caused the changes. Parklike ponderosa stands provide the best places to sample ponderosa birds, but many comparatively dense forests also support the typical species.

Pygmy Nuthatch and Western Bluebird specialize in ponderosas. The pines also attract Williamson's Sapsucker, Northern (Red-shafted) Flicker, Western Wood-Pewee, Plumbeous Vireo, Steller's Jay, Mountain Chickadee, White-breasted Nuthatch, and Western Tanager.

Aspen (7,500 to 10,000 feet)
Quaking aspens form the only deciduous forest in the Colorado Rockies. "By sitting still and watching you can see how the pale shining greenness of new leaves moves up the steep hillsides in the spring and how the duskier reds, oranges, and yellows flow back down in the autumn" (Lavender, in Griffiths, 1984). Coloradans treasure the last half of September for golden aspen gleaming in the sun. Many aspen groves suffer from unwelcome attention by elk and deer, which nibble on the bark, stunt tree growth, and chew seedlings to the ground. They particularly afflict the aspen in Rocky Mountain National Park.

The aspen indicator bird, Warbling Vireo—by far the most abundant species in this habitat—sings from almost every acre of aspen forest and even from patches of only three to five aspens surrounded by conifers. Branches of rustling leaves pro-

Aspen groves form the only deciduous woodlands in the Colorado Rockies.

vide nest sites for vireos and other cup-nesting birds. Woodpeckers and sapsuckers drill holes that swallows, chickadees, nuthatches, wrens, and bluebirds use in the following year(s). One aspen may host five hole-nesting species at once.

Lodgepole Pine (8,000 to 10,500 feet)
Lodgepoles usually grow in dense stands with little undergrowth; they present a uniform habitat and a limited number of birds—both variety and quantity. They host many of the same species that nest in spruce/fir, though the latter habitat supports greater densities of all except Red Crossbill.

Spruce/fir (10,000 to 11,500 feet)
The high-elevation forests of Engelmann spruce and subalpine fir thrive in a moist environment and sustain boreal species. Some of these birds breed at lower elevations, but the spruce/fir forest offers better breeding habitat and supports greater numbers of each species.

Ruby-crowned Kinglets, tiny birds with a huge voice, chirrup every 50 feet along a trail through spruce/fir. Quieter Yellow-rumped (Audubon's) Warbler and Pine Siskin occur almost as densely. Haunting melodies from Hermit Thrushes echo over the high valleys, particularly at dawn and dusk. American Three-toed Woodpecker and Gray Jay move silently through the trees, and the Boreal Owl feeds voraciously on red-backed voles.

Alpine Tundra (11,500 to 13,000 feet)

Plants in the tundra—alpine grassland—merit close study as they grow only a few inches tall. Exquisite flowers carpet the tundra with bright spots of color. Above 13,000 feet the rocky terrain attracts few nesting species; ravens, pipits, and rosy-finches may explore the really high peaks, but they usually nest lower down. Black Swifts, seeking flying ants far from their midelevation waterfalls, may careen past the peak tops.

The two alpine specialties, White-tailed Ptarmigan and Brown-capped Rosy-Finch, prefer different parts of the alpine zone. Ptarmigan, feathered to blend in with the rocks and convinced they are invisible, skulk through grassy hillocks or scoot along and through snowy drifts. (In winter they roost by tunneling into the snow.) They nest on the ground, sometimes on very steep slopes. Rosy-finches (chocolate brown with bellies colored lingerie-pink), build their nests on steep rock faces, finding space in cracks in the cliffs. To feed, they fly from their cliffs to patches of snow. There they search for insects and seeds in receding snowbanks, often far from their nests.

American Pipits, true birds of the tundra, sing in the air and flutter down to grassy knolls to rest, to feed, and to breed. Only four other species nest above timberline: Horned Larks pick drier tundra than pipits. A few Rock Wrens putter among talus slopes (rock slides), and occasionally Prairie Falcon and Common

Engelmann spruce and subalpine fir drape the mountainsides across the Colorado high country, such as here, near Independence Pass.

Summer flowers carpet the tundra with vivid palettes of color.

Raven nest on cliffs. Breeding Wilson's Warbler and White-crowned Sparrow follow willow-covered streams up above timberline.

In late summer other species venture above timberline. Hummingbirds seek lush flower fields, Mountain Bluebirds look for insects, Northern Harriers cruise low over the tundra, and Swainson's Hawks soar above it. American Kestrel and Merlin seek pikas and mice. Then other surprises materialize: a Western Kingbird flycatching from a rock outcropping, a Pygmy Nuthatch piping from stunted spruces.

Foothills Riparian, Willow Carrs, and Montane Meadows (6,500 to 12,000 feet)
Across the state, willow bushes (several species) line high mountain streams in shrubby patches called "willow carrs." Among the willows, scattered aspen, spruce, and fir provide perches and vary the uniformity of the willow brush. At higher elevations 6-foot willows harbor one set of species, 12-foot willows a different mix.

Stream vegetation provides nest sites and singing perches for Dusky Flycatcher, Yellow, MacGillivray's, and Wilson's Warblers, and Song, Lincoln's, and White-crowned Sparrows. Swainson's Thrush and Fox Sparrow favor large willows (taller than 10 feet). Rarely, you may notice a Dusky Grouse furtively stepping by a streamside or mountain meadow.

As mountain streams drop through the foothills, trees move in—narrow-leaf cottonwoods and Colorado blue spruce. At these lower elevations (6,000 to 8,500 feet) taller shrubs such as birch, alder, and maple crowd the streamsides. Foothills riparian trees and bushes—coniferous and deciduous—grow separately as well as in combination. They draw birds from the plains below and the conifer forests above.

Nearby hillsides often have open meadows, in summer festooned with brilliant flowers. Mountain Bluebirds forage, and House Wren and Vesper Sparrow burble. Broad-tailed and Rufous Hummingbirds sample flower fields all the way to timberline and higher.

Shrublands (5,000 to 9,000 feet)

A variety of shrubby habitats grows across the state, most extensively in western Colorado. Gambel oak ("scrub oak") fills foothill canyons south from Denver and blankets mountainsides on the Western Slope. Often other shrubs grow among the oaks: mountain mahogany, three-leaf sumac, squaw currant, snowberry, and others. In the San Juan Basin, scrub oak grows in ponderosa woodlands—and Grace's Warbler and Dusky Flycatcher like that. At higher east-slope elevations and on the Western Slope, taller bushes such as serviceberry, chokecherry, bitterbrush, and buckbrush create thick shrublands.

Scrub oak and montane shrubs support a similar mix of birds: You'll hear the small songs of Orange-crowned, Virginia's, and MacGillivray's Warblers, the more varied Green-tailed and Spotted Towhees songs, and the scratchy voices of Blue-

Scrub oak grows in patches and at the edges of ponderosa (here) and pinyon pines.

The breathtaking view of Unaweep Canyon from Divide Road, Uncompahgre Plateau.

gray Gnatcatchers. From oak brush, Western Scrub-Jays screech and Black-headed Grosbeaks warble.

At mid-elevations sagebrush and other shrubs line hillsides and provide another habitat and subset of birds. In several parts of the state, sagebrush covers the landscape; it grows extensively in Gunnison and Moffat Counties, the southern San Luis Valley, and Dry Creek Basin in western San Miguel County. Sagebrush stands sustain Greater and Gunnison Sage-Grouse, Sage Thrasher, Green-tailed Towhee, Brewer's and Vesper Sparrows, and the ringing songs of Western Meadowlarks. Sage Sparrows prefer the sagebrush of far western Colorado.

Canyon and Mesa Country

Western rivers provide habitat islands like those on the plains, although the surrounding habitat varies from desert to P/J to lush shrubland to high mountains. Narrow-leaf cottonwood replaces plains cottonwood, often with lusher shrubby understories, in Nature Conservancy sites on the Yampa and San Miguel Rivers. Other stretches of the western rivers (and the Arkansas east of Pueblo) have been blitzed by the exotic, water-guzzling, nonbirdy tamarisk bush (aka salt cedar).

Here the birds have a distinct western flavor: Gambel's Quail, Western Screech-Owl, Black-chinned Hummingbird, Lewis's Woodpecker, Black Phoebe, and Bewick's Wren. Land birds migrate more sparsely here, although Ruby-crowned Kinglet and Wilson's Warbler move through in numbers.

These western birds reside in memorable river canyons: the Gunnison through Black Canyon, the San Miguel, the Dolores from Slick Rock to Gateway, and the Yampa and Green Rivers in Dinosaur National Monument.

Semi-desert Shrubland

Parts of the western quarter and the southern tier have a different landscape. Desert, grasslands, and vast expanses of sagebrush, greasewood, and other bushes surround mesas and ridges covered with woodlands of pinyon pines and junipers.

In the western plateau country (4,000 to 6,500 feet) and the San Luis Valley (7,500 to 8,000 feet), low-growing shrubs with narrow, water-saving leaves cover vast expanses; these include greasewood, shadscale, saltbush, and rabbitbrush. Bushes grow a bit taller along watercourses. Few bird species use this habitat (one San Luis Valley *Atlas* block had only six breeding species).

Sometimes we read nostalgically of early ornithologists—the birds they saw and the adventures they faced. Colorado's environment has changed significantly since 1858 when western settlement started to leave indelible marks. Remnants of mining persist throughout the mountains, croplands grow where buffalo grass once dominated, reservoirs pepper the plains. Ranching, logging, urban centers, and recreation all leave marks. Our appetite for fossil fuels, shopping malls, bluegrass lawns, ski slopes, and hiking trails affects birdlife. Some new features bring in rare birds that excite bird-watchers; some make it easier for bird-watchers to find birds. But all somehow affect the landscape and the wildlife. Still Colorado retains such a variety of habitats that visiting birders may indulge in quite satisfactory forays throughout the state.

Birding Ethics

FalconGuides encourage our readers to follow the American Birding Association's Code of Birding Ethics. We hope that everyone who enjoys birds and birding will always respect wildlife, its environment, and the rights of others. In any conflict of interest between birds and birders, the welfare of the birds and their environment comes first.

American Birding Association's Code of Birding Ethics
1. Promote the welfare of birds and their environment.

(a) Support the protection of important bird habitat.

(b) To avoid stressing birds or exposing them to danger, exercise restraint and caution during observation, photography, sound recording, or filming.

Limit the use of recordings and other methods of attracting birds, and never use such methods in heavily birded areas, or for attracting any species that is Threatened, Endangered, or of Special Concern, or is rare in your local area.

Keep well back from nests and nesting colonies, roosts, display areas, and important feeding sites. In such sensitive areas, if there is a need for extended observation, photography, filming, or recording, try to use a blind or hide, and take advantage of natural cover.

Use artificial light sparingly for filming or photography, especially for close-ups.

(c) Before advertising the presence of a rare bird, evaluate the potential for disturbance to the bird, its surroundings, and other people in the area, and proceed only if access

Pine Grosbeaks, a quiet bird of the subalpine forest, fill their crops with seeds to feed their young.

can be controlled, disturbance minimized, and permission has been obtained from private landowners. The sites of rare nesting birds should be divulged only to the proper conservation authorities.

(d) Stay on roads, trails, and paths where they exist; otherwise keep habitat disturbance to a minimum.

2. Respect the law and the rights of others.

(a) Do not enter private property without the owner's explicit permission.

(b) Follow all laws, rules, and regulations governing use of roads and public areas, both at home and abroad.

(c) Practice common courtesy in contacts with other people. Your exemplary behavior will generate goodwill with birders and nonbirders alike.

3. Ensure that feeders, nest structures, and other artificial bird environments are safe.

(a) Keep dispensers, water, and food clean and free of decay or disease. It is important to feed birds continually during harsh weather.

(b) Maintain and clean nest structures regularly.

(c) If you are attracting birds to an area, ensure the birds are not exposed to predation from cats and other domestic animals, or dangers posed by artificial hazards.

4. Group birding, whether organized or impromptu, requires special care. Each individual in the group, in addition to the obligations spelled out in item nos. 1 and 2, has responsibilities as a group member.

(a) Respect the interests, rights, and skills of fellow birders, as well as people participating in other legitimate outdoor activities. Freely share your knowledge and experience, except where code 1(c) applies. Be especially helpful to beginning birders.

(b) If you witness unethical birding behavior, assess the situation, and intervene if you think it prudent. When interceding, inform the person(s) of the inappropriate action, and attempt, within reason, to have it stopped. If the behavior continues, document it, and notify appropriate individuals or organizations.

Group leader responsibilities (amateur and professional trips and tours).

(c) Be an exemplary ethical role model for the group. Teach through word and example.

(d) Keep groups to a size that limits impact on the environment and does not interfere with others using the same area.

(e) Ensure everyone in the group knows of and practices this code.

(f) Learn and inform the group of any special circumstances applicable to the areas being visited (for example, no tape recorders allowed).

(g) Acknowledge that professional tour companies bear a special responsibility to place the welfare of birds and the benefits of public knowledge ahead of the company's commercial interests. Ideally, leaders should keep track of tour sightings, document unusual occurrences, and submit records to appropriate organizations.

Please follow this code and distribute and teach it to others.

The American Birding Association's Code of Birding Ethics may be freely reproduced for distribution/dissemination. Please visit the ABA Web site at www.americanbirding.org.

Map Legend

Interstate	70	Continental Divide	• • • • •
US highway	6	Waterfall	
State highway	133	Parking	P
Road		Picnic area	
River		Peak	▲
Intermittent stream		Dam	
National Park boundary		Pass	) (
Trail		Bridge	
County boundary		Lake	
State boundary		Four-wheel-drive only	

Abbreviations

BLM: Bureau of Land Management

NWR: National Wildlife Refuge

P/J: Pinyon/juniper

RMBO: Rocky Mountain Bird Observatory

RMNP: Rocky Mountain National Park

SWA: State Wildlife Area

Northeast

Northeastern Colorado (and the whole eastern plains), once short-grass prairie and river bottom, changed drastically with settlement. Bison once roamed the prairie in unimaginable numbers, and prairie-dog towns stretched from horizon to horizon. The prairie and prairie-dog towns shrank, and bison disappeared. Streams turned greener, and water arrived in reservoirs for irrigation and flood control; small towns, farms, irrigated crops, and grazing cattle now occupy the former grasslands.

For birds, this means lost opportunities for grassland specialists and new habitat for waterbirds. It means openings for species with different tastes: Ring-necked Pheasant in farmlands, Chimney Swift in towns, Western Kingbird and Mourning Dove in farmsteads and shelterbelts. The green ribbons of the streams bring in riparian species that probably used to occur rarely, if at all. On its way to Nebraska, the South Platte River now flows through continuous cottonwood woodland where public ownership allows access to a few fruitful birding spots. Road networks tempt birders to scrutinize seemingly monotonous habitats that yield surprising migrants.

For bird-watchers, this means new opportunities to find riparian species but limited places for prairie birds such as Mountain Plover, prairie-chickens, and longspurs. The best short-grass prairie left in Colorado, Pawnee National Grassland consists of a checkerboard of public and private sections that sprawls over 1,800 square miles. Roads open the grassland to birders seeking prairie birds. Reservoirs in the South Platte valley attract tantalizing waterfowl, shorebirds, and gulls that would have passed over the prairie 200 years ago. (One wonders: These birds must have flown over the seamless prairie then. Did they survive? Did they land in the shallow rivers? Did they perish for want of suitable habitat? Does the new landscape rescue otherwise doomed birds, or does it attract birds that might otherwise use alternate routes?)

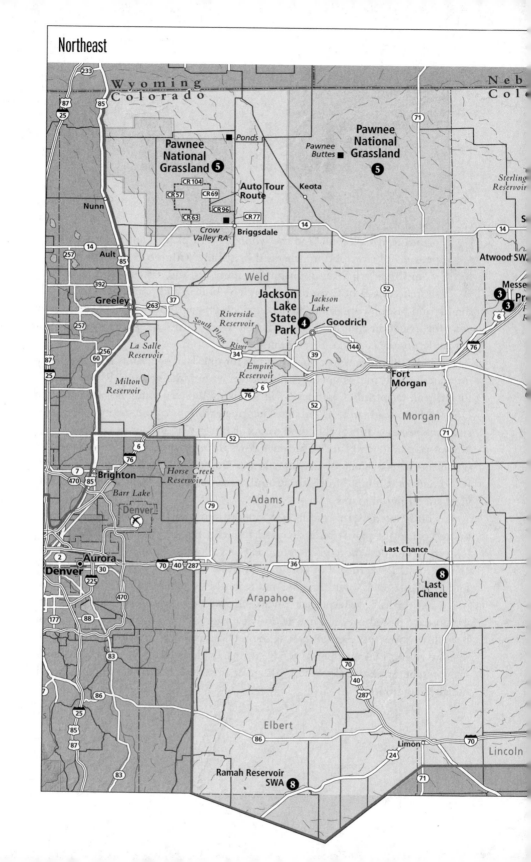

Northeast

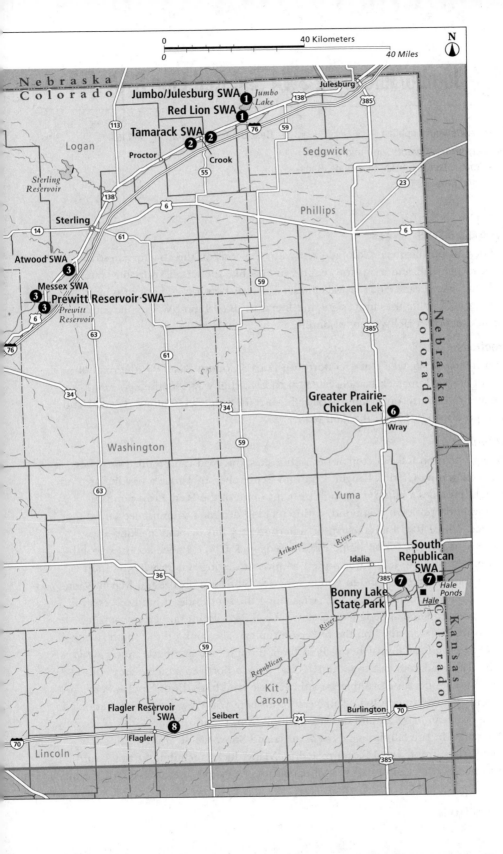

Jumbo/Julesburg SWA and Red Lion SWA

Habitats: Wetlands, riparian.

Specialty birds: *Migrant:* Snow and Greater White-fronted Geese, ducks, shorebirds, Bonaparte's and Sabine's Gulls.

Best times to bird: Spring and fall.

About this site

Birdiness of northeastern Colorado reservoirs depends on three factors: upstream snowpack, rainfall, and irrigation regime. Jumbo, like the rest, has variable water levels and, like several Arkansas Valley reservoirs, has two names, both of which the Division of Wildlife uses in its signs and literature. Red Lion SWA's ponds and marshes support a rich variety of birdlife.

Directions

From Interstate 76, take exit 155 north on Logan County Road 93 (the road on the east end of Tamarack Ranch, Site #2) to U.S. Highway 138, then go east 1 mile and turn north on County Road 95. Easterly, Sedgwick County Roads 1 and 3 also go from US 138 to the dam road.

The birding

Driving north on CR 95, stop at promising sites; this road can produce surprises such as migrating Cassin's Kingbirds in mid-September. In 1 mile a parking area on the right provides a glimpse through trees into one of the **Red Lion** ponds; a nature trail drops down to a pond, with screening designed to minimize bird disturbance. To see Red Lion's marsh or waterbirds, try this or other parking areas, either on Logan CR 95 or a mile east on Sedgwick CR 1. Public access is prohibited from April 15 to July 15, as posted, to protect nesting waterfowl. Red Lion pulls in some shorebirds, and in winter look for Northern Shrike and Marsh Wren.

The dam road, County Road 97, runs along the south side of Jumbo Reservoir and gets renumbered as Sedgwick County Road 24.8. From numerous vantages you can inspect waterfowl on the reservoir. You can also look off the south side at the tall trees and cattail marshes in Red Lion, though trees and birds are far away.

The dam road goes east to County Road 3; turn north to a picnic area with lines of trees (Siberian elms) that sometimes have land birds. Both Eastern Screech-Owl and Great Horned Owl occur here. From here you view a different section of the lake. You can drive around the lake to look from the north side—stop at any parking area. In late fall thousands of Canada and Snow Geese arrive, with a few Greater White-fronted and Ross's mixed in. Many ducks, including, at times, substantial numbers of Canvasbacks (and many more Mallards), use the lake. Migration brings several hundred shorebirds, which might include Ruddy Turnstone or Sanderling. Laughing, Franklin's, Bonaparte's, Lesser Black-backed, and Sabine's Gulls, many Black Terns, and a few Forster's Terns stop here, and this reservoir had the first Colorado Ross's Gull (1983). In 2005 a handful of Common Loons spent the summer here.

Migrating land birds show up in the trees. The list includes Magnolia, Black-burnian, and Palm Warblers, American Redstart, and Golden-crowned Sparrow, along with more usual ones. American Pipits ply the sandy shores and may occasionally become a meal for a Prairie Falcon. Goshawks also show up occasionally.

DeLorme grid: P. 95 A7.

Elevation: 3,700 feet.

Nearest food, gas, lodging: Sterling, food and gas in Julesburg.

Camping: Yes.

For more information: Colorado Division of Wildlife, 317 West Prospect, Fort Collins, CO 80526; (970) 842-6300; http://wildlife.state .co.us/landwater/statewildlifeareas.

Each summer American White Pelicans throng to reservoirs east of the mountains even though they breed at only three to six sites.

② Tamarack SWA 📄

Habitats: Riparian.

Specialty birds: *Resident:* Red-bellied Wood-pecker, Carolina Wren, Eastern Bluebird. *Summer:* Yellow-billed and Black-billed Cuckoos, Red-headed Woodpecker, Bell's Vireo. *Migrant:* Eastern warblers, flycatchers, vireos, and other migrants.

Best times to bird: Year-round, but great during migration.

About this site

Tamarack has the finest riparian habitat in northeastern Colorado. The SWA stretches along 15 miles of the river. It offers excellent birding and, close to the state line, has a bird list that features a large contingent of eastern species, both breeders and migrants.

Tamarack lies along the Overland Trail, heavily used during the Colorado gold rush by prospectors, speculators, and other immigrants, and also by the Pony Express. The map at the entrance to the East section marks sites of four stagecoach stations; despite the map's legend, only one monument exists so far, on County Road 38.5 next to East Area 16.

Directions

The most direct way to this outstanding riparian preserve leaves I–76 at the Crook exit (149) onto Highway 55. The area has East and West sections; the Division of Wildlife has marked "Areas" for parking and access, mainly to accommodate hunters. Enter the East section (0.6 mile north of I–76) by going east on County Road 38.5 for 1.5 miles, and turn left where the sign announces Areas 5–12. (Road 38.5 passes by Areas 1–4, which sit above the river in the grassland.) The map at the east entrance errs in its depiction of Areas 5–12: Despite the map, you're supposed to turn around at Area 12. *Do not* continue east to connect to County Road 38.5. Drive to Area 12, then go back to Road 38.5. You can either go back to Highway 55 and try the west side or follow Road 38.5 east past more numbered areas to County Road 93 and then north to US 138 or south to I–76.

The birding

One could spend a whole day exploring Tamarack's trees, shrubs, and marshes. Park in any Area to walk into the woodland or to walk along the road. Birders spend most of their time closer to Highway 55 simply because they reach those places first and achieve quick gratification.

At East Areas 5–12, shelterbelts stretch south (right) with junipers and Russian olives; some have cottonwoods and wild plums. In weedy fields between the Russian-olive hedgerows, Dickcissel and Field Sparrow sing in June. On the left the woodland stretches a quarter mile or so to the river. (From Highway 55, you can also walk directly into the East section by parking at the entrance to a service road, but don't block the gate.)

The West section (immediately beyond Road 38.5 at a break in the guardrail) has twenty-five Areas that an ambitious birder with ample leisure time can sample. This road dead-ends, so you have to retrace back to Highway 55. You can walk the road or plunge into the riparian habitat between the road and the river from any of the Area lots.

Red-bellied (year-round) and Red-headed (April through October), as well as Hairy and Downy, Woodpecker noisily feed and fly through the tall trees. Eastern Screech-Owl and Eastern Bluebird stay year-round. Breeding species include Black-billed and Yellow-billed Cuckoos, Long-eared Owl, Great Crested Flycatcher (possibly), and Bell's Vireo. Migrants include Eastern Wood-Pewee, Cassin's Kingbird, Blue-headed Vireo, Worm-eating Warbler, Ovenbird, Northern Waterthrush, Northern Cardinal (winters), White-throated Sparrow, Rose-breasted Grosbeak, and Indigo Bunting. In winter a Northern Goshawk, Townsend's Solitaire, Hermit Thrush, or Harris's Sparrow may slip in.

For another habitat, if coming from the west on I–76, try exit 141 to Proctor. Go north 1.4 miles to U.S. Highway 6 and turn right on US 138. From Proctor to Julesburg, the highway passes through agricultural fields and prairie where Upland Sandpiper and Burrowing Owl breed. Look for a 2-mile-long prairie-dog town that starts about a mile northeast of Proctor and spans both sides of County Road 71. Burrowing Owl and other prairie species hang out here; scanning from County Road 71 is probably safer than from the fairly busy US 138.

Birders on forays on backcountry roads report Sprague's Pipit in October and Short-eared Owl and Lapland Longspur in January.

DeLorme grid: P. 95 A6.

Elevation: 3,700 feet.

Hazards: Poison ivy.

Nearest food, gas, lodging: Sterling, food and gas in Julesburg.

Camping: No.

For more information: Colorado Division of Wildlife, 317 West Prospect, Fort Collins, CO 80526; (970) 886-2992; http://wildlife.state .co.us/landwater/statewildlifeareas.

3 Prewitt Reservoir SWA ♿ 📖

Habitats: Wetlands, riparian.

Specialty birds: *Resident:* Northern Bobwhite, Red-bellied Woodpecker. *Migrant:* Rare shore-birds, land birds.

Best times to bird: August to November.

About this site

The 2005 irrigation drawdown of Prewitt produced the most exciting shorebirding in northeastern Colorado that year. The combination of protected wetlands and nearby SWAs with riparian woods produces good birding. The *Atlas* block recorded sixty-eight breeding species.

Directions

From I–76 take exit 102, drive north 0.4 mile, and turn right on US 6 to the entrance (on the right, 3.6 miles; referred to here, for convenience, as Entrance #1). Try going right and then left toward the trees.

To reach Entrance #2, continue 0.6 mile along US 6 and turn right into the parking lot. You can park here and walk below the dam to find land birds or climb up on the dam to scope the reservoir.

The birding

With the reservoir level fluctuating, birders encounter a puzzle of casual roads that approach the reservoir in at least a dozen spots. The northwest and west sides offer the most productive spots for shorebirds. Ducks and pelicans tend to rest on the southeast, generally too far away to pick out any but the largest and most distinctively shaped species (pelicans, cormorants). The dirt tracks go past and through the trees that line the shore; land-bird migrants drop into these groves.

Walk to the edge of the water to look for shorebirds (but don't go so close that you flush them—especially if you're joining a search for some rare species that has magically appeared at Prewitt). You may have an urge to cross the inlet, in which case you should wear mud boots (water depth can vary from a few inches to a foot or more, and you may also encounter mucky mud).

If you go to Entrance #2 and want to find land birds, park by the handicap entrance gate and walk into the shrubs and ponds below the dam.

Prewitt has a third entrance, off County Road 2.5, 0.4 mile northeasterly from Entrance #2. Follow 2.5 for 1.7 miles; turn into Entrance #3 just before the road takes a sharp left. On the left side of the parking lot, walk the road that climbs gradually up the dam and look across to the southeastern side of the water. Halfway along the dam, you can drop down into the riparian forest to look for land birds.

Prewitt's breeding birds include Northern Bobwhite and Red-bellied Woodpecker. Earnest observers have found migrants such as Olive-sided Flycatcher, Cassin's Kingbird, Cassin's, Blue-Headed, and Philadelphia Vireo, White-breasted Nuthatch (eastern), Rock Wren, American Pipit, Tennessee, Nashville, Townsend's, Pine, Black-and-white, Blackpoll, and Canada Warblers, American Redstart, Ovenbird, Northern Waterthrush, and, in fields nearby, Sage Thrasher.

The lake fills up with hundreds or thousands of waterbirds, mainly ducks but also a few loons and grebes. Possible gulls include Franklin's, Bonaparte's, and Lesser Black-backed plus Common, Forster's, and Black Terns. At least two species of jaegers (Parasitic and Long-tailed) come to harass the gulls and shorebirds, and so do occasional Peregrine Falcons.

In 2005 shorebirds stole the show. A very rare Curlew Sandpiper spent five September days on the mudflats. Other out-of-the-ordinary shorebirds among hundreds of Killdeer included Black-bellied, American Golden-, Semipalmated, and Piping Plovers, Willet, Whimbrel, Long-billed Curlew, Marbled Godwit, Ruddy Turnstone, Red Knot, Sanderling, Dunlin, Stilt and Buff-breasted Sandpipers, Short-billed Dowitcher, and Red-necked and Red Phalaropes.

The Division of Wildlife maintains a series of State Wildlife Areas along the South Platte River from Kersey northeasterly to the state line. **Messex SWA,** near Prewitt, presents good habitat for land birds during migration and summer breeding. From County Road 59.5, opposite Entrance #2 to Prewitt, go east 2.5 miles, left onto County Road R, then right onto County Road 59; in 0.8 mile go into the parking area on the left.

You'll find trails at Messex a bit sketchy, so you'll have to improvise on faint hiking and deer trails and one service road. The habitat includes cottonwood and box-elder woodlands, and a thick patch of willows along the stream. Small flocks of migrating land birds flitter through the woodland and shrubs. Look for chickadees, kinglets, Eastern Bluebird, warblers, and migrating sparrows. Typical breeding birds include Eastern Screech-Owl, Red-headed Woodpecker, and Brown Thrasher, but Great Crested Flycatcher also have nested here.

Similar but not as promising, nearby **Atwood SWA** lies a little farther downstream. Go back to US 6 eastward; in 5 miles go right on County Road 29.5 and in a half mile, park on the right just after crossing the South Platte. The woodland here consists of cottonwoods, ash, and box-elder. To return to I–76, drive on for 1 mile; go left on County Road 12 and in 1.7 miles, right on Highway 63 to the interstate.

DeLorme grid: P. 95 C4.

Elevation: 4,070 feet.

Hazards: Muddy roads, insects.

Nearest food, gas, lodging: Sterling.

Camping: No.

For more information: Colorado Division of Wildlife, 317 West Prospect, Fort Collins, CO 80526; (970) 521-0233; http://wildlife.state .co.us/landwater/statewildlifeareas.

4 Jackson Lake State Park ♿ Ⓢ

Habitats: Riparian, wetlands.
Specialty birds: *Migrant:* Rare shorebirds, gulls, land birds. *Winter:* Bald Eagle.

Best times to bird: August to November.

About this site

As mentioned for Prewitt SWA, birdiness of northeastern Colorado reservoirs depends on two factors: rainfall and irrigation regime. Jackson Lake's attraction to waterbirds varies from year to year. From 2002 to 2004 irrigation drawdowns created extensive mudflats that attracted hundreds of shorebirds. In 2005 the reservoir held much more water into the fall and attracted few shorebirds.

In spring and fall migration, land birds pour into the trees on the South Shore entrance and in the campgrounds. Russian olives dominate several campgrounds and, as a non-native tree, do not hold the variety of migrants that native trees might. The park closes several campgrounds from Labor Day until spring; birders can park along the main road or enter open campgrounds to bird.

Directions

From I–76 at exit 66, signs direct you to the park. Go north 5.7 miles on Highway 39. Half a mile north of Goodrich, turn left at the T intersection on County Road Y.5. (Note County Road 3.5, 1 mile from the T, goes north to the dam; more of that later.) County Road Y.5 swings north; in 1.4 miles you pass the South Shore entrance to the park, and 0.6 mile beyond that you come to the main park entrance. Past park headquarters are six campgrounds and a marina.

From Fort Morgan, you can come a different way. From I–76, take Highway 144 westerly 15.8 miles to County Road Y.5 (the intersection half a mile north of Goodrich) and then follow the directions above.

The birding

For land birds, walk the trails around the campgrounds. The second one, Pelican Campground, stays open until after Labor Day. Try its trails through the mainly Russian-olive thickets interspersed with some tamarisk and cottonwoods. Warblers drop in here and may stay a few days while awaiting good migratory winds. Yellow-rumped Warbler and American Robin like it especially because they feed on Russian-olive berries, but you may find other species—the list includes Cassin's Vireo and Townsend's Warbler.

Past the marina you can park at Northview Campground and walk to the tall cottonwoods on the lakeshore to look for migrants and even a Great Horned Owl.

From any campground, look at the lake itself. Throughout the warm months it holds fifty to one hundred American White Pelicans no matter what the water level, and a few Great Blue Herons feed along the edge. If the water level has receded, look for shorebirds.

From the South Shore entrance, you can walk through tall cottonwoods to the lakeshore. Sometimes these trees attract land-bird migrants and, one year, a roosting cluster of Long-eared Owls. You can walk out to the lakeshore on your shorebird search.

During periods of low water, go back to County Road Y-5 and then to County Road 3.5. It provides a shorter way to reach shorebird habitat on the south side of this large reservoir. Go north on Road 3.5 to the parking lot below the dam (just after the road curves right and crosses a canal). From here walk up the dam and trek along it, in whichever direction you spot shorebirds (usually to the right). If you take care, you can climb down the (rather steep) dam to the lake floor and approach the clusters of shorebirds. Among hundreds of Killdeer you may find Black-bellied, American Golden-, or Snowy Plovers, a rare peep, Sanderling, Stilt Sandpiper, Ruddy Turnstone, or Red-necked or Red Phalaropes. Colorado's first Kelp Gull stopped here before winging west to Fort Collins.

When walking the dam, look into the tall cottonwoods on the other side to search for land-bird migrants. Migrating Rock Wrens sometimes crawl along the dam face, and American Pipits fly along the lakeshore. If you find few shorebirds here, Jackson SWA, on the north shore, sometimes attracts them.

In late winter (January or February) the ice breakup heaves up frozen fish, a treat that dozens of Bald Eagles find delectable.

DeLorme grid: P. 94 C1.
Elevation: 4,450 feet.
Nearest food, gas, lodging: Fort Morgan.
Camping: Yes.

For more information: Jackson Lake State Park, 26363 Road 3, Orchard, CO 80649; (970) 645-2551; www.parks.state.co.us.

5 Pawnee National Grassland

Habitats: Short-grass prairie, riparian, wetlands.

Specialty birds: *Resident:* Ferruginous and Red-tailed Hawks, Prairie Falcon. *Summer:* Swainson's Hawk, Mountain Plover, Loggerhead Shrike, Lark Bunting, McCown's and Chestnut-collared Longspurs, Cassin's, Brewer's, and Grasshopper Sparrows. *Migrant:* Eastern passerines. *Winter:* Golden and Bald Eagles, Merlin.

Best times to bird: Year-round.

About this site
The grassland on early June mornings stages a memorable sight-and-sound extravaganza of larking buntings, longspurs, and larks. Lark Buntings, most numerous and most spectacular, rocket into the sky, fold their wings into a V that flaunts their white wing patches, drop slowly in a controlled butterfly-like flight, and sing a loud, varied song as they vie for females and territory. In 1922 C. L. Whittle wrote that they shoot up "as though propelled from guns, pouring out the most infectious and passionate song [of] any bird in the United States." Longspurs, Horned Lark, and Western Meadowlark add to the dawn chorus. Prairie flowers paint the landscape with vivid yellow, blue, white, and orange.

Pawnee National Grassland rose out of the Dust Bowl of the 1930s. The federal government bought failed farms and ranches, created the grassland, and ended up preserving the best short-grass prairie system in Colorado. Public and private land intermix; the Forest Service (administrator of the grassland) leases much of its land for cattle grazing.

The Pawnee has two units: a western one with a fine auto-tour route for birders, and an eastern one that features Pawnee Buttes, which loom over a prairie valley, isolated by erosion from a string of bluffs where raptors and swifts nest.

Directions
Most Pawnee trips start at Crow Valley Recreation Area and follow the **Auto Tour Route:** From U.S. Highway 85 in Ault, take Highway 14 east for 23 miles to County Road 77. Drive north half a mile and turn left into the campground. Roads penetrate the Pawnee from the east, south, and north: Wander at will; it pays to have an atlas of the roads. You can drive into the west section from US 85 from Nunn on County Roads 98, 100, or 108 (north 4 miles); from Highway 14 on County Roads 61, 65, 69, and others; and from the east on diagonal County Road 390.

The birding
Those looking for short-grass prairie birds should skip Crow Valley (famous as a land-bird migrant trap) and take the auto tour, a 27-mile drive through a western

section of the grassland. Start at Highway 14 and County Road 77. The Forest Service puts out an excellent pamphlet that describes the route, with an explanation of stops and likely birds (available from the office listed below). They also caution you not to disturb wildlife by walking out on the prairie. Also heed the advice about "Our Responsibility to Wildlife," which urges us to respect the sensitivity of the birds and mammals of the grassland. The route takes you through habitat where you should find all the Pawnee specialists. Note, however, that birds move around—although the brochure suggests certain species at certain places, birds can defy the printed word and show up elsewhere.

The two longspurs occupy slightly different habitats: Chestnut-collared prefer taller grass, McCown's the short buffalo grass. Horned Larks, the most abundant bird in Colorado, flit all over the prairie and have fledged young by June 1. Young wear confusing plumages that confound birders. Lark Buntings likewise populate most prairie habitats, including some agricultural fields. Longspurs arrive in April, buntings in late May.

Mammals occupy an important place on the Pawnee. Pronghorns (antelope) race across the prairie or stop and retrace their steps with curiosity. (Allegedly Native Americans would wave a white cloth at pronghorns to induce them to come closer.) Fifteen years ago herds of 300 pronghorns raced over the shortgrass; drought and hunting reduced the herds to one or two dozen, though they still pepper the landscape, particularly in the northern part.

PHOTO © WENDY SHATTIL/BOB ROZINSKI

Half of the Mountain Plover in the world breed on the Colorado Prairies.

Mountain Plovers are the hardest prairie birds to find. Plovers often favor prairie-dog towns, as do Burrowing Owls, but just as frequently use prairie swales. Hard to find during incubation, they become more visible after the young hatch (mid-June). Later in summer they gather in small flocks, sometimes close to water holes.

Loggerhead Shrikes nest in small trees in small stands (five to ten trees). Often they perch on fence posts while out on feeding forays. The auto tour doesn't pass through good Swainson's Hawk habitat; they need at least a few trees for breeding, though they roam several miles when searching for food.

In winter Horned Larks remain abundant, and Lapland Longspurs mix into their winter flocks. Raptors—Golden and Bald Eagles, Prairie Falcon, and Merlin—become conspicuous.

Crow Creek flows south from Wyoming and culminates, for Colorado birders, at *Crow Valley Recreation Area*. The dense riparian zone of cottonwoods, box-elders, and rose bushes provides cover for migrant birds, lured by the oasis of trees surrounded by prairie and croplands. The Pawnee's enormous bird list owes its length to this migrant trap. The checklist of 301 species, last updated in 2000, will add several more in its next revision. It includes 35 species of warblers, 20 sparrows, 14 flycatchers, 7 vireos, 6 thrushes, and even 4 hummingbirds. May and August/September are peak times for these migrants. Test the trails, mainly on the left as you drive into the campground.

Ponds: Two readily accessible water holes contribute most of the waterfowl and shorebirds. Both lie about 2 miles west of County Road 77 (the road north from Briggsdale), the better pond on County Road 124, the other on Road 120.

The east section features the anomalous *Pawnee Buttes:* 15 miles east of Briggsdale, turn north on County Road 105; bear left (after 4 miles) on County Road 390 a quarter mile to Keota; or go north from Briggsdale on County Road 77 for 5 miles, then right on Road 100, east on Road 100, 13 miles to Road 390, then southeast 0.8 mile to Keota.

From Keota, look for the signs to Pawnee Buttes. Go right on County Road 98.5 and left in 0.7 mile on County Road 105. Along County Road 105, note the mile-long prairie-dog town on the right—look for Burrowing Owl. After 3 miles go right on Road 104 for 3 miles, then left on Road 111. After another 3 miles, jog right on Road 110 for a mile and left a mile on Road 113. Finally, in half a mile, where Road 113 turns right, a grassland road bears left into the Pawnee Buttes area. The grassland road climbs over a hill, and the buttes suddenly rise majestically in front of you.

The buttes have a 1.5-mile trail that leads to the West Butte through a prairie landscape dominated by bluffs and buttes. The less-common prairie land birds don't occur here, although you can see the cliff-nesting raptors (Golden Eagle, Prairie Falcon) and White-throated Swifts zoom around the cliffs. One trailhead starts 1.5 miles beyond the turnoff into the buttes from County Road 113, and a second trailhead is 0.7 mile farther; this trail meets the one from the first parking lot. From the second trailhead, a half-mile road leads to an overlook that's open from July through February but closed during raptor–nesting season.

DeLorme grid: West unit, p. 21 B5–B7; east unit, p. 96 A1–A2.

Elevation: 4,900 feet.

Hazards: Running out of gas; dehydration; sudden storms; roads may become impassable when wet or snowy, although most on the auto tour have well-graveled surfaces; rattlesnakes.

Nearest food, gas, lodging: Greeley, Fort Morgan, Brush; B&B on the Pawnee.

Camping: Yes.

For more information: Pawnee National Grassland, 2150 Centre Avenue, Building E, Fort Collins, CO 80526-8119; (970) 295-6600; www.fs.fed.us/r2/arnf.

Pawnee National Grassland features a suite of short-grass specialists such as Ferruginous Hawk, Mountain Plover, Burrowing Owl, and two longspur species. (Note Pawnee Buttes in the background.)

6 Greater Prairie-Chicken Lek 💲

Best time to bird: April.

About this site

The courtship dance of the Greater Prairie-Chicken presents a droll and exceptional wildlife spectacle. At daybreak dozens of birds descend on a lek (dancing ground) to compete for females by twirling, jumping, and strutting as they inflate their orange throat sacs. Colorado prairie-chickens live in the sandhills of eastern Yuma County; all leks are on private property.

Due to their location on private ranches, you can experience these displays only on guided tours. The chamber of commerce in Wray sponsors lek tours. You can opt for one- or two-night tour packages that include accommodations, educational lectures, and some meals. With tours limited to weekends only, from late March through April, reserve space way in advance.

DeLorme grid: P. 102 D2.

Elevation: 3,700 feet.

Hazards: Skip your morning coffee before you go as the blind has no facilities.

Nearest food, gas, lodging: Wray.

Camping: No.

For more information: Wray Chamber of Commerce; (970) 332-3484; wraychamber @plains.net.

Ferruginous Hawk breed on the prairies, and in winter they frequent prairie-dog towns.

PHOTO © WENDY SHATTIL/BOB ROZINSKI

7 Bonny Lake State Park $ ♿ 🦅 IBA and South Republican SWA 📄

Habitats: Riparian, wetlands, grassland, shrubland.

Specialty birds: *Resident:* Eastern Screech-Owl, Red-bellied Woodpecker, Brown Thrasher. *Summer:* Red-headed Woodpecker, Logger-head Shrike, Bell's Vireo, Eastern Bluebird, Baltimore and Orchard Orioles. *Migrant:* Eastern vagrants (flycatchers, vireos, warblers), Clay-colored Sparrow. *Winter:* Long-eared and Short-eared Owls, White-breasted Nuthatch (eastern form), Harris's Sparrow, Snow Bunting (rare).

Best times to bird: Year-round; fall and spring for migrants.

About this site

Bonny has the most extensive, varied, and accessible habitats in eastern Colorado. During migration, myriad migrants drop into its woods and water, making it a prime destination for two to three days of birding. Interlocked with the state park, South Republican SWA embraces several riparian miles along the South Fork of the Republican River.

Bonny's north side has mature gallery forests and shelterbelts. The south side has easier car access to woodlands and more shrubby habitats. From both, scan the lake for waterbirds and see where the shoreline might have lured a few sandpipers.

Bonny Dam, unlike most eastern Colorado irrigation reservoirs, serves solely as a flood control project. Due to a series of dry years starting in 1998, it hasn't captured much water lately, and the water level has dropped substantially. At the upper end this creates a sandy/muddy shoreline used by migrating shorebirds, grazing teal, and dabbling ducks. With the water shortage, extensive cattail marshes upstream from the now-diminished lake dried up and lost many nesting and migrant species. With the pool at least temporarily way below capacity, a curious combination has grown up: tall cottonwoods on the land side and dense, head-high cottonwoods in the lake bed, trees that sprouted as the water level dropped. Still, Bonny has its summer complement of American White Pelican and Double-crested Cormorant (and Canada Goose).

Land birds have an eastern (or midwestern) flavor, with breeding species such as Eastern Screech-Owl, Red-bellied and Red-headed Woodpeckers, Bell's Vireo, Eastern Bluebird, Brown Thrasher, and Baltimore and Orchard Orioles. Other breeders include Swainson's Hawk, Rock Wren (look on the dam), and Lark Sparrow. The *Atlas* block found sixty-nine breeding species. Spring trips typically record one hundred species or more, and the Christmas Count records around seventy-five species.

Directions

Bonny State Park lies east of U.S. Highway 385, between Idalia and Burlington. The North entrance (County Road 3) lies 6 miles south of the intersection of U.S. Highways 385 and 36 east of Idalia; a mile south the South entrance (County Road 2) is 20.5 miles north from the intersection of U.S. Highways 385 and 24 on the east side of Burlington.

The arcane operation of Western water law may lead to the complete drainage of Bonny Reservoir by 2012; drying it up will affect both birds and birding, although no one yet knows how. Check with State Parks before you plan a weekend at Bonny.

The birding

Birders can roam freely into woodlands, shelterbelts, marshes, and lakeshores (and the lake itself, if you have a boat). Taking advantage of this openness can consume several days if done systematically. For the most part, trails don't exist in or to these habitats, so you have to find your own way through them—and negotiate fallen trees, poison ivy, and insidious stickers that, in the fall, attack your shoelaces and pants legs.

The park has campgrounds on both sides. Foster Grove, on the north, sits amid towering cottonwoods, with at least six shelterbelts within walking distance. Wagon Wheel Campground, on the south side, is more open, fancier, and favored by boaters. From it, birders can examine lakeside trees and a few shelterbelts. A third campground, North Cove, on the northeast side near the dam, offers little in the way of birding.

North side: Turn east from US 385 into the park. The first grove of cottonwoods on the left, Schoolhouse Grove (so-called from a collection of school desks abandoned amid the trees, now long gone), sometimes perks birders' interest. It can have such specialties as Red-bellied Woodpecker, Eastern Bluebird, Brown Thrasher, Northern Cardinal, warblers, and other migrants.

A cattail marsh on the right dried up because of the drought. If the water returns, it may again attract Pied-billed Grebe, teal and other dabblers, and Common Yellowthroat. Just beyond, the road comes close to the river woodland of willows mixed with cottonwoods, which sometimes produces interesting migrants. A mile farther, past a park entrance station, a right turn takes you to *Foster Grove.* Park in the campground (not in a camping space) to spend a couple of hours walking through the campground and the shelterbelts between it and the entrance road. Eastern Screech-Owl and Red-bellied Woodpecker nest in Foster Grove.

Sometimes migrants throng the shelterbelts: sparrows (Chipping, Brewer's, Clay-colored, White-crowned) and warblers (Orange-crowned, Yellow-rumped, Yellow, Wilson's) like them. Among them you may find less likely species: Bell's Vireo, warblers such as Townsend's (fall) and Black-and-white, and White-throated Sparrow. Look for Red-headed Woodpecker and Spotted Towhee (and maybe an Eastern Towhee, but check carefully for both plumage and call).

By day, Red-bellied and Red-headed Woodpeckers weave through the cottonwoods at Foster Grove Campground in Bonny Lake State Park. At night an Eastern Screech-Owl may whinny to its mate.

From the southwest corner of the campground, a road leads to a parking area located on the edge of the lake until the drought. Walk either right or left (no formal trails), through tall cottonwoods, willows, and box-elders. To the left nests a small cluster of Great Blue Herons, along with Eastern Bluebird, Yellow Warbler, Common Yellowthroat, and Baltimore Oriole. To the right a similar (former) lakeside forest leads to a big cattail marsh (dry now) and an expansive cottonwood forest. Its grassy understory limits the variety and number of birds. You can trek through it to the edge of the Republican River (2 to 3 feet wide, not very deep). An old roadbed lends some habitat and bird variety.

Past the Foster Grove turnoff, the park road passes two productive shelterbelts and several coves with small groves of trees and shrubs. About a mile beyond Foster Grove, the road turns left; although it passes several shelterbelts and skirts the North Cove, this section does not produce many birds (despite the nature trail shown on the park map). During high water North Cove can attract some water and marsh birds. In winter the park often closes the road at Foster Grove.

US 385 between the North and South entrances sees heavy, high-speed traffic, including lots of trucks. From it, two pull-offs on the east access the river and adjacent woodlands. Cliff Swallows nest under the bridge across the river.

South side: Going east on County Road 2, stop in a half mile at the shelterbelt on the right; this is the most reliable place in Colorado to find Bell's Vireo, which sing their wheezy song from the wild plums. Also look for Brown Thrasher and Western Meadowlark. In fall migrating *Spizella,* Vesper, and Lark Sparrows dart among the bushes.

A quarter of a mile farther, a left-hand track leads to a big (now dry) cattail marsh called *Hopper Ponds.* The entrance road turns right in a quarter mile; park straight ahead. The cattails on the left have dry feet after several years of drought, and therefore don't harbor the marsh birds of yore such as American and Least (rare) Bitterns, herons, teal and other dabbling ducks, rails, Marsh Wren, and Common Yellowthroat. Walk along the dike trail (straight ahead) into more cattails, closer to the lake, with possible water for marsh birds. Woods on the right may produce land birds as you meander through the trees and poison ivy.

From the right turn, stop at the Texas crossing to look and listen, then swing around to the left for half a mile to **South Republican SWA.** A left turn at the sign goes to the edge of the same cattail marsh. At some times of the year (most likely autumn), the whoosh at dusk of thousands of Red-winged Blackbirds coming into roost can stagger your powers of sight and sound. A right-hand road goes almost a mile along a ditch with a dense growth of cottonwoods, Russian olives, and shrubs. Spurs on the left lead to the edge of the former lakeshore. Land-bird migrants often feed quietly in both lakeside cottonwoods and roadside thickets.

Wagon Wheel area: Back on the entrance road, continue easterly 1.5 miles to a T intersection (County Road JJ goes right; see below for a side trip to a large prairie-dog town); go left to a second T, then left again to the south park entrance and visitor center. Past the visitor center, go left (the route straight ahead goes into Wagon Wheel campground). Go left again at the Y intersection; this road passes two picnic areas on the edge of the lake and then enters a woodland like that on the South Republican spur road. Drive or walk the half mile to the end (actually, just across from the end of the South Republican spur—a dirt berm blocks the two roads). On the left, away from the lake, negotiating an often productive shelterbelt has become challenging because of overgrown shrubs, thorn bushes, Russian olives, and wild plums. On the right the lakeshore cottonwoods and thickets often produce satisfying bird lists.

By going right at the Y, you pass the store (with fairly limited, mostly summer-time, hours) on the way to the boat ramp and a large parking lot. Park there, inspect the lake from the ramp, and walk along the edge of the lake bed toward the campground. Trees here trap lots of migrants, especially in spring when northbound birds discover Bonny as the first green space in 150 miles. If you go back out past the Wagon Wheel campground and straight (instead of left to the exit), a road inside the park skirts the Wagon Wheel arm and leads off to a second arm of the lake where shorebirds occasionally stop to feed.

Back at the T intersection just south of the visitor center, go left on County Road 3 for 1.5 miles to an intersection with the dam road (County Road KK) and County Road 3.5. Cliff Swallows, the main attraction of the dam road, nest on the spillway at the far end of the dam. You can also peer down into the wetlands and woodlands below the dam (use a scope) or onto the lake for resting waterbirds (use a scope), but while on the dam don't leave your car; you're not supposed to park there.

County Road 3.5 takes you to *Hale* and the Hale Ponds. In 2 miles turn left on County Road LL.5 past Hale (three houses and a closed general store on the right) and jog right on County Road 4. In a half mile, stop under the cottonwoods that arch across the road; migrants such as Great Crested Flycatcher and Wood Thrush like it here and Red-headed Woodpecker and White-breasted Nuthatch (eastern form) breed here.

The sandsage shrubland starting in 3 miles on the right has nesting Cassin's Sparrows. Another 3.5 miles takes you to the first of three entrances into *Hale Ponds,* on the left. (If you stay on County Road 4, it turns left and follows the state line, with Kansas on the right and Hale Ponds on the left. In another half mile the road turns right into Kansas.) Take the first entrance and contemplate the extensive cottonwood gallery forest. The road edges along the ponds, with several spots where you can walk into the woodlands and reach the river, a whopping 3 feet wide and 6 to 12 inches deep, but lined with willows and sometimes with birds. After the last pond the road turns right and comes out at the Kansas corner.

Hale Ponds themselves rarely keep the ducks and Pied-billed Grebe that test their waters, because of numerous fishermen. Woodlands around the ponds feature typical eastern Colorado birds but few migrants. Breeding species include Wild Turkey, Northern Bobwhite, Yellow-billed Cuckoo, Hairy Woodpecker, Northern (Yellow-shafted) Flicker, Rough-winged Swallow, Eastern Bluebird, and Orchard and Baltimore Orioles.

Way back at the intersection of County Roads 3 and JJ, near the visitor center, go south on County Road JJ. One mile south of the intersection, a prairie-dog town stretches for a mile to the next road (County Road Zero). Burrowing Owls nest here, as do Horned Lark and Western Meadowlark, and you might see a Ferruginous Hawk.

DeLorme grid: P. 102 B4.

Elevation: 3,700 feet.

Hazards: Poison ivy, thorny plants; in fall, nasty stickers.

Nearest food, gas, lodging: Burlington, Idalia.

Camping: Yes.

For more information: Bonny Lake State Park, 30010 County Road 3, Idalia, CO 89735-9674; (970) 354-7306; www.parks .state.co.us.

8 Plains Oases

Habitats: Wetlands, riparian.

Specialty birds: *Summer:* Red-headed Woodpecker. *Migrant:* Tired land birds, ducks, shorebirds.

Best times to bird: Spring and fall.

About this site

To migrating birds in the middle of the high plains, little clumps of green trees must look like oases amid deserts of wheatfields and grasslands. These green spots, large and small, formal and informal, draw both birds and birders for brief forays on their ways elsewhere. Don't plan these places as destination sites.

We recommend three sites here, though you might find others along roadsides or spot some in the atlas that you carry.

Breeding in scattered colonies, Black-crowned Night-Herons fan out 10 to 20 miles to seek food for themselves and their nestlings.

The birding

To reach **Flagler SWA** from the west, exit I–70 at Flagler; go north on Ruepner Avenue for 0.2 mile, and right on East 2nd (County Road U) 3.7 miles to the SWA boundary. From the east, exit I–70 at Seibert and go north 0.4 mile to US 24 (not a conspicuous intersection). Go left on US 24 for 3.3 miles, jog right and then left onto County Road U, and in 1.5 miles jog right and left again, then it's half a mile to the SWA boundary. Straight ahead leads to a boat ramp with a side road to the left. A right turn loops around the reservoir, where you can look at the shelterbelt and lakeside trees on the left.

Though you rarely see rafts of birds here, the reservoir can bring in migrant waterfowl including ducks and grebes, and occasionally shorebirds stop, especially on the east side. The list includes Eared, Western, and Clark's Grebes, Great Blue Heron and Black-crowned Night-Heron, some ducks (Ruddies seem to like it), White-faced Ibis, Virginia Rail, Sora, American Coot, and sixteen species of shore-birds, including Semipalmated Plover, White-rumped and Stilt Sandpipers, and Red-necked Phalarope.

To reach the most productive land-bird site, park on the east side of the dam (0.4 mile from the east entrance) and walk down to the wooded stream bottom. Possible birds include Red-headed (breeds) and Hairy Woodpeckers, Willow Fly-catcher, Blue-gray Gnatcatcher, Eastern Bluebird, Brown Thrasher, Orange-crowned, Black-and-white, Pine, Worm-eating, and Wilson's Warblers, Clay-colored and Lincoln's Sparrows, and Lazuli Bunting, plus an Inca Dove on the road from Flagler. A Varied Thrush also snuck in one January.

Ramah Reservoir SWA sits north of US 24, 28 miles southwest of Limon and 37 miles northeast of Colorado Springs. As at Bonny, the water level drops during dry periods; it dried up completely in 2006. The southwest third is private property, but drive around to the north side to look south into the lake. Ramah's birds include twenty-three species of shorebirds including American Golden-Plover, Semipalmated Plover, Black-necked Stilt, Willet, Marbled Godwit, White-rumped (mid-May to early June) Sandpiper, Dunlin, Sanderling, and Red-necked Phalarope, plus Least and Black Terns. Land-bird migrants include Cordilleran Fly-catcher, Cassin's Kingbird, Sedge Wren, Blue-gray Gnatcatcher, Tennessee Warbler, and hordes of sparrows: Chipping, Brewer's, Clay-colored, Vesper, Savannah, and White-crowned. Least Flycatcher may nest: Listen at the first set of trees on both sides of the road.

Last Chance rest area sits at the southwest corner of the intersection of US 36 and Highway 71. A small parking area and scruffy restroom mark the site. Siberian elms and brushy weeds flank a stream course, with a small pond (dry in drought years). Last Chance fills with lots of Swainson's Thrush in late May (and an occasional Hermit Thrush or Veery) and Wilson's Warbler in early September. It collects a sur-prising variety of strays. A partial list includes twelve warblers (odd ones include

Tennessee, Bay-breasted, MacGillivray's, Hooded, Northern Parula, American Redstart, Northern Waterthrush, Ovenbird), four vireos (Bell's, Plumbeous, Cassin's, and Warbling), and seven sparrows (among them, Clay-colored, Lark, Lincoln's, and White-throated). It even has records of are Scarlet Tanager, Rose-breasted Grosbeak, Red-breasted Nuthatch, Ruby-crowned Kinglet, Blue-gray Gnatcatcher, and Great Horned Owl. Bizarrely, the list includes Green and Little Blue Herons and Solitary Sandpiper.

DeLorme grid: Flagler, p. 97 C5; Ramah, p. 96 D1; Last Chance, p. 96 B3.

Elevation: 4,700, 6,200, and 4,780 feet, respectively.

Hazards: Biting bugs.

Nearest food, gas, lodging: Limon, Burlington; gas and food at Flagler and Last Chance.

Camping: No.

For more information: Colorado Division of Wildlife, 4255 Sinton Road, Colorado Springs, CO 80807; (719) 227-5200; http://wildlife.state.co.us/landwater/statewild lifeareas.

Mainly a plains bird, Swainson's Hawk usually nest in sparser stands of trees than the more ubiquitous Red-tailed Hawk.

Southeast

Reservoirs in the Arkansas Valley from Rocky Ford to Lamar draw an amazing variety of waterbirds. Each has its own coterie of species, although all share some birds in common (White Pelican, Killdeer, American Avocet, for example). In midsummer, when temperatures hit the 90s and 100s, interesting species persist, and in fact, birders find some unusual species during very hot weather.

Scattered sites attract migrating land birds, both rare and not so rare: flycatchers, vireos, warblers, and sparrows. Bring a scope to these reservoirs, as some have quite large expanses and limited access. Also, the birds inevitably decide to use the parts of the reservoir farthest from the place you choose to look at them.

Several of the lakes, "playas," sit in natural depressions, enhanced by irrigation waters, for example, Great Plains reservoirs and Blue Lake. All—playas and otherwise—lead an uncertain existence. Water levels depend on the vagaries of weather and local irrigation demands. In addition, thirsty cities in metro Denver own water rights in the valley to augment municipal water supplies.

The valley boasts Colorado's only breeding populations of two endangered species: Piping Plover and Least Tern. They don't always use the same sites from one year to the next because of changing water levels, encroachment by vegetation, and depredations by various predators ranging from kangaroo rats to foxes to ATVs. During their breeding season, the Colorado Division of Wildlife and Army Corps of Engineers post nesting areas as off-limits to people. Please honor these roped-off areas. You can walk up to posted boundaries and see plovers and terns.

All reservoirs attract an appealing selection of shorebirds. Look along shorelines and inspect the points, where pelicans rest. American White Pelicans spend the summer at all of the reservoirs. Ducks congregate in migration, and large flocks of geese (Snow, Ross's, Canada, and Cackling) throng open water in winter.

Driving between reservoirs, you can see birds of the high plains such as Mountain Plover, Long-billed Curlew, Chihuahuan Raven, Horned Lark, Cassin's and Grasshopper Sparrows, Lark Bunting, and Dickcissel. Towns along U.S. Highway 50 from Fowler to Lamar all have populations of Mississippi Kites, a striking sight as they cruise over residential areas hawking insects.

Lamar celebrates the High Plains Snow Goose Festival in February. The affair offers sunrise and sunset bird tours, lectures, an arts and crafts fair, and a Saturday night dinner (www.lamarchamber.com/goose).

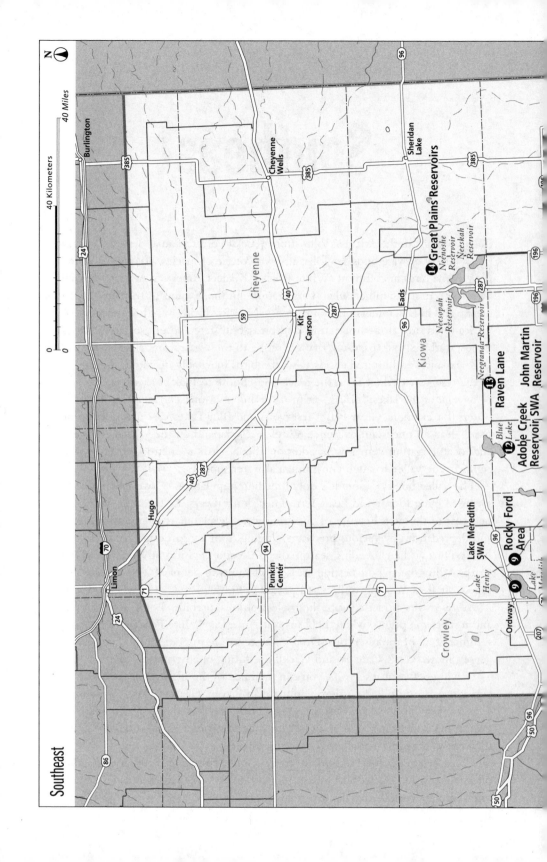

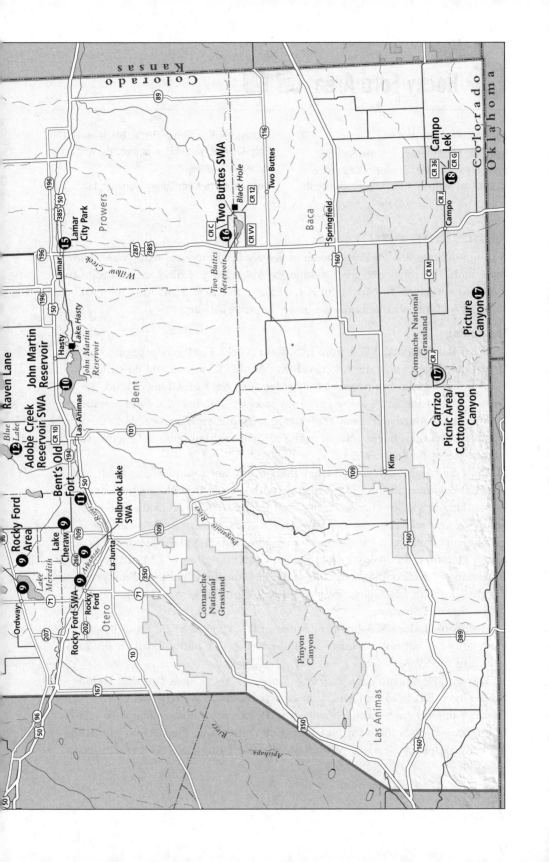

⑨ Rocky Ford Area 🗎 ♿

Habitats: Wetland, riparian.

Specialty birds: *Resident:* Bewick's Wren, Great-tailed Grackle. *Summer:* Waterbirds, shorebirds, Northern Bobwhite, Eared Grebe, Mississippi Kite, Snowy Plover, Black-necked Stilt. *Migrant:* Waterbirds, shorebirds, White-throated Sparrow.

Best times to bird: Spring, summer, fall.

About this site
A group of State Wildlife Areas north of Rocky Ford produces many water and shore birds. The mix varies from nesting Eared Grebes and Black-necked Stilts to migrating shorebirds to Mississippi Kites. Except at Rocky Ford and Holbrook Lake SWAs, lake and lakeshore constitute the main habitats.

The birding
To reach **Rocky Ford SWA** from U.S. 50 in Rocky Ford, go north on Highway 266; at the bridge across the Arkansas River (2 miles), look up and down for Cliff Swallows and ducks. Just north of the bridge, turn right on County Road 805 (note a sign for the SWA at the corner). Use either the first or second parking lot to enter the wooded and sunny trails that traverse the riparian area along the north side of the Arkansas River. (North of the road, the section opposite the first two lots also lies within the SWA.)

Trails ramble through shaded lanes, thick brush, open meadows, ag fields, and ponds. Bobwhites call from thickets along with singing Bewick's and House Wrens, Brown Thrasher, Yellow-breasted Chat, and Blue Grosbeak. From the trees, Red-headed Woodpecker, Eastern and Western Kingbirds, American Redstart, and Orchard and Bullock's Orioles chatter and sing. Cattails at the edge of the ponds harbor Common Yellowthroat, and overhead you may glimpse a Mississippi Kite or American Kestrel. Look for migrants such as Mountain Chickadee, Ruby-crowned Kinglet, Virginia's, MacGillivray's, and Wilson's Warblers, Western Tanager, and White-throated Sparrow.

Holbrook Lake SWA lies 4 miles east of Rocky Ford SWA. From Rocky Ford, go north and east 6.5 miles on Highway 266 to County Road 25 and turn right into the SWA.

This shallow lake attracts a variety of water and shore birds. Breeders include Eared Grebe, Redhead, and American Coot, and maybe Western and Clark's Grebes. Migrants range from Black Tern to Bonaparte's Gull to various shorebirds. In the cottonwoods, listen for Northern Bobwhite. Other breeders include Red-headed Woodpecker, (eastern) Warbling Vireo, and Eastern and Western Kingbirds,

Northern Bobwhites call from wooded patches in the wildlife areas north of Rocky Ford.

Barn Swallow, Northern Mockingbird, Brown Thrasher, Yellow Warbler, Blue Grosbeak, Orchard and Bullock's Orioles.

Lake Cheraw attracts a myriad of shorebirds and other waterbirds. From US 50 in La Junta, take Highway 109 north 7 miles. Highway 109 crosses an arm of the lake, and at high water you can stop on the broad shoulder and look for shorebirds. Follow Highway 109 as it turns right into Cheraw, to inspect the lake from the Main Street promontory. Proceed to Main Street and there turn right to follow Main out to the lake. Stop at the small parking area and walk to the end of the dike.

Nesting species include Killdeer, Snowy Plover, American Avocet, Black-necked Stilt, and Wilson's Phalarope. American White Pelican, Franklin's and Ring-billed Gulls, and Forster's Tern use the lake. Migrant shorebirds (many of which show up during the breeding season, when birders debate about whether they are headed north or south) include almost every shorebird that visits Colorado. A partial list: Black-bellied (fall), Piping, and Semipalmated Plovers, Willet, Long-billed Curlew, and Sanderling, plus Black Tern and White-faced Ibis.

Along the Main Street dike, look for Blue Grosbeak, Brown Thrasher, and Northern Mockingbird in the snippets of vegetation, and, in town, Eurasian

Collared-Dove. In 2005 a Greater Roadrunner trotted along the shore mimicking a shorebird.

Lake Meredith has its best birds March to May and mid-August to mid-November. To reach Meredith from US 50 on the west side of Rocky Ford, take Highway 71 north 10 miles to County Road G in Ordway; turn right (Highway 96 goes left). In about a mile, check the effluent pond opposite a cattle stockyard. In summer Black-necked Stilts breed here (one of its few Colorado sites), and you may see baby stilts teetering on gangly legs. Also look for White-faced Ibis and other shorebirds. The stockyards collect lots of blackbirds; you might find Yellow-headed Blackbird or Great-tailed Grackle among the flocks, especially during migration and sometimes in winter.

At a T (3 miles from Ordway), turn right to the SWA entrance. The huge expanse of Lake Meredith demands a scope for coverage. Clark's Grebes probably breed here, although not many other waterbirds use the lake in midsummer. A remote arm of the lake may have breeding Black-crowned Night-Heron, Great Blue Heron, and White-faced Ibis.

Particularly in late August and September, you might find several thousand migrants: ducks, shorebirds—at least twelve species including Black-necked Stilt, Wilson's (thousands), Red-necked (hundreds), and Red Phalaropes—Franklin's (hundreds), Laughing (rare), Ring-billed, and California Gulls, and Black, Common, and Forster's Terns. On hot summer days recreationists fish and swim in the lake, although maintenance of the outhouses seems slapdash.

DeLorme grid: P. 98 D3.

Elevation: 4,000 to 4,370 feet.

Nearest food, gas, lodging: Rocky Ford, La Junta, and Las Animas; food and gas in Ordway, gas in Cheraw.

Camping: *Meredith:* Okay but no facilities.

For more information: Colorado Division of Wildlife, 2500 South Main Street, Lamar, CO 81052; (719) 336-6600; http://wildlife.state .co.us/landwater/statewildlifeareas.

10 John Martin Reservoir State Park and SWA ⑤ ♿ IBA 📄

Habitats: Riparian, wetland, shrubland.

Specialty birds: *Resident:* Red-bellied Woodpecker, Eastern Bluebird. *Summer:* Piping Plover, Least Tern, Black-billed Cuckoo (rare), (eastern) Warbling Vireo, Orchard Oriole.

Migrant: Warblers, vireos, flycatchers, kinglets. *Winter:* Cackling, Snow, and Ross's Geese, Marsh and Sedge (rare) Wrens, LeConte's (rare), Swamp, and Savannah Sparrows.

Best times to bird: Year-round.

About this site

Quite big (12 miles long) and the only Arkansas Valley reservoir actually on the river, John Martin offers a plethora of birdy places. At the upper end near Fort Lyon, a huge expanse of cattails, probably the biggest marsh in Colorado, extends for 2.5 miles. Nearby riparian groves attract many migrant, breeding, and wintering birds. The Christmas Bird Count routinely counts over one hundred species.

The birding

Most Colorado birders approach John Martin from the west—they come from either Pueblo or Limon—so this guide starts at the west end of the reservoir, at Fort Lyon. Here marsh and land birds populate the extensive cattail marshes lined with clumps of trees. Turn south off US 50 on County Road 13, 4 miles east of Las Animas. From mid-June through July, look for Dickcissel along Road 13. Turn right on County Road HH (a quarter mile) to the *Fort Lyon easement.* A marsh in half a mile and the huge marsh at the end of Road HH support a full complement of Arkansas Valley marsh birds: Black and Virginia Rails, Sora, American Bittern (and an occasional Least Bittern), Great Blue Heron, American Coot, and Redwinged and Yellow-headed Blackbirds. Common Yellowthroat hiccup throughout the marsh.

For ten years, a small contingent of LeConte's Sparrows wintered in the marsh at the end of HH, but not since 2004–2005, because the marsh dried up. However, with springs still flowing, sedges and sapling cottonwoods have sprouted, so they may return. Other winter sparrows include Swamp, Savannah, and Lincoln's, plus Marsh, and, rarely, Sedge Wren.

Between the two marshes, in Siberian elm groves north and south of Road HH, and in the elms opposite the Veteran's Cemetery, an impressive variety of breeding and migrant land birds have occurred, but drought and disease killed many of the trees. Brown Thrashers and Orchard Orioles breed here. Migrants include most warblers recorded in Colorado, including such rarities as Northern

John Martin Reservoir State Park and SWA

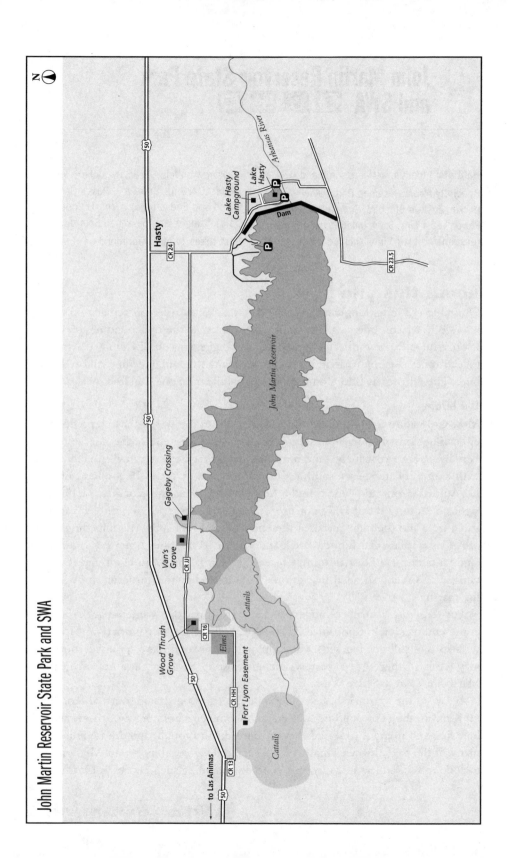

Parula, Black-throated Green, Hermit, Palm, and Cerulean. In winter this forest has lured a Northern Cardinal and mountain birds such as Northern Saw-whet Owl, Steller's Jay, and Varied Thrush.

Turn left on County Road 16. At the southeast corner of Roads 16 and JJ, *Wood Thrush Grove,* has attracted, yes, a Wood Thrush, and an array of eastern warblers including Prothonotary, Worm-eating, and Blackburnian, and once, a White-eyed Vireo. Breeding birds include Northern Mockingbird, Brown Thrasher, Yellow Warbler, and Blue Grosbeak. Unfortunately, half the trees were cut in 2005, severely damaging the habitat.

Go right on County Road JJ for 2 miles to *Van's Grove.* Park by the entrance road, where one or two mulberry trees stand guard over a path into a grove of widely spaced Siberian elms. Blue Grosbeak, Northern Mockingbird, and Brown Thrasher breed here. The list of warblers probably tops twenty-five species, including migrating Blue-winged, Golden-winged, Magnolia, Chestnut-sided, Mourning, Kentucky, and Hooded, plus White-eyed Vireo.

Just beyond Van's Grove, the spot where Gageby Creek crosses Road JJ is known as *Gageby Crossing.* The cattails lining the creek there sometimes harbor rarities such as Tri-colored Heron, Black Rail, Red Knot, and, once, Sharp-tailed Sandpiper. More typical are White-faced Ibis, Common Yellowthroat, and Red-Winged Blackbird in summer and Marsh Wren in winter.

John Martin State Park occupies the east end of the reservoir and below the dam. From Van's Grove, keep on JJ for 6.5 miles and turn right on County Road 24 to reach *Lake Hasty Campground.* Or from Hasty (on US 50, 14 miles east of Las Animas and 21 miles west of Lamar), turn south on Road 24 and drive 2 miles to the visitor center and a half mile down to the campground.

Good-size trees dot the campground, which boasts two resident eastern species: Eastern Bluebird and, sporadically, Red-bellied Woodpecker. The campground holds a variety of land birds; in summer Western Kingbird, (eastern) Warbling Vireo, and Bullock's and Orchard Orioles breed here. You might also find a Black-billed Cuckoo. Migrant songbirds drop into its green trees for food and rest; rarities include Vermilion Flycatcher, Gray-cheeked Thrush, Northern Parula, Worm-eating and Black-and-white Warblers, American Redstart, and Painted Bunting. Other oddballs sneak in, for example, a Black Vulture among roosting Turkey Vultures and an Olivaceous Cormorant among hundreds of Double-cresteds. *Lake Hasty,* a large pond, attracts many waterfowl and some shorebirds. Least Terns occasionally feed here. Geese, ducks, grebes, and a few shorebirds also use it. Four swans—three Trumpeters and one Tundra—spent one winter here. You can walk around the pond, look at it from the campground and various stops on the west side, or drive to a view point on the east side.

Below the dam the Arkansas River resumes its flow from a "stilling basin"; though lined with tamarisk (an eradication project began in 2006), it often has migrant or wintering land birds of interest—Greater Roadrunner, Bewick's Wren,

Ruby-crowned Kinglet, Wilson's Warbler, Blue Grosbeak, and Painted Bunting stand out.

In winter large flocks of Snow and Ross's Geese rest on the reservoir and fly up and down the river for daytime feeding. Skeins of these white honkers make a winter visit memorable. With them, flocks of Canada Geese often include Cackling Geese.

You can approach the reservoir on a road behind the visitor center (SWA Habitat Stamp required) or drive to the south side of the dam to a series of dirt two-tracks. Along the south shore summertime exclusions protect nesting Piping Plover and Least Tern. Other shorebirds also favor this side throughout the long migratory season (February to November). A winter closure applies from November 15 to April 1.

The prairie south of the reservoir looks barren, but in winter you can find Ferruginous Hawk and among the large flocks of Horned Larks, an occasional clutch of Lapland Longspurs—listen for their rattly call, different from the tinkly notes of the larks. Brewer's Blackbirds may hang around cattle pens in winter, and the area supports a contingent of winter shrikes—half Northern, half Loggerhead. In summer Cassin's Sparrows sing from the shrubby sections.

DeLorme grid: P. 99 D5-6.

Elevation: 3,900 feet.

Hazards: High centering and getting stuck in sand or mud.

Nearest food, gas, lodging: Las Animas, Lamar.

Camping: Hasty.

For more information: John Martin Reservoir State Park, 30703 Road 24, Hasty, CO 81044; (719) 829-1801; www.parks.state .co.us. Colorado Division of Wildlife, 2500 South Main Street, Lamar, CO 81052; (719) 336-6600; http://wildlife.state.co.us/land water/statewildlifeareas.

Bent's Old Fort National Historic Site

Habitats: Cattail marsh.

Specialty birds: *Summer:* Black Rail, Common Yellowthroat, Great-tailed Grackle.

Best times to bird: Dusk or dawn.

About this site

Bent's Old Fort traces its history back to the early 1800s, when it operated as a fort on the Santa Fe Trail. An appealing and authentic restoration by the National Park Service evokes images of its heyday. Well worth a time-out from birding to visit, it will reward you with a friendly reception and fascinating stories of early Colorado.

In the cattails by the highway entrance (fee not required), birders found the first Colorado Black Rails, which, it turns out, occur widely in the marshes of the lower Arkansas River. Most vocal from April to June, they lurk in shallow water among the reeds, not only at Bent's Fort but also in most cattail complexes from La Junta to Lamar.

Directions

From Las Animas, go west from the intersection of US 50 and Highway 194, north of the town, for 13 miles. From La Junta, go north from US 50 on Highway 109 to Highway 194, then east on 194 for 5 miles to the fort.

The birding

You can park at the DAR memorial, hop the wooden fence, and walk down to the marsh. Black Rails call most frequently from dusk to 10:00 P.M.—as do their marsh companions, Sora and Virginia Rail. Please refrain from using tape recorders, which may disturb them. Other birds in the marsh include American Coot, Red-winged and Yellow-headed Blackbirds, and Great-tailed Grackle.

In the fort you can see Barn Swallow and peacocks (not listable, but apparently legitimate as a denizen during fur-trading days).

DeLorme grid: P. 99 D4.

Elevation: 4,000 feet.

Hazards: Thistles.

Nearest food, gas, lodging: La Junta, Las Animas.

Camping: No.

For more information: Bent's Old Fort National Historic Site, 35110 Highway 194 East, La Junta, CO 81050; (719) 373-5010; www.nps.gov/beol.

12 Adobe Creek Reservoir SWA (Blue Lake) 📑 IBA

Habitats: Wetland.

Specialty birds: *Summer:* Piping and Mountain Plovers, Least Tern. *Migrant:* Shore-birds, terns. *Winter:* Lapland, McCown's, and Chestnut-collared Longspurs.

Best times to bird: Spring, summer, fall.

About this site

A good place to find shorebirds, Blue Lake, like other Arkansas Valley reservoirs, has varying dimensions that depend on rainfall, mountain snowpack, and irrigation demands. In high-water years an island forms on which terns, gulls, and plovers may nest. A continuing drought, coupled with no water inflow for four years, in 2005 brought the lake to its lowest level in fifty years and turned the island into a point of land. In 2006 the water level went up again and re-created the island; 2007 also has good water levels.

Directions

From the intersection of US 50 and Highway 194, on the north side of Las Animas, go west one-quarter mile, turn right (north) on County Road 10, and follow it to Blue Lake.

The birding

Three miles north of Las Animas, the road crosses one of the biggest unmolested short-grass prairies in the area. Unfortunately the harsh drought affected soil moisture severely, and plants (grasses and herbs) deteriorated. Prairie birds persist though: Among the abundant Horned Larks, look for Lark Bunting, Western Meadowlark, Long-billed Curlew, and, north of a stock pond on the right (9 miles), Mountain Plover. In winter the pond freezes, but the sun melts the fringe and longspurs come here to drink: Lapland, McCown's, and Chestnut-collared (less frequently). Shorebirds use the pond in migration. From here north, Mountain Plovers occur more commonly; so do jackrabbits.

At 12.5 miles County Road 10 meets County Road VV; in good weather stay on 10, but if it's rainy, watch out for muddy roads and detour right on VV and left on Road 11. On Road 10 the lake is one more mile away. At low water levels you can drive directly into the lake area. Try the dirt tracks to locate shoreline where you can find shorebirds. The north side of this lake is private, but you can explore the other three sides.

From February to November Blue Lake hosts an impressive variety of shorebirds and gulls. They include Snowy, Piping, and Black-bellied (September) Plovers, Black-necked Stilt, Willet, Hudsonian (rare) and Marbled (April and late June to August) Godwits, White-rumped (mid-May to mid-June), Stilt (late May), and Buff-breasted (rare) Sandpipers, Dunlin (rare), Sanderling, and Red-necked (regular in late May) and Red (rare) Phalaropes. In late June and July, Mountain Plovers stage in the hundreds and Long-billed Curlews around fifty; look for them on relatively bare ground, rather than on the shoreline or in taller vegetation.

Forster's, Common, and Black Terns come regularly, with occasional visits by Caspian and Arctic Terns and Sabine's Gull. White-faced and Glossy (rare) Ibis have stopped coming. The lake even has records of Reddish Egret and Little Blue Heron.

In good water years Least Tern and Piping Plover nest on the island in the lake, as long as the Division of Wildlife keeps the vegetation at bay. These birds don't nest amid vegetation, and if cottonwoods sprout on the island, they go elsewhere. In late 2005 water storage resumed. Water started to fill burrows where white-footed mice lived, and at least one hundred Northern Harriers streamed to the lakeshore to take advantage of the resulting bonanza of disoriented prey.

DeLorme grid: P. 99 D4.
Elevation: 4,128 feet.
Hazards: Getting stuck in sand or mud.
Nearest food, gas, lodging: Las Animas.
Camping: No.

For more information: Colorado Division of Wildlife, 2500 South Main Street, Lamar, CO 81052; (719) 336-6600; http://wildlife.state.co.us/landwater/statewildlifeareas.

Nonbreeding White Pelican loiter at Adobe Creek Reservoir.

13 Raven Lane

Habitats: Short-grass prairie.

Specialty birds: *Resident:* Raptors, Chihuahuan Raven. *Summer:* Mountain Plover, Long-billed Curlew, Grasshopper, Lark, and Cassin's Sparrows, Dickcissel. *Winter:* Lapland Longspur.

Best times to bird: Year-round.

About this site
Roads between Blue Lake and Queens SWA pass through short-grass habitat where you can find a variety of prairie birds, from raptors to sparrows.

Directions
You can run this route from Blue Lake to the Queens SWA or from Queens to Blue Lake. From Blue Lake, take County Road C from Road 19 to Road 27; jog north 2 miles to Road E, then right 4 miles to Road 31, south 1 mile to Road D, east (left) 5 miles to Road 36, north again 1 mile to Road E, and east 2.5 miles to Road 40. This takes you to the westernmost of the Queens reservoirs, Neesopah.

The birding
A power line runs along the north side of Road C, whose poles Chihuahuan Ravens deem excellent as nest sites. When Road C comes to a T intersection at Road 27, the power line veers off southeasterly; go left on the route described above, where you may encounter other plains specialties. During breeding season look for prairie sparrows: Lark Bunting and Grasshopper, Lark, and Cassin's. Cassin's prefer fields with several layers of vegetation. Dickcissel like somewhat taller vegetation and arrive later than other plains nesters, the bulk in mid-June. Look for Long-billed Curlew from April to June. On Road 27, Mountain Plovers breed (May/June). Scaled Quail and Burrowing and Short-eared Owls are also possible.

Look for raptors year-round: Northern Harrier, Swainson's (summer), and Red-tailed and Ferruginous Hawks, and in winter Golden Eagle, Merlin, and Prairie Falcon.

DeLorme grid: P. 99 D4–6.

Elevation: 4,000 feet.

Hazards: Muddy roads, blizzards.

Nearest food, gas, lodging: Las Animas, Lamar, Eads.

Camping: No.

Raven Lane, Great Plains Reservoirs

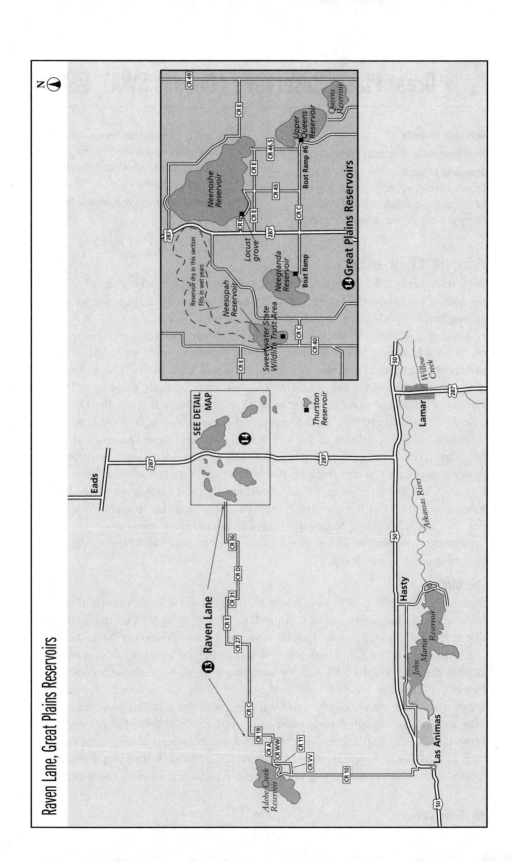

See map on page 61.

Habitats: Wetland, riparian, grassland.

Specialty birds: *Summer:* Yellow-billed Cuckoo, Red-eyed and (eastern) Warbling Vireos, Blue Grosbeak, Orchard Oriole. *Migrant:* Black-bellied, American Golden-,

Snowy, and Semipalmated Plovers, Red Knot, Sanderling, Red-necked Phalarope, Clay-colored Sparrow, Chestnut-collared and McCown's Longspurs.

Best times to bird: Spring, summer, fall.

About this site

Each reservoir in this group, also called Queens Reservoirs, holds a slightly different mix of birds. Limited access restricts viewing opportunities, but plan to spend at least half a day. Visit as many of the lakes as you can in one day.

Changing water levels from month to month mean that you may have to drive on two-track roads to get close enough to the water to see the birds. Shorebird variety abounds from April through October, so you want to get close to the shoreline to find them. Look where you see resting pelicans. In some years Piping Plovers nest at Neenoshe and Neegranda Reservoirs; when they do, the Division of Wildlife ropes off nesting areas to protect these endangered little runners.

Expect to find a plethora of shorebirds at Neenoshe, Upper Queens, and Neesopah Reservoirs, particularly from late July to September: numerous American Avocets and Baird's Sandpipers, plus Black-bellied, American Golden-, Semipalmated, and Snowy Plovers, Solitary, Stilt, and Pectoral Sandpipers, peeps, Red Knot, Sanderling, and Red-necked (rare) Phalarope. From fall to spring large numbers of Canada, Cackling, Snow, and Ross's Geese use these reservoirs.

Waterfowl closures in winter restrict access to Neenoshe and Neegranda; even land-birding areas are closed.

The birding

Start on U.S. Highway 287 going north from Lamar; go 4.5 miles north of the Kiowa County line to the *second* County Road E (there seem to be two here, the first at 4 miles) and turn right. This takes you to *Locust Grove* along *Neenoshe Reservoir.* Turn right at the T and park where a small patch of locusts comes up to the edge of the road (on the left). A dense understory grows beneath the locusts; beyond, an open cottonwood woodland beckons. Look for land birds—a big variety of flycatchers, vireos, kinglets, and warblers move through this little patch in May and August through October (for example, Eastern Phoebe, Eastern and Mountain Bluebirds, Black-and-white Warbler and Northern Waterthrush, strays such as Red-naped Sapsucker, Clark's Nutcracker, and Lazuli Bunting). Breeding species include Yellow-billed Cuckoo, Western Kingbird, Red-eyed and (eastern)

Warbling Vireo, Brown Thrasher, Blue Grosbeak, and Orchard and Bullock's Orioles. Great Horned (and maybe Long-eared) Owls breed and winter here, and Barn Owls migrate regularly. Nearby fields may collect Clay-colored Sparrow and Chestnut-collared and McCown's Longspurs.

Follow along the edge of the trees until you come to County Road 45, turn left toward the lake, and drive on two-tracks (how far depends on the water level—the habitat is transitory) until you get close enough to see the shore and water. All the terns on the Colorado list have visited this reservoir, including Arctic, Royal, and Caspian; also Reddish Egret and Sabine's Gull. It's a good place to look for ducks, grebes, shorebirds, and gulls.

Return to County Road 45; you can either stay on the road that skirts the trees or go out to the other Road E and turn east (right) for a mile to County Road 46.5. South 2 miles to County Road C, a road leads (left) to Boat Ramp #6 on *Upper Queens Reservoir.* Geese, ducks, pelicans, and shorebirds like to rest on the point to the right. Several hundred shorebirds can stop here, a prime spot for Long-billed Curlew and Whimbrel. Colorado's first Curlew Sandpiper stopped here. Cottonwoods on the left often hold eastern migrants.

Go back to County Road C and go left (west) 3 miles, across US 287, toward the Boat Ramp on *Neegranda Reservoir.* As at Neenoshe, check the two-tracks for views of water and shoreline. You might spot Black-bellied, Snowy, and Piping Plovers, Long-billed Curlew, and Whimbrel.

Return to US 287 and drive north 3-plus miles to Road F on the left. This passes Cottonwood Park campground (private) and swings south as County Road 41.2. Turn right at County Road C and in a mile, right on County Road 40. In 1.5 miles turn right to *Sweetwater State Wildlife Trust Area,* on *Neesopah Reservoir.* Neesopah, depending on water supply, covers a small to huge area—it can stretch the 4 miles over to US 287—but in recent years it shrank to a small area at Sweetwater. It sometimes has a good collection of shorebirds. Most of the lake is inaccessible to the public but camping is permitted on the right (no facilities).

If you return to US 287, you can check out *Thurston Reservoir SWA:* 4 miles south of the county line, go left (east) on County Road SS for 5 miles to County Road 7, then north to the reservoir. This shallow reservoir collects great numbers of ducks and shorebirds during their respective migrations. Sandhill Cranes use it in autumn and from February to April. One fall a Whooping Crane even stopped here for a couple of weeks.

DeLorme grid: P. 99 C6-7.

Elevation: 3,850 feet.

Hazards: Don't try two-track roads during rain, snow, or when they're muddy; rattlesnakes.

Nearest food, gas, lodging: Lamar, Eads.

Camping: No.

For more information: Colorado Division of Wildlife, 2500 South Main Street, Lamar, CO 81052; (719) 336-6600; http://wildlife.state.co.us/landwater/statewildlifeareas.

15 Lamar

Habitats: Riparian, urban.
Specialty birds: *Summer:* Mississippi Kite.
Winter: Carolina Wren. *Migrant:* Songbirds.

Best times to bird: April to October.

About this site
The birding

Two to three dozen pairs of Mississippi Kites have nested in **Lamar City Park** (Willow Creek Park) since the 1960s; a summer walk or drive through the park will yield many sightings of these graceful insect-eaters as they cruise around seeking prey. Go south on US 287 from the US 50 intersection in downtown Lamar half a mile to Cedar; turn left in half a mile to Parkview Avenue and right to the park. Take your picnic lunch and watch the kites' elegant flight maneuvers.

A 1-mile stretch of **Willow Creek** behind Lamar Community College attracts a fine variety of migrant songbirds. Follow US 287 south from US 50 1 mile to Lamar Community College; turn left and go behind the college buildings, where limited parking exists. Several trails, official and unofficial, provide entry into the dense riparian growth along Willow Creek. Take any of the trails that wind along the stream; upstream probably has more potential for finding birds. The Rocky Mountain Bird Observatory has run a banding station here each spring since 2003. Social trails and banding trails ramble all over the stream bottom, but please don't follow the net trails during banding, and don't walk between trails because concentrated birding here has created enough trails—leave habitat for the birds!

Spring attracts the biggest diversity. A sampling: Broad-winged Hawk, Red-bellied Woodpecker, White-Eyed Vireo, Cassin's Vireo, Carolina Wren (into winter), Brown Thrasher, Hermit and Varied (spent the winter) Thrushes, Orange-crowned, Cape May, Blackpoll, and Wilson's Warblers, Western Tanager, Clay-colored and Field Sparrows, Indigo Bunting, and Rose-breasted Grosbeak. Occasionally, Northern Cardinals nest. In fall other species may pass through such as Yellow-billed Cuckoo and White-breasted (eastern race) and Red-breasted Nuthatches.

DeLorme grid: P. 99 D7.
Elevation: 3,650 feet.
Hazards: Biting insects.

Nearest food, gas, lodging: Lamar.
Camping: No.

16 Two Buttes SWA W⊕ 🗎

Habitats: Riparian, cliff, grassland, wetlands.

Specialty birds: *Resident:* Greater Roadrunner. *Summer:* Barn Owl, Yellow-billed Cuckoo, Say's and Eastern Phoebes, Cliff Swallows, Northern Mockingbird, Canyon Towhee. *Migrant:* Vireos, warblers.

Best times to bird: Spring and fall.

About this site

Colorado birders journey a long way to Two Buttes to seek rare and elusive migrants, especially eastern vireos and warblers. Between US 287 and the dam, grasslands attract Lark Bunting, and Cassin's Sparrow lark above the grass, sagebrush, and yucca. Cassin's, while rather nondescript, has an ethereal song: a sweet trill followed by two deliberate chips.

Directions

Fill up with gasoline before venturing here. Go south from the junction of US 50 and US 287 in downtown Lamar for 29 miles; turn left on County Road C, then right on County Road 12, just before Two Buttes (the actual buttes, not the town). In 2 miles, just before Two Buttes Dam, a well-hidden track on the left drops below the dam (opposite the edge of a small "village").

PHOTO © WILLIAM EDEN

Migrating eastern warblers, such as this Black-and-white Warbler, lure Colorado birders to Two Buttes.

The birding

Stop in the first parking lot and drive or walk the trails and down the road to the turnaround. *Black Hole,* a luxuriant riparian bottomland with several ponds and a red sandstone cliff, can attract an interesting mix of migrant and breeding birds. Don't let the extensive trash strewn all over dismay you—the birds ignore it. Lush growth entices migrants to stop for a day or two before they move on. Prowl along the various trails and the road that runs down the north side of the small canyon. Tall cottonwoods, thick box-elders, Russian olives, and dense shrubby thickets supply habitat for the variety of birds here.

Breeding birds comprise an odd mix of eastern and western species. They include Barn Owl, Yellow-billed Cuckoo, Say's and Eastern Phoebes, Cliff Swallows in abundance, Northern Mockingbird, Brown Thrasher, Yellow Warbler, Canyon Towhee, Blue and Black-headed Grosbeaks, and Bullock's Oriole. Colorado birders have found such exotic (for Colorado) species as Green Heron, Bell's and White-eyed Vireos, Golden-winged, Tennessee, Northern Parula, Magnolia, Chestnut-sided, Blackpoll, and Black-and-white Warblers, Summer Tanager, and Painted Bunting. January can produce Ladder-backed Woodpecker, (eastern) White-breasted Nuthatch, Winter and Carolina Wrens, Hermit Thrush, Curve-billed Thrasher, and Rufous-crowned Sparrow.

When it has water, *Two Buttes Reservoir* attracts both diving and dabbling ducks, Snow Goose, Western Grebe, and long-legged waders including Snowy Egret, White-faced Ibis, Whimbrel, and Stilt Sandpiper. To reach it, cross the dam and go west (right) on County Road VV toward US 287. Look on the right for the rough dirt roads that provide access to the reservoir in several spots.

On County Road VV, about 3.5 miles from the dam, look for an outhouse; turn right on an unmarked dirt road just beyond it. A trail leads into a cottonwood gallery forest, with lots of birds, though of limited variety. In spring and summer expect the typical nesting species of such groves: Eastern and Western Kingbirds, Loggerhead Shrike, Northern Mockingbird, Brown Thrasher, Lark Sparrow, and Bullock's Oriole. Warbling Vireos here probably belong to the eastern subspecies, perhaps destined to become a separate species.

From here west, VV traverses sagebrush and grassland where you can encounter Horned Lark, Cassin's Sparrow, and Lark Bunting. In migration expect hundreds of Chipping, Clay-colored, Vesper, and Lark Sparrows.

DeLorme grid: P. 101 B7.

Elevation: 4,200 feet.

Hazards: Fill up with gas before setting out; Saurday night beer parties.

Nearest food, gas, lodging: Springfield, Lamar.

Camping: Permitted but not recommended.

For more information: Colorado Division of Wildlife, 2500 South Main Street, Lamar, CO 81052; (719) 336-6600; http://wildlife.state.co.us/landwater/statewildlifeareas.

Carrizo Picnic Area/Cottonwood Canyon and Picture Canyon

Habitats: Pinyon/juniper, riparian, cactus grassland.

Specialty birds: *Resident:* Greater Roadrunner, Chihuahuan Raven, Curve-billed Thrasher, Bewick's and Canyon Wrens, Canyon Towhee. *Summer:* Long-billed Curlew, Eastern Phoebe,

Mississippi Kite, Western Screech-Owl, Ladder-backed Woodpecker, Cassin's Kingbird, Rufous-crowned Sparrow, Painted Bunting. *Migrant:* Warblers, sparrows.

Best times to bird: Spring, summer, fall.

About this site

Carrizo/Cottonwood pulls in birders like a magnet. It attracts a curious mix of eastern, prairie, and southwestern avifauna, including species rare in the rest of Colorado. The odd mix includes Mississippi Kite, Western Screech-Owl, Yellow-billed Cuckoo, Ladder-backed Woodpecker, Ash-throated Flycatcher, Cassin's Kingbird, Bewick's and Canyon Wrens, Canyon Towhee, Blue Grosbeak, and Painted Bunting.

The road crosses a cactus-clad prairie to Carrizo and Cottonwood Canyons, both with lush growths of junipers, cottonwoods, box-elders, and chokecherry.

Directions

Fill up with gas before you leave the highway. Avoid back roads during thunderstorms: Baca County roads can turn to mud pie. From the intersection of US 287 and 160 in Springfield, go south on 287 for 16 miles and turn right on County Road M. A sign advises that it's 16 miles to Picture Canyon, 22 to Carrizo.

The birding

Immediately west of US 287 along Road M, east and west of County Road 23, a mile-long prairie-dog town hosts Burrowing Owls. Other likely birds along the road: Long-billed Curlew, Horned Lark, Chihuahuan Ravens (which nest on power poles), and Lark Bunting. Also look for pronghorns and savor the big sky. Brown signs along the road mark pastures administered by the Comanche National Grassland. This part of Baca County excels at sparrow migration: During May you can encounter hundreds of Chipping, Clay-colored, and Lark Sparrows, dozens of Brewer's and Vesper Sparrows, and thousands of Lark Buntings.

Try **Picture Canyon** only if you have extra time; Carrizo/Cottonwood has much more allure. Picture Canyon has fewer birds, but it also has Native American rock art—petroglyphs as well as pictographs (battered by time and latter-day "artists")—along the canyon walls. Some of the original petroglyphs may have had astronomical significance. Cliffs only 100 to 200 feet high line the half-mile- to 1-mile-wide canyon floor.

Eight miles from the turnoff from US 287 on Road M, turn left (south) on County Road 18; in 8 miles, turn right (south) at the Picture Canyon road sign (Forest Road 533), then proceed 1 mile to the parking area.

This site excels as a place to see Rufous-crowned Sparrow. Two loop trails, 4 and 8 miles long, provide scenic vistas and unusual rock formations. A shorter walk takes you along the east side of the canyon. Rufous-crowned Sparrows sing their tinkly song from rocks on the side of the canyon. Within a half mile you come to small stands of hackberry trees and a couple of small, marshy ponds with cattails. In the trees look for Bewick's Wren and Blue Grosbeak. (Another half-mile trek takes you across the broad valley floor to the Oklahoma border.)

Make sure you have plenty of time for Carrizo/Cottonwood; 14.5 miles from the Picture Canyon turnoff, turn left into the **Carrizo Picnic Area.** A short loop trail drops to Carrizo Creek and goes upstream and over a ridge back to the parking area. A big colony of Cliff Swallows nests along the stream. Other likely birds

A disparate selection of eastern, southern, and western species populate the riparian forests in Cottonwood Canyon.

include Western and Cassin's Kingbirds, Ash-throated Flycatcher (also look for these in the cottonwoods on the road into the picnic area), Eastern and Say's Phoebes, Bewick's and Rock Wrens, Northern Mockingbird, and Blue Grosbeak, and in the cactus, Curve-billed Thrasher.

Return to Road M and stay on it as it winds over a juniper-covered mesa (Lark Sparrow and Western Kingbird) and, in 5 miles, drops down into **Cottonwood Canyon.** Stop anywhere in the next mile and a half. Mississippi Kites wheel gracefully over the canyon hawking insects. Turkey Vultures and Red-tailed Hawks soar over the canyon, too. Maybe a roadrunner will zip across in front of you. In the trees look for Yellow-billed Cuckoo, Black-chinned Hummingbird, Lewis's Woodpecker, Bewick's Wren, Yellow Warbler, Blue Grosbeak, and Bullock's Oriole. Canyon Wrens sometimes nest in abandoned adobe buildings. The hillsides resound with noisy Rock Wrens. For several years birders have found Painted Bunting up a side canyon. P/J boasts the usual species. If you camp, you'll probably hear and maybe see a Western Screech-Owl.

The road crosses a fence with a PRIVATE PROPERTY sign; it's okay to drive it as long as you stay on the road; don't leave the road looking for those elusive birds. This section can have Rufous-crowned Sparrow and Canyon Towhee singing from the sparsely vegetated hillsides; Ladder-backed Woodpeckers may flit through the scrub oak beside the road. The road turns into County Road J and loops back to CR M (10 miles). Across M, look in the field to the right for Long-billed Curlew. Surprisingly hard to see despite their size (towering over the short grass), curlews call attention to themselves with noisy calls uttered in flight.

DeLorme grid: Carrizo/Cottonwood, p. 101 D5; Picture Canyon, p. 99 D6.

Elevation: 4,300 to 4,900 feet.

Hazards: Rattlesnakes and cacti.

Nearest food, gas, lodging: Springfield.

Camping: Yes.

For more information: Carrizo Unit, Comanche National Grassland, 27204 U.S. Highway 287, P.O. Box 127, Springfield, CO 81073; (719) 523-6591; www.fs.fed.us/ r2/psicc/coma.

18 Campo Lek W⊕ IBA

Habitats: Grassland.

Specialty birds: *Resident:* Lesser Prairie-Chicken. *Summer:* Cassin's Sparrow.

Best time to bird: April.

About this site

Lesser Prairie-Chickens put on lively dances at this site, Colorado's only public lek for seeing them. As always with any lek, *please:*
- **arrive before** the birds start displaying (i.e. before dawn).
- **stay in your car.**
- **leave** only **after** they finish.

Directions

From Springfield, go south 21.5 miles on US 287/385 to Campo. Go left (east) 8 miles on County Road J, right (south) on County Road 36 for 2 miles, left (east) on County Road G for almost 4 miles to a small two-track on the right, marked by a large sign with many bullet holes. (If you go over the small bridge at just over 4 miles, you went too far.) Follow the two-track a little over a quarter mile to a parking lot on the right.

The birding

The Forest Service installed a blind here for lek watchers. You can arrange in advance to pick up a key in Springfield. Views from the car usually satisfy birdwatchers who don't use the blind. Your car is warmer, especially in March and April.

In late April or May you will almost certainly hear the Cassin's Sparrows that abound in this area, and Chestnut-collared Longspurs stop during migration in early April. A bird tour leader reported Eastern Meadowlark here too.

DeLorme grid: P. 103 D7.

Elevation: 4,300 feet.

Hazards: Cold temperatures; black widow spiders in the blind.

Nearest food, gas, lodging: Springfield; Campo for breakfast.

Camping: No.

For more information: Carrizo Unit, Comanche National Grassland, 27204 U.S. Highway 287, P.O. Box 127, Springfield, CO 81073; (719) 523-6591; www.fs.fed.us/r2/psicc/coma.

Northern Front Range

The heavily urbanized corridor from Denver north to Fort Collins offers bird-watchers a rich assortment of bird-watching places, courtesy of city, county, state, and federal open-space programs. Coloradans call it the "Front Range," although mountaineers apply that term to the mountain range that stretches from Wyoming to Pikes Peak. Fort Collins and Boulder have outstanding open-space programs that protect plains habitats that suburbia would otherwise blanket. National forest lands occupy much of the foothills and mountains, and Rocky Mountain National Park shines as the showpiece of the high country. South of the park the Indian Peaks Wilderness protects another 30-mile stretch of glaciated magnificence.

Parks and open space span every habitat, from short-grass prairie and lowland riparian to alpine tundra. In most cities, trails parallel one or more streams that run through them; open-space properties encompass natural areas and irrigation reservoirs, stream bottoms and gravel ponds, conifer-clad hillsides, and well-grazed pastures. All these lands, depending on the level of human disturbance, serve as magnets for birds and bird-watchers.

Countless waterbirds throng to bodies of water such as old gravel pits and irrigation reservoirs. Land birds pile into the cottonwood-lined streams. Native western birds breed in numbers in the foothills and high mountains despite encroaching suburbs and second homes. Prairie natives find a few places not converted to wheat, corn, or houses. In all, the Front Range folds in a grand diversity of birdlife in a splendid setting.

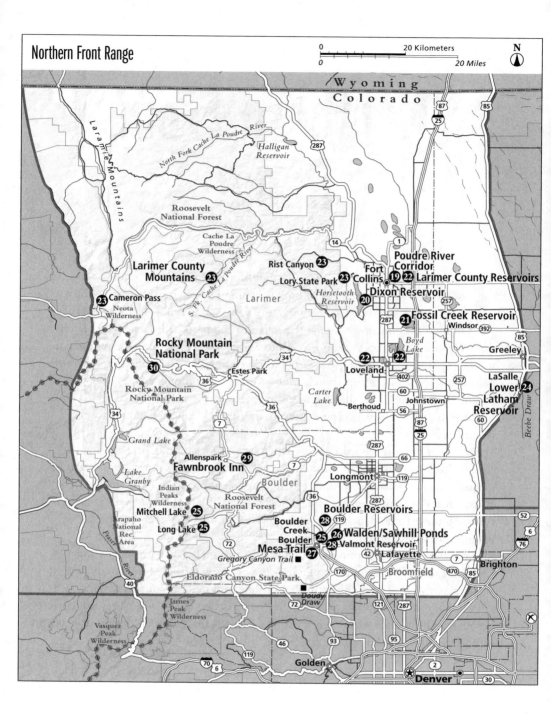

⑲ Poudre River Corridor ♿

Habitats: Riparian, wetlands.

Specialty birds: *Resident:* Eastern Screech-Owl. *Summer:* Egrets, herons, American Bittern, Virginia Rail, Sora, Marsh Wren, Yellow-headed Blackbird, Great-tailed Grackle. *Migrant:* American White Pelican, White-faced Ibis, warblers, flycatchers, sparrows. *Winter:* Waterfowl, geese; Barrow's Goldeneye possible.

Best times to bird: Spring and summer.

About this site

The City of Fort Collins owns a battery of natural areas along the Cache la Poudre River. A trail parallels the stream all the way through the city from Interstate 25 west to Overland Trail (road). Sand and gravel mining left behind over a dozen pits, now filled with water, that the city turned into natural areas for wildlife-watching, hiking, and other recreation. These sites offer great opportunities for half-day or all-day wildlife walks, as well as city bird-watching before breakfast or during breaks from more mundane activities.

Directions

The city trail has many access points, from Riverside Avenue, Mulberry Avenue, and other streets in the city. The best bird-watching sites cluster at the east end of the city in a contiguous group of natural areas. Among several sites off Prospect Road, on the south side try *Cottonwood Hollow* and *Environmental Learning Center,* a mile west of I–25 (exit 268); *Riverbend Ponds* on the north side, just west of the Cottonwood Hollow lot; and *Prospect Ponds,* west 0.5 mile to Sharp Point Drive and south to the parking area.

The birding

Within the natural areas, trails lead to viewing spots for ponds, marshes, and cottonwood riparian zones. Nesting species include Wood Duck, egrets, herons, American Bittern, Killdeer, and Red-winged and Yellow-headed Blackbirds. Green Herons sometimes nest here, and summer-long sightings of Caspian Terns tantalize birders about possible nesting. A hacking project for Osprey failed to establish a nesting population, though Osprey do stop during migration. Other species use the wetlands: Western and Clark's Grebes, White Pelican, and, occasionally in winter, Barrow's Goldeneye. In April a few shorebirds show up: Killdeer, both yellowlegs, and Wilson's Snipe. In summer Eastern and Western Kingbirds, Marsh Wren, and Song Sparrow inhabit the marshes and uplands. In fall geese move in: lots of Cacklings among the Canadas, and a few Greater White-fronted, Snow, and Ross's.

On riparian trails, migrant warblers can include a variety of eastern strays such as Northern Parula, Northern Waterthrush, Townsend's, Blackburnian, Black-and-

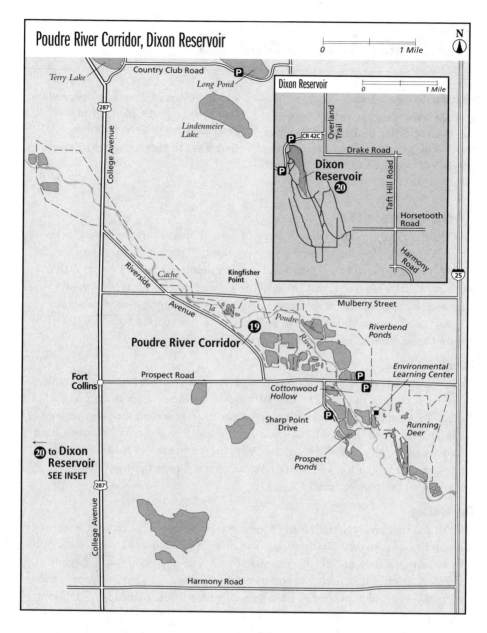

Poudre River Corridor, Dixon Reservoir

N

0   1 Mile

Dixon Reservoir

0   1 Mile

Terry Lake

Country Club Road

Long Pond

Lindenmeier Lake

287

College Avenue

Overland Trail

CR 42C

Drake Road

Dixon Reservoir

20

Taft Hill Road

Horsetooth Road

Harmony Road

25

Riverside

Cache

Kingfisher Point

la

Mulberry Street

Poudre

Avenue

Poudre River

19

Riverbend Ponds

Poudre River Corridor

Fort Collins

Prospect Road

Environmental Learning Center

Cottonwood Hollow

Sharp Point Drive

Running Deer

20 to Dixon Reservoir
SEE INSET

287

College Avenue

Prospect Ponds

Harmony Road

white, Prothonotary (a week in September 2005), Kentucky, and Hooded Warblers. Among the regular migrating flycatchers, vireos, and such, you might find thrushes—Veery, Hermit, and lots of Swainson's (late May).

A feed lot next to Cottonwood Hollow lures blackbirds in winter: Red-winged, Yellow-headed, and Brewer's, plus starlings and crows. For three winters, observers spotted a Harlan's Red-tailed Hawk here.

DeLorme grid: P. 20 D2.
Elevation: 5,000 feet.
Nearest food, gas, lodging: Fort Collins.
Camping: Fort Collins.

For more information: Natural Areas Program, P.O. Box 580, Fort Collins, CO 80522-0580; (970) 416-2815; www.fcgov.com/natural areas.

An American Bittern, thinking itself invisible, may stand stockstill in the marsh.

Dixon Reservoir (Pine Ridge Natural Area)

See map on page 74.

Habitats: Riparian, wetlands, shrubland.

Specialty birds: *Resident:* Great Horned Owl.

Summer: Blue Grosbeak. *Migrant:* Flycatchers, warblers, sparrows.

Best times to bird: May, August to September.

About this site

This migrant trap in southwest Fort Collins provides an oasis of deciduous trees for passerines ready to rest after a long night. Cottonwood, willow, and box-elder trees rise above Russian-olive, chokecherry, honeysuckle, and hawthorn thickets; they provide food for insect hunters ready to replenish after an evening journey. The lake pulls in some waterfowl during migration, but few in summer.

Dixon Reservoir shines during spring migration, with a diverse complement of migrating songbirds.

Directions

From exit 265 on I–25, go west on Harmony Road 7.5 miles to Taft Hill Road, then right 1.5 miles, left on Drake, right at the T intersection on Overland, and left on County Road 42C a half mile to the trailhead. Turn around there and park on the south side of the road. (Or about a half mile farther, you can go left into a parking lot for the Natural Area and walk down to the riparian sections.)

The birding

From the first, lower parking area, enter through the walk-around next to a metal gate. Keep within the fences (i.e., don't trespass) and follow the formal trail or social trails on either side of Dixon Dam. Migrants and breeders populate the thick stand of cottonwoods, box-elders, and Russian olives. You can walk along the dam and the east side of the reservoir to bands of cottonwoods that sometimes trap spring migrants.

Spring migration brings regular warbler migrants plus eastern ones: Golden-winged, Tennessee, Black-throated Gray, Blackburnian, Worm-eating, Blackpoll, and Northern Waterthrush. Other migrants include flycatchers—Eastern Phoebe, Ash-throated Flycatcher, and *Empidonax* flycatchers including Gray Flycatcher—swallows and thrushes (mainly Hermit and Swainson's), Brown Thrasher, White-crowned and Lincoln's Sparrows, and Orchard Oriole. On the lake, waterfowl pass through in March and April, as well as Osprey, Sora, and Wilson's Snipe. Killdeer nest along the shore.

Nesting species include common riparian species plus Gray Catbird, Common Yellowthroat, Yellow-breasted Chat, Spotted Towhee, and Lesser and American Goldfinches.

From the parking lot half a mile farther up Road 42C, a trail follows a power line along a shrubby hillside (mainly mountain mahogany) with Western Kingbird, Blue-gray Gnatcatcher, Bushtit (sporadic), Spotted Towhee, and House Finch.

DeLorme grid: P. 20 D1.

Elevation: 4,900 feet.

Hazards: Park carefully to avoid traffic, blocking gates, and parking restrictions.

Nearest food, gas, lodging: Fort Collins.

Camping: No.

For more information: Natural Areas Program, P.O. Box 580, Fort Collins, CO 80522-0580; (970) 416-2815; www.fcgov.com/natural areas.

21 Fossil Creek Reservoir

Habitats: Wetlands, riparian, grassland.

Specialty birds: *Resident:* Great Horned Owl. *Summer:* Clark's Grebe, Marsh Wren, Yellow-headed Blackbird, Orchard Oriole. *Migrant:* Geese and ducks, loons, grebes, sandpipers.

Winter: Bald Eagle, waterfowl, American Tree Sparrow.

Best times to bird: April to May, October to November.

About this site

This new park provides a great overlook from which to view most of the lake, ringed by a narrow line of trees. Operated by Larimer County for wildlife and open space, the park should develop into a major stopover for migrating waterfowl; it allows no boats or fishing. Short paved paths lead to picnic tables and the overlook, and dirt trails lead to other sections. Because you look from the south, over-the-shoulder light provides good viewing all day. For three years, before the park opened officially, Fort Collins Audubon conducted monthly surveys of the park and produced a 197-species bird list, half of them waterbirds—a high proportion for Colorado.

Bird watchers in Fort Collins continue to add species to the list for Fossil Creek Reservoir.

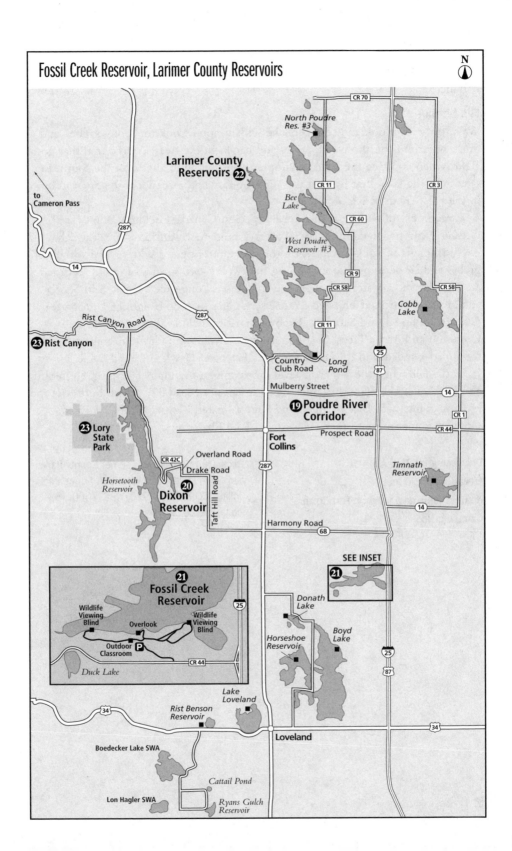

Fossil Creek Reservoir, Larimer County Reservoirs

N

to Cameron Pass

287

14

Larimer County Reservoirs 22

North Poudre Res. #3

CR 70

CR 11

CR 3

Bee Lake

CR 60

West Poudre Reservoir #3

CR 9

CR 58

CR 58

Cobb Lake

Rist Canyon Road

287

23 Rist Canyon

CR 11

Country Club Road

Long Pond

25

87

Mulberry Street

14

23 Lory State Park

19 **Poudre River Corridor**

CR 1

Fort Collins

Prospect Road

CR 44

CR 42C

Overland Road

287

Timnath Reservoir

Horsetooth Reservoir

Drake Road

20 **Dixon Reservoir**

Taft Hill Road

14

Harmony Road

68

SEE INSET

21

21 **Fossil Creek Reservoir**

25

Donath Lake

Wildlife Viewing Blind

Overlook

Wildlife Viewing Blind

Horseshoe Reservoir

Boyd Lake

Outdoor Classroom

P

CR 44

25

Duck Lake

87

Lake Loveland

34

Rist Benson Reservoir

Boedecker Lake SWA

Loveland

34

Cattail Pond

Lon Hagler SWA

Ryans Gulch Reservoir

Directions

From exit 262 on I–25, go west 0.5 mile on County Road 32 to the park entrance.

The birding

Walk to the overlook and scan the lake with a scope. Look for loons, grebes, and other waterbirds on the water, eagles and hawks in the trees. Try the trail that goes right (when you face the lake) to another overlook, with a view of the southeast section of the lake (best light in the afternoon), where occasional scoters stop by in the fall. Stay on the trails, please.

Large flocks of geese can include six species (Canada, Cackling, Brant [rare], Greater White-fronted, Snow, and Ross's). Trumpeter Swans drop in, although rarely. Big rafts of ducks often sit on the water, interspersed with several species of grebes and an occasional loon. Among the twenty-two species of ducks recorded are Canvasback, Greater Scaup among the Lesser, Long-tailed Duck, Surf Scoter, and Hooded and Red-breasted Mergansers. Gulls include Laughing, Bonaparte's, Glaucous-winged, and Sabine's. Reported rarities include Brown Pelican and Common and Arctic Terns. In summer expect Swainson's Hawk, in migration look for Broad-winged, and in winter for Rough-legged Hawk and Bald Eagle.

In the fall, when the reservoir level drops, migrant sandpipers appear. Shorebirds also like Duck Lake (another mile west on County Road 32), which buttresses the usual migrants with Black-bellied and Semipalmated Plovers, Willet, Marbled Godwit, Sanderling, and Red-necked and Red Phalaropes.

DeLorme grid: P. 30 A2.
Elevation: 5,200 feet.
Nearest food, gas, lodging: Fort Collins.
Camping: No.

For more information: Larimer County Parks and Open Lands, 200 West Oak Street, Fort Collins, CO 80521; (970) 498-7000; www.co.larimer.co.us/parks.

22 Larimer County Reservoirs

See map on page 79.

Habitats: Wetlands.

Specialty birds: *Migrant:* Waterbirds, fifteen gull species. *Winter:* Short-eared, Long-eared, and Barn Owls.

Best times to bird: Spring and fall.

About this site

A surfeit of reservoirs surrounds Fort Collins, most of which hold water for irrigation and follow the typical Colorado pattern: They fill up from October to March, then irrigators draw them down from April to September. Birders tour these reservoirs in fall and spring to find loons, grebes, geese, ducks, and gulls.

Gulls especially intrigue local bird-watchers, with thirteen species seen from fall 2004 to spring 2005. Typical species include Ring-billed, Herring, and California. Fall migrants among the hundreds of gulls include Franklin's, Bonaparte's, and Sabine's; fall through spring brings a few Glaucous, Thayer's, Lesser Black-backed, and Great Black-backed Gulls. The area has one record each of Slaty-backed (it spent lots of time at the dump) and Kelp (probably the same bird that appeared at Jackson Lake a week earlier) Gulls.

The birding

Among the dozens of reservoirs, try some of these. For *Long Pond* (ducks and gulls), drive north on Lemay Avenue for 2.5 miles and turn right on Country Club Road. This privately owned lake has only one viewing spot, shortly after the road curves to skirt the lake. In late fall diving ducks and a smattering of gulls congregate here.

Lakes along County Road 11 also feature ducks and gulls. From Long Pond, drive east to Turnberry Road/CR 11, turn left, and in 3.5 miles turn right on County Road 58. In 0.8 mile, turn left on Highway 9 and proceed to County Road 60, which angles north to skirt *Bee Lake* and then goes north to *North Poudre Reservoir #3*. Even with high water levels, they attract a few spring shorebirds—the list includes White-faced Ibis, Willet, Marbled Godwit, Long-billed Dowitcher, and Red-necked Phalarope—and in the fall, Sandhill Crane.

Across I–25, County Road 3's series of lakes pick up ducks, gulls, marsh birds, a variety of sparrows, and, in winter, Short-eared, Long-eared, and Barn Owls. From exit 281 (I–25) north of Wellington, go east on County Road 70 to Road 3. Drive south (right) past a series of reservoirs and wildlife areas. Look from the road at the reservoirs; some SWAs permit walk-ins except during waterfowl-nesting or hunting season. Road 3 comes to a T intersection, where you can peer into *Cobb Lake* from a pull-off to the right. Go east 1 mile to the county line; to the right a colony of prairie dogs hosts nesting Burrowing Owls and may, in winter, attract Ferruginous Hawks. Two miles south of Highway 14, the road provides a limited view of *Timnath Reservoir.*

South of Fort Collins at another collection of lakes, a procession of gulls moves back and forth during the winter and early spring. Directions: From I–25 exit 257, take U.S. Highway 34 west 3 miles to Madison Avenue then jog right on East 37th Street to a right turn on North, then north (left) on County Road 11C. *Boyd Lake* is on the right, *Horseshoe Reservoir* on the left. For *Donath Lake,* go north on 11C to the T intersection and turn left in half a mile. Boats and anglers make Boyd a poor place to find birds from April to October, but in other months it and nearby reservoirs attract a good mix of waterfowl and gulls. Gulls come in to roost in late afternoon on *Lake Loveland* in downtown Loveland. Like Boyd, it receives heavy recreational use year-round, but a few migrants use it. Follow US 34 through the city till it curves around the south side of the lake; west of this, go north on Taft about a mile to the park entrance on the right. West of Lake Loveland 1.5 miles on US 34 (north side), *Rist Benson Lake* picks up winter gulls.

All these lakes have similar lists of gulls and ducks. Waterfowl can include the expected as well as a rare Long-tailed Duck, Greater Scaup, or Common Loon. Each year exploring birders discover other reservoirs where they find similar mixes of waterbirds.

DeLorme grid: P. 20 C2-3, D2-3, p. 30 A2.
Elevation: 5,200 feet.
Nearest food, gas, lodging: Fort Collins, Loveland.
Camping: Yes.

For more information: Colorado Division of Wildlife, 1424 NE Frontage Road, Fort Collins, CO 81524; (970) 416-3329; http://wildlife .state.co.us/landwater/statewildlifeareas.

23 Larimer County Mountains 〔w〕

Habitats: Ponderosa, shrubland, foothills riparian, spruce/fir.

Specialty birds: *Resident:* Boreal Owl. *Summer:* Ovenbird.

Best times to bird: Year-round.

About this site
Habitats here range from shrubland to conifer forests, montane grasslands, and mountain riparian streamsides. The foothills and mountains west of Fort Collins beckon birders.

The birding
Trails in **Lory State Park** lead into shrubland, ponderosa, and foothills riparian habitats, although birding from the road offers only limited opportunities. To get there from nearby Dixon Reservoir, drive up County Road 42C; turn right at the top and drive north along the edge of Horsetooth Reservoir. In 5 miles turn left on County Road 25G and follow it 1.5 miles to the entrance to Lory. Alternatively,

The secretive Northern Saw-whet Owl hides itself well during the day, but in late winter and early spring utters its monotonous single hoot as often as 120 times per minute.

from U.S. Highway 287, turn west on County Road 54G; after 3.5 miles, turn south at the Bellevue Store on County Road 23; go 4 miles to County Road 25G and on to the park.

The winding road up **Rist Canyon** produces ponderosa birds. Directions: North of Fort Collins on US 287, go past LaPorte, turn west on County Road 54G, then in 1.5 miles turn left on County Road 52E, the Rist Canyon Road (look for Vern's Restaurant).

Stop at wide spots to look and listen for ponderosa species, possibly including, at night, Flammulated and Northern Saw-whet Owls. Look for hummingbird feeders by houses, and in 10 miles listen for Ovenbird, a rare Colorado breeder. In another 5 miles, at a T at Stove Prairie Road, turn right to Poudre Canyon and Highway 14. Heavy recreational traffic on the river and highway make this section a dubious place for bird-watching, except in winter.

Evenings in late winter (March and April), you can drive up Poudre Canyon to **Cameron Pass** and the site of Colorado's first Boreal Owl observations. North of Fort Collins, turn off US 287 at Ted's Place onto Highway 14; drive about 60 miles to Chambers Lake.

Listen for the owl's haunting tremolo, similar to a winnowing snipe. We urge you to refrain from playing tapes due to the number of people who seek these little owls and the deleterious effect of such antics on birds. Stop at safe turnouts to listen. Though Boreals occur on both sides of the pass, most reports come from the east side. Some years observers find several; some years they have a hard time finding even one. In summer the pass and the roads leading off provide excellent spruce/fir birding.

DeLorme grid: Lory and Rist Canyon, p. 19 D7, p. 20 C1; Cameron Pass, p. 18–19 C4–7, D3–4.

Elevation: Lory and Rist Canyon, 5,300 to 7,800 feet; Cameron Pass, 10,276 feet.

Nearest food, gas, lodging: Fort Collins.

Camping: Yes.

For more information: U.S. Forest Service, 2150 Centre Avenue, Building E, Fort Collins, CO 80526; (970) 295-6700; www.fs.fed.us/ r2/arnf.

24 Lower Latham Reservoir

Habitats: Wetlands.
Specialty birds: *Summer:* Cinnamon Teal, Sandhill Crane, American Avocet, Black-necked Stilt, Wilson's Phalarope, Marsh Wren,

Great-tailed Grackle. *Migrant:* Ducks, herons and egrets, shorebirds.
Best times to bird: Spring and summer.

About this site

Lower Latham offers splendid viewing of ducks and shorebirds. Although you can view birds in this wetlands complex only from county roads, ponds and marshes on the south side of the reservoir harbor a surprising variety of visible marsh and water birds. The shallow ponds attract migrants and nesting species that move around and offer good views in good light.

Directions

From U.S. Highway 85, exit at La Salle, go southeast on 1st Avenue and east on Todd Avenue (County Road 50) for 2.5 miles. At the T intersection, go south (right) 1 mile on County Road 43 (check the pond on the left), then left on County Road 48, on the south side of the reservoir. Ponds and wetlands line County Road 48 for the next mile.

The birding

Survey the ponds on both sides of County Road 48. Shorebird migrants include Semipalmated Plover, Marbled Godwit, White-rumped Sandpiper (late May and early June), and Red-necked Phalarope. Common migrating ducks use the wetlands; occasionally so do less common ones such as Snow Goose, Canvasback, and Greater Scaup (all most likely in March and April). A Peregrine Falcon sometimes scours the marsh for prey. Large migrating flocks of blackbirds include Red-winged, Yellow-headed, and Brewer's, Great-tailed and Common Grackles, and Brown-headed Cowbird.

During breeding season the cattails buzz with singing Marsh Wren, Common Yellowthroat, Savannah Sparrow, Yellow-headed Blackbird, and Great-tailed Grackle. Breeders in the marsh include American Bittern, Cinnamon and Blue-winged Teal, Northern Harrier, White-faced Ibis, Sora, Virginia Rail, Black-necked Stilt, Wilson's Snipe, and Wilson's Phalarope. Cattle Egrets stalk insects among the grazing cattle and probably nest nearby. American White Pelicans soar overhead and rest on the reservoir. In 2005 a pair of Sandhill Cranes fledged a chick, the first Colorado nesting record for this bird east of the Continental Divide.

To the south, check County Roads 40 and 42 between Roads 45 and 47. Where *Beebe Draw* crosses them, and at a cow pond on the north side of Road 42,

Marsh Wrens nest in only a few Colorado sites—Lower Latham Reservoir on the Eastern Slope, the San Luis Valley, and Browns Park National Wildlife Refuge.

migrants sometimes stop: dabbling ducks and such surprises as Great and Snowy Egrets, White-faced and Glossy (rare) Ibis, Marbled Godwit, Red-necked Phalarope, and American Pipit.

On Road 47 north of Road 48, a large prairie-dog colony sometimes produces a Burrowing Owl. From several vantage points on Road 47, you can also look down to the reservoir; but at the quarter-mile distance, you need a scope.

DeLorme grid: P. 31 B5.

Elevation: 4,670 feet.

Hazards: Traffic—pull off to the side of the road.

Nearest food, gas, lodging: Greeley and neighboring towns.

Camping: No.

25 Boulder Area Ⓦ Ⓗ

About this site

Twenty years of open-space sales taxes have blessed Boulder with a sterling set of natural areas. Everywhere you drive east of the city, you'll see signs for trails and ponds. Both the city and the county have Web sites, with the city's particularly informative (see the Walden and Sawhill Ponds, Mesa Trail, and Boulder Reservoirs sites). With El Dorado State Park, Roosevelt National Forest, and Rocky Mountain National Park added in, Boulder offers excellent birding.

The birding

Below the University of Colorado campus, **Boulder Creek** attracts vagrants during migration; birders caption the section below Folsom Field as "Warbler Woods." It can produce, for example, Townsend's or Magnolia Warblers, Broad-winged Hawk, Red-eyed Vireo, and mountain-bound migrants such as Hermit Thrush and White-crowned Sparrow. In winter look for Brown Creeper, Winter Wren, and American Dipper.

If you drive to the trail instead of walking from the campus or downtown, go to Folsom Street, turn west just north of the bridge, and drive past Lot 169 to Lot 168 for unrestricted parking.

The mountains west of Boulder offer the usual mountain species. You can try driving to the **Long Lake** and **Mitchell Lake** trailheads ($) on the Brainard Lake road (a left turn 1 mile north of Ward off Highway 72). Look for the quiet Three-toed Woodpecker, Williamson's Sapsucker, and Gray Jay (anomalous among their noisy corvid relatives). Swainson's and Hermit Thrushes pour out their fluty songs, and Wilson's Warblers pick up territories in late May even when that territory is still covered with a foot of snow.

Ambitious birders can climb above timberline—maybe even up Mount Audubon—to look for White-tailed Ptarmigan and, in August, Baird's Sandpiper (as migrants, they show up at high altitudes in western North America).

DeLorme grid: Boulder Creek, p. 30 D1; Brainard Lake, p. 29 D6.

Elevation: Boulder Creek, 5,325 feet; Brainard Lake, 10,345 feet; Mount Audubon, 13,223 feet.

Hazards: Sun, altitude; carry water.

Nearest food, gas, lodging: Boulder.

Camping: Brainard Lake.

For more information: Brainard Lake: U.S. Forest Service, 2140 Yarmouth Avenue, Boulder, CO 80301; (303) 541-2500; www.fs.fed.us/r2/arnf/recreation/brainard.

Boulder Area, Walden and Sawhill Ponds, Mesa Trail, Boulder Reservoirs

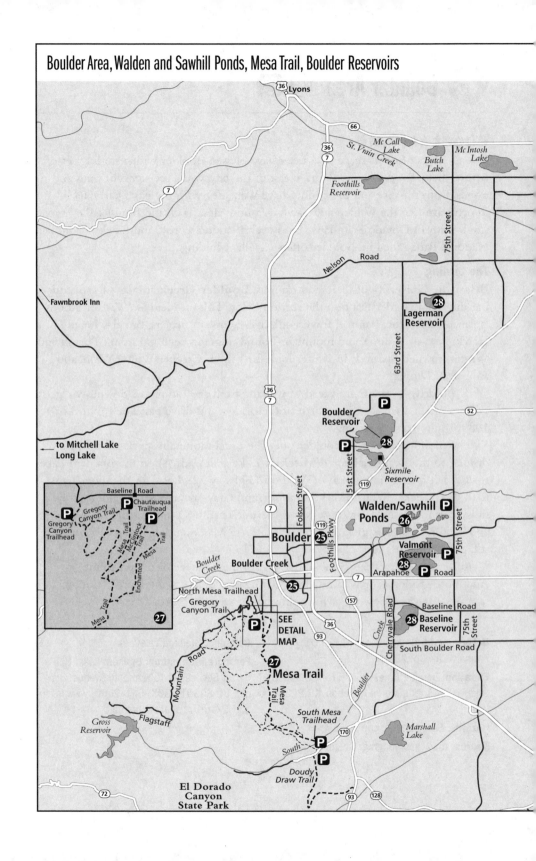

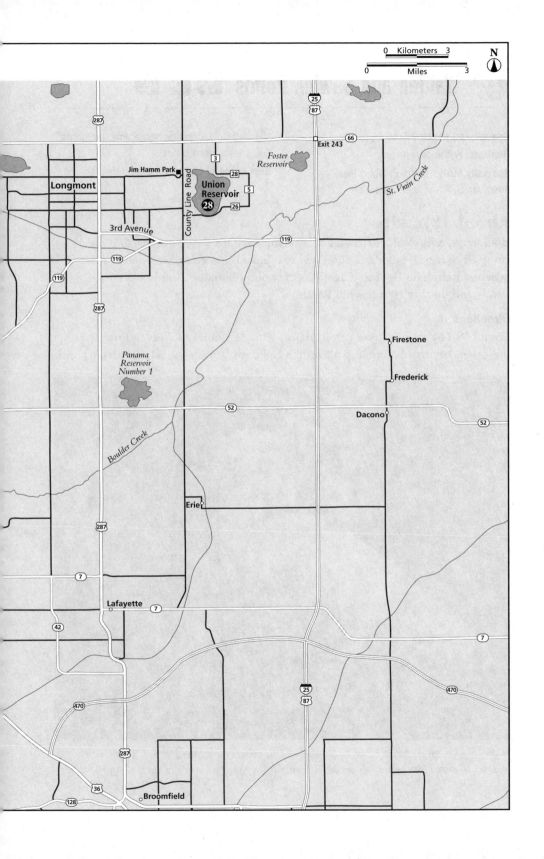

287

25
87

Exit 243 66

3

Foster
Reservoir

St. Vrain Creek

Jim Hamm Park

Longmont

28

Union
Reservoir
28

5

26

County Line Road

3rd Avenue

119

119

119

287

Firestone

Frederick

Panama
Reservoir
Number 1

52

Dacono

52

Boulder Creek

Erie

7

Lafayette 7

7

42

25
87

470

470

287

36

128

Broomfield

See map on pages 88–89.

Habitats: Wetlands, riparian.

Specialty birds: *Summer:* Wood Duck, American Bittern, Green Heron, rails.

Migrant: Ducks, grebes, shorebirds, landbirds.

Winter: American Dipper.

Best times to bird: Spring, summer, fall.

About this site

Boulderites relish Walden/Sawhill as a premier site for water and marsh birds. A complex of reclaimed gravel pits, these two linked sites comprise ponds, cattail marshes, and, along Boulder Creek, cottonwoods. Boulder County operates Walden Ponds, and the city runs Sawhill Ponds.

Directions

From U.S. Highway 36, go east on Arapahoe for 2.5 miles to 75th and north 1 mile, then left. In a half mile, park on the right at Cottonwood Marsh parking area.

PHOTO © WILLIAM EDEN

Numbers of breeding Snowy Egret have declined in the state over the last fifty years, with colonies at Barr Lake and the San Luis Valley, but they migrate and feed throughout the state.

The birding

Cottonwood Lake, where you park, is an excellent place to study waterbirds, with the sun over your back. It attracts ducks, gulls, and a few Great Blue Herons and Great Egrets that nest a couple of miles to the east. Take the Cottonwood Marsh boardwalk—look for sparrows, and listen for Sora and Virginia Rail. Then go left through a fence into the Sawhill complex. The ponds attract disparate species depending on depth; most are shallow and draw geese and dabbling ducks (including Wood Duck). The trail west leads to cottonwood groves where land-bird migrants may hide. You could spend all day sampling various trails and ponds.

Green Heron might, and American Bittern do, breed; rare visitors include Little Blue Heron and Least Bittern. Osprey, Bald Eagle, and Sharp-shinned Hawk may fly by. A sampling of migrants: Yellow-billed Cuckoo, Olive-sided, Willow, Least, and Dusky Flycatchers, Yellow-throated Vireo (rare), Brown Creeper, Marsh Wren, Swainson's Thrush, Northern Waterthrush, Western Tanager, Brewer's and Clay-colored among the Chipping Sparrows, Fox Sparrow, and Blue and Rose-breasted Grosbeaks. Occasionally seen here are Bobolinks and Orchard Oriole, which breed nearby. American Dippers sing and feed along Boulder Creek in winter.

DeLorme grid: P. 30 D1.

Elevation: 5,100 feet.

Nearest food, gas, lodging: Boulder.

Camping: No.

For more information: City of Boulder Open Space & Mountain Parks Department, P.O. Box 791, Boulder, CO 80306; (303) 441-3440; www.bouldercolorado.gov (click on "Departments," then "Open Space and Mountain Parks"). Boulder County Parks & Open Space, 2045 13th Street, P.O. Box 471, Boulder, CO 80306; (303) 441-3950; www.co.boulder.co.us/openspace.

27 Mesa Trail

See map on pages 88–89.

Habitats: Ponderosa, lowland riparian, grassland.

Specialty birds: *Summer:* Peregrine Falcon, small owls, Veery, Gray Catbird, Ovenbird. *Migrant:* Land birds: flycatchers, vireos, thrushes, warblers.

Best times to bird: Spring, summer, fall.

About this site

Boulder birders scour these trails during migration for common and less common land birds and year-round for ponderosa birds. Branching off Mesa Trail, a network of paths offers short and long hikes. Boulderites use them extensively—expect to encounter joggers and dogs. The city has 130 miles of hiking trails; the best for birding lie south of the city, between Baseline Road and Highway 170. You can obtain a trail map at the North Mesa Trailhead or the park office there.

Directions

North Mesa Trailhead: Turn into Chautauqua, off Baseline 1 mile west of Broadway, into the first pair of parking lots.

McClintock and Enchanted Mesa Trails: Drive on into Chautauqua, turn left for the auditorium, and park on its south side.

Gregory Canyon ($): Turn left where Baseline Road ends (1.5 miles west of Broadway, just before it turns right to climb Flagstaff Mountain).

South Mesa Trailhead and Doudy Draw: From Highway 93 and South Boulder Road, go south 3.5 miles to Highway 170, then west 1.5 miles to the Mesa trailhead on the right and Doudy Draw on the left.

The birding

Gregory Canyon's tangled riparian stream bottom, both above and below the small parking lot, produces a plethora of migrants. A half mile up from the lot, the trail enters ponderosa pine woodlands.

North Mesa Trailhead connects a maze of trails that stretches west and south over grasslands and ponderosa forests at the base of the slanting red-rock Flatirons. The main stem runs south 6 miles to the South trailhead.

At *South Mesa Trailhead,* cottonwoods and a tangle of shrubs surround the South Boulder Creek parking area. Trails climb uphill to the north; Homestead and Towhee Trails form a loop that traverses grassland, sparse streamside bushes, and some ponderosas. The Mesa Trail itself heads straight north through ponderosas to the north terminus at Chautauqua (6 miles).

On these trails, look and listen for Least, Dusky, and Cordilleran Flycatchers, Hermit Thrush, Veery, Gray Catbird, Cedar Waxwing, warblers, Green-tailed and

The network of trails around Boulder provides many splendid places for birdwatchers to stroll or to hike year-round—here the South trailhead of the Mesa Trail.

Spotted Towhees, Black-headed and Blue Grosbeaks, and Lazuli and Indigo Buntings. Yellow-breasted Chats make a ruckus along streams. You may glimpse a Peregrine Falcon on a foray from the Flatirons aerie, or Cooper's Hawk, Prairie Falcon, or Merlin. A nighttime journey may net an Eastern Screech-Owl along South Boulder Creek, and Common Poorwill, Common Nighthawk, and Pygmy, Saw-whet, or Flammulated Owl up Mesa Trail.

Doudy Draw's trail, across Highway 170 from the South Mesa trailhead, climbs up through grassland and copses of bushes and small trees. Grassy fields bring in numerous sparrows: Chipping, Field (rare), and Clay-colored. Also look for flycatchers: Ash-throated and Olive-sided, Say's Phoebe, and Cassin's Kingbird. In August, Sage Thrashers move through regularly. Grasshopper Sparrows, numerous along the Big Bluestem Trail, also inhabit a weedy field on Highway 170 near El Dorado Springs.

DeLorme grid: P. 40 A1.

Elevation: 5,600 to 6,000 feet.

Nearest food, gas, lodging: Boulder.

Camping: No.

For more information: City of Boulder Open Space & Mountain Parks Department, P.O. Box 791, Boulder, CO 80306; (303) 441-3440; www.bouldercolorado.gov (click on "Departments," then "Parks and Recreation").

28 Boulder Reservoirs ♿

See map on pages 88–89.
Habitats: Wetlands, riparian, grassland.
Specialty birds: *Migrant:* Ducks, gulls. *Winter:* Ducks and other waterbirds (Valmont), Bald Eagle.

Best times to bird: Fall and spring.

About this site

Like other Front Range cities, Boulder boasts a bunch of reservoirs for fall and spring birding. They collect a mix of waterbirds similar to the Larimer County and Denver-area impoundments.

The birding

These reservoirs have similar bird lists: the usual duck species, loons, grebes, lots of coots, shorebirds, gulls, and terns. Less common birds include Surf and Black Scoters, Long-tailed Duck, Red-necked Grebe, Great and Snowy Egrets, Red and Red-necked Phalaropes, Lesser Black-backed and Sabine's Gulls, Black-legged Kittiwake, and Common Tern.

The power plant at **Valmont Reservoir** discharges warm water so that waterbirds find sustenance and safety all winter. From Foothills Parkway (Highway 157), go east 2.5 miles on Arapahoe Road and turn left into Legion Park. Go up the hill to the parking area, and get your scope. The faraway impoundments require long-distance visual assistance.

Wintering birds include geese, ducks (over one hundred each of Hooded and Red-breasted Mergansers), grebes, a few loons, and a multitude of American Coots. On late winter afternoons, gulls flock in for the night: The assemblage can include Mew, Ring-Billed (thousands), California, Herring, Thayer's, Lesser Black-backed, Glaucous, and Great Black-backed. A second place to look at this throng (closer views, but still take your scope) requires a mile-long walk from city Open Space headquarters, off 75th Street a half mile north of Arapahoe; the gate closes at 4:00 P.M. Park outside if you plan to stay later.

View privately owned **Baseline Reservoir,** immediately west of town, from roads on the west and north. From US 36, exit right to South Boulder Road; in a mile, turn left on Cherryvale. In 0.25 mile, park by the gate at the southwest corner of the lake. Look at the gulls on the sandbar on the left. Scope the lake from here and along Cherryvale all the way to Baseline Road (0.75 mile). The bird list includes Red-breasted and Hooded Mergansers, Ruddy Duck, loons, and grebes. Turning right on Baseline, you won't find good pull-offs, but you can look into the reservoir from a parking area on the northeast corner.

To reach **Boulder Reservoir,** take the Diagonal (Highway 119) and, at Jay Road, turn left and then immediately right on 51st Street (by the firehouse). The park entrance lies 1.5 miles north. Avoid this park during the summer, when hordes of swimmers and boaters shell out $6 per person to get in. After the summer season, enter via the exit gate. Drive down to the edge of the lake and to the boathouse for views of the water. At the boathouse also go up to the fence on the south to look into *Sixmile Reservoir,* a private lake. It often has more birds because

PHOTO © WENDY SHATTIL/BOB ROZINSKI

Great Blue Heron breed in around 100 breeding colonies (properly termed "heronries," not rookeries), most in cottonwoods surrounded by lakes or rivers, though small colonies exist in anomalous sites such as ponderosa pine woodlands.

they encounter less human disruption here. Wilson's Snipe sometimes feed on the shore in the open.

To look at the far part of Boulder Reservoir, go north from the entrance. Northern Harriers cruise over marshes and grassland and you may see other raptors. After 51st Street swings right, stop in 1.5 miles at a right-hand parking lot and walk down to the lake.

Raptors, visible in winter from roads north of the reservoir, haunt prairie-dog towns (abundant in extensive open-space acquisitions by the county); they include Bald and Golden Eagles, Ferruginous Hawk, and Prairie Falcon. At the T intersection where 51st Street ends, turn right, left in a mile, and right in 2 miles on Prospect, and follow it around past Swede Lakes to **Lagerman Reservoir.**

East of Longmont, **Union Reservoir** (private; aka Calkins Lake) has long produced sterling waterbirds. To reach it from I–25, take exit 243 and go west 4 miles to County Line Road, left 1.5 miles to County Road 26, and left to the south side of the reservoir. From Longmont, go east on 3rd Avenue and north on County Line Road to Road 26. Entry to Union is restricted, but you can view the water from Road 26 as it swings around the south end. In the fall Union collects thousands of gulls and ducks, and many loons and grebes, including most rare species listed above. Gulls and other waterbirds sometimes rest on the pond in *Jim Hamm Park,* on the west side of Union where County Road 28 comes in. A short path around the northeast side sometimes yields interesting land birds.

DeLorme grid: P. 30 C–D 1–2; p. 40 A1.   **Camping:** No.
Elevation: 5,300 feet.
Nearest food, gas, lodging: Boulder, Longmont.

29 Fawnbrook Inn [w]

Habitat: Bird feeders.
Specialty birds: *Summer:* Hummingbirds, Band-tailed Pigeon. *Winter:* Rosy-finches, Northern Pygmy-Owl.
Best times to bird: Winter, late summer.

About this site

Fawnbrook Inn has become the easiest place near Front Range cities to find all three species of rosy-finch in winter, from January to March (more often in stormy weather). In summer the restaurant maintains an impressive array of hummingbird feeders. At both times of year, they welcome birders, as long as we behave: Please park in the lot, away from the feeder complex, so as not to disturb the plantings or the birds. (In January the restaurant's closed, but the feeders are full.)

The inn, open for a quarter century, offers upscale and well-reviewed dinners (open from 5:00 P.M.). It's best not to infringe on their parking after this time unless you stay for a good meal. The owners appreciate cards of thanks and gifts of sugar in summer and birdseed in winter. The Colorado Field Ornithologists presented the inn with a plaque that signifies the birding community's appreciation of their welcome.

Directions

From Lyons, go west on Highway 7 to Allenspark; turn on the business route (2.2 miles beyond Highway 72); the inn is 0.9 mile from there. From Estes Park, go south on Highway 7 for 14 miles, then 0.3 mile on the business route (north exit).

The birding

In winter watch for the hundreds of rosy-finches that throng the feeders. Other visitors: Hairy Woodpecker, Steller's Jay, Clark's Nutcracker, Black-capped and Mountain Chickadees, and Pine Siskin. One observer watched a Northern Pygmy-Owl catch a rosy-finch and pluck it—not an everyday occurrence.

In the summer at least three varieties of hummingbirds career around the feeders: Broad-tailed, Rufous, and Calliope. Band-tailed Pigeons sometimes perch on wires next to Crystal Springs, just beyond the inn and visible from the parking area.

DeLorme grid: P. 29 C6.
Elevation: 8,300 feet.
Hazards: Icy roads.
Nearest food, gas, lodging: Estes Park, Lyons; lodging and food in Allenspark; food at the Fawnsbrook Inn.

Camping: No.
For more information: (303) 747-2556.

30 Rocky Mountain National Park

Habitats: Ponderosa, aspen, mountain meadow, lodgepole, spruce/fir, tundra.

Specialty birds: See below.

Best times to bird: June to September.

About this site

The premier mountain bird-watching place in Colorado, Rocky Mountain National Park (RMNP) has fine examples of every mountain habitat in Colorado; 450 miles of streams and 150 lakes punctuate the landscape in each ecosystem. Superb scenery, excellent facilities, and lots of birds (262-bird checklist; Global IBA) make Rocky a prime destination. Easy access to each habitat and its complement of breeding species lends enchantment to a visit.

You can see mountain birds in RMNP from your car and on short or long hikes. The park offers a grand menu of trails (355 miles worth), through and to magnificent glaciated valleys, lakes, and peaks. Many short trails are wheelchair-accessible.

The park has a few ponderosa pine sites, all on the east side, all below 8,000 feet. Roads into Estes Park from the east travel through ponderosa woodlands, much of it in Roosevelt National Forest.

If you walk along a trail with your eyes closed (see "Hazards," below), you'll know you're in an aspen grove when you hear a singing Warbling Vireo. Sapsuckers, woodpeckers, and flickers drill holes in aspen that later provide cavities for chickadees, nuthatches, swallows, wrens, and bluebirds.

Lodgepole pine forests, rather depauperate compared with other park habitats, still have Mountain Chickadee, Ruby-crowned Kinglet, Hermit Thrush, Yellow-rumped Warbler, and Red Crossbill. High-elevation spruce/fir forests provide abundant nesting sites for the lodgepole birds and Three-toed Woodpecker (a quiet bird that favors recently dead trees), and its look-alike, Hairy Woodpecker; also Hammond's and Olive-sided Flycatchers, Gray Jay, Clark's Nutcracker, Red-breasted Nuthatch, Brown Creeper, Golden-crowned Kinglet, Townsend's Solitaire, Western Tanager, Pine Grosbeak, and Cassin's Finch.

Two alpine specialties, White-tailed Ptarmigan and Brown-capped Rosy-Finch, can be hard to find, but during your search, tundra flowers, which hug the ground in rainbows of color, enhance your sensory experience. Broad-tailed and Rufous Hummingbirds sample flower fields all the way to timberline and above.

The park has a few wetland specialists: American Dippers live along streams, Ring-necked Ducks breed in some lakes and beaver ponds, Wilson's Snipe call *peent* in wet meadows, and Spotted Sandpiper ply the banks of streams and ponds.

One *Colorado Breeding Bird Atlas* block spanned a big elevation differential (8,526 to 11,722 feet), from Endovalley to the east section of Trail Ridge, and recorded ninety-three species—more than any other Colorado mountain block. The Estes Park block included the town and Gem Lake: It recorded eighty species. High mountain blocks listed thirty-eight to forty-eight species.

Directions

East side: Go west on US 36 from Lyons or US 34 from Loveland to Estes Park. **West side:** From US 40 in Granby, go north on US 34 past Grand Lake to the park entrance.

The birding

First, an explanation: In Colorado *mountain* nomenclature the word "park," when used in place names, refers to an open meadowland or grassland ringed by high mountains, for example, Estes Park, Moraine Park, Horseshoe Park.

From downtown Estes Park, turn left at the main intersection and drive 2 miles on US 36 to the *visitor center* (left) to learn about "Rocky." A mile beyond the visitor center, the road forks; the right (Deer Ridge Road) climbs up to Trail Ridge and the left goes to Bear Lake.

Going left from the fork, a half mile takes you to Moraine Park Museum (left), with exhibits and naturalist programs. Just beyond it turn right on the *Moraine Park* road. Meadows and a meandering stream fill the broad glacial valley, with ponderosa pine/aspen woodlands on the right,

Despite this one probing an aspen, Hairy Woodpeckers tend to favor coniferous forests while their smaller congeners, Downy Woodpeckers, prefer deciduous habitats.

Rocky Mountain National Park

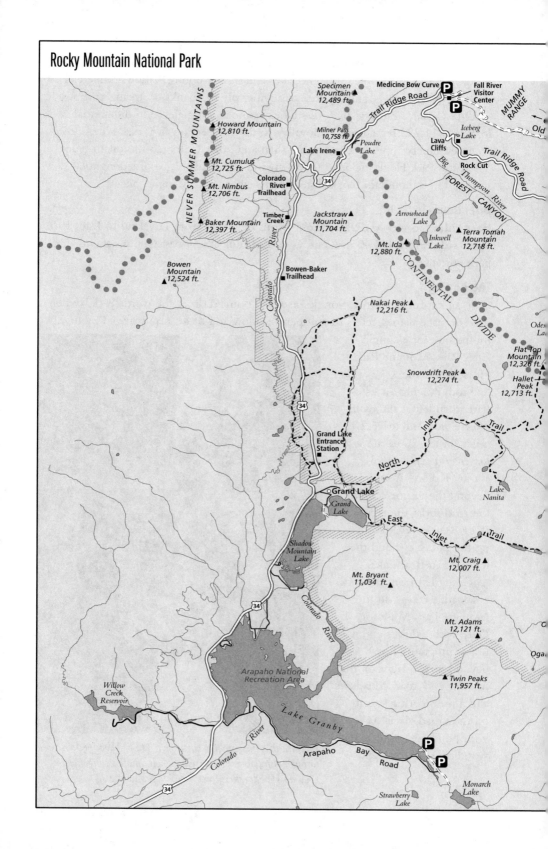

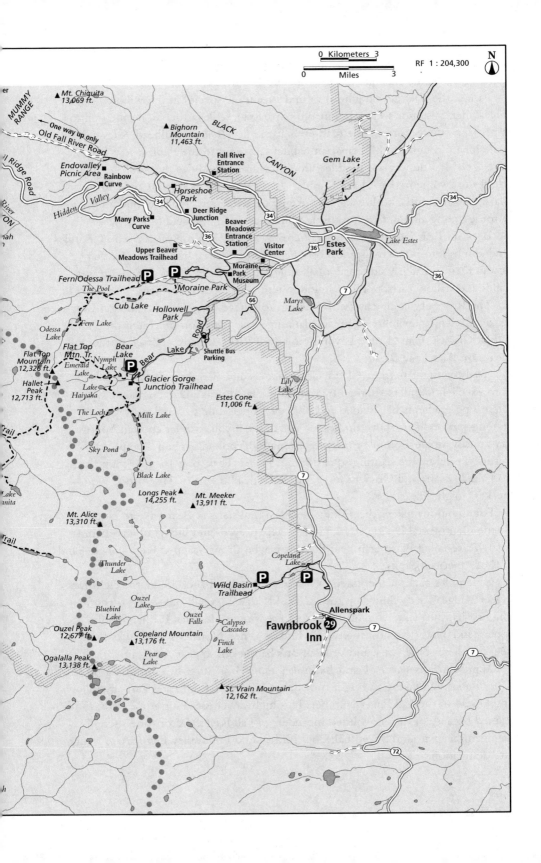

including the Moraine Park Campground. Red-naped and Williamson's Sapsuckers, Pygmy Nuthatch, and Western Bluebird live here.

Park at the *Cub Lake* trailhead to find streamside species in the willows (Dusky Flycatcher, Swainson's Thrush, Lincoln's Sparrow); walk farther along the trail to aspen and conifer forests. The road ends at the *Fern/Odessa* trailhead. A level 2-mile hike through foothills riparian habitat takes you to the Pool, where Fern Creek swirls around giant boulders (look for dippers). Above the Pool the trail climbs to two gems: Fern Lake (2 miles, 1,250 feet elevation gain) and Odessa Lake (another mile), both walled by craggy peaks. Rarely, you may find a Dusky Grouse hiding alongside a streamside trail or squiring a passel of grouselets.

Back on Bear Lake Road, the trail crosses the Big Thompson River in 0.5 miles and climbs into ponderosa pine. Look here for ponderosa birds if you haven't found them already. A side road a half mile on leads to *Hollowell Park,* with wetlands and willow carrs, plus dry hillsides with Green-tailed Towhees.

The Park Service operates a shuttle bus to relieve the parking crunch at Bear Lake; this lends flexibility to hikers planning circle trips. You can catch the shuttle bus at Glacier Basin (1 mile beyond Hollowell Park) or drive yourself to the trailheads on Bear Lake Road.

Trails that radiate from *Glacier Gorge Junction* and *Bear Lake* (9,475 feet) lead into excellent conifers rimmed by rugged glaciated peaks. Dazzling lakes, with increasing gradients of distance and difficulty, a half mile to 5 miles away, rest among spruce/fir or above timberline in tundra, if you hike far enough. You can try an easy amble around Bear Lake, among lodgepole pines and clumps of spruce/fir below the slanting square top of Hallett Peak, or a 10-mile round-trip to Lake Haiyaha and Glacier Gorge. Look for dead trees that Three-toed Woodpeckers might like.

For ambitious hikers, the *Flattop Mountain* trail starts at Bear Lake to climb up to the Continental Divide at 12,324 feet. Sharp-eyed (and lucky) observers can find White-tailed Ptarmigan near the top, maybe Brown-capped Rosy-Finch—and lots of American Pipits.

Nine miles back, at the junction of Bear Lake Road and US 36, the right fork (Deer Ridge Road) climbs up toward Trail Ridge. In a half mile a left turnoff (at the first hairpin) takes you 1.5 miles to *Upper Beaver Meadows.* Rather scruffy aspens and pines here host interesting birds at times: Northern Goshawks (hard to see) nest here some years, and Williamson's Sapsuckers appear regularly.

Approach *Horseshoe Park* and *Endovalley Picnic Area* either by continuing up to Deer Ridge and taking the right turn down US 34 or, from Estes Park, by following US 34 to the Fall River entrance. This highway crosses Horseshoe Park, so named because of the convoluted meanders of Fall River. Visitors often see bighorn sheep around Sheep Lake, but birders find Endovalley Picnic Area a sure-fire destination.

In the deep spruce woods at Endovalley or nearby aspen groves, expect the usual birds, plus Williamson's Sapsucker, Hammond's and Olive-sided Flycatchers, Western Bluebird, Pine Grosbeak, and Cassin's Finch. Nearby willow bottoms could harbor an unusual Fox Sparrow. One year a summer Winter Wren sang from a hillside above Fall River Road. Where the stream drops down through eddying currents, look for American Dipper. Atlasers found an amazing inventory of owls: Flammulated, Boreal, Great Horned, Saw-whet, and Pygmy. Fall River Road starts here as a one-way, up-only, gravel road (closed in winter) to the Fall River Visitor Center (11,796 feet) at the far side of Trail Ridge Road.

Starting at Deer Ridge Junction, *Trail Ridge Road* ascends through all Colorado mountain habitats. Pull-offs and parking areas provide plentiful birding opportunities. (The highway closes from Many Parks Curve on the east side to the Colorado River trailhead on the west from October till June, when snowplows finally clear 12- to 15-foot snowdrifts to open it.)

Two miles beyond Deer Ridge Junction, Ring-necked Ducks nest in beaver ponds, although human traffic makes them hard to find. A quarter mile beyond, go right to Hidden Valley for spruce/fir birds. Many Parks Curve, at the next hairpin, offers a spectacular view over mountain parks and their protective moraines and mountains, but few birds live in its lodgepole pines. Three more miles takes you to Rainbow Curve, where park visitors routinely ignore strictures against feeding wildlife and draw in not only chipmunks and ground squirrels but also Gray and Steller's Jays and Clark's Nutcracker.

Two miles farther, the road climbs above timberline. For 8 miles, Trail Ridge (high point 12,183 feet) presents a magnificent mountain panorama of Longs Peak, the Continental Divide, Mummy Range, and Never Summer Mountains. It swings through alpine tundra where birders can watch alpine birds surrounded by soaring scenery. American Pipit and Horned Lark populate grassy expanses. With a scope, you might pick out Brown-capped Rosy-Finch feeding on the snowbanks at Iceberg Lake, at the foot of the Lava Cliffs. A Common Raven or even a Prairie Falcon might wing by.

Birders find White-tailed Ptarmigan at two sites. A trail from the Rock Cut climbs gently, and one on the right of Medicine Bow Curve (the next hairpin a quarter mile after the Fall River Visitor Center) contours up a mountainside. In 2005 visitors reported ptarmigan within 50 yards of the curve, and also 0.5 mile farther. Please stay on the trails—the sensitive tundra crumbles when feet clomp on it.

Dropping down the west side, test the spruce forest just below Milner Pass at Lake Irene if you still seek that set of birds. The road drops through lodgepole pine to the broad Kawuneeche Valley—headwaters of the Colorado River. You can stop at Bowen/Baker or Coyote Valley trailheads to sample the lush willow-covered streamside.

At Grand Lake, the North Inlet and East Inlet Trails lead to a good mix of park habitats. Both have aspen and spruce/fir birds; no ponderosas grow on the west side of Rocky. South of Grand Lake (the largest *natural* lake in Colorado), two larger reservoirs, Shadow Mountain and Granby, form the nucleus of *Arapaho National Recreation Area*. Ospreys nest on Shadow Mountain and sometimes work Lake Granby. Look in Shadow Mountain around the island at the south end.

The trail at Arapaho Bay off Lake Granby enters habitats less available on the east side of the park. Turn east on the dam road and go all the way to the end. Walk to Monarch Lake and beyond to sample midelevation willow carrs—lusher here than on the east side (Swainson's Thrush, MacGillivray's Warbler, Fox Sparrow)—and aspen and spruce/fir. From Monarch Lake, you can hike into the Indian Peaks Wilderness to Crater Lake, set in spruce/fir at the foot of spectacular Lone Eagle Peak, or toward Arapaho Pass through a long stretch of spruce/fir to timberline (both hikes 8 to 10 miles).

Add two sites on the east side to your itinerary. For ponderosa species, the *Gem Lake* trail leads to the lake perched among boulders. Check at the visitor center for directions: The park plans to relocate this trailhead.

South of Estes Park 12 miles on Highway 7, you can explore *Wild Basin's* trails to lakes blessed with bird names: Finch, Ouzel, and Bluebird. Stop first at Copeland Lake picnic area, where you might find Red-naped Sapsucker, Mountain Chickadee, and all three nuthatches. From here a 2-mile drive takes you to the trailhead.

Calypso Cascades and Ouzel Falls, a 2-mile hike, convey possible American Dipper (ornithologists' name for John Muir's water ouzel) and Black Swift (more likely at dawn and dusk). The trail passes through rather dense conifers, mainly lodgepole pine, where it's hard to find many high-country birds. The country opens up more beyond Ouzel Falls, through spruce/fir toward Ouzel, Bluebird, or Thunder Lakes, the latter two perched at timberline.

DeLorme grid: P. 28-29 A-D 4-6.

Elevation: 7,500 to 14,255 feet.

Hazards: Altitude; thunderstorms; bears; animals crossing the road; traffic, including cars stopped to see megafauna such as deer and elk; slipping on snow and ice fields; walking blindfolded through an aspen grove.

Nearest food, gas, lodging: Estes Park, Grand Lake, Granby.

Camping: Yes.

For more information: Rocky Mountain National Park, Estes Park, CO 80517; (970) 586-1206; www.nps.gov/romo.

Denver Metro Area

The Mile High City offers a variety of habitats and elevations for resident and visiting bird-watchers. The South Platte River bisects the city and in winter offers fabulous close views of dabbling and diving ducks. Reservoirs at three state parks (Barr, Cherry Creek, and Chatfield) attract a large variety of waterbirds (ducks, loons, grebes, waders, shorebirds, and gulls). These parks also have trails through first-class riparian habitats where breeding and migrant land birds congregate—and have bird lists larger than those of some states.

South of Denver birders can sample scrub oak and ponderosa pine woodlands. Jefferson County, west and south of downtown, has a particularly fine collection of foothills parks. National forests between the city and the Continental Divide parade high-country habitats, from ponderosa pines up to ptarmigan haunts on Guanella Pass and 14,260-foot Mount Evans.

The Denver Field Ornithologists group probably has more field trips than any other bird club in the United States. It schedules trips every Saturday and Sunday all year long. The trips fan out throughout metro Denver and to other sites mentioned in this guide. Check its Web site—visitors welcome.

Visiting birders can learn about Colorado habitats in Mead Hall at the Denver Museum of Nature and Science, located in City Park (entrance at Colorado and Montview Boulevards, equivalent to 20th Avenue, in east Denver). These exhibits show birds in the principal Colorado habitats and depict actual places (for example, Pawnee National Grassland and Longs Peak). Denver city parks offer birdless landscapes of sterile blue grass and non-native eastern shade trees (Canada Geese like them), but City Park does have two lakes with islands where Double-crested Cormorants, Black-crowned Night-Herons, and Snowy Egrets nest (in years that the Parks Department doesn't drain the lakes in order to clean up droppings from the nesting colony).

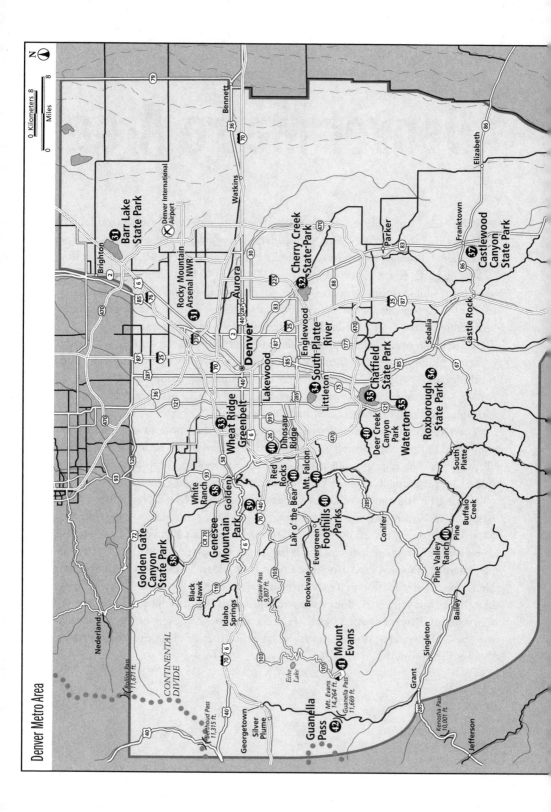

Denver Metro Area

31 Barr Lake State Park $ ♿ 🐦 IBA

Habitats: Wetlands, riparian, grassland.

Specialty birds: *Resident:* Bald Eagle, Northern Harrier. *Summer:* Western Grebe, Great Blue Heron, Black-crowned Night-Heron, Snowy Egret, Swainson's Hawk, Yellow-headed Blackbird. *Migrant:* Ducks, grebes, shorebirds, gulls, flycatchers, warblers, sparrows. *Winter:* Merlin, Prairie Falcon.

Best times to bird: Spring, summer, fall.

About this site

A 1,900-acre reservoir maintained for irrigators, Barr Lake has shone as a premier birding spot for over a century, now as a state park comanaged for irrigation and recreation (nature study, fishing, and hunting). Colorado's pioneer ornithologists, Bob Niedrach and Alfred Bailey of the Denver Museum of Natural History, did extensive field work here and found many first state records and other memorable observations. The park bird list tops 350 species.

The deed to the Oasis Water Supply Park and Improvement Co., filed August 5, 1892, recited that the company "is desirous of establishing a large reservoir for supplying water for irrigating purposes and also to be used as a lake for a pleasure resort and for boating fishing and other gaming purposes. . . [sic]." The deed described a property "as has been surveyed by Peter O'Brian a practical surveyor and designated and marked by stakes and small mounds of manure chips. . . ." The irrigation company apparently enlarged a buffalo wallow.

Now cottonwoods line the edge of the reservoir, with grasslands spreading out beyond that. A road/trail circles the reservoir; an irrigation ditch runs along the east side. Below the dam lies a maze of cattail marshes. Colorado State Parks manages Barr for wildlife (south half), limited fishing and boating (north half), and waterfowl hunting (north of the dam). Rocky Mountain Bird Observatory has its office at the northeast corner of the park and in the fall maintains a banding station near the Barr Lake Nature Center.

Typical of irrigation reservoirs in Colorado, the lake fills from October to April; irrigators call for the water May to September. Consequently, water laps at the edge of the perimeter road in spring; the drawdown creates extensive shoreline and mudflats beginning in midsummer.

Directions

Take Interstate 76 to Bromley Lane and go east three-quarters of a mile; turn south (right) on Picadilly Road and drive 1 mile to the park entrance, on the right.

Past the park entrance station a quarter mile, turn left at the Y intersection for the Barr Lake Nature Center and the perimeter road/trail. (You can also turn right and park at the fishing access lot, which also has a bridge to the trail.)

The birding

From the Barr Lake Nature Center, cross the bridge to the *Perimeter Trail,* which goes in both directions. For the ambitious, the 10-mile trail circles the lake. Cottonwoods and willows that hug the high waterline harbor many migrating and breeding birds. Follow the Perimeter Trail in either direction, from either the nature center or the boat-ramp parking lot. To protect the pair of Bald Eagles that nests here, a southern section of the trail closes during nesting season.

Walks in spring and fall yield migrants in the trees and rafts of ducks and other waterbirds on the lake. While Western Wood-Pewee, Western and Eastern Kingbirds, House Wren, American Robin, European Starling, Yellow Warbler, and Bullock's Oriole are the most common breeders, look also for Swainson's Hawk, Great Horned Owl, Tree Swallow, Loggerhead Shrike, and Warbling Vireo. Western Meadowlarks sing from adjacent fields. In cattail marshes you can find Virginia Rail, Sora, Common Yellowthroat, and Red-winged and Yellow-headed Blackbirds.

Frequently seen land-bird migrants include Swainson's Thrush, Orange-crowned, Yellow-rumped, and Wilson's Warblers, and White-crowned Sparrow. Less often observers find others of the twenty species of flycatchers and thirty-four species of warblers on the park list, as well as migrant thrushes, thrashers, kinglets, and sparrows. Spring sees the flashiest migrants.

The banding station operates from late August to mid-October (from the Barr Lake Nature Center, across the bridge and 0.25 mile to the right along the Perimeter Trail). It bands more Wilson's Warblers (over half) than any other species. In 2004 RMBOers banded 1,929 birds of 59 species, 991 of them Wilson's Warblers; next highest were 187 White-crowned Sparrows, 129 Song Sparrows, 85 Dark-eyed Juncos, 72 House Wrens, and 63 Orange-crowned Warblers.

If you turn left from the bridge, in 100 yards a short side trail, named for Bob Niedrach, branches off to the right. It follows the edge of the lake and has a walkway across a section of water in spring (dry in fall). It returns to the Perimeter Trail, from which a boardwalk (1.25 miles) leads to a gazebo a quarter mile out into the lake (in spring; in fall into a dry lake bed). From the gazebo you can view the eagles' nest and see nesting herons and cormorants (a scope helps). In some years Western Grebes nest at this end of the lake. By midsummer the lake retreats from the gazebo and the high-water mark; nesting done, the birds scatter. This is when shorebirds arrive.

Park rules allow off-trail access to the retreating lake *only* north of the banding station. A set of buoys marks the south limit of permissible off-trail use. (To the south, birders must stay on established trails and view birds through binoculars and spotting scopes.) Exploring the (retreating) lake edge can produce a variety of migrating shorebirds. Less common species include Black-bellied, American Golden, and Semipalmated Plovers, Willet, Marbled Godwit, Sanderling, Stilt, Buff-bellied and Pectoral Sandpipers, and Red-necked Phalarope. Franklin's, Ring-billed, and California Gulls rest on the lake. Black Terns occasionally migrate through. Rarely, jaegers or peregrines harry the gulls and shorebirds, causing them to rise into clouds of swirling birds. Later in the season look at the ducks, geese, grebes, pelicans, and coots. November's geese include thousands of Cackling plus Greater White-fronted, Ross's, and Snow.

South of Barr Lake lies **Rocky Mountain Arsenal National Wildlife Refuge** (IBA), a Superfund site that will soon offer premier wildlife viewing. The refuge presently permits access only on weekends, starting at 6:00 A.M. To reach the entrance at 56th Avenue and Havana Street, drive north on Havana from Interstate 70 about a mile; from the gate, continue north 1.5 miles to the visitor center. From here trails access two lakes and locust and cottonwood woodlands. Refuge-conducted tours travel a greater area in trolley buses.

Birds run the gamut from ducks to grassland species, from shorebirds to warblers. Spring and fall counts produce eighty to one hundred species. A winter roost shelters twenty-five to fifty Bald Eagles. Ferruginous Hawks like to feast in prairie-dog towns, especially in winter. (You may find Ferrugs stalking prairie dogs north of the refuge.)

North of the Arsenal toward Barr Lake, prairie-dog towns host Burrowing Owls from May to September. Go north on Tower Road (exit I–70 east of Havana or from Pena Boulevard) and, west of Tower, explore 104th, 112th, and 120th Avenues. Also, if you park at Buckley Road (1 mile west of Tower) and 88th, you can walk down Buckley just outside the Arsenal fence and look for owls and hawks near prairie-dog colonies within.

DeLorme grid: P. 41 A4.

Elevation: 5,100 feet.

Hazards: Weather, ants.

Nearest food, gas, lodging: Brighton and Denver, gas and food along Interstates 70 and 76.

Camping: No.

For more information: Barr Lake State Park, 13401 Picadilly Road, Brighton, CO 80603; (303) 659-6005; Nature Center (303) 659-1160; barr.lake.nature.center@state.co.us. Rocky Mountain Bird Observatory, 14500 Lark Bunting Lane, Brighton, CO 80603; (303) 659-4348; www.rmbo.org. Rocky Mountain Arsenal NWR, Building 121, Commerce City, CO 80020; (303) 289-0930; www.rocky mountainarsenal.fws.gov.

32 Cherry Creek State Park $ & 🦜

Habitats: Wetlands, riparian, grassland.
Specialty birds: *Resident:* Northern Harrier.
Summer: Virginia Rail. *Migrant:* Ducks, six
grebe species, gulls. *Winter:* Common

Merganser, Bald Eagle, gulls, American Tree
Sparrows.

Best times to bird: October to April.

About this site

This flood-control reservoir (880 acres) attracts surprising numbers of waterfowl and myriad gulls. The park claims the highest visitation rate of any in Colorado: over 1,500,000 people annually. Most come for reasons unrelated to wildlife-watching, such as boating, swimming, and jogging, and most come in summer. Other seasons of the year, the people press becomes less disruptive to wildlife, and local birders assemble to see flocks of gulls, ducks, loons, and grebes. Bring a scope.

In addition to a state parks pass, visitors must purchase a $3.00 Water Quality Surcharge decal, good for one calendar year.

Directions

For the West Entrance, take exit 1 (Tamarack) from Interstate 225, follow Frontage Road 0.5 mile, turn right on Yosemite, and proceed 0.5 mile to Union Avenue.

Grassland and shrubland such as Cherry Creek State Park attract winter flocks of American Tree Sparrow.

Turn left, proceed 0.5 mile, and turn right at a traffic light (don't go on the Dam road) to the park entrance on the left. For the East Entrance off Parker (Leetsdale) Road (Highway 83), go south 1.5 miles beyond I–225 to the entrance on the right.

The birding

Birds on the lake move around and always seem to favor the middle or the other side, as far from the observer as possible. With a scope (and help from other birders), you may find many specialties that flock here before and after the summer hordes of people. In fall look for Common and Pacific Loons, six grebes (Red-necked rare), flocks of ducks including rafts of Ruddy Duck (early fall) and Common Merganser (2,000 by December), and occasionally Snow and Ross's Geese among the Canada and Cackling Geese. American White Pelicans may stop over, but few stay through the summer onslaught of boat traffic.

At the wetlands by Cottonwood Creek Loop and the Cherry Creek parking area, marsh birds can include Green Heron, Black-crowned Night-Heron, American Bittern, Snowy and Great Egrets, and White-faced Ibis. From riparian sites, the park has records of Vermilion and Hammond's Flycatchers, Cassin's Kingbird, Plumbeous Vireo, Red-breasted Nuthatch, Golden-crowned Kinglet, Gray Catbird, and Green-tailed Towhee. The twenty-five-species warbler list includes Orange-crowned, Virginia's, Townsend's, and Wilson's as regulars and rare ones including Black-throated Gray, Blackburnian, and Pine. Over the water on cloudy days, look for six swallow species and, hovering over grasslands, migrating Mountain Bluebird.

From the *West Entrance,* just past the entrance station, the park perimeter road turns right; go left to the *marina.* Most gull searchers start their quests here. In fall (October to December) gulls perch on the pilings next to the concession building. A walkway on the right side of the marina leads to a good spot to inspect the pilings and the reservoir.

The gull list includes: year-round—California (few in winter) and Ring-billed; migrants—Franklin's, Bonaparte's, and Sabine's (September); fall, winter, and spring—Herring, Glaucous, and Thayer's (uncommon), and, rarely, Laughing, Mew, Lesser Black-backed, Glaucous-winged, and Great Black-backed Gulls, and Black-legged Kittiwake. Terns include regular Forster's and Common and infrequent Black and Caspian. Even an occasional jaeger shows up; a Pomarine that arrived in early September 2005, joined by a second one in October, spent two months on the lake despite daily pestering by motorboats and Jet Skis.

Back on the perimeter road, you can see more of the reservoir from the shade shelters close to the waterline and at three loops on the left. The third one, *Cottonwood Creek Loop,* overlooks a shallow bay, another good site (depending on water level) for gulls and terns, plus shorebirds.

The perimeter road swings left and, just before it enters the riparian woodland, you can park on the left at the *Cherry Creek Trail parking area.* In the small cattail marsh next to the lot, Virginia Rails frequently scurry about in plain sight. Try trails along the edge of the woodland on either side of the road, toward the lake or upstream, for migrants: sparrows, warblers, flycatchers, and others. Great Horned and Long-eared Owls sometimes nest in these woods. Walk along the road where it crosses Cherry Creek to look in the wet-footed woods on both sides. A short distance beyond the creek crossing, a road on the right climbs to the park office. For several summers Black-chinned Hummingbirds (rare in the Denver area) have hovered nearby. Across from this another trail leads into the woodland bordering Cherry Creek.

Back on the perimeter road, at a T intersection, go left to a parking area. From here you can walk to the water's edge and survey the inlet side of the lake. Gulls roost here, and more shorebirds show up here than in other parts of the park. Shorebirds peak March to May and August to September. The park lists thirty-five shorebird species including Willet, Red Knot, Sanderling, White-rumped Sandpiper, and Red-necked Phalarope.

Go back toward the *East Entrance* and take two lefts, to a boat ramp and picnic shelters. The *East picnic shelters* proffer good views of the lake and its waterbirds. Back on the perimeter road, the campground on the right has a nice stand of tall trees, sometimes hosting land birds. A little farther, *Dixon Grove* picnic area has good trees and a short spit with the best view of the northeast part of the lake. The road ends at Tower Loop, yet another place to inspect the water.

DeLorme grid: P. 40 C3–4.
Elevation: 5,600 feet.
Nearest food, gas, lodging: Denver area.
Camping: Yes.

For more information: Cherry Creek State Park, 4201 South Parker Road, Aurora, CO 80114; (303) 650–1166; www.parks.state .co.us.

33 Wheat Ridge Greenbelt ♿

Habitats: Riparian, wetlands.

Specialty birds: *Resident:* Eastern Screech-Owl. *Summer:* Double-crested Cormorant, Great Blue Heron. *Migrant:* Greater Scaup.

Best times to bird: Spring, summer, fall.

About this site

Greenbelt paths, on both sides of Clear Creek, border several gravel pits, cattail marshes, and cottonwood woodlands. They offer close-up opportunities to see the typical waterbirds and woodland species of the Denver area. Even with heavy foot traffic, birders find a good variety of species along its trails and using its ponds.

Directions

From I–70 turn south on Kipling to 44th Avenue; turn right on 44th and proceed to Robb (street names here are alphabetical) and left into the park. A discreet sign at the turn announces PROSPECT PARK.

The birding

Immediately after you turn into the park, look over Prospect Pond. It attracts many ducks, including Greater Scaup and Hooded Merganser. Swing around the pond to the parking lot. The trail that heads west (on the right as you drive in) goes by a gravel pit with nesting Great Blue Heron and Double-crested Cormorant. It crosses Clear Creek; then go left along the trail and right on the dike.

In the large pond on the right, ducks and gulls often rest at the far end. (Walk up either side.) On the left a pond lined with cattails brings in dabbling ducks. To see it well, return along the dike and go right. Trails traverse the woodland to a bridge over Clear Creek and back to the parking lot.

Alternatively, start at the bridge; going either right or left, trails lead through cottonwoods and shrubby undergrowth. Spring and fall migrants drift into these woods, particularly in May. Up one trail, Colorado's only recorded Red-faced Warbler spent just one day (May 3, 1993), to the delight of about one hundred birders.

The trail left from the bridge (actually a patchwork of several trails) eventually arrives at another parking lot and park entrance. Turn around here and go back west along the trail. From a hole in a tree at the first clump of cottonwoods, an Eastern Screech-Owl often pokes out its head. (We've seen it once in twenty tries.)

DeLorme grid: P. 40 B2.

Elevation: 5,600 feet.

Hazards: Bicycles.

Nearest food, gas, lodging: Metro Denver.

Camping: No.

For more information: Park Naturalist; (303) 205-7554; www.ci.wheatridge.co.us/govsite.

34 South Platte River   ♿ 🦅 IBA

Habitats: Riparian, wetlands.

Specialty birds: *Resident:* Great Blue Heron, Black-crowned Night-Heron, Red-tailed Hawk. *Summer:* Green Heron, Swainson's Hawk, Northern Rough-winged and Bank Swallows.

Winter: Long-tailed Duck, Barrow's Goldeneye, Hooded Merganser, other ducks.

Best times to bird: Winter for ducks; year-round for South Platte Park.

About this site

A great place to see ducks at close range, the South Platte River through Denver fills with ducks each winter. Constant foot and bike traffic accustoms them to humans, and most don't flush if you stop to look at them. Their tolerance allows superb, close-up views of the twenty or so species that winter along the river. South Platte Park in Littleton has a network of trails that offers good riparian bird-watching year-round.

Directions

A paved trail follows the South Platte River from Chatfield Dam to the far north side of Denver. You can access it from several major cross streets: Dartmouth, Evans, Florida, Alameda, Confluence Park, 64th, 88th, and 104th Avenues, and Highway 224.

The birding

For winter ducks, walk the river trail from any cross street; you don't need a scope. Waterfowl sport their most vivid plumage during winter; a walk along the path makes for memorable duck-watching. You can encounter Black-crowned Night-Heron (in winter, between Dartmouth and Evans; in summer from 64th north). Flocks of ducks and a few other waterbirds use the river near bridge crossings at 74th and 88th Avenues from October to March. Besides the usual species, 88th may produce a Long-tailed Duck and sometimes a Barrow's Goldeneye.

For spring and summer birding, try the sections from 64th north. Limited riparian habitat improves on the outskirts of the city. May migrants include swallows, Yellow-rumped Warbler, Western Tanager, Green-tailed and Spotted Towhees, and White-crowned Sparrow. Bank Swallow pick transitory nest sites—temporary gravel piles connected with construction activities that disappear from one season to the next. They have nested between Dartmouth and Evans and near Highway 224. You might also find a Snowy Egret or Green Heron (at the north end, 64th to 74th).

For **South Platte Park (IBA),** turn west off Santa Fe Drive at Mineral Avenue (2 miles north of C–470); on the far side of the RTD (Regional Transportation

District) lot, turn right and follow signs to Theo Carson Nature Center (limited parking). The city of Littleton developed this floodplain park as an alternative to channelizing the river. Reclamation involved planting 10,000 native trees to restore natural vegetation and wildlife habitat after thirty-four years of sand and gravel mining. The park has become a lush riparian zone with six lakes. The park bird list has 225 species. Trails extend in two directions from the nature center and form part of the Chatfield-to-Denver trail. Bald Eagles winter here, as do many river ducks, but viewing them doesn't come as easy as in the city. The riparian habitat picks up migrant warblers, vireos, sparrows, and nesting land birds.

Winter walks along the South Platte will produce dozens of handsome male Hooded Mergansers and "bad hair-do" females.
PHOTO © WILLIAM EDEN

Other metro-area sites may merit a trip if you have a couple of hours or a half day. **Marston Lake** (south of U.S. Highway 285 on Sheridan Boulevard to Bow Mar Drive, then right; view from the street) collects an impressive variety of waterbirds during migration and winter: scoters and other ducks, loons, grebes, and gulls. **Belmar Park** (in Lakewood off Wadsworth between Alameda and Mississippi) features nesting American Avocets and, occasionally, notable land birds. **Sloan's Lake,** in northwest Denver at 17th and Sheridan, attracts migrating waterbirds including Western Grebe and various gulls. South Metro walkers like to explore the **Highline Canal Trail** that winds through Littleton, Centennial, Englewood, and Denver. **Bear Creek Greenbelt** (from Sheridan to Wadsworth to Kipling) can produce interesting land-bird migrants and nesting Cliff Swallows (unless some vandal knocks them down). Bald Eagles nest at **Standley Lake,** in Westminster off West 88th.

DeLorme grid: P. 40 B3–D2.
Elevation: 5,280 feet.
Hazards: Fast-moving bicyclists.
Nearest food, gas, lodging: Denver, Littleton.
Camping: Denver, Chatfield.

For more information: Carson Nature Center, South Platte Park, 3000 West Carson Drive, Littleton, CO 80120-2968; (303) 730-1022; www.littleton.org/clubs/carson.asp.

35 Chatfield State Park and Waterton

Habitats: Wetlands, riparian, grassland.

Specialty birds: *Resident:* Common Merganser, Great Blue Heron, Virginia Rail, American Dipper. *Summer:* Wood Duck, American White Pelican, Least Flycatcher, Red-eyed Vireo, Gray Catbird, American Redstart, Yellow-breasted Chat, Lazuli Bunting, Spotted Towhee, Lesser Goldfinch. *Migrant:* Ducks, Western and other grebes, loons, Osprey, Broad-winged Hawk, flycatchers, vireos, swallows, warblers, Western Tanager. *Winter:* Common Goldeneye, Bald Eagle, Northern Harrier, Winter Wren (uncommon).

Best times to bird: Year-round.

About this site

The bird list for Chatfield/Waterton tops 360 species—it and Barr Lake have longer bird lists than any other Colorado state park. An array of migrants, eastern strays, and mountain species swells the list. The *Atlas* block here recorded 79 breeding species.

Chatfield State Park centers on a good-size reservoir fed by two streams, Plum Creek and the South Platte River. The reservoir draws a dazzling assortment of waterbirds. A perimeter road leads to a dozen viewing sites of water and riparian habitats.

Plum Creek has cottonwood woodlands, extensive willow and box-elder thickets, and large cattail marshes. The South Platte River bottom, a finger of green thrusting out from the foothills, features tall cottonwoods, sprawling box-elders, and an understory of willows, wild plums, hawthorns, and other shrubs that draw droves of migrating land birds.

Upstream from the reservoir, Waterton refers to the area along the Platte within 2 miles of the Waterton Road bridge across the river. Downstream from the bridge, a river trail leads to Chatfield; upstream the Colorado Trail follows an old railroad grade into the foothills. (*Note:* The Denver Water Board in 2004 proposed to raise the reservoir 10 to 20 feet, which would inundate riparian habitat for a mile or more up both streams and create major changes in bird-watching opportunities. In 2005 Congress passed enabling legislation, but environmental studies will precede any drastic changes.)

At Waterton the *Denver Audubon Nature Center* conducts classes for schoolchildren, and RMBO operates a spring banding station. The center so far does not open for visitors except for classes and meetings.

On the first Sunday of each month, a 3-mile "Walk the Wetlands" hike that samples habitats along the river leaves from the nature center (8:00 A.M. in summer, 9:00 A.M. in winter). A bulletin board posts the birds seen on previous walks.

Chatfield offers a morning bird walk on the last Saturday of each month (7:00 A.M. in summer, 8:00 A.M. in winter), which starts on the east side of Kingfisher Bridge.

Directions

Located in southwest metro Denver.

Chatfield, main entrance: 1 mile south of C–470 on Wadsworth, on the left.

Waterton: Turn left on Waterton Road 3.4 miles south of the main Chatfield entrance (a brown sign announces Waterton Canyon and Roxborough State Park), as the road curves right. Park in the first parking lot on the left (Audubon Center at Chatfield and Discovery Pavilion), the second parking lot on the left (for hikers and bikers going upstream into Waterton Canyon), or just beyond, on the side of the road before the road crosses the South Platte River.

The birding

More than fifty species nest along the streams; most abundant are the ever-noisy House Wren and Yellow Warbler. Other breeders include Wood Duck, Common Merganser, Great Horned Owl, Belted Kingfisher, Western Wood-Pewee, Black-capped Chickadee, Gray Catbird, MacGillivray's Warbler, Black-headed Grosbeak, Lazuli Bunting, Bullock's Oriole, and Lesser and American Goldfinches. Yellow-breasted Chats sing lustily from late May to late June, after which they skulk secretively in the shrubbery. Chatfield/Waterton has Colorado's only regularly nesting Least Flycatchers and American Redstarts. Western Meadowlarks sing beside all park roads. One or two pairs of American Dippers may breed, starting in March; lately they used two sites—one under or close to Waterton Bridge and another 1.5 miles downstream.

Migrant flycatchers, vireos, swallows, thrushes, warblers, and sparrows spice up birders' April and May quests. On May and June days with low clouds or rain, thousands of migrating swallows (six species) feed over streams, reservoir, and gravel pits. Among warblers, Yellow-rumped predominate. Regulars include Orange-crowned, Virginia's, Townsend's (fall, mainly), MacGillivray's (a few stay to nest), and Wilson's. Frequent but less common: Northern Parula, Black-throated Gray, Chestnut-sided, Blackpoll, and Black-and-white, Northern Waterthrush, and Ovenbird. Fall migrants differ somewhat from the spring birds; Wilson's outnumber all other warblers combined (August 15 to September 15) whereas Yellow-rumps arrive in numbers after the Wilson's leave. Sparrows like rabbitbrush, especially in fall migration: Chipping, Brewer's, Clay-colored, Vesper, Lark, and White-crowned; a few Lincoln's may lurk in streamside shrubs. The prolific list of rarities includes Yellow-throated and White-eyed Vireos, nine flycatchers, and fifteen other warblers, mostly eastern vagrants.

Ospreys sometimes ply the river and perch on snags or power poles. Other regular migrants include Broad-winged Hawk (spring), Western Tanager, Green-tailed Towhee, and Rose-breasted and Evening Grosbeaks. Marsh Wrens join rails and blackbirds in cattail marshes.

In fall and spring the reservoir collects an exemplary collection of migrating waterbirds. They range from abundant Western Grebes and many ducks to extraordinary rarities such as Brown Pelican and Long-billed and Ancient Murrelets. In November a few loons spice the birder's day—usually several Commons, but each year a handful of Pacifics and, rarely, a Yellow-billed or Red-throated. Over the course of the fall, the lake can hold six species of grebes. You get best views of the lake from the Heronry Overlook in the morning, the marina all day, and Fox Run in afternoon.

Cottonwood woodlands quiet down in winter, with a few mixed flocks of chickadees, White-breasted Nuthatch, and Brown Creeper, perhaps joined by a Downy Woodpecker and a Ruby-crowned Kinglet. A sharp-eyed (sharp-eared) birder may find a Winter Wren hiding in willows bordering the river. A few Virginia Rails remain in cattail swamps with open water, joined by a few Marsh Wrens and Swamp Sparrows. Driven downstream by upstream freezing, ten to twenty American Dippers patrol the South Platte between Waterton and Chatfield Lake, their calls rivaling the rattle of Belted Kingfishers. A few Bald Eagles watch the river or perch a half mile away in tall cottonwoods from which they survey their territories.

Chatfield: From the West entrance, turn right at the T intersection. Two parking lots, *Catfish Flats* and *Fox Run,* provide good views of the South Platte arm of the reservoir. In migration, pelicans and many ducks, grebes, and gulls rest here.

The road crosses the South Platte on *Kingfisher Bridge:* Trails go upstream on both sides of the bridge. The west-side one, better for birding, threads through towering cottonwoods and shrubby thickets, with periodic views of the river. Migrants use these woods—flycatchers, vireos, warblers, Western Tanager. This trail offers the best place to find breeding songbirds.

On the east side of Kingfisher Bridge, a half-mile, wheelchair-accessible trail leads to a platform at the river's edge after passing through tall cottonwoods. A dirt trail proceeds south through willow bottoms, climbs to an overlook of a handsome stretch of river, passes through box-elder and cottonwood groves, and comes to two ponds that often attract waterfowl in both summer and winter.

Back at the perimeter road, half a mile on, make a sharp left to the *Heronry Overlook.* The herons departed when their nest trees toppled (flooding and ice action did them in), but now this platform affords an excellent vantage over the south arm of the reservoir. During spring and fall migration, viewers see ducks, gulls, and grebes (including thousands of Western Grebes in spring). (From this site in October, counters tally the most species of any Colorado Big Sit! In 2003 the count hit sixty-one species. The Big Sit! Observers count all the birds they see or hear while within a circle with a 17-foot—yes, *foot*—diameter.)

The road arrives at a three-way intersection; bear left. (The right fork goes out the park's south entrance; Burrowing Owls may nest opposite the entrance station.) Almost immediately, a road on the right leads to *Plum Creek "Nature Area"* (about a mile). A trail goes upstream (south) across grasslands, by the stream and cattail marshes, to an extensive cottonwood woodland with shrubby thickets. Plum Creek has breeding and winter birds similar to the South Platte but fewer migrants. A January 1993 ski tour produced Colorado's second record of Long-billed Thrasher.

The perimeter road, past the nature area road, ends at a T intersection. Go right to *Plum Creek Delta* (0.25 mile). There, on the left, a quarter-mile walk toward the lake (take your scope) leads to mudflats where ducks, geese, gulls, and a few shore-birds assemble during migration.

A left-hand turn at the T leads to two parking lots near the *marina;* at the first, park in the center or right side. Migrating warblers and sparrows feed in the sparse willows on the sand spit, and from the end you can inspect the spit for shorebirds, the lake for waterbirds. From the second parking lot (another quarter mile) you can walk out a similar spit to look for waterbirds. A wheelchair-accessible fishing platform provides a good view of the reservoir. (Scopes help on both sand spits.) From these vantages Denver birders have found many of the rarities that make Chatfield an exciting destination (for example, loons, grebes, and murrelets).

Waterton: Denver birders come here to see spring and fall migrants—warblers, kinglets, and flycatchers—in the shrubs and cottonwoods that line the Platte River. Waterton entertains many of the same birds as Chatfield, and its list includes Summer and Scarlet Tanagers and Orchard and Baltimore Orioles. Colorado's first Blue-winged and Prairie Warblers appeared within 200 yards of the Waterton Bridge, as did its first Common Black-Hawk and second Scott's Oriole (now known to breed along the western state border).

Trails from the end of the *Audubon Center* parking lot, past the restrooms, lead to two ponds (old gravel pits) lined with cattails and willows and to the river. The ponds rarely hold waterfowl due to frequent foot traffic, although in the cattails that separate them, you might find Virginia Rail and Red-winged Blackbird. Song Sparrow and Yellow Warbler sing from the willows. Walk east toward the river and go right to *Redstart Woods,* a patch of tall cottonwoods with a thick understory. American Redstarts nest here, one of their few Colorado breeding sites, and a Least Flycatcher may call *'che-bec.'* The riverside trail from Waterton Bridge comes in here.

If you park at *Waterton Bridge,* follow the trail downstream along the river (on the left side as you face downstream). In migration and summer, thickets of hawthorn, willows, and wild plum shelter shrub-lovers. This trail arrives at Redstart Woods in a mile (after ducking through some dense willow thickets).

From Redstart Woods, walk downstream as the trail skirts the river through groves of cottonwoods and shrubby thickets. In June, chats sing loudly, you might hear the monotonous song of a Red-eyed Vireo, and Western Wood-Pewees build nests at eye level. About 1.5 miles downstream, a narrow pond ends in a cattail marsh where Sora and Virginia Rail hide, the latter year-round unless the water freezes. Common Yellowthroats breed here, and Marsh Wrens stop in migration.

Sometimes in summer Cinnamon Teal flush from the marsh. From here you can stay along the river to Kingfisher Bridge in Chatfield (2 miles), turn back, or turn west to the gazebo.

The Gazebo Trail crosses a grassland (rather than walk on the bicycle road, go along the cattails and fence; Tree Swallows use the bird boxes) and a dry irrigation ditch and swings south to the *Wetlands Gazebo*. From its shade, you can scan ponds created to mitigate wetlands destroyed by C–470. The ponds usually have dabbling ducks and Killdeer. A few migrating shorebirds use the wetlands: White-faced Ibis, American Avocet, yellowlegs, and Spotted Sandpiper. A prairie-dog town across Wadsworth from the overlook sometimes lures raptors, especially Bald Eagle and Red-tailed and Ferruginous Hawks. Perhaps a Bald Eagle, watching from a mile away, may hurtle over to pirate prey from a smaller hawk. Golden Eagles occasionally join in feeding here. Return to the parking lot (0.25 mile) on the road/trail that goes straight south. (On this road you can reach the gazebo directly from the parking lot.)

Back at Waterton Road, the second parking lot, between Audubon Center and Waterton bridge, serves as a trailhead for hikers, bikers, and anglers to walk up the Platte through *Waterton Canyon*—the north terminus of the 470-mile long Colorado Trail. The first half mile passes shrubby hills and riparian woods, a good place to find Blue-gray Gnatcatcher, Lesser Goldfinch, and migrating Lazuli Bunting. In a half mile the canyon narrows, box-elders line the stream, and mountain mahogany and other shrubs cover the steep hillsides, but fewer birds live here. Rock Wrens trill among scattered piles of rock, Canyon Wrens sing from the cliffs, and Song Sparrows from streamside shrubs. Winter brings Common Merganser and American Dipper, along with rather tame bighorn sheep.

DeLorme grid: P. 40 D2.

Elevation: 5,300 feet.

Hazards: Poison ivy, knapweed, thistles.

Nearest food, gas, lodging: Littleton, Englewood, Lakewood, and Denver.

Camping: Yes.

For more information: Chatfield State Park, 11500 North Roxborough Park Road, Littleton, CO 80125; (303) 791–7275; www.parks .state.co.us. Audubon Society of Greater Denver, 9308 South Wadsworth Boulevard, Littleton, CO 80128; (303) 973–9530; www .denveraudubon.org.

36 Roxborough State Park

Habitats: Scrub oak, grassland.

Specialty birds: *Resident:* Golden Eagle, Prairie Falcon, Western Scrub Jay, Canyon Wren. *Summer:* Blue-gray Gnatcatcher, Virginia's Warbler, Spotted Towhee, Lazuli Bunting.

Best times to bird: Year-round.

About this site

A stunning panorama of red-rock spires and cliffs, Roxborough features scrub-oak birds amid soaring scenery. The only road goes to the visitor center, no farther. On the trails, which fan out from the visitor center, the park allows no bicycles, horses, or motorized vehicles, and it has no camping or picnic facilities. The park offers an active series of volunteer-led nature walks.

Directions

From C–470, exit at Santa Fe Boulevard (U.S. Highway 85), then drive 3.5 miles south and turn west on Titan Road. In 3 miles Titan swings south and becomes Rampart Range Road. In 3.7 miles, just before a subdivision's parkway entrance, turn left and then immediately right by the fire station onto the park road.

The birding

The visitor center, with a back wall of Lyons sandstone, usually has a nearby Canyon Wren. From it, trails go in two directions. Fountain Valley Trail (2 miles) loops through scrub oak and grassland, with a side trip to the Lyons Overlook. Willow Creek Trail (1.5 miles) loops around for a short hike, or take a longer loop to the South Rim (3 miles). Carpenter Peak Trail (6.5 miles) climbs to the highest point in the park, 7,160 feet.

The ramparts pull in summer visitors such as White-throated Swift and Violet-green Swallow that swoop around the sandstone pillars, as do Common Raven, Golden Eagle, and Prairie Falcon. Listen for the music of the Canyon Wren. Noisy scrub-jays will welcome you, Black-headed Grosbeak and Lazuli Bunting sing from the brush, Spotted Towhees scrabble in the scrub oak, Bushtits nest, and both Lesser and American Goldfinches fly around.

DeLorme grid: P. 50 A2.

Elevation: 6,000 to 6,500 feet.

Hazards: Rattlesnakes, poison ivy. Bring water.

Nearest food, gas, lodging: Littleton, metro Denver.

Camping: No.

For more information: Roxborough State Park, 4751 Roxborough Drive, Littleton, CO 80125; (303) 979-3959; www.parks.state .co.us.

37 Castlewood Canyon State Park

Habitats: Scrub oak, ponderosa/Douglas-fir forest, foothills riparian, cliff.

Specialty birds: *Resident:* Steller's Jay, Common Raven, Canyon Wren. *Summer:* Turkey Vulture, White-throated Swift, Broad-tailed Hummingbird, Cordilleran Flycatcher, Lazuli Bunting, Lesser Goldfinch. *Winter:* Townsend's Solitaire, Dark-eyed Junco, Pine Siskin.

Best times to bird: May to September.

About this site

Castlewood claims the largest roost of Turkey Vultures in Colorado; spectacular flights swirl around the west side from April to September. The park has two main habitats: scrub oak and mixed conifers. It merits IBA status because Prairie Falcon, Cordilleran Flycatcher, Virginia's Warbler, and Western Tanager breed here.

Directions

The park has two entrances: one to the visitor center atop the rimrock and one through the canyon that Cherry Creek cut when, on August 3, 1933, the Castlewood dam burst.

Visitor center: From the one and only traffic light in Franktown (intersection of Highways 83 and 86), drive south 5 miles on Highway 83 to the park entrance, on the right just after a highway bridge crosses Cherry Creek. The gate opens at 8:00 A.M.

Cherry Creek: From the traffic light in Franktown, go west 0.25 mile, just across Cherry Creek, and go south (left) on Castlewood Canyon Road to the park, which is 2 miles south. This road is always open. This side of the park offers better bird-watching.

The birding

Birders can encounter the park's excellent foothills scrub habitat from short and long trails. Next to and beyond the *visitor center,* trails start from several parking lots. Birdhouses along the entrance road attract both Mountain and Western Bluebirds. Asphalt wheelchair-accessible trails follow the rim of the canyon. From any of these trails (collectively called *Canyon View Nature Trail),* you can find vultures, towhees, and bluebirds; Canyon Wrens sing from the cliffs and occasionally hop into view for patient and observant birders.

Cherry Creek Canyon has three main parking lots—in order from the north: Homestead, Middle, and Falls—with a network of trails. *Homestead Trail* drops easterly downslope to Cherry Creek, where it forks. The left fork, *Rimrock Trail,* crosses a small riparian patch along Cherry Creek and climbs through scrub oak and a small patch of conifers to a rimrock cliff. The trail extends south for 2.25 miles, drops down to Cherry Creek, and meets *Inner Canyon* and *Falls Trails.* Hikers can turn around anytime and return to the parking lot or make a complete circle.

In scrub oak, Western Scrub-Jay, Black-capped Chickadee, Blue-gray Gnat-catcher, Virginia's Warbler, Spotted Towhee, Lazuli Bunting, and Black-headed Grosbeak flourish. One or two pairs of Yellow-breasted Chats nest in the shrubs that line Cherry Creek. On the first part of the rimrock climb, birders sometimes find an Indigo Bunting singing among the Lazulis. Along the rimrock, vultures soar by at eye level, adding to the spectacular view across the canyon to the Rockies.

Try the right-hand fork if you haven't found all the scrub-oak birds. It traverses oak groves and scattered ponderosa/Douglas-fir patches: It's 1.5 miles to the Middle parking lot or 2 miles to the Falls parking lot and *Falls Trail*. The latter leads upstream along Cherry Creek to the ruins of Castlewood Dam (2 miles). Usually not many birds are produced here, although winter trips occasionally yield a Winter Wren.

Castlewood Canyon State Park features a large roost of Turkey Vultures, Canyon Wrens singing from cliffs, and both Mountain and Western Bluebirds using bird boxes.

On the west side of the road, conifer groves, composed of ponderosa pine, Douglas-fir, and Rocky Mountain juniper, harbor Broad-tailed Hummingbird, Cordilleran and Hammond's Flycatchers, Plumbeous Vireo, Mountain Chickadee, White-breasted and Pygmy Nuthatches, Western Tanager, and Dark-eyed Junco. Turkey Vultures roost in tall pines and on the cliff rim (often visible early in the morning from the parking lots).

Three short but primitive west-side trails ascend 300 feet through pines and Douglas-fir to the cliff base (and provide a cool place to walk on hot summer days). Each traverses the base of the cliff to meet the other trails: *Cliff Base Trail* from the Falls lot, *Cave Trail* and *Climber's Trail* from the Middle lot. White-throated Swift and Cliff and Violet-green Swallows nest on the cliff faces and swoop around the rim, and Turkey Vultures sometimes allow fairly close approach. Common Poorwills call at dusk and dawn. You can also see breeding Broad-tailed Hummingbird and Cordilleran Flycatcher.

On the east side of the road, trails from the Middle and Falls parking lots lead into scrub oak and a pine/Douglas-fir/oak woodland. Pygmy Nuthatch commonly occur here, as well as Plumbeous Vireo, Western Scrub Jay, Blue-gray Gnatcatcher, and some of the pine birds mentioned above.

Local birders like to drive through the park to the *Winkler Ranch*. A one-hundred-box roadside bluebird trail houses nesting Western and Mountain Bluebirds, as well as Violet-green and Tree Swallows. Say's Phoebes perch on fence lines. The road passes stone pillars on the left (4.5 miles from the Falls parking lot, 2 miles from the broken dam at the park's south end); 0.2 mile farther, look back at the rock inscription on the west side: MEMORIAL CONRAD MOSCHER MASSACRED BY INDIANS AUGUST 21, 1864. Past this marker 0.25 mile on the right, bushes surrounding two metal stock tanks attract thirsty birds. Across the road, look in the hayfields for Bobolink, Dickcissel, Brewer's Blackbird, and maybe a Grasshopper Sparrow (a scope helps). The road ends at a T intersection where you can go left to Highway 83, right into Castle Rock, or back on Castlewood Canyon Road.

DeLorme grid: P. 51 B4.

Elevation: 6,150 to 6,600 feet.

Hazards: Rattlesnakes (rarely encountered), poison ivy, trails relatively primitive except on visitor center rimrock—hikers should step carefully. In winter, snow and ice on all trails except paved trails near the visitor center.

Nearest food, gas, lodging: Castle Rock, Parker; food and gas in Franktown.

Camping: No.

For more information: Castlewood Canyon State Park, 2989 South Highway 83, Franktown, CO 80116; (303) 688-5242; www.parks.state.co.us.

38 Golden Gate Canyon State Park

Habitats: Foothills riparian, ponderosa, Douglas-fir, aspen, lodgepole.
Specialty birds: *Resident:* Dusky Grouse,

nuthatches, Brown Creeper. *Migrant:* Townsend's Warbler.
Best times to bird: May to October.

About this site

A good place to find birds of the lower mountains, Golden Gate provides many spots for bird-watching near your car, and has an appealing array of trails, both short and long.

Directions

From Golden, go north on Highway 93 to County Road 70 (about a mile), Golden Gate Canyon Road; turn left and, in a slow, winding 12 miles, you'll reach the park.

The birding

As you enter the park, you come first to the visitor center, situated beside *Ralston Creek*. Trails run in each direction along the stream, to rewarding streamside and hillside habitats. Turn right and drive along the stream; park at any pull-off. From *Bridge Creek* to the *Red Barn Picnic Area,* the valley opens up to a series of ponds and trails in three habitats: foothills riparian, scrubby hillside, and low-elevation conifers (ponderosa pine and Douglas-fir).

Along the willow carrs that line the stream, you can find Broad-tailed Hummingbird, Dusky and Cordilleran Flycatchers, and Lincoln's, Song, and Fox (rare) Sparrows. You can also find Red-naped Sapsucker, Hairy Woodpecker, Warbling Vireo, Tree and Violet-green Swallows, House Wren, Swainson's Thrush (rare), Yellow and MacGillivray's Warblers, and Black-headed Grosbeak. The scrubby hillsides above harbor Green-tailed Towhee and Virginia's Warbler. In the conifers you might encounter Williamson's Sapsucker (scarce), Hammond's Flycatcher, Steller's Jay, Mountain Chickadee, all three nuthatches, Brown Creeper, Ruby-crowned Kinglet (unusual at this low elevation), Western Bluebird, Yellow-rumped Warbler, and Western Tanager. You might stumble across a Dusky Grouse on one of the trails.

Back past the visitor center, at an intersection where the county road goes straight, turn right on the park road. At the pay station you might see swallows—Barn and Cliff—as well as Brewer's and Red-winged Blackbirds. The park road, though paved, climbs rather steeply to *Bootleg Bottom* and has essentially no places to stop a car. The park prohibits RVs, oversized vehicles, and trailers from this road because of steep grades and tight curves.

Cliff Swallows have expanded by adapting to man-made nest sites such as bridges and condominiums. In cities they often feed around intersections near bridges.

At Bootleg Bottom, a ponderosa/Douglas-fir hillside on the north provides more chances to find the species listed for Ralston Creek. In an aspen grove on the south side, look for cavity drillers: Red-naped Sapsucker, Hairy and Downy Woodpeckers, and Northern Flicker. Cavity users, who depend on the drillers for the nest holes, include Tree and Violet-green Swallows, House Wren, and Mountain Bluebird. Western Wood-Pewee, Dusky Flycatcher, and juncos also use the aspen. Hermit Thrushes sing from the conifers and sometimes from aspen. In the aspen groves some years ago, the local bird club consistently found a Flammulated Owl at dusk. The park probably has nesting Northern Saw-whet, Northern Pygmy-, and Great Horned Owls.

Continue on up the hill and, instead of going into the campground, turn right along the road to *Panorama Point.* You won't see many birds here (maybe a soaring Red-tailed Hawk or a Prairie Falcon), but you will enjoy a striking view of the high peaks of the Front Range.

The park's intricate network of trails goes through all park habitats. The visitor center has maps of the park and trail guides; with two cars you can arrange a downhill trek from Panorama Point or one of the campgrounds to the visitor center.

Try another Jefferson County park, **White Ranch,** to look for Dusky Grouse from March to May. Follow the directions to Golden Gate, but go only 4 miles on County Road 70, to County Road 37 (Crawford Gulch) for 4 miles to the park road (right); the park entrance is 1.5 miles farther. Go into the first parking area, on the upper side, and walk the trails on the south. Dusky Grouse display along the trails (sometimes). Other trails, from this lot and the main one, lead to pine and aspen woods.

DeLorme grid: P. 39 B7; White Ranch, p. 40 B1.

Elevation: 7,690 to 10,200 feet.

Nearest food, gas, lodging: Golden, metro Denver.

Camping: Yes.

For more information: Golden Gate State Park, 92 Crawford Gulch Road, Golden, CO 80403; (303) 582-3707; www.parks.state .co.us. Jefferson County Open Space, 700 Jefferson County Parkway, Golden, CO 80401; (303) 278-5925; www.co.jefferson.co.us/openspace.

39 Genesee Mountain Park W⊕

Habitats: Ponderosa.

Specialty birds: *Resident:* Red Crossbill (erratic). *Summer:* Williamson's Sapsucker, Cordilleran Flycatcher, Violet-green Swallow, Townsend's Solitaire, Western Bluebird.

Best times to bird: May to October.

About this site

Probably the best and most accessible place near Denver to find Williamson's Sapsucker, Genesee (a Denver Mountain Park) has a single road that climbs through ponderosas, with several parking areas where birders can stop and look for typical ponderosa specialists. Its picnic facilities and volleyball courts attract crowds of people on summer-weekend afternoons—best to get here in early morning.

Directions

Take exit 254 from I–70, turn left, cross the overpass, and turn right at the T intersection.

The birding

Stop at the first turn (0.25 mile) to look around. An almost boreal Douglas-fir forest lines the next section but lacks safe stops. The road turns right—you can park at the first wide place on the right (0.75 mile) and walk up the hill to the top (no real trail; about a mile, 250-foot elevation gain) or follow the road to several other parking spots. (Note the road on the left, which leads to Chief Hosa, 0.5 mile from that first wide spot.) The road goes to the top of Genesee Mountain, with specialty birds at any stop.

Williamson's Sapsuckers have holes in several trees between the first parking lot and the top. You should also encounter Steller's Jay, Pygmy Nuthatch, Violet-green Swallow, Western Bluebird, and possibly Cassin's Finch and Red Crossbill. The park has an abundance of venerable restrooms; look for Cordilleran Flycatchers nesting on their eaves, especially the one at the top. Rarely, Dusky Grouse perch in the pines, and they could hide in Douglas-firs on the steep northern slope.

The Chief Hosa Road crosses Interstate 25 at exit 253: Turn right (below the freeway fill), toward a parking area (1 mile) and trails (1 to 2 miles) out to a promontory.

DeLorme grid: P. 40 C1.

Elevation: 7,400 to 8,800 feet.

Hazards: Errant volleyballs or horseshoes.

Nearest food, gas, lodging: Metro Denver, Evergreen; Bergen Park for gas.

Camping: No.

40 Foothills Parks ⓦ ♿

Habitats: Ponderosa, montane grassland, foothills shrubs.

Specialty birds: *Resident:* Common Raven,

Red Crossbill. *Summer:* American Dipper, Western and Mountain Bluebirds, Ovenbird.

Best times to bird: May to September.

About this site

Jefferson County Open Space operates a splendid set of parks with trails, mainly into ponderosa pine and related montane meadows. Its informative Web site (see below) describes the parks and trails, and you can download maps.

The birding

Dinosaur Ridge (IBA), the only regular Colorado hawk watch, operates from mid-March to early May (cloudy days, after 9:00 A.M., in April are best). It tallies modest numbers of hawks so the official hawk-watchers have time for friendly discussion about identification and hawk ecology. From I–70, go south from exit 259 and park on the left (southeast quadrant of the intersection) in the Stegosaurus lot. The hawk-watch site is a thirty-minute, steep hike south on the hogback. Daily hawk counts run from 10 to 250 (usually on the lower side). Though it claims the best Ferruginous Hawk migration site in the world (241 in the peak year), it tallies more Red-tailed Hawks, American Kestrels, Turkey Vultures, and Cooper's Hawks, plus, most surprising for Coloradans, 55 to 200 Broad-winged Hawks. Thousands of White-throated Swifts also zoom by. (The hawk-watch did not operate in 2007.)

Just to the south, off Highway 26 between Morrison (U.S. Highway 285) and I–70, **Red Rocks Park** mixes massive, upthrust, red-sandstone slabs with scrub-oak birds, essentially the same mix as Roxborough Park's. Trails emanate from most parking areas and feature swifts and swallows, Western Scrub-Jay, Canyon Wren, Virginia's Warbler, Spotted Towhee, and Lazuli Bunting. The Trading Post maintains a winter feeder, which occasionally nets a Golden-crowned Sparrow.

American Dippers nest along Bear Creek at **Lair o' the Bear.** A Chestnut-sided Warbler in June may represent an outlying breeding attempt. Reach it from Morrison (off C–470 or past Red Rocks Park, 4 miles south of I–70) by driving 4 miles up Highway 74; the park entrance is on the left. A mile-long trail runs along Bear Creek.

Mount Falcon's trails, all traversing ponderosa habitat, loop around and into each other. Birders can link a hike anywhere from 1 to 5 miles. Castle Trail leads to the ruins of a castle that John Brisben Walker started building in 1909 but that lightning destroyed nine years later; Brisben dreamed of creating a summer White House for U.S. presidents. Tower Trail leads to two overlooks, one of the mountains

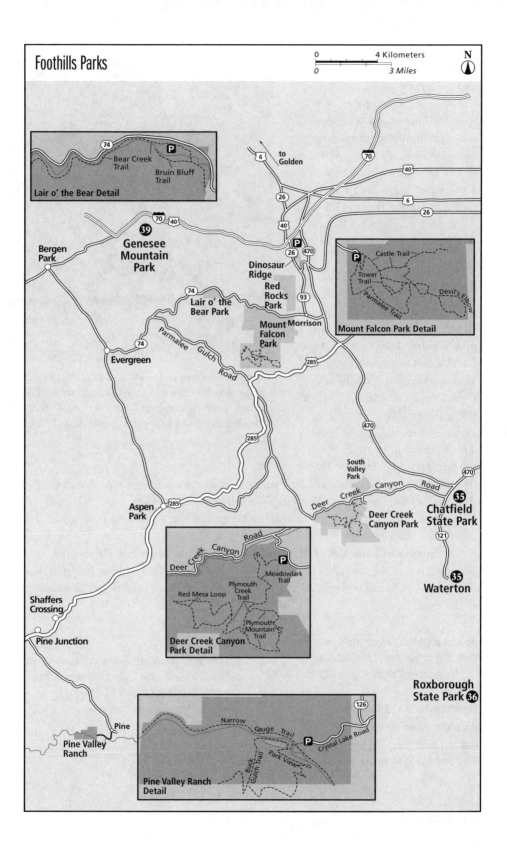

Foothills Parks

0   4 Kilometers
0   3 Miles
N

Lair o' the Bear Detail
74
Bear Creek Trail
Bruin Bluff Trail
P

to Golden
6
70
40
26
6
26
40
40
26
470

Bergen Park

Genesee Mountain Park
39

70
40

74

Dinosaur Ridge
Red Rocks Park

P
Mount Falcon Park Detail
Castle Trail
Tower Trail
Parmalee Trail
Devil's Elbow
P

93

Lair o' the Bear Park
74

Parmalee Gulch Road

Evergreen
74

Mount Falcon Park
Morrison

285

285

South Valley Park

Deer Creek Canyon Road
470

Aspen Park
285

Deer Creek Canyon Park

Chatfield State Park
35
121

Waterton
35

Deer Creek Canyon Road
Deer Creek Canyon
Meadowlark Trail
P
Plymouth Creek Trail
Red Mesa Loop
Plymouth Mountain Trail
Deer Creek Canyon Park Detail

Shaffers Crossing

Pine Junction

Roxborough State Park
36

Pine
Pine Valley Ranch

Narrow Gauge Trail
Buck Gulch Trail
Park View
P
Crystal Lake Road
126
Pine Valley Ranch Detail

to the west, the other toward metro Denver.

If you see dying pines or firs, look for Three-toed Woodpeckers, sporadically reported from Mount Falcon. From C–470 exit to US 285 "south" to Fairplay; at 4 miles turn right on Parmelee Gulch Road (to Indian Hills); at 2.8 miles turn right on Picutis Road then left on Mount Falcon Road to the park.

Near Chatfield State Park, **Deer Creek Canyon Park** trails start in foothills shrubland and climb quickly up into ponderosa pine/scrub-oak woodlands. From C–470, exit southbound on Wadsworth; go 0.25 mile to Deer Creek Canyon Road (first traffic light). Drive west for about 2 miles to Grizzly Drive and the parking lot, 0.25 mile on the left. Take Meadowlark Trail

PHOTO © GLENN WALBEK

Mountain Bluebirds, originally tied to cavities carved by woodpeckers into aspen trees, now benefit mightily from bluebird trails—networks of birdhouses—as do Western Bluebirds, Tree and Violet-green Swallows, and House Wrens.

(hikers only) on the right—it hasn't suffered from ditch-digging mountain bikes. Among the ponderosa birds, Virginia's Warbler, Spotted Towhee, and Dark-eyed Junco predominate. Ovenbirds nest at the far end of the Red Mesa loop, about 3.5 miles from the parking lot.

Dying trees in **Pine Valley Ranch** occasionally lure American Three-toed Woodpecker as well as ponderosa birds. Go south on US 285 to Pine Junction, left on Pine Valley Road (County Road 126) 5.8 miles to Pine, then follow the signs to the park.

DeLorme grid: Dinosaur Ridge, Red Rocks Park, Lair o' the Bear, Mt. Falcon, p. 40 D1; Deer Creek Canyon, p. 40 D2; Pine Valley, p. 49 A7.

Elevation: 6,000 to 7,800 feet.

Hazards: Lightning, bad weather.

Nearest food, gas, lodging: Metro Denver; food and gas in Morrison, Pine Junction.

Camping: No.

For more information: Jefferson County Open Space, 700 Jefferson County Parkway, Golden, CO 80401-6018; (303) 271-5993; www.co.jefferson.co.us/openspace.

41 Mount Evans

Habitats: Spruce/fir, alpine.

Specialty birds: *Summer:* White-tailed Ptarmi-gan, Gray Jay, Clark's Nutcracker, Pine Gros-beak, Brown-capped Rosy-Finch.

Best time to bird: Summer.

About this site

The highest auto road in the country climbs to 14,130 feet on Mount Evans. Along the way it rises from the spruce/fir forest around Echo Lake through stunted conifers at Goliath Natural Area to tundra and rocky cliffs above timberline. Determined exploration may net you a ptarmigan, and Rocky Mountain goats, pikas, and marmots haunt the roadsides—don't feed them!

Directions

Two choices from I–70: exit 256 onto Highway 74 to Bergen Park, right on Highway 103 over Squaw Pass (9,807 feet) to Echo Lake; or exit 240 at Idaho Springs onto Highway 103 to Echo Lake. Follow directions to the Mount Evans highway (28 miles from Idaho Springs to the top). Closed in winter.

The birding

From the entrance station at Echo Lake, proceed to Summit Lake, at 12,830 feet. Walk around the lake and inspect the cliffs and snowbanks for feeding rosy-finches and pipits. Rock Wrens may trill from the rock piles. The road climbs up to a hairpin turn where you can look down on a saddle covered with tundra. Here pipits abound, and you have a chance of finding ptarmigan if you spend time and look diligently for the well-concealed birds. After many hairpin turns (you might find rosy-finches on cliffs or snowbanks as you climb up), the road reaches a visitor center, 134 vertical feet below the summit of 14,264 feet. A vast panorama of mountains stretches out north, west, and south; the Great Plains occupy the east horizon.

DeLorme grid: P. 39 C5–7, D5–6.

Elevation: 10,599 to 14,264 feet.

Hazards: Altitude, sudden weather changes—snow in July.

Nearest food, gas, lodging: Idaho Springs, Evergreen, metro Denver.

Camping: National forest campgrounds on Highway 103.

For more information: USDA Forest Service, 101 Chicago Creek Road, P.O. Box 3307, Idaho Springs, CO 80452; (303) 567-3000; www.fs.fed.us/r2/arnf. For road conditions: (303) 639-1111; www.dot.state.co.us (under "Travel Info").

Habitats: Spruce/fir, aspen, alpine.
Specialty birds: *Resident:* White-tailed Ptarmigan. *Summer:* American Pipit, Wilson's Warbler, Pine Grosbeak, Brown-capped Rosy-Finch.

Best times to bird: Year-round.

About this site

Denver and visiting birders most often try for ptarmigan (white in winter, brown in summer) on Guanella. The huge expense of keeping the road open all winter led Clear Creek County to close it in 2006–2007. The road will reopen in late spring, probably June, and stay available until the snows of October and November start to accumulate. A return to winter plowing seems doubtful.

Please exercise constraint in your ptarmigan search. Heavy birder traffic has the Forest Service apprehensive about allowing this viewing opportunity. Don't harass the birds.

Directions

From I–70, take exit 228 at Georgetown; drive through town to the highway, County Road 381; or from US 285, turn right at Grant on Forest Road 118.

The alpine stretches of Guanella Pass, Trail Ridge Road, and most high peaks host White-tailed Ptarmigan that hide quite effectively among the grasses, flowers, and rocks.

The birding

The road climbs from Georgetown through aspen and spruce/fir forests and willow bogs to the summit (11,669 feet). Several hiking trails branch out into the forest habitats.

For your ptarmigan quest, park at the top. During the nesting season the birds scatter widely over the large basin below Mount Bierstadt. By fall they form flocks that migrate to willow patches, on whose leaves they feed all winter. Ptarmigan descend from the tundra only as far as necessary to find exposed patches of their primary food.

The summer tundra offers other delights: American Pipit and, if you hike far enough on the Mount Bierstadt trail, Brown-capped Rosy-Finch nesting on the cliffs and feeding on snowbanks, plus the subtle kaleidoscope of miniature alpine wildflowers.

DeLorme grid: P. 39 C5–D5, p. A6–7.

Elevation: 10,000 to 12,000 feet.

Hazards: Altitude, sudden changes in weather. If the road reopens in winter, deep snow into May and blizzards in winter.

Nearest food, gas, lodging: Georgetown, Idaho Springs, Bailey.

Camping: Yes.

For more information: U.S. Forest Service, 101 Chicago Creek Road, P.O. Box 3307, Idaho Springs, CO 80452; (303) 567-3000; www.fs.fed.us/r2/arnf.

South-Central

Flanked on the north by "America's most famous mountain," Pikes Peak, south-central Colorado offers more habitats than the rest of the Front Range. Mountains extend south into New Mexico. It has plains and conifer habitats, pinyon/juniper, and a taste of the desert Southwest. Pinyon/juniper woodlands from the Garden of the Gods south to Raton Pass boast most P/J species. Cactus grasslands east and south of Pueblo bring in Southwestern species such as Scaled Quail, Greater Roadrunner, and Curve-billed Thrasher. Pueblo County has all the habitats except for extensive alpine tundra, and a county list of almost 400 species.

Pueblo Reservoir picks up many unusual waterbirds: loons, grebes, ducks, gulls, and terns. The Arkansas River, from Cañon City downstream, intercepts migrating land birds, and many stay to breed. Pikes Peak serves as a major tourist destination, although its mountain habitats, due to a granitic soil layer, lack the variety of plants and birds that other Colorado mountains provide.

Pike and San Isabel National Forests occupy substantial portions of the mountains and provide good access, and at least two state parks present good bird-watching opportunities. El Paso County (Colorado Springs) operates several superb parks that entice bird-watchers year-round.

New in 2007, the Colorado Birding Trail came online with an impressive array of eastern Colorado birding sites. The list includes all the sites listed in this guidebook plus forty-eight private ranches, some SWAs, and a few driving routes. The Birding Trail comprises fourteen sub-trails that spread over four of this guide's regions: mainly South Central and Southeast, with a few in the Northeast and Central Rockies.

Go to www.coloradobirdingtrail.com to explore this rich resource.

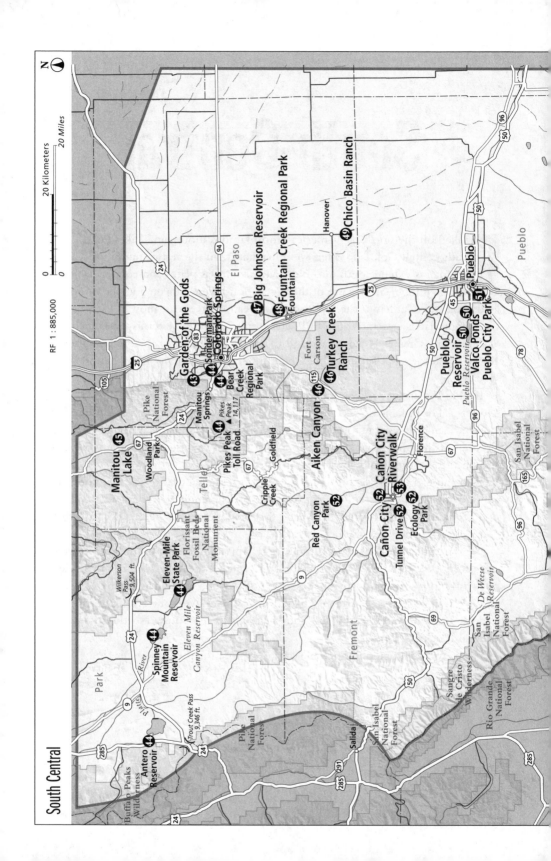

South Central

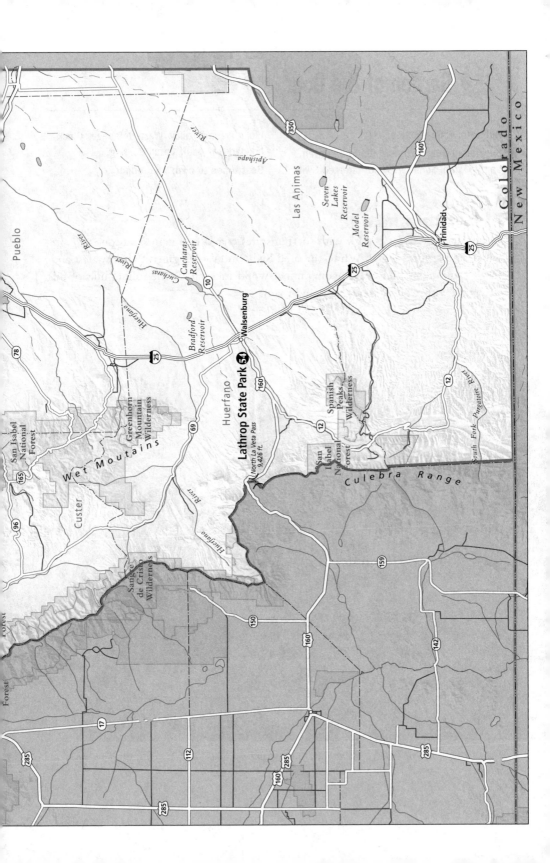

43 Garden of the Gods

Habitats: Pinyon/juniper, cliffs.

Specialty birds: *Resident:* Common Raven, Canyon Wren. *Summer:* White-throated Swift, Violet-green Swallow, Western Tanager, Black-headed Grosbeak, Lazuli Bunting.

Best times to bird: Year-round.

About this site

A spectacular red-rocks park with soaring spires of red Fountain sandstone in which and around which White-throated Swift and Violet-green Swallow nest and soar all summer. Extensive pinyon/juniper woodlands carpet the rolling hills of this city park, with well-laid-out trails and roads.

The soaring spires in Garden of the Gods inspire soaring birds such as swifts, swallows, and falcons.

Directions

From Interstate 25 take exit 141 and go west on U.S. Highway 24 (Cimarron Avenue); turn right on 30th Street and proceed north to the visitor center, on the right. Alternatively, from exit 146 on I–25, follow Garden of the Gods Road to 30th, turn left, and drive south to the visitor center.

The birding

Stop at the visitor center for a map of roads and trails. Take Gateway Road to Juniper Way Loop; stop at the first parking area (North Main) for your first views of the sandstone spires and of swifts and swallows careening about. Across the road, a little to the left of the lot, a trail leads into P/J woodland. Keeping left to stops #6 or #7, trails to the base of the sandstone spires pass by a few P/J birds. Prairie Falcons nest on the east side of the Kissing Camels formation.

It's a one-way loop, so drive around again and then turn right at the fork, on Garden Drive. Past Juniper Loop, try P/J from any of the parking lots. You can drive up Rampart Range Road a mile or two through more P/J. Exit the park on Garden Drive to US 24 or go back on Garden Lane to Gateway Road.

DeLorme grid: P. 62 B3.
Elevation: 6,450 feet.
Nearest food, gas, lodging: Colorado Springs.
Camping: No.

For more information: Garden of the Gods Visitor and Nature Center, 30th Street and Gateway Road, Colorado Springs, CO 80904; (719) 634-6666; www.springsgov.com.

44 Colorado Springs Area

Habitats: Riparian, scrub oak, ponderosa, spruce/fir.

Specialty birds: *Summer:* Cordilleran Flycatcher, Ovenbird, Lesser Goldfinch. *Migrant*

(fall): Ducks, scoters (Spinney and Eleven-Mile Reservoirs).

Best times to bird: Year-round; summer on Pikes Peak.

About this site

Colorado Springs has several urban parks besides the Garden of the Gods. For a mountain experience, the Toll Road up Pikes Peak climbs from near Manitou Springs almost 7,000 feet to the summit, at 14,110 feet.

The birding

On the southwest side of the city, **Bear Creek Regional Park** presents a network of trails, well marked and of various lengths, full of options for bird walks. To reach it, go west on US 24 (Cimarron Avenue; exit 141 from I–25) to 26th Street; turn south on 26th Street, across Lower Gold Camp Road to the Bear Creek Nature Center (open Tuesday through Saturday).

Bear Creek rushes noisily through a narrow stream bottom filled with cottonwoods, scrub oak, birch, maple, and alder, and surrounded by hills covered with scrub oak. Thick ground cover hides secretive ground-dwelling species. Listen for the elusive MacGillivray's Warbler's short but loud song; the singer lurks at eye level in thick brush. Warbling Vireos sing from the tops of cottonwoods, Lesser Goldfinches flit through. One trail plies the brushy bottomland, others climb the hillsides.

Turn left out of the nature center and follow *Bear Creek Road;* stop at pullouts to listen for Ovenbirds and Cordilleran Flycatchers. Additional trails in *Bear Creek Canyon Park* may tempt you to test the foothills habitat in this narrow canyon.

An urban surprise, **Sonderman Park** offers a delightful spot to prowl in the morning before heading for a meeting or work. Cottonwoods, willows, Siberian elms, and single stands of spruce and pine form a canopy over an understory composed of willow, chokecherry, lilac, and honeysuckle. To reach it (740 West Caramillo Street), leave I–25 at exit 144 (Fontanero); go west and, almost immediately, at the first stop sign, turn left (south) on Chestnut. In 0.25 mile turn left where you see the sign for Beidleman Environmental Learning Center and Sonderman Park; the parking area is a short hop away.

A collection of paths covers the park and its habitats. (The Mesa Valley Trail stretches north from the park for several miles.) Look in trees and bushes for migrants as well as the usual lowland riparian breeders, plus Black-chinned Hummingbird, Yellow-breasted Chat, Black-headed Grosbeak, Lazuli Bunting, and Lesser Goldfinch. So many Spotted Towhees sing here that it seems the park has one towhee for each other bird.

Migrants can include Broad-tailed Hummingbird, Olive-sided and Gray Flycatchers, Plumbeous Vireo, Gray Catbird, Orange-crowned, Tennessee, Yellowrumped (Audubon's and Myrtle), and Wilson's Warblers, Northern Parula, Western Tanager, Lark Sparrow, and Pine Siskin. A Sharp-shinned Hawk may cruise through the woods looking for small birds, and you might see a Red-tailed Hawk overhead. Among the limited winter species, something special can show up, such as a Harris's Sparrow.

The **Pikes Peak Toll Road** rises from ponderosa pine woodlands through rather desolate Douglas-fir/aspen patches into a fine spruce/fir forest at Glen Cove. It ascends above timberline through rocky scree fields and tundra to the summit at 14,110 feet (19 miles). To reach the Toll Road, take US 24 west from Manitou Springs to Cascade (10 miles from I–25).

Glen Cove (11,425 feet, Mile 13) produces the most interesting birds, the spruce/fir species that typify Colorado high-country habitat. Above timberline American Pipit and Horned Lark nest close to the road, but chances of finding rosy-finches or ptarmigan are exceedingly slim. Late-summer drives might net a few migrants that have moved up-mountain such as Mountain Bluebird or Swainson's Hawk.

In winter rosy-finches attend feeders west of Colorado Springs. Take US 24 to Divide, drive south on Highway 67 through Cripple Creek to Victor, turn north to *Goldfield,* and look for the feeders.

Fifty-five miles west of Colorado Springs off US 24, two reservoirs in South Park produce scoters each fall. To reach **Spinney Mountain Reservoir,** turn left on County Road 23; in 2.8 miles, turn right on County Road 59 for 1.1 miles to the park. You'll find the best viewing from the dam, at the south end. For **Eleven-Mile State Park,** return to the Spinney entrance; go right (southerly) on Road 59 for 2 miles to the park. Several parking areas on the westerly side provide views into the lake.

In October these reservoirs fill up with waterfowl: 10,000 to 15,000 birds. Ducks include the common dabblers (thousands) and divers (hundreds), scoters regularly (all three species), and Long-tailed Duck. Other waterbirds: Trumpeter and Tundra Swans, Common, Pacific, and Red-throated Loons, five species of grebe, and five gull species. In November you might find all three species of rosy-finches feeding on the rocky hillsides beside Eleven-Mile, and possibly Lapland Longspur among flocks of Horned Larks.

Antero Reservoir, west of Spinney and Eleven-Mile on US 24, reopened in fall 2006 to rave reviews from Colorado birders. It collects waterfowl in big numbers (25,000 ducks in October 2006) and a variety (for example, diving ducks, scoters, loons, and gulls). Historically, American White Pelican, California Gull, and

Colorado Springs Area, Manitou Lake, Big Johnson Reservoir, Fountain Creek Regional Park

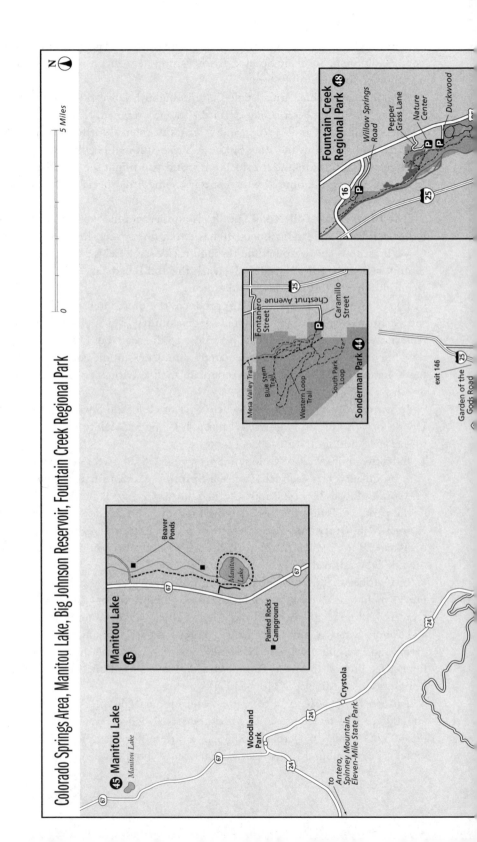

0 ⊢─────┴─────┴─────┴─────┤ 5 Miles

45 Manitou Lake
Manitou Lake

Manitou Lake
45

Beaver Ponds

Manitou Lake

67

Painted Rocks Campground

67

Woodland Park

67

24

24

Crystola

to Antero, Spinney Mountain, Eleven-Mile State Park

24

Sonderman Park 44

Mesa Valley Trail

Blue Stem Trail

Western Loop Trail

South Park Loop

Fontanero Street

Chestnut Avenue

Caramillo Street

25

Garden of the Gods Road

exit 146

25

Fountain Creek Regional Park 48

Willow Springs Road

Pepper Grass Lane

Nature Center

Duckwood

16

25

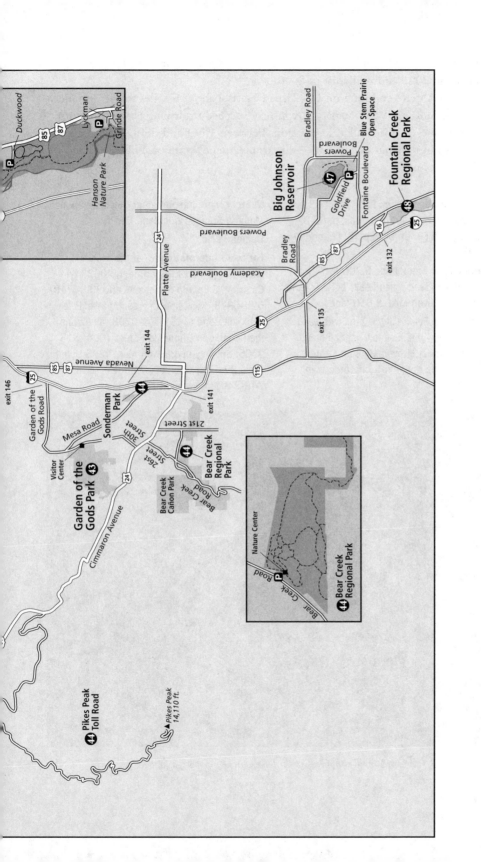

Snowy Plover nested here. The Denver Water Board, which owns Antero, drained it for repairs in 2002 and refilled it in 2006.

To reach Antero, continue on US 24 past Hartsel about 6 miles to the entrance. Depending on the DWB's managers, you may succeed in driving along the south side, north side, or not at all. (Negotiations between CFO and the DWB opened up access to birders but not anglers—this arrangement, we hope, will continue . . . for birders, at least.)

DeLorme grid: Bear Creek Park, p. 62 B3; Sonderman, p. 63 B4; Pikes Peak, p. 62 B2–3; Spinney and Eleven-Mile, p. 49 D5 and p. 61 A5–6.

Elevation: Bear Creek Park, 6,200 feet; Sonderman, 6,100 feet; Pikes Peak, 14,110 feet; Spinney and Eleven-Mile, 8,650 feet.

Hazards: *Pikes Peak:* Fill the tank with gasoline. Driving downhill, use low gears instead of brakes. *Spinney, Eleven-Mile, and Antero:* Ground blizzards make travel hazardous in South Park.

Nearest food, gas, lodging: Colorado Springs, Manitou Springs, Woodland Park.

Camping: No.

For more information: Bear Creek Park, El Paso County Parks Department, 2002 Creek Crossing, Colorado Springs, CO 80906; (719) 520-6375; www.elpasoco.com/parks. Pikes Peak Toll Road (719) 473-0208; directions, road conditions, hours, and fees (800) 318-9505. Spinney and Eleven-Mile, 4229 County Road 92, Lake George, CO 80827; (719) 748-3401; www.parks.state.co.us.

Yellow-Headed Blackbirds prefer marshes with deep water—at least a foot deep.

45 Manitou Lake W$ 🚹 IBA

See map on pages 142–43.

Habitats: Ponderosa, wetlands, willow carr.

Specialty birds: *Resident:* Red Crossbill.

Summer: Western Bluebird. *Migrant:* Mountain species, raptors.

Best times to bird: Year-round.

About this site

Manitou Lake and nearby facilities present the most accessible place near Colorado Springs to sample ponderosa birds. The Manitou Lake picnic area charges a fee for day use as well as camping. It has several trails through the pines and along Trout Creek (several active beaver ponds) below the dam.

Directions

From Woodland Park, take Highway 67 (at the west end of town) north 7.5 miles to the Manitou Lake turnoff on the right.

The birding

Besides the usual ponderosa birds, Red Crossbills throng the area in seasons with good cone crops. Breeders include Virginia Rail, Wilson's Snipe, Willow, Dusky, Hammond's, and Cordilleran Flycatchers, and Common Yellowthroat.

High numbers of migrants—100 to 1,000 in late September—include big counts of Ruby-crowned Kinglet, Mountain Bluebird, and Orange-crowned, Yellow-rumped, and Wilson's Warblers, plus such surprises as Gray Catbird, Black-and-white Warbler, Chipping, Clay-colored, Brewer's, Swamp, and Fox Sparrows, and Rose-breasted Grosbeak. Raptors slip in: Northern Harrier, Osprey, Sharp-shinned, Red-tailed, and Rough-legged Hawks. Only a few duck species use the lake (a mere five acres) and its marshes.

You may find Manitou Lake crowded in midsummer, in which case you can try other nearby ponderosa spots. The Painted Rock campground (half a mile south of Manitou Lake) sits amid ponderosas and grotesque, 20-foot-tall red-rock goblins. The road to Manitou Experimental Forest, 1.25 miles past Manitou Lake, provides a view of Trout Creek beaver ponds and passes through more pines.

North from Manitou Lake, Highway 67 drops down to Deckers on the South Platte River and passes through the 2002 Hayman Fire area, which burned 138,000 acres of mainly ponderosa pine. Woodpeckers have finished with the dead skeletons, but you can see how other birds move in as the forest recovers. Look for House and Rock Wrens, Mountain Bluebird, and American Robin in the burned-over areas, and where the fire spared the trees, for cottonwood and ponderosa birds.

DeLorme grid: P. 50 D2.

Elevation: 7,750 feet.

Nearest food, gas, lodging: Woodland Park.

Camping: Yes.

For more information: Pikes Peak Ranger District, Pike National Forest, 601 South Weber, Colorado Springs, CO 80903; (719) 636–1602; www.fs.fed.us/r2/psicc.

46 Aiken Canyon ⓦ◈ IBA and Turkey Creek Ranch Recreation Area

Habitats: Riparian, short-grass prairie, pinyon/juniper, scrub oak, montane shrubland, ponderosa, mixed conifer.

Specialty birds: *Resident:* Wild Turkey, Sharp-shinned and Cooper's Hawks, Golden Eagle, Lewis's Woodpecker, Clark's Nutcracker, Red-breasted Nuthatch, Brown Creeper, Canyon Wren, three bluebird species. *Summer:* Common Poorwill, White-throated Swift, Olive-sided, Hammond's, and Cordilleran Flycatchers, Say's Phoebe, Northern Rough-winged, and Bank Swallows, Yellow-breasted Chat, Lark Sparrow, Lazuli and Indigo (breeds most years) Buntings, Lesser Goldfinch. *Migrant:* Northern Harrier, Cedar Waxwing. *Winter:* Clark's Nutcracker, Golden-crowned Kinglet, Townsend's Solitaire, Cassin's Finch.

Best times to bird: *Aiken:* summer; *Turkey Creek:* February to June; September to November for both sites.

About this site

These two sites, across the highway from each other, open up varied habitats. Although you can combine trips to both, each merits its own half-day.

You can visit Aiken year-round, dawn to dusk, but *only* **on Saturday, Sunday, and Monday.** Aiken Canyon's mosaic of habitats includes shrublands, tall-grass meadows, pinyon/juniper woodlands, and mixed coniferous woodlands. The Nature Conservancy preserves two globally rare plant communities here: pinyon pine/one-seeded juniper/Scribner needlegrass woodland and scrub oak/mountain mahogany shrubland. Mammals include black bear, gray fox, mountain lion, and tufted-eared squirrels.

Turkey Creek Ranch, on Fort Carson, has permanent water that attracts birds and other wildlife, including deer, elk, bobcat, and coyote. Picnic grounds and trails make for easy walking.

Directions

From I–25 take exit 135 (Academy Boulevard) west to Highway 115, then south 11.5 miles to Turkey Canyon Ranch Road (0.1 mile south of milepost 32). Turn right in 200 yards to the Aiken parking lot; left to Turkey Creek Ranch, through a gate.

The birding

Aiken: A 4-mile-loop trail begins from the parking lot. You don't have to walk the whole loop to see the most birds but it's worthwhile, especially during flower season. Leaving the field station, the trail, with interpretive signs, passes through scrub oak, grassland, and P/J. It provides opportunities to see Golden Eagle, Plumbeous

Vireo, Western Scrub-Jay, Pinyon Jay (rare), Blue-gray Gnatcatcher, Virginia's Warbler, and Black-Headed Grosbeak, and to hear Common Poorwill.

At the loop junction, go clockwise. In a quarter mile the canyon narrows and you come to the birdiest spot (a mixture of montane conifer, P/J, scrub oak, and canyon habitats, with intermittent water). Expect Common Raven, Tree and Cliff Swallows, Bushtit, three types of nuthatches, Brown Creeper, Canyon Wren, Ruby-crowned Kinglet, Western and Mountain Bluebirds, Townsend's Solitaire, and Western Tanager.

On up the trail, across a low saddle, a three-quarter-mile spur winds up-canyon through dense Douglas-fir/blue spruce. A pair of Golden Eagles nests nearby, along with Hairy Woodpecker, Olive-sided, Cordilleran, and Hammond's Flycatchers, Plumbeous Vireo, Hermit Thrush, MacGillivray's Warbler, and Ovenbird. In winter numerous Townsend's Solitaires join the abundant, resident Spotted Towhees. Continuing around the loop into ponderosas, you might see species you missed on the way up, plus Wild Turkey, Gray and Dusky Flycatchers, Spotted Towhee, and Vesper Sparrow.

Turkey Creek Ranch: Drive to the stables; at a T intersection turn right and park by the big old Penrose House, and bird west along the creek and in the grove of large crack willows. Next, drive back past the stables east to the Kit Carson and Tombstone picnic areas. Walk south through foothills riparian habitat (a permanent spring, good cover, and large dead cottonwoods), which often hosts Lewis's Woodpecker, Gray-cheeked (rare) and Swainson's Thrushes, Gray Catbird, Brown Thrasher, and Lincoln's Sparrow. Then drive north on Road 4 about a mile and park where a smaller road branches to the right, before a culvert. Walk back down the drainage, south and east—good for *Empidonax* flycatchers in migration, Red-tailed Hawk, Cooper's Hawk, sparrows, and often three bluebird species.

DeLorme grid: P. 62 D2-3.

Elevation: 6,200 to 8,500 feet.

Hazards: Brush, cactus, maybe a rattlesnake! Wear sturdy boots.

Nearest food, gas, lodging: Colorado Springs.

Camping: Yes, by reservation.

For more information: Aiken: The Nature Conservancy, 121 East Pikes Peak, Suite 206, Colorado Springs, CO 80903; (719) 632-0534; www.nature.org/wherewework/ northamerica/states/colorado/preserves/ art517.html. Turkey Creek: Fort Carson MWDI, (719) 526-3905.

See map on pages 142–43

Habitats: Wetlands, short-grass prairie.

Specialty birds: *Migrant:* Eighteen duck species, Common and Pacific Loons (fall), four grebe and eight gull species.

Best times to bird: February to December.

About this site

During migration thousands of ducks and coots, hundreds of gulls, and some loons and grebes collect at Big Johnson. It's the best place near Colorado Springs to find common and rare waterbirds.

Directions

From I–25 exit 135, go east on Academy Boulevard (Highway 83) and exit in 1 mile on Bradley Road. Follow it east and south until it dips down by the reservoir dam and then climbs up to Bluestem Prairie Open Space in 4.5 miles.

The birding

A trail from the Open Space parking lot leads around the south and east sides of the reservoir and provides good views in good light—but *take a scope*—a fence restricts the trail to several hundred yards away from water's edge. The trail traverses

California (above) and Ring-billed dominate flocks of gulls that congregate at Colorado reservoirs.

PHOTO © WENDY SHATTIL/BOB ROZINSKI

short-grass prairie and an impressively large prairie-dog town, which should produce Burrowing Owl and maybe Mountain Plover in summer. The barren shoreline provides little cover for breeding birds though a few shorebirds (Killdeer, American Avocet) stay to breed.

Starting in February when the lake ice melts, grebes, ducks, and gulls collect. In April they disperse as shorebirds arrive. Fall migration starts in September, with loons, ducks, and gulls remaining into mid-December, when the lake usually freezes. The eighteen duck species include Greater Scaup, White-winged Scoter, and Red-breasted Merganser. Among the geese, look for Greater White-fronted, Snow, and Cackling among the Canadas. Bonaparte's, Lesser Black-backed, Thayer's, Mew, and Sabine's Gulls have also showed up. The shorebird list, though slim, does include Red and Red-necked Phalaropes, and both Snowy and Great Egrets may appear. Raptors cruise in from the open prairie to spook the waterbirds: Look for Bald and Golden Eagles, Ferruginous Hawk, Prairie Falcon, and Northern Harrier.

DeLorme grid: P. 63 C5.
Elevation: 5,825 feet.
Hazards: Rattlesnakes, prairie-dog fleas.
Nearest food, gas, lodging: Colorado Springs.
Camping: No.

For more information: Parks, Recreation & Cultural Services, City of Colorado Springs, 1401 Recreation Way, Colorado Springs, CO 80905-1975; (719) 385-5940; www.springs gov.com.

See map pages 142–43.

Habitats: Riparian, wetlands.

Specialty birds: *Resident:* Brown Thrasher.
Summer: Green Heron (rare), Swainson's Hawk,
Black-chinned and Broad-tailed Hummingbirds,
Red-headed Woodpecker, Eastern Kingbird,
Northern Rough-winged Swallow, Yellow-
breasted Chat, Great-tailed Grackle, Lesser
Goldfinch. *Migrant:* Twenty-three duck, thirty-
nine warbler, and eighteen sparrow species;
Clark's, Western, and Horned Grebes, Broad-
winged Hawk, Swainson's and Hermit Thrushes,
Canyon Towhee, Orchard and Baltimore Orioles,
Cassin's Finch, Evening Grosbeak.

Best times to bird: Year-round.

About this site

Migrants moving along the edge of the Colorado foothills find shelter in this
floodplain habitat now disturbed only by hikers and nature-watchers. Lowland
riparian breeders include the typical plus a few southeastern Colorado specialties.
Winter sees fewer species—cottonwoods seem unattractive to winter passerines.

The park spans the broad floodplain on the east side of Fountain Creek. Groves
of tall cottonwoods intersperse with grassy meadows, spring-fed ponds, and cattail
marshes. Trails encompass fine riparian corridors and lead to a great variety of
migrants and breeding species. The checklist contains 256 species.

Directions

The park has four entrances. From I–25 take exit 132, then proceed east on Highway
16 for 0.5 mile. Exit to the U.S. Highway 85/87 junction; turn right on US 85/87.

To get to the first entrance, the *Willow Springs trailhead,* turn right immediately
after turning onto US 85/87, onto Willow Springs Road. The parking area is 0.5
mile down the road. A trail leads south along the stream into the main part of the
park; two ponds attract migrating waterbirds, and the cattails attract marsh birds.

The *Fountain Creek Nature Center* provides the best access to the network of
trails, including the ponds also available from Willow Springs. Drive down US
85/87 for half a mile, turn right (just south of Mesa Road on the left), and follow
Pepper Grass Lane to the nature center (open Tuesday through Saturday; trails
always open).

For the second-best place to sample the trails, including one that follows a
shaded irrigation ditch that hugs the bluff on the east side of the floodplain, *Duckwood Active-use Area,* follow US 85/87 another half mile and turn right on Duckwood Road; the parking lot is straight ahead, past the playing fields. For the
southernmost, fourth, access point, *Hanson Nature Park,* go past Duckwood Road 1
mile—look for a car wash and the Salvation Army store—turn right and go to the
end of Lyckman, then right on Grinde Road to the parking lot, on the left. A

Wide paths traverse the riparian groves of Fountain Creek Regional Park.

footbridge leads into the park. Follow Fountain Creek and the lush cottonwood groves that line the stream.

The birding

Western Wood-Pewee, House Wren, Yellow Warbler, Common Yellowthroat, and Bullock's Oriole dominate the trails in summer. Other regular breeders include Swainson's and Red-tailed Hawks, Black-chinned and Broad-tailed Hummingbirds, Red-headed Woodpecker, Northern Rough-winged Swallow, Yellow-breasted Chat, Great-tailed Grackle, and Lesser and American Goldfinches. Rare migrants include Gray-cheeked and Wood Thrushes and Purple Finch. In summer 2005 a Vermilion Flycatcher spent a week at the Hanson Nature Park, flycatching over two ponds and from a large cottonwood

Winter counts produce forty-five to fifty species—ten species of ducks including Hooded Merganser, five raptors, and land birds such as American Pipit and Yellow-rumped Warbler.

DeLorme grid: P. 63 C5.

Elevation: 5,600 feet.

Nearest food, gas, lodging: Fountain, Colorado Springs, Pueblo.

Camping: No.

For more information: El Paso County Parks Department, 2002 Creek Crossing, Colorado Springs, CO 80906; (719) 520-6745; www.elpasoco.com/parks.

49 Chico Basin Ranch $

Habitats: Riparian, wetlands, grassland.
Specialty birds: *Migrant:* Flycatchers, vireos, thrushes, warblers, sparrows.

Best times to bird: Spring and fall.

About this site
Southeast of Fountain, Chico Basin Ranch, a working cattle and dude ranch covering 87,000 acres, allows daily bird-watching. This oasis—3 miles of green nestled amid dry grassland—attracts weary migrants. Habitats include towering cottonwoods, Siberian elms, thickets of Russian olives, and three ponds lined with cattails, willows, and cottonwoods. An RMBO banding station brought attention to this sanctuary.

Directions
To bird the ranch, contact the owners in advance by telephone or e-mail. **Access is by permission only.** To drive there, turn east from exit 122 on I–25 and go east and north on Old Pueblo Highway a mile to Hanover Road. Follow that south and east 13 miles to Hanover; turn south on Peyton Highway. In 2 miles you'll come to a ranch gate over the road. Follow the signs to ranch headquarters, where you obtain your birding permit ($10 per day).

The birding
The ranch bird list includes twelve species of shorebirds, twenty-two warblers, and ten sparrows. Warblers include rarities such as Blue-winged, Tennessee, Black-throated Blue, Yellow-throated, Prairie, Palm, Bay-breasted, Blackpoll, Black-and-white, and Mourning. Mountain species drift in: Northern Goshawk, Band-tailed Pigeon, Flammulated Owl, Williamson's Sapsucker, and Pygmy and Red-breasted Nuthatches. The list includes strays such as Scissor-tailed Flycatcher, White-eyed, Cassin's, and Philadelphia Vireos, Long-billed Thrasher (Colorado's third record), Hepatic Tanager, Eastern Towhee, and Painted Bunting. In fall the oasis effect traps hundreds of Western Wood-Pewee and Wilson's Warbler. A prairie-dog town supports breeding Mountain Plover and Burrowing Owl.

DeLorme grid: P. 63 D7, p. 73 A7.
Elevation: 5,100 feet.
Nearest food, gas, lodging: Pueblo, Colorado Springs.
Camping: No.

For more information: Chico Basin Ranch, 2250 Peyton Highway South, Colorado Springs, CO 80928; (719) 683-7960; www.chicobasinranch.com; kim@chicobasinranch.com.

Pueblo Reservoir and Valco Ponds

Habitats: Wetlands, pinyon/juniper, riparian.
Specialty birds: *Resident:* Scaled Quail.
Summer: Osprey. *Migrant and Winter:* Loons,
grebes, waterfowl, gulls. *Winter:* Mountain
Bluebird, Sage Thrasher, Spotted Towhee.
Best times to bird: Fall and winter.

About this site

These two adjacent sites occupy 75 percent of Pueblo birders' birding time. The reservoir, from fall to spring, attracts a mighty assemblage of abundant and rare water species. Lake Pueblo State Park occupies the east end of Pueblo Reservoir and a State Wildlife Area takes up the west end. The bird list includes four loon, six grebe, and fifteen gull species, and all likely and unlikely ducks. Ospreys and Great Blue Herons nest at the upper end. Valco Ponds produces land birds of note, especially in late fall, and a few waterbirds.

Arkansas Valley Audubon, the Division of Wildlife, and the state parks sponsor Bald Eagle Days, usually the first or second weekend of February.

Directions

From I–25 exit 101, go west 2.5 miles on U.S. Highway 50 to Highway 45 (Pueblo Boulevard); turn left (south) and proceed 4 miles to Highway 96.

From Highway 45, it's 2.3 miles on Highway 96 to Valco Ponds and another 1.5 miles to Lake Pueblo State Park. The visitor center is 0.6 mile from the park entrance; take the first right to the day-use area or go straight ahead to the Southshore Marina.

To reach the north side of the reservoir, follow Juniper Road (just before the visitor center) 1.4 miles to Cottonwood Road. Turning east on Cottonwood Road takes you to stream bottom trails: 0.4 mile to Rock Canyon and 1.8 miles to Osprey Picnic Area. Two miles farther on Juniper Road is Northshore Marina Road (left) or, in 1.4 miles, Hobie Cat Road (right). To the west, the SWA road leads to views of nesting Osprey and Great Blue Heron.

You can reach the north side from US 50: 3.5 miles past Pueblo Boulevard, go left on Nichols Street 4.5 miles to an entrance to both Lake Pueblo State Park and Pueblo SWA. The SWA has a west entrance, off Swallows Road (3.5 miles west of Nichols Street).

The birding

Birders hightail it back and forth between the *Southshore Marina* and north-side sites such as the *sailboat launching area, Northshore Marina,* and *Hobie Cat.* Gulls like to perch on the marina breakers on the south side (best seen in early morning or late afternoon; in midday they fan out to various landfills, garbage dumps, and

Pueblo Reservoir and Valco Ponds

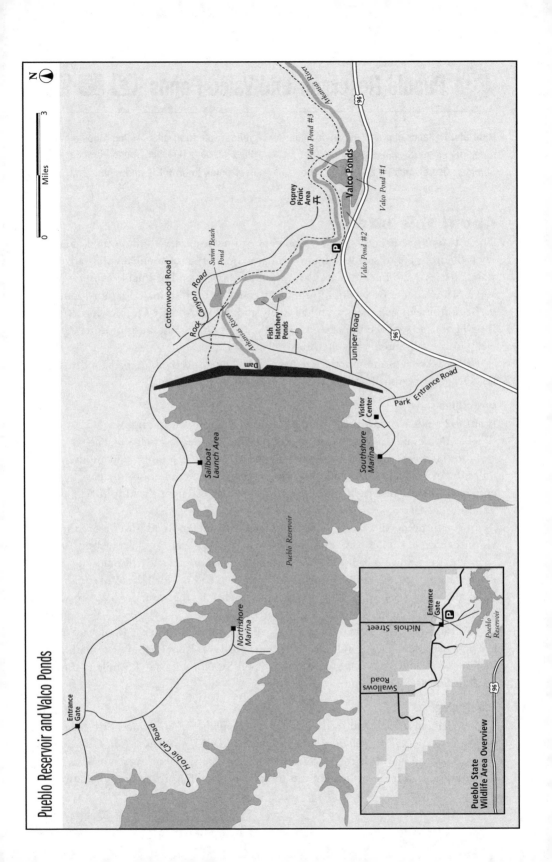

Pueblo State Wildlife Area Overview

other gull attractions). Finding and identifying the gulls and waterbirds requires patience, a scope, and a strong constitution on blustery winter days; triumph rewards the diligent.

The thousands of gulls in 2005 included the usual—Ring-billed, California, and Herring—plus Franklin's, Bonaparte's, Mew, Little, Thayer's, Iceland, Glaucous, Lesser Black-backed, Great Black-backed, and Sabine's. Many stay through the winter. When gulls fly up frantically, look for jaegers—the park has records of Long-tailed and Pomarine. Abundant ducks include thousands of Common Goldeneyes and Common Mergansers, and Barrow's Goldeneye, Surf Scoter, and Long-tailed Duck. Look for loons and grebes. Sandhill Cranes stage fall flyovers. Shorebirds can include unusual ones such as Black-bellied Plover, Willet, and Whimbrel. Occasional oddities show up in winter: Dunlin and late-occurring Spotted and Least Sandpipers.

P/J birds inhabit the woodland near the park office. Look for Scaled Quail, Sage Thrasher, and Canyon Towhee. In winter expect lots of Mountain Bluebirds, and check the tops of junipers for Townsend's Solitaire. Both Loggerhead and Northern Shrikes terrorize the local mice. Winter raptors include both eagles, occasional Ferruginous Hawks and Peregrines, and Merlin.

Rock Canyon, with its interesting rock features—horizontal layers along cliff edges—offers good habitat for land birds. A sampler of migrants: Red-naped Sapsucker, Hairy Woodpecker, Plumbeous and Cassin's Vireos, Eastern Bluebird, Townsend's and Cape May Warblers, and Spotted Towhee. After summer, waterbirds use the swim beach pond: Cackling Geese, ducks, a few gulls such as Bonaparte's and Sabine's, Common, Least, and Caspian Terns (all rare), and shrikes; even Great Horned Owls find solitude of a sort.

To study **Valco Ponds,** you have two choices: To see the pond closest to Highway 96, park on the shoulder but well off the highway. From the parking lot a bit farther, a trail (right) along a dike provides views into the other two ponds. For land birds, follow the trails to the left along the river. You can also enter by crossing the bridge from the Osprey Picnic Area off Rock Canyon Road.

Land-bird possibilities include Broad-winged Hawk, Black, Eastern, and Say's Phoebes, Cassin's and Blue-headed Vireos, Winter Wren, American Pipit, Tennessee, Magnolia, Black-throated Green, Townsend's, Blackburnian, and Bay-breasted Warblers, Northern Waterthrush, and White-throated Sparrow. The ponds can hold ducks (dabbling and diving), Sabine's Gull, and terns. A Green Heron may lurk in the shrubbery, a Peregrine Falcon may careen by, or an Osprey may cruise overhead.

DeLorme grid: P. 73 B4-5.
Elevation: 4,900 feet.
Hazards: Rattlesnakes.
Nearest food, gas, lodging: Pueblo.

Camping: Yes.
For more information: Lake Pueblo State Park, 640 Pueblo Reservoir Road, Pueblo, CO 81005; (719) 561-9320; www.parks.state .co.us.

51 Pueblo City Park, Arkansas River Trail

Habitats: Plains riparian, wetlands, urban park.

Specialty birds: *Resident:* Bushtit, Bewick's Wren, Wood Duck, Mandarin Duck. *Summer:* Green Heron, Mississippi Kite, Black-chinned Hummingbird. *Migrant:* Waterfowl, gulls, songbirds. *Winter:* Yellow-bellied Sapsucker (city park), waterfowl, gulls.

Best times to bird: Fall, winter, spring.

About this site

Pueblo's City Park, built on a bluff overlooking the Arkansas River, hosts many migrant and winter songbirds due to the mixture of big deciduous and coniferous trees. The Arkansas River Trail system, underused by birders, has, on the west end, a wetland known as Olive Marsh, and Runyon Lake on the east. Fed by warm water from a power plant, this lake attracts a wide variety of waterfowl, and winter is a good time to visit as it rarely freezes. Paved trails between these areas run along the Arkansas River. Under the guise of fisheries habitat improvement, the Army Corp of Engineers recently enhanced the river with many new weirs and pools; it attracts increasing numbers of gulls, shorebirds, and waterfowl. New plantings of native tree and shrub species plus removal of invasive species, also part of the plan, should improve the already good birding.

Directions

From I–25 exit 101, go west on US 50 for 2.5 miles to Highway 45 (Pueblo Boulevard), then 3 miles south to the park entrance (Goodnight Avenue, at the first stoplight after crossing the Arkansas River).

The birding

The old-growth urban forest of **City Park,** including pines and sycamores, attracts numerous songbirds in migration. Birding is best around the duck pond and along a small creek near the disc golf course. Blue-winged, Black-throated Gray, Townsend's, Blackburnian, Blackpoll, Yellow-throated, and Pine Warblers have visited in spring or fall migration. In winter the duck pond hosts a variety of waterfowl. Eurasian Wigeons regularly appear among the many American Wigeons. Mew Gulls sometimes show up with the Ring-billed Gulls. Yellow-bellied Sapsuckers appear in the park every winter: Look for them and their sap-wells in large pines at the east end of the park. Townsend's Solitaire, Golden-crowned Kinglet, Yellow-rumped Warbler, and other mountain birds winter in the park.

The **River Trail** follows the Arkansas River through Pueblo. Enter from the north side of City Park or the west side of Runyon Lake (check the map). You can also reach it from near the Union Avenue Bridge or 4th Street Bridge in central

Pueblo City Park, Arkansas River Trail

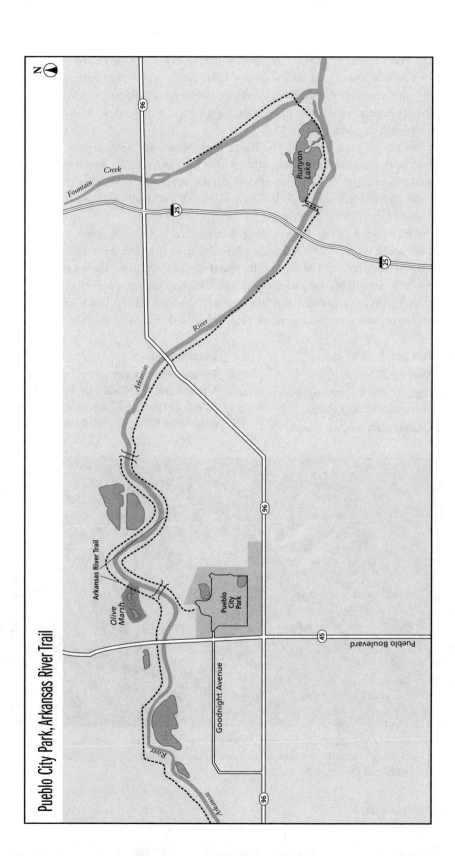

Pueblo. Footbridges cross the river: below City Park, in central Pueblo below Dutch Clark Stadium, and near Runyon Lake. North of the first bridge, *Olive Marsh,* with a series of beaver ponds, draws assorted birds during migration. Birders suspect Summer Tanagers of nesting, Green Herons have nested, and Swamp Sparrows stop in winter.

Anything can turn up along the River Trail. Mississippi Kites appear overhead anytime in the summer. Check overhead lines near the trail for perching Black-chinned Hummingbird. Introduced over twenty years ago, Mandarin Ducks (not accepted on the Colorado state list) have endured; the small population most often stays west of the central footbridge.

The River Trail circles *Runyon Lake.* You can reach it directly from I–25 exit 98A: Go south on Santa Fe Avenue to Locust Street (just before crossing the Arkansas River), left on Locust past the baseball field, and over the levee to the lake parking area. Trees around the lake and the river attract songbirds during migration. In winter, because the lake is a well-stocked fishery, Black-crowned Night-Heron, mergansers, and other fish-eating birds frequent the lake.

DeLorme grid: P. 73 B5-6.

Elevation: 4,700 feet.

Hazards: Bike riders, poison ivy (Runyon, River Trail), flying frisbees (City Park).

Nearest food, gas, lodging: Pueblo.

Camping: No.

For more information: City of Pueblo Parks & Recreation, 800 Goodnight, Pueblo, CO 81005; (719) 553-2790); www.pueblo.us/ documents/Parks_Recreation/ParkMap.pdf.

During their breeding sequence, American Avocets set up three successive territories: a pre-egg-laying one around a feeding site, then a small one surrounding the nest during incubation, and the last a mobile, chick-centered one.

52 Cañon City

Habitats: Desert shrub, cliff, pinyon/juniper.

Specialty birds: *Resident:* Ladder-backed Woodpecker (occasional), Canyon Wren, Canyon Towhee, Rufous-crowned Sparrow.

Summer: White-throated Swift, Say's Phoebe, Rock Wren. *Winter:* Clark's Nutcracker, Townsend's Solitaire.

Best time to bird: Summer.

About this site

Several sites around Cañon City reward birders seeking foothills and riparian species.

The birding

A recently discovered (2000) population of Rufous-crowned Sparrows lives along **Tunnel Drive.** This has proved a reliable and accessible place to find this inconspicuous sparrow, at the northernmost inland location in its range. On US 50 drive west past the Colorado Territorial Prison; just after the highway makes a sharp right (0.3 mile), turn left onto Tunnel Drive and go 0.7 mile to the parking lot.

In spring and summer hike the trail that climbs up a small gully to a level grade and then turns left along the grade of an old water line; you may find the sparrows along here, especially in side canyons with tall brush. Listen for the two-trilled song (second trill a bit lower in pitch), but beware of the similar-sounding Virginia's Warbler. Other species include Turkey Vulture and Blue-gray Gnatcatcher. The trail continues for about 2 miles, through three tunnels, and ends at the edge of the Arkansas River. On the cliffs in mid-May, you can enjoy brilliant blooming cactus. In winter take the riverside trail and walk to a pump station, less than a quarter mile away. Rufous-crowned Sparrows lurk in the grass and brush in the flats here.

Outstanding P/J woodlands blanket **Red Canyon Park.** From US 50, go north on Raynolds; jog left and then right at the T intersection, which puts you on Field Avenue. Ten miles from US 50, turn left into the park entrance.

The road climbs up to a small ridge; look for Gray Flycatcher. Stop at the first picnic area (a mile in) and walk up the draw through narrow red-sandstone cliffs. Wild plum, currants, and scrub oak line the sides of the canyon. In about an eighth of a mile, a tributary comes in from the left; keep to the right. You can walk about a mile up this attractive, cool defile and see species that don't depend totally on P/J, such as Virginia's Warbler and Bushtit.

Drive a half mile farther, park at the second picnic area, and prowl for P/J birds; as usual with this habitat, you have to cover a good amount of ground to find them. If you climb the ridge across the road from the picnic area, you'll see nice views of the valley, two red-sandstone towers, and mountains beyond.

Cañon City, Cañon City Riverwalk

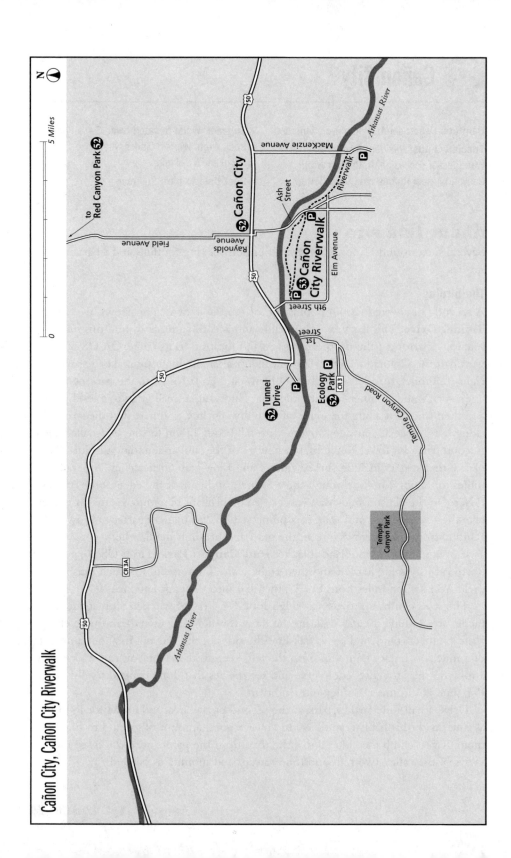

On the way back to Cañon City, stop 3 miles from the Red Canyon Park entrance at the BLM exhibit and trailhead for the *Garden Park* fossil quarries. Signboards describe the excellent dinosaur finds from this site, and you might see a few desert birds along the trail.

The high school environmental club, with help from many in the community, led an effort to revegetate an old dump and turned it into **Ecology Park.** The park itself consists of a large grassy plain with limited bird-watching potential, but in adjacent BLM lands, two trails are more attractive.

To get there, drive south on 1st Street (opposite the prison); at 1 mile, go right at a Y intersection (sign to Temple Canyon Park) on County Road 3 for 0.8 mile to the parking lot for Ecology Park. (Three miles farther along Road 3, Temple Canyon Park used to draw local birders to its P/J birds but has lost its luster in the last few years.)

To the left of the parking lot, twenty-two birdhouses perch on fence posts. By mid-May several species use them: Mountain Bluebird, Juniper Titmouse (occasional), and Ash-throated Flycatcher. Straight ahead, walk to a T intersection; the right-hand trail winds to and down a side canyon that leads to Grape Creek, a perennial stream. Shrubs, mainly, grow in the two canyons—rabbitbrush, squaw currant, chokecherry, saltbush, and willow, as well as a few cottonwoods. Birders occasionally find Rufous-crowned Sparrow in these canyons. More usual are Scaled Quail, Say's Phoebe, Rock Wren, Blue-gray Gnatcatcher, Mountain Bluebird, Virginia's Warbler, Canyon and Spotted Towhees, Lark and Vesper Sparrows, Black-headed Grosbeak, and House Finch (in its native habitat). Along a ridge between a side canyon and Ecology Park, a trail through well-spaced pinyons and junipers may yield Ash-throated Flycatcher, Pinyon Jay, Juniper Titmouse, and Western and Mountain Bluebirds.

DeLorme grid: P. 72 A1; Red Canyon Park, p. 62 D1.
Elevation: 5,400 to 6,400 feet.
Hazards: Rattlesnakes.
Nearest food, gas, lodging: Cañon City.

Camping: No.
For more information: Cañon City Recreation & Park District, 503 Main, Cañon City, CO 81212; (719) 275-1578.

53 Cañon City Riverwalk

See map on page 160.

Habitats: Riparian, wetlands.

Specialty birds: *Resident:* Great Blue Heron, Scaled Quail, Bewick's Wren. *Summer:* Green Heron (a few), Cooper's Hawk (fledged August 4, 2005), Black-chinned Hummingbird, Gray Catbird, Cedar Waxwing, Yellow-breasted Chat, Lazuli Bunting. *Migrant:* Osprey, Bald Eagle, Eastern Phoebe, Marsh Wren, Orange-crowned and Virginia's Warblers, Western Tanager, Blue and Evening Grosbeaks. *Winter:* Greater White-fronted Goose, Bald Eagle, Mountain Chickadee, Bushtit, Brown Creeper, American Dipper, Ruby-crowned Kinglet, White-crowned Sparrow.

Best times to bird: Year-round; better in migration.

Habitat along the riverwalk in Cañon City attracts a surprising variety of unusual species, such as Common Black-Hawk, Carolina Wren, and Black Phoebe.

About this site

The 3-mile riverwalk provides excellent riparian habitat with scattered cattail marshes. Cañon City birders find a sizable array of species; an old checklist (out of print) listed 198 species, and since that printing birders have added at least 25 more.

Directions

The Riverwalk has three access points from US 50:

- South on 9th Street; just across the Arkansas River, turn left on Sells to the parking lot.
- South on Raynolds Avenue (in the east part of town) and across the river; the road turns left, with a long parking lot on the right.
- South on MacKenzie Avenue: Cross the river, turn right on the first road (Santa Fe); go one-quarter mile to the parking lot.

The birding

Walk along the river path from any of the three parking sites. The more productive section runs between Raynolds and MacKenzie. Cottonwoods bring in migrating songbirds such as flycatchers, vireos, warblers, and seed-eaters. Cattail marshes and riverside wetlands attract waders and shorebirds. Regular migrants include Snowy Egret, Franklin's Gull, Common Nighthawk (more in fall), Rufous and Calliope Hummingbirds, Olive-sided Flycatcher, Plumbeous Vireo, Townsend's Solitaire, and Western Bluebird. The list has rarities such as Great Egret, Yellow-crowned Night-Heron (very rare), Common Black-Hawk (very rare), Broad-winged Hawk, Peregrine Falcon, Red-eyed Vireo, Carolina Wren, Hooded Warbler (second Colorado nesting record), and Swamp Sparrow.

In nearby residential areas, feeders in summer attract Black-chinned Hummingbirds. Try going south on Raynolds; it turns into Ash, from where you can turn left onto any street to look for front-yard feeders. Almost anywhere around the fringes of Cañon City, you stand a chance of seeing Scaled Quail scurry across the road, and perhaps even a Roadrunner.

DeLorme grid: P. 72 A1.
Elevation: 5,300 feet.
Hazards: Fast bicyclers.
Nearest food, gas, lodging: Cañon City.

Camping: Cañon City.
For more information: Cañon City Recreation & Park District, 503 Main, Cañon City, CO 81212; (719) 275-1578.

54 Lathrop State Park Ⓦ Ⓢ ♿ 🐦

Habitats: Pinyon/juniper, grassland, wetlands.   **Best times to bird:** Spring, summer, fall.

About this site

Two reservoirs perched amid a sprawling pinyon/juniper woodland spice up bird-watching at this 1,600-acre park. The Spanish Peaks tower to the south, their narrow volcanic dikes fanning out from the base.

Directions

From Walsenburg, drive west 3 miles on U.S. Highway 160 to the park entrance, on the right.

The birding

Park roads circle both lakes; stop at pull-offs to search promising habitats or when you spot a bird. P/J birds require a lot of space; you have to cover a lot of ground to find them. Pinyon Jay, Juniper Titmice, Bushtit, and other P/J specialties flit through the trees (not recorded: Gray Flycatcher and Gray Vireo, Black-throated Gray Warbler). Bluebirds (the park has all three species—Eastern, Western, and Mountain) sparkle in the sun. Lesser Goldfinches add color to the summer. In winter look for Townsend's Solitaire perched in the tops of berry-laden junipers.

The lakes often have waterfowl; the park has nineteen ducks on its list, including Greater and Lesser Scaup and Common and Hooded Mergansers. Marshy areas attract Sora and coots, blackbirds, and Marsh Wren. Pied-billed Grebes breed and Western Grebe, coots, and Double-crested Cormorant persist despite the boat traffic. Occasional loons (including Red-throated), Great and Snowy Egrets, American Bittern, Green Heron, and White-faced Ibis come through. Turkey Vulture and Osprey migrate through (fifteen Ospreys at dusk one April evening). Land birds include Common Black-Hawk (accidental), Black Phoebe, Golden-crowned, White-throated, and White-crowned Sparrows, Black-headed Grosbeak, and Great-tailed Grackle.

On the north side of the park, the 2-mile-long *Hogback Trail* offers a taste of the park's upland habitats. A core sample aged a cliff-edge juniper as 200 to 400 years old. To find the trail, follow the main park road between the two lakes and turn left toward Pinon Campground; park at the trailhead on the left (north), one-quarter mile from the turn. The trail crosses through P/J and prairie as it climbs to the top of the hogback that lies on the north edge of the park. From here enjoy the splendid views—north to Greenhorn Mountain, south to the Spanish Peaks, and west to the Sangre de Cristo Mountains.

On the way out, check the cattail pond on the south side, west of the entrance, what the park brochure calls "Bird Watch Area."

DeLorme grid: P. 83 D4.

Elevation: 6,400 feet.

Nearest food, gas, lodging: Restaurant at nearby golf course; Walsenburg.

Camping: Yes.

For more information: Lathrop State Park, 70 CR 502, Walsenburg, CO 81089; (719) 738-2376; www.parks.state.co.us; lathrop@csn.net.

PHOTO © GLENN WALBEK

Spotted Towhees reach their greatest abundance in scrub-oak habitat, where they sing from before dawn to after dusk.

Northwest

A combination of mountains, parklands, riparian corridors, sagebrush, ranchland, and canyons vary the landscape over this big country. Its eastern rampart is North Park, 35 miles wide and 45 miles long, rimmed on the east, south, and west by mountains: the Never Summer, Medicine Bow, Rabbit Ears, and Park ranges. Meandering streams spread over the basin floor and merge to form the headwaters of the North Platte River that flows north into Wyoming. Irrigated meadows fill the floodplains while sagebrush grasslands occupy ridges that rise above. Lt. John Charles Fremont described it in 1844: "a beautiful circular valley walled in all around with snowy mountains, rich with water and grass, fringed with pine on the mountain sides below the snow, and a paradise to all grazing animals."

North Park's short summer entices legions of waterbirds to its wildlife areas. Ducks, grebes, cormorants, shorebirds, and gulls nest; Colorado's only breeding Northern Waterthrushes (a handful) slip through the willows of braided streams. The *Atlas* block on the Arapaho refuge recorded seventy-five breeding species. Winter, cold and long, drives out most birds, though the streams and sagebrush hills fill up with elk and deer. Christmas Bird Counts typically tally only twenty-five species, mostly birds sheltering in the conifers (jays and chickadees); most frequent birds of the open areas are Greater Sage-Grouse, Golden Eagle, and Common Raven.

To the west, Steamboat Springs sits at the foot of snowy Rabbit Ears Pass. Steamboat has nine nesting sparrow species, and more Veery (sparse) and Green-tailed Towhee (abundant) than elsewhere in Colorado. The state's nesting Sandhill Cranes center in mountain parks a few miles north; their flamboyant calls resound over wet meadows. Flower fields sparkle, from yellow snow lilies as the snow melts to lush blue larkspur and monkshood in midsummer to golden sunflowers in August. Trillium and rhododendron grow in Colorado only north of Steamboat.

Splendid mountain roads and trails make the area a target for summer birdwatching and winter skiing. The Yampa River flows west, with a fine riparian section preserved by The Nature Conservancy near Hayden, and then on to the incomparable canyons of Dinosaur National Monument. Both Greater Sage- and Sharptailed Grouse perform their centuries-old dances on leks in the region; we can recommend one site for each. Browns Park National Wildlife Refuge, in the northwest corner of the state, qualifies as Colorado's most remote bird-watching site.

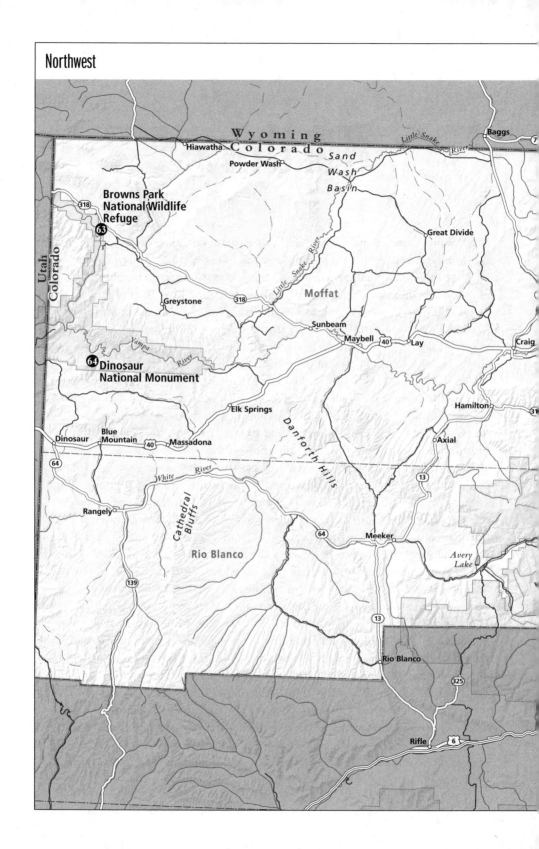

Wyoming
Colorado
Utah Colorado

Baggs

Hiawatha

Powder Wash

Sand Wash Basin

Little Snake River

Great Divide

Browns Park National Wildlife Refuge

318

63

Greystone

318

Moffat

Little Snake River

Sunbeam

Maybell

40

Lay

Craig

Yampa River

64 Dinosaur National Monument

Elk Springs

Hamilton

31

Danforth Hills

Axial

Dinosaur

Blue Mountain

40

Massadona

13

64

White River

Rangely

Cathedral Bluffs

64

Meeker

Avery Lake

139

Rio Blanco

13

Rio Blanco

325

Rifle

6

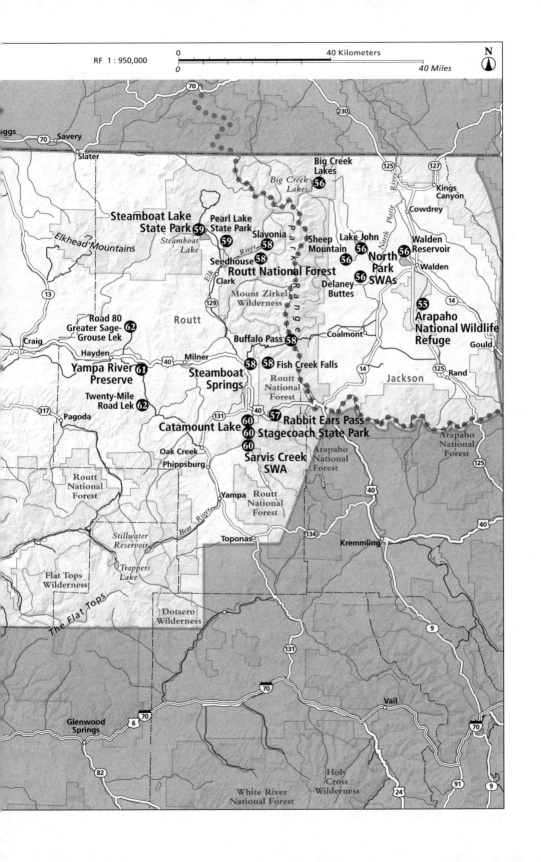

RF 1 : 950,000

0   40 Kilometers

0   40 Miles

70

230

ggs

70 Savery

Slater

Big Creek
Lakes **56**

*Big Creek
Lakes*

125

127

Kings
Canyon

Cowdrey

**Steamboat Lake
State Park** **59**

Pearl Lake
State Park

Slavonia

Park

Sheep
Mountain

Lake John

Walden
Reservoir

55

14

**Steamboat
Lake**

59

58

56

56

**North
Park
SWAs**

Walden

Elkhead Mountains

Elk River

Seedhouse **58**

Routt National Forest

Clark

129

Mount Zirkel
Wilderness

Delaney
Buttes

56

Range

13

Routt

Road 80
Greater Sage-
Grouse Lek **62**

Coalmont

55

**Arapaho
National Wildlife
Refuge**

Craig

Hayden

40 Milner

Buffalo Pass **58**

14

Jackson

Gould

125 Rand

**Yampa River
Preserve** **61**

Twenty-Mile
Road Lek **62**

58 **58** Fish Creek Falls

**Steamboat
Springs**

Routt
National
Forest

317

Pagoda

131

40

60

57 **Rabbit Ears Pass**

Arapaho
National
Forest

125

Catamount Lake

60 **Stagecoach State Park**

Oak Creek

Phippsburg

60

**Sarvis Creek
SWA**

Arapaho
National
Forest

Routt
National
Forest

Yampa Routt
National
Forest

Bear River

Toponas

134

Kremmling

40

*Stillwater
Reservoir*

*Trappers
Lake*

Flat Tops
Wilderness

The Flat Tops

Dotsero
Wilderness

131

9

40

70

Vail

70

Glenwood
Springs

6 **70**

70

82

Holy
Cross
Wilderness

24

91

9

White River
National Forest

55 Arapaho National Wildlife Refuge

Habitats: Wetlands, riparian, grassland, shrubland.

Specialty birds: *Resident:* Greater Sage-Grouse. *Summer:* Willet, Burrowing and Short-eared Owls, Marsh Wren, Savannah and Brewer's Sparrows.

Best times to bird: Spring, summer, fall.

About this site

The refuge checklist has 198 species, with the emphasis on those that depend on ponds and marshes. Fourteen duck, six shorebird, and fourteen marsh species nest here. Refuge biologists direct a complex system of ditches to irrigate meadows and to manipulate water levels in several ponds for waterfowl breeding. Pond levels affect aquatic vegetation that provides food and cover. Insects and other invertebrates produced in the ponds feed female waterfowl during egg-laying and, later, ducklings and goslings.

Though migrants may appear anywhere in Colorado, Willets breed in the state only at the wildlife refuges in North Park.

Moose, reintroduced to North Park in the 1970s, have become a common sight, along with other mammals such as coyote, beaver, weasel, mink, mule deer, and raccoon.

Directions

From the intersection of Highways 125 and 14 in Walden, go south on Highway 125 for 4 miles to the Wildlife Tour Route (on the right, west) and 4 more miles to refuge headquarters (on the left, east).

The birding

The Wildlife Tour Route travels beside a series of ponds. Primary breeding waterfowl are Gadwall, American Wigeon, Mallard, Cinnamon Teal, Northern Pintail, Northern Shoveler, Redhead, Lesser Scaup, Ruddy Duck, and Canada Goose. Arapaho has a few dozen breeding Willets, as well as numerous Killdeer, American Avocet, and Wilson's Phalarope. You might see a Black-crowned Night-Heron or a Great Blue. Listen for the whinnying sound that Wilson's Snipe make with their wings while Marsh Wrens titter from the cattails. Savannah and Brewer's Sparrows breed in the meadows and Lincoln's Sparrow in riparian sections. Swainson's and Red-tailed Hawks, American Crow, and Common Raven may fly overhead, and Northern Harriers cruise close to the cattails. Short-eared and Burrowing Owls nest here, too.

From the turnoff to refuge headquarters, a sign directs you to a nature trail, half a mile to the right. This mile-long trail rambles through wetlands and willows along the Illinois River. Here you can encounter Marsh Wren, plus herons, Mallard, Gadwall, Green-winged and Cinnamon Teal, Wilson's Snipe, and Yellow Warbler. Past refuge headquarters another auto tour (County Road 31) flanks the Illinois River on the east and provides views into the willows that line the river. If open, it runs north 6 miles and joins Highway 14 east of Walden.

DeLorme grid: P. 17 C7-D7, p. 18 C1.
Elevation: 8,200 feet.
Hazards: Muddy roads.
Nearest food, gas, lodging: Walden.
Camping: No.

For more information: Arapaho National Wildlife Refuge, 953 JC Road #32, Walden, CO 80480; (970) 723-8202; http://arapaho.fws.gov.

56 North Park SWAs 🆔 📧 W🌐

Habitats: Wetlands, sagebrush.
Specialty birds: *Resident:* Golden Eagle, Prairie Falcon. *Summer:* Eared and Western Grebes, Willet, Franklin's Gull, Forster's Tern.

Migrant: Ducks, grebes, loons, gulls, terns, and shorebirds.
Best times to bird: Spring, summer, fall.

About this site

A North Park specialty, Greater Sage-Grouse perform mating dances on leks on private property. Sites previously available for watching closed in 2006; as of this writing no public viewing exists. Hopeful viewers can try contacting the North Park Chamber of Commerce, 491 Main Street, Walden, CO 80480 (970–723–4600), or the Colorado Division of Wildlife, Watchable Wildlife Coordinator, 711 Independent Avenue, Grand Junction, CO 81505 (970–255–6181).

The Division of Wildlife operates several wildlife refuges in North Park worth visiting. Each has a slightly different mix of birds.

The birding

Several species of waterbirds nest on islands in **Walden Reservoir** (IBA). In migration it attracts a varied assortment of migrating waterbirds: ducks, grebes, loons, gulls, terns, and shorebirds.

From the intersection of Highways 14 and 125 in Walden, go west half a mile; when the road turns left, go straight on County Road 12W, then in a quarter mile, turn right on County Road 15. The reservoir is on the left, although a pond on the right may have a few birds. Go left at the Y intersection to stay along the north side of the reservoir. Take any of the dirt tracks to obtain closer views.

Breeding waterbirds include White Pelican, Double-crested Cormorant, Franklin's and California Gulls, and Forster's Tern. Western, Clark's, and Eared Grebes may nest here. In summer the lake's complement of dabbling and diving ducks includes Cinnamon Teal, Canvasback, and Redhead. Look for Willet, Long-billed Curlew, and Killdeer. In the sagebrush Sage Thrasher and Brewer's Sparrow sing.

The main reservoir at **Lake John** attracts migrating waterfowl in spring and fall and fishermen in summer. *Lake John Annex* attracts migrant species and in summer has an appealing assortment of nesting and non-nesting waterbirds.

From the intersection of Highways 14 and 125 in Walden, go west half a mile; when the road turns left, go straight on County Road 12W (signs for Lake John and Delaney Buttes). In 5 miles turn right on County Road 7 and continue 10 miles to the Lake John entrance.

When the road first hits the edge of the water, look in the bulrushes for Gadwall, Redhead, Canvasback, and Ruddy Duck and in the shallows for Killdeer,

American Avocet, and Wilson's Phalarope. North Park has Colorado's only nesting Willets (far from their more common seashore haunts), which you may find here. Go as directly as you can all the way around Lake John—the road runs along the west and south sides—to the dike that separates lake from annex.

The annex has more cover and a couple of islands. View its marshes from the dike; please don't disturb the breeding birds. Up to 150 pairs of Eared Grebes build platform nests in shallow water here, but not every year—it depends on water levels. Other summer species include American Wigeon, Cinnamon Teal, Lesser Scaup, Western Grebe (Clark's possible), and White Pelican. California and Franklin's (possible breeder) Gulls roost on the far shore; Yellow-headed as well as Red-winged Blackbirds nest in the marshes. In July look for American Coots and their bizarre red-headed babies. Savannah Sparrows chirp their *tseeee-lick* from the marshes; Sage Thrasher and Brewer's Sparrow sing from the shrubby uplands. Barn and Tree Swallows and House Wren favor the structures and trailer park.

West of Lake John, **Sheep Mountain** has nesting raptors: Red-tailed Hawk, Golden Eagle, and Prairie Falcon. To look for them, return to County Road 12W and go west (right) until it turns north, toward the cliffs on the west side of the mountain. Another raptor spot, **Big Creek Lakes,** hosts nesting Ospreys. A nature trail traverses the west side of the larger lake. To get there, go north from Walden on Highway 125 to Cowdrey (9 miles), then left on County Road 6W to Pearl (19 miles). Turn left on Forest Road 600 and proceed 6 miles to Big Creek Lakes campground.

Like most State Wildlife Areas, **Delaney Buttes** receives heavy use by fishermen. It lacks obvious nesting cover but nevertheless attracts some waterbirds. Take County Road 12W from Walden (same as Lake John), but when it turns right, continue straight onto County Road 18; turn left at the T intersection with County Road 5 to the SWA.

Delaney has more Forster's Terns than other North Park sites; they cruise the south lake. Other species here include Lesser Scaup, Western Grebe, White Pelican, Double-crested Cormorant, American Avocet, and Franklin's and California Gulls. You can find Horned Lark along lake edges, Vesper and Savannah Sparrows in the prairie, and Yellow Warbler and Red-winged and Yellow-headed Blackbirds along the shore. Common Nighthawks may sail overhead, seeking insects.

DeLorme grid: Walden, p. 17 C7; Lake John and Sheep Mountain, p. 17 B6; Big Creek Lakes, p. 17 A5; Delaney Buttes, p. 17 C6.

Elevation: 8,050 to 8,100 feet.

Hazards: Muddy roads.

Nearest food, gas, lodging: Walden.

Camping: Lake John.

For more information: Colorado Division of Wildlife, 346 Grand County Road 362, Hot Sulphur Springs, CO 80451; (970) 725-6200; wildlife.state.co.us/landwater/state wildlifeareas.

57 Rabbit Ears Pass ⟨W-⟩

Habitats: Spruce/fir, willow carr.

Specialty birds: *Resident:* Boreal Owl, American Three-toed Woodpecker. *Summer:* Wilson's Snipe.

Best times to bird: Year-round.

About this site

The Rabbit Ears Pass highway crosses a rolling, high-altitude plateau, over 6 miles long and dotted with spruce/fir copses, willow carrs, and wet meadows. Meadows blaze with bright yellow snow lilies in June, marsh marigolds and globeflowers in July, and still later, paintbrush, arnica, and columbines. The *Atlas* block on Rabbit Ears Pass recorded forty-seven species, with the most abundant breeders Mountain Chickadee, Hermit Thrush, Yellow-rumped Warbler, Lincoln's and White-crowned Sparrows, Pine Grosbeak, Cassin's Finch, and Pine Siskin.

Directions

U.S. Highway 40 crosses this pass, between Kremmling and Steamboat Springs. Directions start on the east, at Muddy Pass (20 miles beyond the Gore Pass road, Highway 134).

The birding

Half a mile past Muddy Pass, a pull-off provides a view of *Muddy Pass Lake,* where Ring-necked Ducks breed. Other birds around the edge of the lake include Spotted Sandpiper, Wilson's Warbler, and White-crowned Sparrow.

Going west on US 40, look in the conifers for spruce/fir birds. Try any of these side roads:

- 1.5 miles west of Muddy Pass Lake, a dirt track to the north; it takes you to a stream lined with willows and a couple of beaver ponds. American Three-toed Woodpeckers nested here in 2007.
- West 3 miles from Muddy Pass Lake, the *Muddy Creek trailhead* on the north and opposite it on the south, *Buffalo Park Road* (Forest Road 100). The latter, well graveled once it opens for the summer, goes all the way south to Gore Pass, through stands of conifers interspersed with open meadows and occasional ponds.
- West 3.5 miles from Muddy Pass Lake, on the north, a paved road to the *Dumont Lake* picnic area and campground, and Forest Road 251 on the south. Dumont Lake sees a fair amount of attention from anglers.
- 6 miles west of Muddy Pass Lake, the *west summit,* with a parking area on the south side. You can climb up the hillside across the highway into the conifers.

All these roads offer similar habitats and all boast stunning flower fields in season. Closely spaced Ruby-crowned Kinglets sing loudly; adding to the chorus,

Olive-sided Flycatcher, Hermit Thrush, Chipping, Song, Lincoln's, and White-crowned Sparrows, Cassin's Finch, Pine Grosbeak, and, of course, American Robin. Less musically gifted species include Hammond's and Dusky Flycatchers, Red-breasted and White-breasted Nuthatches, and Dark-eyed Junco. With very good luck at night, you might encounter a Boreal Owl (but watch out for Wilson's Snipe; both make their similar sounds at night).

Two miles below the West Summit, check *Ferndale Picnic Area* for Steller's Jay and Red-naped Sapsucker.

DeLorme grid: P. 27 A4.

Elevation: 9,000 to 9,500 feet.

Hazards: High-speed traffic on US 40; Rabbit Ears Pass is infamous for winter driving hazards.

Nearest food, gas, lodging: Steamboat Springs, Kremmling.

Camping: Yes.

For more information: Hahns Peak Ranger District, Routt National Forest, 925 Weiss Drive, Steamboat Springs, CO 80487-9315; (970) 879-1870; www.fs.fed.us/r2/mbr.

PHOTO © GLENN WALBEK

Shy and quiet post-breeding interlopers from the northwest, Calliope Hummingbirds filter into Colorado in July to sample flower fields and feeders.

58 Routt National Forest ⓌⒺ ♿ and Steamboat Springs

Habitats: *Forest:* Spruce/fir, aspen, willow carr, stream. *Town:* Wetlands, riparian, urban.

Specialty birds: *Resident:* American Dipper, Red Crossbill. *Summer:* Swallows (especially Tree and Cliff), Gray Catbird, Cassin's Finch. *Winter:* Gray Jay, Pine Grosbeak.

Best times to bird: May to October.

About this site
Famous for its skiing, Steamboat had a ski-jumping hill in the 1930s and still boasts a marching band that moves out on skis. The Yampa River runs through Steamboat with access at several points. The nearby national forest provides an extensive assortment of roads and trails.

The birding
At **Fish Creek Falls,** close to Steamboat, two short trails, one wheelchair-accessible, provide stunning views of a cascading waterfall. Local rumors claim that the logo of a nationally known Colorado beer pictures this waterfall. From Lincoln Avenue in Steamboat Springs (the main street, US 40), turn north on 3rd; take the first right onto Fish Creek Falls Road and drive 4 miles to the parking lot.

The upper trail offers treetop views of Western Wood-Pewee and Western Tanager and a watering hole (marked by an interpretive sign) that birds enjoy on hot afternoons. When walking the trails in June, you're never out of earshot of at least two Warbling Vireos. The lower trail files down to the roaring stream, the noise of which smothers any birdsong, and onto a bridge where misty spray from the waterfall coats your binoculars. Energetic birders can follow the trail past the falls to sample spruce/fir species and, if they go far enough, more aspen birds.

Likely birds include Broad-tailed Hummingbird, Downy Woodpecker, Cordilleran Flycatcher, Steller's Jay, Tree Swallow, both chickadees, House Wren, Swainson's Thrush, Townsend's Solitaire, Orange-crowned and MacGillivray's Warblers, Western Tanager, Green-tailed Towhee, Black-headed Grosbeak, and Bullock's Oriole.

The graveled **Buffalo Pass** road crosses the Continental Divide at 10,300 feet. From Lincoln Avenue (US 40) in Steamboat Springs, go north on 7th Street 4 blocks; bear right on Missouri Avenue; in 3 blocks turn left (north) on North Park; in another 3 blocks turn right onto Strawberry Park Road (County Road 36); turn right in 2 miles onto County Road 38, which becomes Forest Road 60, the Buffalo Pass road. Snow keeps the road closed into June beyond Dry Lake Campground; check to determine road status.

At its lower reaches it passes through tall mountain shrubland, lodgepole pine, and aspen on its way to spruce/fir. The *Atlas* block tallied forty-seven breeders, the commonest Broad-tailed Hummingbird, Ruby-crowned Kinglet, Hermit and Swainson's Thrushes, Wilson's Warbler, and Red Crossbill. On the top a dirt track leads south along the ridge, the Continental Divide, where you'll find scattered copses of spruce/fir on both sides and one or two ponds. On an outside chance, look for Bufflehead in the ponds, although they nest north of here in ponds lower down on the east side.

The road to the **Seedhouse** campground and the **Slavonia** trailhead travels montane wetlands, aspen, and spruce/fir; the *Atlas* block recorded a commendable sixty-six species. From the west side of Steamboat Springs, drive north 17.5 miles on Highway 129

Easy access makes Fish Creek Falls a popular destination. Birders can look at Warbling Vireo singing in the treetops at eye level.

to CR 64, left 8.5 miles to Seedhouse, and 3 more miles to Slavonia.

Between Seedhouse and Slavonia, the road passes through several fine aspen forests. The trees abound with Red-naped Sapsucker, Hairy Woodpecker, Northern Flicker, Western Wood-Pewee, Warbling Vireo, Tree and Violet-green Swallows, and Yellow-rumped Warbler. Broad-tailed Hummingbirds zoom through the aspen and across flower-bedecked meadows. Listen for the hoarse squawking of Clark's Nutcracker high on the hillsides. On brushy hillsides look for Dusky Flycatcher and Green-tailed Towhee. Some side roads cross the stream; look under bridges for nests of American Dipper and along the streams expect Willow and Cordilleran Flycatchers, Yellow Warbler, and Lincoln's Sparrow.

Trailheads at Slavonia take you to the Mount Zirkel Wilderness and several mountain lakes with striking scenery. The forest here holds Olive-sided and Hammond's Flycatchers, Golden-crowned and Ruby-crowned Kinglets, Western Tanager, Green-tailed Towhee, and Red Crossbill.

Right in Steamboat Springs, the *Yampa River Core Trail* follows the Yampa River through town for 7 miles. Cottonwood trees, shrubby riparian thickets, and open fields provide bird habitat, with the trail sometimes a barrier between urban Steamboat and riverine open space. Benches and picnic spots make for a leisurely bird walk. From south to north, you can reach the Core Trail from Walton Road,

Pine Grove Road to Fetcher Park, Trafalgar Drive (see botanic park below), Yampa Avenue and 2nd Street, 13th Street, and James Brown Bridge on Shield Drive.

Riparian species include swallows, warblers, Cedar Waxwing, and Pine Siskin and maybe a mink on the river shore. At *Yampa River Botanic Park* (open dawn to dusk, May 1 to October 31), volunteer gardeners maintain an eye-catching assortment of plants that grow in this demanding climate. A hummingbird garden and feeders attract primarily Broad-tailed, but also, starting in July, Rufous and Calliope. Feeders attract Cassin's Finch and Lesser Goldfinch. Turn off US 40 (Lincoln Avenue) onto Trafalgar Drive, left on Pamela Lane, and on to the far-end parking lot. The gardens lie beyond the soccer field.

At the upper (south) end of the Yampa River, not quite attached to the Core Trail, the *Chuck Lewis SWA* comprises wet meadows and dense willow thickets along the river. From Steamboat Springs go south on US 40 to Highway 131; go right half a mile, then right again onto County Road 14F to two parking lots: one before the Yampa River crossing, one on County Road 14. Walk along any of the informal angler trails to look for Wilson's Snipe, Willow Flycatcher, and sparrows that use these lush and damp bottomlands. Occasionally, birders find Bobolink in the fields between the railroad tracks and US 40.

Steamboat ski area operates a bird feeder where, during ski season, you might find Gray Jay, Mountain Chickadee, Red-breasted Nuthatch, Pine Grosbeak, and Red Crossbill.

DeLorme grid: P. 16 A3, p. 26 A3.

Elevation: Fish Creek Falls, 7,600 feet; Buffalo Pass summit, 10,300 feet; Slavonia trailhead, 8,425 feet; Town, 6,800 feet

Hazards: Ticks, especially in spring; mosquitoes; fast bicyclists on the Core Trail

Nearest food, gas, lodging: Steamboat Springs.

Camping: Seedhouse, Buffalo Pass.

For more information: Hahns Peak Ranger District, Routt National Forest, 925 Weiss Drive, Steamboat Springs, CO 80487-9315; (970) 879-1870; www.fs.fed.us/r2/mbr. Botanic Park, P.O. Box 776269, Steamboat Springs, CO 80477; (970) 879-4300; www.steamboatsprings.net—click on Parks and Open Space or Botanic Park.

59 Steamboat Lake State Park

Habitats: Shrubland, sagebrush, spruce/fir/lodgepole pine, wetlands.

Specialty birds: *Summer:* Sandhill Crane, Western Grebe, seven species of sparrows.

Best times to bird: Spring and summer.

About this site

Set in a mountain park amid sagebrush and aspen hillsides, this lovely spot features a splendid mix of Colorado montane birdlife. On the north side, sagebrush flats and conifer woodlands border the lake; on the west and south, wet meadows. Several pairs of Sandhill Cranes nest in the wetlands, along with ducks and grebes. On weekends boats and fishermen jam the lake; it's better to bird here on weekdays.

Directions

From the west side of Steamboat Springs, take Highway 129 north 24.5 miles to the park.

Besides the striking setting, seven sparrow species and Sandhill Cranes spice up a visit to Steamboat Lake State Park.

The birding

At the first park entry, opposite the village of Hahns Peak, a dirt road leads to the lake. In June a sparrow serenade of Brewer's, Lark, Savannah, and White-crowns fills the sagebrush with song. Killdeer run along the shore and distant cranes bellow. Look for Swainson's Hawk and Mountain Bluebird in the open fields.

A half mile beyond the first turnoff is the visitor center on the left. Just beyond it, plan to spend a couple of hours exploring for forest birds on the fine, mile-long *Nature Trail*. The trees resound with montane species in habitats from sunny lodgepole woodlands and aspen glens to shaded spruce forests. Views of the lake may also yield a grebe or a pair of Sandhill Cranes. You can add Chipping, Lincoln's, and Song to your sparrow list (and Dark-eyed Junco). Both Ruby-crowned and Golden-crowned Kinglets sound off, along with Hairy Woodpecker, Olive-sided, Hammond's, and Dusky Flycatchers, Red-breasted Nuthatch, Hermit Thrush, and maybe Red Crossbill. In winter, snowshoes make the Nature Trail a rewarding outing to find such winter specialties as Pine Grosbeak and Red Crossbill.

Back on Highway 129, drive 0.8 mile to County Road 62 and turn left to the park marina and campground (Long-eared Owls have nested here). Lakeshore trails from the marina lead in both directions. On Road 62, stop at stream crossings; Willow Flycatchers call their sneezy *fitz-bew* from tall willows. Turn into *Meadow Point* (1.3 miles past the marina turnoff). In the wet meadows that border the parking area, unmated Sandhill Cranes sometimes gather. Wetlands south along the lakeshore shelter nesting ducks such as Green-winged and Cinnamon Teal, plus Western Grebe.

Back 2.5 miles toward Steamboat Springs on Highway 129, County Road 209 turns off to **Pearl Lake State Park.** At 1.4 miles the road, before it reaches the park, crosses an extensive willow flat. Stop to listen for Willow Flycatcher and Lincoln's Sparrow.

The road leads into the park's spruce/fir forest; campground sites spotted among the trees bring campers close to the birds. Look here for Olive-sided Flycatcher, Mountain Chickadee, Ruby-crowned Kinglet, Hermit Thrush, and Dark-eyed Junco. Few waterbirds use the lake itself, although one or two pairs of Sandhill Cranes may have territories around the north side. A 1-mile trail leads to the Pearl Lake dam, and a longer one takes you higher into the spruce/fir forest. The dam trail goes through habitats similar to those of the Steamboat Lake Nature Trail.

DeLorme grid: P. 16 B2.

Elevation: 8,000 feet.

Hazards: Deer on the roads at night.

Nearest food, gas, lodging: Hahns Peak, Clark, Steamboat Springs.

Camping: Yes.

For more information: Steamboat Lake & Pearl Lake State Park, P. O. Box 750, Clark, CO 80428; (970) 879-3922; www.parks .state.co.us.

60 Catamount, Stagecoach, and Sarvis Creek

Habitats: Wetlands, riparian, montane shrubland.

Specialty birds: *Summer:* Cinnamon Teal, Ring-necked Duck, Common Merganser, American White Pelican, Bald Eagle, Willow Flycatcher, Veery, MacGillivray's Warbler, Green-tailed Towhee, Fox Sparrow, Lazuli Bunting. *Migrant:* Waterfowl.

Best times to bird: Spring, summer, fall.

About this site

Steamboat birders like to go to three sites south of town, off Highway 131. One has the best waterbirds locally, one has an attractive wetlands walk, and the third offers several habitats including shrubland, streamside riparian, and (via a trail) montane forest.

The prime location around Steamboat for migrating waterfowl, **Catamount Lake,** is privately owned. Good numbers of ducks and geese, grebes, gulls, pelicans, and cormorants use the lake. An occasional loon may show up, especially in the fall. The lake edge attracts sandpipers and other shorebirds.

The birding

From Steamboat Springs, drive south on US 40 to Highway 131. Go south 4.5 miles and left on County Road 18. You can set up a scope in the parking lot next to the restaurant. At 1.8 miles the road comes close to an arm of the lake that provides a good view (park carefully). A mile farther turn left on County Road 18C, but go only to the Yampa River crossing because there the road becomes private. Turn around at the first sign, just across the Yampa River, that announces private roads.

During breeding season the lake supports seventy-five non-nesting American White Pelicans, Double-crested Cormorants, and a variety of ducks and gulls. Look for nesting Bald Eagle and Sandhill Crane. In the willows look and listen for Veery, Western Wood-Pewee, and Willow Flycatcher. In the wetlands listen for winnowing or chattering Wilson's Snipe and singing Savannah Sparrows. Both Yellow-headed and Red-winged Blackbirds use the marshes. Dry shrublands support both Green-tailed and Spotted Towhees.

The reservoir at **Stagecoach State Park** (fee, handicap-accessible) sees some waterfowl during spring and fall migration, but heavy boat traffic keeps birds off the water during the warm months. Six miles south of US 40 on Highway 131, go left on County Road 14 to the park; at the junction with County Road 18 (see Sarvis Creek SWA, below), go right to the junction with County Road 16 (to Lynx Pass); take an immediate right into a parking area.

A short nature trail through the *Wetland Habitat Preserve* (0.75 mile) has two ponds, extensive wet meadows, and a willow-lined stream in a relatively secluded spot. You can hear snipe winnowing, peer through a blind at the ducks on one of the ponds (Cinnamon Teal, Ring-necked Duck, and Common Merganser nest here), and seek out willow-nesting birds such as Willow Flycatcher, Yellow Warbler, and Lincoln's Sparrow. Common Yellowthroats breed here, one of Routt County's few sites.

Sarvis Creek SWA, below Stagecoach, hosts different species. (Some maps call this "Service" Creek; the SWA spelling reflects how Coloradans pronounce the common tree-shrub, serviceberry.) At the junction of County Roads 14 and 18, turn left on County Road 18 and drive around the northeast side of Stagecoach Lake to a narrow, bumpy, potholed dirt road that drops below the dam and leads to this wildlife area.

The road passes through tall shrubs with MacGillivray's Warbler, Green-tailed Towhee, and Lazuli Bunting. In 3 miles it reaches the wildlife area, on the right. (The road continues on to Catamount Reservoir but remains closed until mid-summer.) Fox Sparrows inhabit tall willows at the Yampa River crossing as do the more common Song Sparrow, Yellow Warbler, Warbling Vireo, and Cliff Swallow. From a parking area across the river, a trail leads into aspen and conifer forests with their usual complement of birds.

DeLorme grid: P. 26 B3.

Elevation: 7,000 feet.

Nearest food, gas, lodging: Steamboat Springs; food and gas at Oak Creek and Yampa.

Camping: Stagecoach.

For more information: Stagecoach State Park, P.O. Box 98, Oak Creek, CO 80467; (970) 736-2436; www.parks.state.co.us.

61 Yampa River Preserve 🦅 IBA ♿

Habitats: Riparian.

Specialty birds: *Summer:* Swainson's Thrush, Veery, Gray Catbird, Cedar Waxwing, Bobolink, Cassin's Finch, Lazuli Bunting, American and Lesser Goldfinches.

Best times to bird: Spring, summer, fall.

About this site

The Nature Conservancy protects this river bottom along the Yampa River because of its unique ecosystem of trees and shrubs: narrow-leaf cottonwood, box-elder, and red-osier dogwood. The broad stream bottom holds surprisingly varied birdlife. The birds have an eastern flavor; only about a third have ranges restricted to the West. The *Atlas* block recorded ninety-seven breeding species, the highest count in western Colorado.

A contingent of eastern species, such as Veery, Swainson's Thrush, and American Redstart, mixes with western ones, such as Cassin's Finch, Lazuli Bunting, and Lesser Goldfinch, to breed in the lush stream bottom of the Yampa River Preserve.

Directions

From Milner on US 40, drive west 8.5 miles; immediately after crossing the Yampa River, look for a small parking area on the left. From Hayden, go 5 miles east on US 40.

The birding

The 1.5-mile trail through this superb habitat (foot traffic only) starts out along an irrigation ditch with willows and the river on the left and a shrubby hillside on the right. In about a half mile, where a power line crosses, a dirt trail leads to the river bottom.

During breeding season, both Swainson's Thrush and Veery sing from the shrubs. Treetops resound with the songs of Yellow Warbler and Warbling Vireo; House Wrens burble from the shrubs. Other likely species include Willow and Cordilleran Flycatchers, Blue-gray Gnatcatcher, Gray Catbird, Cedar Waxwing, Fox Sparrow, Black-headed Grosbeak, Cassin's Finch, Lazuli Bunting, Bullock's Oriole, and American and Lesser Goldfinches. You might find a Great Horned Owl family, an American Redstart, or Plumbeous Vireo. On the cliffs across the river (and Highway 40) nesting species include Red-tailed Hawk, Golden Eagle, and Cliff Swallow.

Just west on Highway 40 (1.4 miles) from the preserve trail, *Carpenter Ranch,* full of history, has a similar trail along the Yampa stream bottom. The Conservancy operates this as a working ranch—open to the public May 15 to Labor Day, Thursday to Saturday from 9:00 A.M. to noon. You can arrange a guided tour by prior arrangement.

As you drive into the ranch, look for Bobolink on either side of the road. (You can also search for them along any dirt roads in the vicinity adjacent to hay meadows.) One or two pairs of Sandhill Cranes nest near the ranch.

Across the Yampa (north) from the preserve trail (closer to Milner), County Road 70 runs between agricultural fields and sagebrush hillsides. Three species of grouse (Sharp-tailed, Dusky, and Greater Sage-) may strut and feed in the fields or perch on fence posts along this road. Typical summer birds include American Kestrel, Vesper and Savannah Sparrows, Western Meadowlark, and Brewer's Blackbird.

DeLorme grid P. 26 A1.

Elevation: 6,500 feet.

Hazards: Unrelenting summer mosquitoes.

Nearest food, gas, lodging: Steamboat Springs, Craig; food and gas in Hayden.

Camping: No.

For more information: The Nature Conservancy; (970) 276-4626; nature.org/where wework/northamerica/states/colorado/preserves/.

62 Grouse Sites 〔W〕🌐

Habitats: Sagebrush, aspen, spruce/fir.

Best time to bird: April.

Specialty birds: *Resident:* Greater Sage-Grouse, Sharp-tailed Grouse. *Summer:* Purple Martin.

About this site

Near Hayden two grouse species—Greater Sage-Grouse and Sharp-tailed Grouse—perform centuries-old mating dances on leks (dancing grounds). We list two viewing opportunities and urge your adherence to cardinal rules when observing the spectacle of lekking grouse:

- **Stay** in your car.
- **Do not disturb** the birds by approaching them, slamming car doors, or waving your arms.
- **Arrive** at dawn and keep quiet.
- **Leave** only **after** they finish.

Also, the Colorado Division of Wildlife offers tours guided by a District Wildlife Manager.

The birding

To reach **Road 80 Greater Sage-Grouse lek,** turn north on Walnut Street in Hayden, right in 0.8 mile at the T intersection on County Road 80, and in 3 miles, left on the California Park Road (still Road 80). Count cattle guards. Greater Sage-Grouse favor a lek a quarter mile beyond the third cattle guard, at 3.5 miles. Stop at the top of a hill, at Milepost 7, near the JIMMY DUNN GULCH sign. Listen for the sounds of dancing grouse and look on the left side of the road. Grouse use the lek from mid-March to mid-May; April sees the most active dancing. Get here before dawn, and to watch, pull well off the road (which sees moderate traffic) and stay in your car so you don't disturb the birds.

Sometimes along the road, birders see three species of grouse: Greater Sage-, Sharp-tailed (near second cattle guard), and Dusky (which sometimes display *in* the road!). Later in the season, after the grouse scatter, you can find dozens of Vesper Sparrows along with Mountain Bluebird and Western Meadowlark in the sagebrush. Blue-gray Gnatcatcher, Green-tailed Towhee, and Chipping Sparrow favor brushy hillsides. In roadside stock ponds you may see a pair of Cinnamon Teal, noisy Killdeer, and perhaps a cruising Northern Harrier. The road climbs through aspen woodlands (look for Purple Martin) into spruce/fir at the top of a pass. (Limited camping okay; no facilities.) In the spruce you might find Olive-sided

Flycatcher, Clark's Nutcracker, and Hermit Thrush. From here into California Park, the Forest Service closes the road until midsummer to protect nesting Sandhill Crane.

Sharp-tailed Grouse use **Twenty-Mile Road lek** south and east of Hayden. Between the Carpenter Ranch and Yampa River Preserve, County Road 27 (Twenty-mile Road) goes south (just east of the Hayden power plant). In 6.6 miles, at the top of a hill, look for two gates on the left (landmarks to warn you when you're close: a pond on the right at 5.5 miles and a 55 mph sign at 5.8 miles). By the gates two 8-foot poles stick up, probably snowplow markers. Turn around to face back down the road. The lek is on the other side of the road (west), on a knoll several hundred yards below. Even though you could drive closer, this spot provides the best vantage.

Like Sage-Grouse, Sharp-tails dance from mid-March to mid-May and peak in April. Get here before dawn, and to watch, stay in your car—don't disturb the birds.

DeLorme grid: Road 80, p. 15 D7, p. 16 D1 and C1; 20-Mile Road, p. 26 A1.

Elevation: 7,000 feet.

Nearest food, gas, lodging: Steamboat Springs, Craig; food and gas in Hayden.

Camping: No.

Tour booking and information: Colorado Division of Wildlife; (970) 276-3338; wildlife.state.co.us/.

The cold days of early spring inspire Greater Sage-Grouse to strut their extraordinary courtship dances on leks in the sagebrush.

63 Browns Park NWR $ 🦆 IBA

Habitats: Wetlands, pinyon/juniper, sage-brush, riparian.

Best times to bird: Spring through early fall.

About this site

Way up in the northwest corner of the state, Browns Park National Wildlife Refuge straddles the Green River just before it plunges into Canyon of Lodore in Dinosaur National Monument. In the late 1800s Browns Park became a major hideout for horse thieves and cattle rustlers; they readily crossed state lines to escape the jurisdiction of pursuing law officers.

Directions

Turn north from US 40 at Maybell (31 miles west of Craig) on Highway 318; refuge headquarters and the start of the auto tour route are another 55 miles.

The birding

The 13,000-acre refuge shelters ducks and other waterbirds in its wetlands complex. Nesting Mallard, teal, Redhead, and Canvasback produce 2,500 ducklings annually. More ducks come during spring and fall migration. Other nesting species include Pied-billed Grebe, American Bittern, and White-faced Ibis in the marshes.

Golden Eagle and Peregrine Falcon soar over during spring and summer. Bald Eagles visit in winter. Other habitats include P/J, sagebrush, and lowland riparian, where you might find Black-chinned Hummingbird, Loggerhead Shrike, Juniper Titmouse, Brewer's Sparrow, and Bullock's Oriole.

An 11-mile auto tour samples all the habitats. The refuge closes its marshes to visitors March 1 to July 31 to protect nesting waterfowl. Visitors should remain on the road during this period.

Across the road from refuge headquarters, trails lead into the Willow Creek SWA through a foothills riparian gully worth exploring.

DeLorme grid: P. 12 A1.
Elevation: 5,500 feet.
Nearest food, gas, lodging: Craig, Rock Springs, Wyoming.
Camping: No.

For more information: Browns Park National Wildlife Refuge, 1318 Highway 318, Maybell, CO 81640; (970) 365-3613; www.fws.gov/brownspark/.

Habitats: Canyon, pinyon/juniper, sagebrush, riparian.

Best times to bird: Spring through early fall.

About this site

Originally established because of a dinosaur bone quarry in Utah, Dinosaur National Monument expanded into Colorado to embrace the rugged canyons of the Green and Yampa Rivers. The rivers provide critical habitat for two endangered fish, and rock art tells something of the history of prehistoric people. That you can marvel at these canyons instead of boat on a lake 1,000 feet higher stems from a major conservation battle in the 1950s that resulted in a law forbidding construction of dams in national parks and monuments.

Directions

Dinosaur Visitor Center: 88 miles west of Craig on US 40. The Harpers Corner Road starts there.

The birding

The road in, *Harpers Corner Scenic Drive* (closed in winter), crosses through excellent P/J habitat and takes you into Utah to a striking overlook of the canyon country. You can stop at wide spots in the road and troll for P/J birds.

Just before the road enters the monument (an hour from the visitor center), a rough side road branches back into Colorado and drops down to *Echo Park* and the river junction—a rare chance to drive into a western canyon. Don't try it in wet weather or with a low-slung car. The Dinosaur brochure warns that only high-clearance vehicles should try it (though we made it with a VW). The road drops down through P/J to the junction where the Green and Yampa Rivers have carved out massive Steamboat Rock.

A few cottonwood patches line the river, with some western lowland riparian species. Peregrine Falcons nest here, along with other canyon specialties such as White-throated Swift and Canyon Wren.

DeLorme grid: P. 22 A1, B1, p. 12 D1.

Elevation: 5,075 (Echo Park) to 8,000+ feet.

Nearest food, gas, lodging: Craig, Vernal, Utah.

Camping: Yes.

For more information: Dinosaur National Monument, 4545 East Highway 40, Dinosaur, CO 81610-9724; (970) 374-3000; www.nps.gov/dino/.

Central Rockies

The epitome of Colorado—Ski Country USA—scenery unsurpassed. And birds, too! Anywhere you go in the Colorado Rockies, you can find excellent birding spots. This guide calls out a few, but they by no means come close to all the tantalizing places. National forests cover 75 percent of the land mass; their networks of roads and trails offer visitors endless opportunities for rewarding bird-watching amid breathtaking mountain scenery.

The Rockies consist of a series of ranges, most running north to south; Colorado's highest peaks soar above the Arkansas River headwaters between Leadville and Salida, although the mountains south of Aspen have more rugged features. Wilderness areas hug the spines of most high ranges, although most 14,000-foot peaks have well-trodden trails to the top.

Habitats include all Colorado conifers and all mountain grasslands, including alpine tundra. Pinyon/junipers grow around Buena Vista, Eagle, and Glenwood Springs; ponderosas around Buena Vista. Lodgepole pines poke straight up in dense forests, and give way to spruce/fir stands that cover the 2,000 feet below timberline. Aspen woodlands cover entire hillsides, montane meadows complement the forests throughout, and streams lined with willow carrs drain every peak. Sagebrush hills surround Gunnison.

In this part of the state, you must use your feet to discover alpine species—a feat that will make you proud of the birds you find. Three highways climb above timberline: Loveland Pass (Denver to Dillon), Independence Pass (Leadville to Aspen), and Cottonwood Pass (Buena Vista to Gunnison). From their summits, you can trek up the tundra to look for ptarmigan, pipits, and rosy-finches.

Mining history shows up almost everywhere, with abandoned mines sprinkled up many valleys. Leadville's old mines and opera house support the National Mining Hall of Fame. Other nineteenth-century mining towns have turned into small (St. Elmo) or glitzy (Aspen) tourist destinations, and old mine roads penetrate much of the high country.

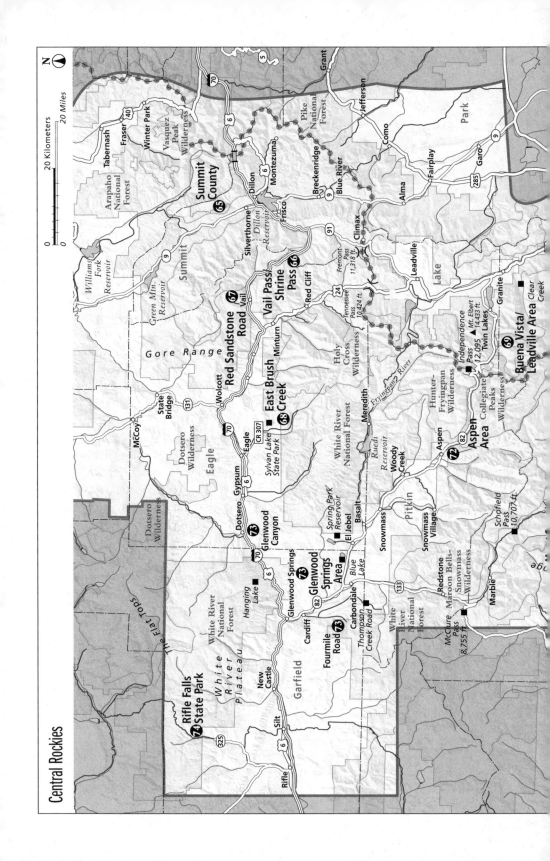

Central Rockies

N

20 Kilometers
0

20 Miles
0

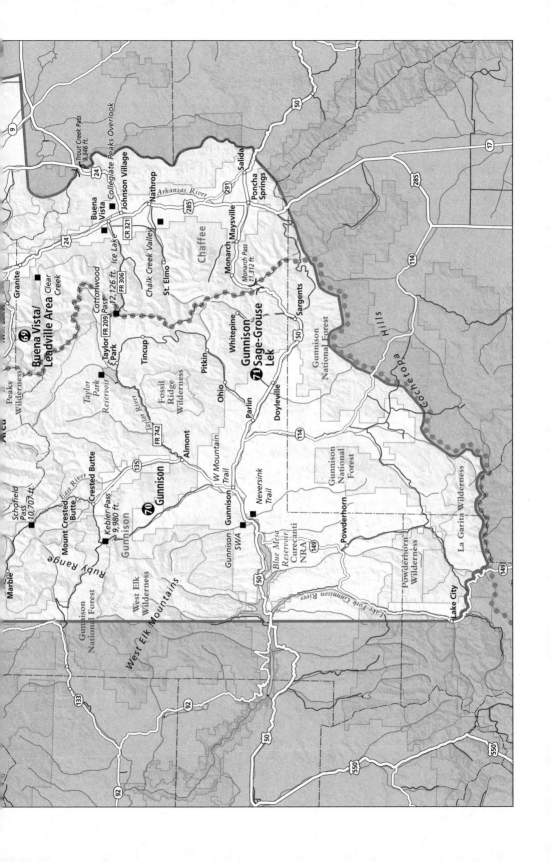

(65) Summit County [W]

Habitats: Lodgepole, aspen, spruce/fir, foot-hills riparian, willow carr, alpine.

Specialty birds: *Resident:* Golden Eagle, White-tailed Ptarmigan (hard to find), Three-toed Woodpecker (also hard to find), American Dipper, Pine Grosbeak, Brown-capped Rosy-Finch, Cassin's Finch. *Summer:* Osprey, Broad-tailed and Rufous Hummingbirds, Olive-sided, Cordilleran, Dusky, and Hammond's Flycatch-ers, Golden-crowned Kinglet, Swainson's and Hermit Thrushes, MacGillivray's Warbler, Fox Sparrow. *Winter:* Barrow's and Common Gold-eneyes, all three rosy-finches.

Best times to bird: Summer and winter.

About this site

Summit County lies west of the Continental Divide, 60 miles west of Denver. With 90 percent of the land publicly owned, three towering and spectacular mountain ranges, and good roads and trails, it offers enterprising birders mountain species amid gorgeous scenery.

All year long birders can find western conifer specialists along roads and trails. The Blue River bisects the county north and south, interrupted by Dillon Reservoir and Green Mountain Reservoir, both part of Denver's Pacific-to-Atlantic water-delivery system, and neither a premier waterbird destination. Willow brush and narrow-leaf cottonwoods populate stream bottoms. Up from the streams, forests cover the mountainsides: Lodgepole pine and aspen (sometimes mixed, sometimes separate) give way, at about 10,000 feet, to spruce/fir forests, succeeded by alpine tundra.

Birders who visit in winter to "Ski the Summit" (Breckenridge, Copper Mountain, Keystone, and A Basin) may take a day off to search for Summit's bird special-ties. You can drive to several locations, and national forests that flank the valleys offer a plethora of trails for ski touring or snowshoeing and for summer hiking.

Directions
Access via Interstate 70 from east or west, or Highway 9 from north or south.

The birding
Ski areas (winter): Gray Jays cluster around ski area restaurants. Riding the lifts, an observant birder may notice Common Raven, Mountain Chickadee, and Pine Grosbeak. A friend claims to have seen a Northern Pygmy-Owl from one chairlift.

River watch (winter): Downstream (north) from Silverthorne, Highway 9 follows the Blue River on its path to the Colorado River. From Silverthorne, 2.8 miles from the Wildernest/Rainbow Drive traffic light, or 2 miles north of the last traffic light (Annie Street), the *Silverthorne Sewage Ponds* lie on the right. They can hold six to eight species of ducks, including Barrow's and Common Goldeneyes.

North 3 miles, park in a lot on the right (at County Road 1870). Walk to the edge of the Blue River. Look for American Dippers in riffles, especially downstream; they nest under the bridge. Continuing north, stop at each parking area to look for dippers and possibly Barrow's Goldeneye.

Summer: Try the same drill except for the sewage pond (though it may have a few species, including Common Merganser). Ospreys nest about a mile north of Silverthorne in a huge nest on a power pole on the west, conspicuous from the highway. In the willows you can find moose, Wilson's Snipe, Swainson's Thrush, Yellow Warbler, and Fox, Savannah, and Song Sparrows. Check *Blue River Campground* (7.5 miles) for conifer birds in lodgepole pines and Swainson's Thrush in willow thickets across the Blue River. You can park by the highway and walk around the campground.

PHOTO © WILLIAM EDEN

The American Dipper's "music is that of the streams refined and spiritualized. The deep booming notes of the falls are in it, the trills of the rapids, the gurgling of margin eddies, the low whispering of level reaches, and the sweet tinkle of separate drops oozing from the ends of mosses and falling into tranquil ponds."—John Muir, 1894

Opposite Blue River Campground on the left, *Rock Creek Road* (County Road 1350) climbs steeply up through lodgepole and aspen to spruce/fir. At 1.3 miles don't go straight into the subdivision, instead turn sharp left, down and up the side of the hill, and continue 1.6 miles (over a rough road, but passable by passenger car) to the parking lot, where you have two choices—or three.

You can go either right or left on the Gore Range Trail: Right (north) provides more habitats, including beaver ponds where you might find Spotted Sandpiper, Red-naped Sapsucker, and Three-toed Woodpecker. The left-hand segment drops down to Rock Creek in order to climb up the ridge to the south through dense conifers, mainly lodgepole at first.

Summit County, Vail Pass/Shrine Pass, Red Sandstone Road

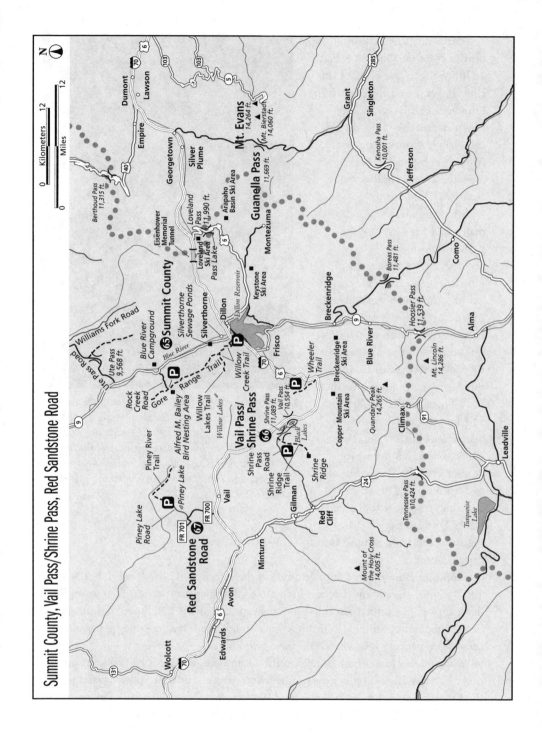

N

Kilometers
0   12

Miles
0   12

Williams Fork Road

Ute Pass Road

Berthoud Pass
11,315 ft.

Empire

Dumont

Lawson

Georgetown

Silver
Plume

Eisenhower
Memorial
Tunnel

Loveland
Pass
11,990 ft.

Loveland
Ski Area

Mt. Evans
14,264 ft.

Mt. Bierstadt
14,060 ft.

Arapaho
Basin Ski Area

Guanella Pass
11,669 ft.

Grant

Singleton

Kenosha Pass
10,001 ft.

Jefferson

Ute Pass
9,568 ft.

Blue River
Campground

Summit County

Silverthorne
Sewage Ponds

Silverthorne

Blue River

Dillon

Pass Lake

Dillon Reservoir

Keystone
Ski Area

Montezuma

Boreas Pass
11,481 ft.

Como

Rock
Creek
Road

Gore
Range Trail

Willow
Lakes Trail

Willow Lakes

Willow
Creek Trail

Frisco

Breckenridge

Wheeler
Trail

Hoosier Pass
11,539 ft.

Alma

Piney River
Trail

Alfred M. Bailey
Bird Nesting Area

Vail Pass/
Shrine Pass

Shrine Pass
11,089 ft.

Vail Pass
10,554 ft.

Breckenridge
Ski Area

Blue River

Mt. Lincoln
14,286 ft.

Piney Lake
Road

Piney Lake

FR 701

FR 700

Red Sandstone
Road

Vail

Shrine
Pass
Road

Shrine Pass
Ridge Trail

Gilman

Black
Lakes

Shrine
Ridge

Copper Mountain
Ski Area

Quandary Peak
14,265 ft.

Climax

Minturn

Red
Cliff

Tennessee Pass
10,424 ft.

Mount of
the Holy Cross
14,005 ft.

Turquoise
Lake

Leadville

Wolcott

Edwards

Avon

The other trail choice follows an old road up the valley, past the EAGLES NEST WILDERNESS sign and the Gore Range Trail to a large willow-filled stream bottom (1.5 miles). Some years ago, the Rocky Mountain Bird Observatory (RMBO) operated a research site and banding station, centered on the stream bottom, dubbed the *Alfred M. Bailey Nesting Area* (IBA). Dr. Bailey photographed nesting Fox Sparrows here in 1964. The site achieved IBA status because of the RMBO research and because the site contains six different representative habitats within a small area. RMBO picked its logo from the MacGillivray's Warblers they found here. Roam through here to look for species that specialize in willow carrs, spruce/fir, lodgepole pine, aspen, and marshy bogs and beaver ponds.

A year-round road, on the right off Highway 9, 9.5 miles from the sewage ponds (11.5 miles from Annie Street), *Ute Pass* has views as spectacular as any Colorado highway, and few people know about it. The craggy peaks of the Eagles Nest Wilderness dominate the western skyline—you'll know you're in Colorado. Before the view, look for Brewer's Sparrow in the sagebrush and rabbitbrush (in June studded with blue lupine and red paintbrush) and for Golden Eagles cruising overhead. Drive 3+ miles to the Forest Service boundary and 2 more to the top of the pass (9,568 feet). Stop at pull-offs for conifer birds and aspen species such as Red-naped Sapsucker, Hairy and Downy Woodpeckers, and Mountain Bluebird.

At the top, which is marked by a cattle guard, a trail goes right through deep forest (hike in summer, snowshoe in winter)—look for it at the end of the parking lot farthest from the cattle guard. The trail climbs briskly uphill via switchbacks through a dense forest of spruce/fir and lodgepole pine with an understory of myrtle whortleberry and twinberry. Ruby-crowned Kinglets and Pine Grosbeaks warble from the spruces; within the first mile, patches of dead trees host Three-toed and Hairy Woodpeckers and flickers. The trail levels off in a mile, above a meadow with a spectacular view of the Eagles Nest Wilderness. If you press on, it drops downhill through a forest with woodpeckers and spruce/fir birds, then turns back and up to climb above timberline on Ute Peak (12,303 feet), 1.5 more miles with a 2,700-foot elevation gain.

You can drive over Ute Pass and north to Williams Fork Reservoir; the inlet sometimes has rewarding willow species such as Willow Flycatcher and Swainson's Thrush.

U.S. Highway 6 over *Loveland Pass* traverses tundra habitat with possible rosy-finches and ptarmigan. The high-altitude *Atlas* block here counted only thirty-two breeders. In summer visitors can hike in either direction from the summit (11,990 feet). Going west (right if coming from the Denver direction) provides more habitat for ptarmigan—a long shot, but possible.

West below the summit a half mile, *Pass Lake* (summer), on the right, may tempt you. Cliffs around this mountain tarn sometimes attract Brown-capped

Rosy-Finches to feed. Other possibilities are Green-winged Teal, American Pipit, and White-crowned Sparrow. Farther down the pass—3 miles or so—stop at the third hairpin turn; a big willow carr hosts nesting Wilson's Warblers.

South from Breckenridge, Highway 9 climbs *Hoosier Pass,* a good spot in summer for spruce/fir species. At 11,539 feet Hoosier lies a couple of hundred feet below timberline. Park at the top and look for high-mountain spruce/fir birds such as kinglets, juncos, and Pine Grosbeak. Above timberline it's possible, though unlikely, to find White-tailed Ptarmigan.

Summit County has many national forest trails where you can find high-mountain specialties. *Willow Creek Trail* (year-round—skis or snowshoes in winter) passes through mountain meadows and lodgepole/aspen into a vast willow bottom along South Willow Creek (3 miles). (In winter, go *no farther* up the valley than the willow bottoms in order to avoid avalanche chutes.) The trail presents everything from Green-winged Teal, Sora, and Lincoln's Sparrow (0.5 mile, 200 feet below the trail, in a willow-ringed pond) to Red-naped Sapsucker, three nuthatches (Pygmy Nuthatches use lodgepole pines here), Ruby-crowned Kinglet, Wilson's Warbler, Green-tailed Towhee, and Red Crossbill.

From Highway 9 in Silverthorne, at the traffic light at Wildernest/Rainbow Drive, turn west onto Wildernest Drive, cross the Blue River, turn right on Adams and then left immediately onto Royal Buffalo Drive. Up the hillside about a mile, Royal Buffalo bears left, but keep right (straight) on Lord Gore Road and turn right at a T intersection onto Royal Red Bird Road. In a quarter mile (where Royal Red Bird turns left), go left into the lot for the Willow Creek trailhead.

The *Wheeler Trail* (summer), a steep challenge across I–70 from Copper Mountain, climbs 2,500 feet to timberline, in 4 miles. Only when going west on I–70 can you reach the trailhead, from the Scenic Area between Officers Gulch and the Copper turnoff. (If you're staying at Copper, go east on I–70 to Officers Gulch and turn around.) The trail traverses open forests where birders can find spruce/fir birds, including, if you're really lucky, Dusky Grouse (I once stepped on one there while working on the *Colorado Breeding Bird Atlas;* we found fifty-eight species in the block).

DeLorme grid: Blue River, p. 38 C2, B1; Ute Pass, p. 38 B1-2; Loveland Pass, p. 38 C2-3; Hoosier Pass, p. 48 A2-3, B2-3; Willow Creek Trail, p. 38 C2; Gore Range Trail, p. 38 C1.
Elevation: 9,000 to 13,000 feet.
Hazards: Altitude, sudden storms (lightning in summer, blizzards in winter), avalanche chutes in winter.

Nearest food, gas, lodging: Breckenridge, Dillon, Silverthorne, Frisco, Copper Mountain, Keystone.
Camping: Forest Service operates several campgrounds.
For more information: USDA Forest Service, 680 River Parkway, Silverthorne, CO 80498; (970) 468-5400; www.fs.fed.us/r2/whiteriver.

66 Vail Pass/Shrine Pass

Habitats: Spruce/fir, montane grassland, willow carr, alpine.

Specialty birds: *Summer:* Broad-tailed and Rufous Hummingbirds, Olive-sided and Hammond's Flycatchers, Gray Jay, Mountain Bluebird, Townsend's Solitaire, Hermit Thrush, Cassin's Finch, Red Crossbill.

Best times to bird: June to September.

About this site

Spectacular vistas of the Gore Range (north), Ten-Mile Range (east), and Mount of the Holy Cross (west) make this somewhat rough dirt road a pleasure. Spruce/fir birds sing and swoop through incomparable mountain scenery. The road often doesn't open until July 1—check with the Forest Service before you try it.

Directions

Take I–70 to the summit of Vail Pass (11 miles west of Frisco, 10 miles east of Vail).

The birding

At the top of Vail Pass (10,666 feet; exit 190), exit right and go left over the bridge (from Frisco) or right (from Vail). On the right a frontage road parallels I–70; drive

The Shrine Pass trail traverses high-mountain meadows and spruce/fir copses on a 2.5-mile route to timberline on Shrine Ridge.

down 2 miles to Black Lakes. Look and listen for Yellow-rumped Warbler, Dark-eyed Junco, Pine Grosbeak, and Cassin's Finch; abundant Lincoln's and White-crowned Sparrows chorus vigorously from willows that surround the lake.

Go back up and go right, up a dirt road (straight ahead you can use the highway rest stop). This rough road, to Shrine Pass (11,089 feet; named for its views of Mount Holy Cross), starts you on scenic bird stops. Spruce/fir grow in scattered copses with open meadows that offer views across the valley and up to the peaks. Stop wherever you hear or see something tempting. Birds breeding along the road include Hammond's Flycatcher and Pine Grosbeak.

At Shrine Pass summit (3 miles), stop at the parking area for a 2-mile trail hike to *Shrine Ridge*. The trail threads through willow thickets, spruce/fir woodlands, and mountain meadows to the ridgetop. Great wildflowers—penstemon, paintbrush, elephantella, and arnica—festoon the mountain with blue, red, pink, and yellow flowers. You'll also find willow carr and spruce/fir birds. The ridge, barely above timberline at 11,977 feet, provides more terrific mountain views and will reward you with a few American Pipits but not the other alpine species.

Back at the car you can either return to Vail Pass or go down the rough road (okay for passenger cars, but use low gears) to Red Cliff. At Red Cliff, U.S. Highway 24 goes south to Leadville or north to Minturn, I–70, Vail, and Eagle.

DeLorme grid: P. 38 D1.

Elevation: 10,500 to 12,000 feet.

Hazards: Altitude, sudden storms, drop in temperature, rough road.

Nearest food, gas, lodging: Summit County, Vail.

Camping: Yes.

For more information: U.S. Forest Service, 24747 U.S. Highway 24, Minturn, CO 81645; (970) 827-5715; www.fs.fed.us/r2/whiteriver.

67 Red Sandstone Road 🔾⊛

Habitats: Lodgepole, spruce/fir, aspen, montane shrub, montane meadow.

Specialty birds: *Resident:* American Three-toed Woodpecker.

Best time to bird: Summer.

About this site

Three-toed Woodpeckers have found congenial territory along Red Sandstone Road. As you scan the mountains around Vail, you'll see lots of dead lodgepole pines, their rust-colored needles contrasting with the deep green of healthy lodge-poles and lighter green of aspens. A borer beetle has attacked many lodgepoles, and during the first year or two of infestation, woodpeckers of several species are drawn here because of it. Three-toeds, quietest of the montane woodpeckers, tap quietly on the trees, and vocalize only rarely. Stop and listen for quiet rapping as they calmly seek beetles, often at eye level. Hairy Woodpecker (noisier and superficially similar in plumage) and Northern Flicker frequent the same stands of dying trees. The lodgepole-pine beetle has created massive stands of dead and dying trees throughout the mountains. American Three-toed Woodpeckers reap the bonanza, and birders might find them in stands of dying or recently dead lodgepoles. Locations vary from year to year.

Directions

From exit 176 off I–70 (the middle Vail exit), go around the traffic circle and down-valley (westerly) 1 mile; turn right on Red Sandstone Road.

The birding

Red Sandstone Road rises quickly out of Vail Valley into a series of montane habitats and a potpourri of birds. At 0.7 mile stay straight on Forest Road 700 (don't turn right on the hairpin). Within 2 miles you enter conifer habitat, and here you can start looking for woodpeckers. Look particularly for trees that have both green and rust needles; Three-toeds seem to prefer these. We found two the third time we stopped.

At 2.7 miles Forest Road 700 bends right, to Lost Lake. Consider walking instead of driving the first quarter mile: In the first patch of dying conifers up this rough road, observers found Three-toed Woodpeckers in 2005. This road soon becomes rutty, rocky, and bumpy, so return to the junction and go left on Forest Road 701. At a fork—road numbers change on the map, but not on signs—*Lost Lake Trail* goes through thick timber, mainly (healthy) lodgepole pines with an understory of blueberry bushes 6 inches high. As lodgepole stands go, this has a few birds, but other habitats yield more.

Piney Lake Road (Forest Road 701) leads off to the left through wooded glades and open meadows that provide views of wilderness peaks. At 1.5 miles the road skirts high above a string of beaver ponds where you can look down on Green-winged Teal, Mallard, Spotted Sandpiper, Willow Flycatcher, and Wilson's Warbler. The road enters mixed conifers of pine, spruce, and fir. Watch out: It's slippery when wet.

Back at the fork, follow the signs to *Piney Lake.* With the habitat variety here, you can encounter

Red Sandstone Road leads to Piney Lake and an easy trail into the Eagles Nest Wilderness.

most montane species before you reach Piney Lake. You might list Broad-tailed and Rufous Hummingbirds, Red-naped Sapsucker, Cordilleran and Willow Fly-catchers, Violet-green, Tree, and Cliff Swallows, Gray and Steller's Jays, Common Raven, Red-breasted Nuthatch, Brown Creeper, American Dipper (a nest, inactive by midsummer, 0.9 mile beyond the Lost Lake Road), Townsend's Solitaire, Hermit Thrush, Western Tanager, Pine Grosbeak, and Red Crossbill.

At Piney Lake, park just before the ranch gate (restaurant, boat rentals) and walk along the trail that leads into Eagles Nest Wilderness—up a broad flat valley toward the precipitous mountains of the Gore Range (Mount Powell on the left, and eighteen peaks named C to T in the center and right). The trail leads through montane meadows filled with hummingbirds, willow carrs with Lincoln's and White-crowned Sparrows and Wilson's Warbler, aspen groves with swallows and Warbling Vireo, and conifers with woodpeckers, thrushes, chickadees, and nuthatches.

DeLorme grid: P. 37 C6.

Elevation: 8,200 to 9,300 feet.

Hazards: Road slippery when wet; side roads mainly for four-wheel-drive vehicles.

Nearest food, gas, lodging: Vail; food and lodging at Piney Lake.

Camping: Informal camping along the road.

For more information: Holy Cross Ranger District, White River National Forest, 24747 U.S. Highway 24, Minturn, CO 81645; (970) 827-5715; www.fs.fed.us/r2/whiteriver.

Habitats: Foothills riparian, montane meadow, spruce/fir, aspen.

Specialty birds: *Summer:* Broad-tailed, Rufous, and Black-chinned Hummingbirds,

Red-naped Sapsucker, Cordilleran and Willow Flycatchers, American Dipper, Western Tanager, Savannah and Fox Sparrows.

Best time to bird: Summer.

About this site

East Brush Creek attracts an impressive variety of birds because of its many habitats. Different seasons produce different surprises.

Directions

Take exit 147 off I–70 into Eagle; at the traffic circle (0.3 mile) go right, then take the first left onto Capitol; in 0.7 mile go left at the stop sign onto Brush Creek Road (County Road 307) and right in another 0.7 mile to stay on it.

The birding

The road traverses a broad valley along tall willow wetlands spotted with tall cottonwoods. Stop at willow patches (where the shoulder provides enough room) to

PHOTO © WILLIAM EDEN

A quarter will fit over the top of a Broad-tailed Hummingbird's nest.

find Cordilleran and Willow Flycatchers and Savannah and Song Sparrows. A feeder attracts an astonishing mass of hummingbirds. Patches of tall scrub oak succeed the willows, and you might find Williamson's Sapsucker, Green-tailed Towhee, and Lazuli Bunting.

The road enters *Sylvan Lake State Park* (9 miles); for birders, the two roads through the park offer more potential than the lake itself (more attractive to anglers). At the Y intersection, go left up East Brush Creek, the less-traveled road, with several pull-offs (no trails). Stop to sample birds in the stream bottom dominated by tall narrow-leaf cottonwoods; alders, aspens, willows, chokecherries, currants, and hawthorns form a lush understory. Here you can find Red-naped Sapsucker and American Dipper. In 3 miles the road crosses the stream and winds for a mile through extensive aspens to the park boundary (the park rents four yurts here for overnight stays). The road opens out into Yeoman Park, a broad willow-filled valley with a Forest Service campground in conifers on the right. Check these for spruce/fir species, and walk the half-mile Discovery Trail (wheelchair-accessible) by turning into campground Loop A.

Forest Road 418 (rough) climbs up through splendid examples of the birds and habitats of the central Rockies to Fulford, an old mining town now composed of summer homes, some old and some new.

Back at the Y intersection, the right fork traverses a wider valley through meadows and cottonwoods with a shrubby understory. In addition to the species listed above, you might find American Kestrel, Western Tanager, and Fox Sparrow. Field workers for RMBO have found nesting Northern Pygmy- and Boreal Owls along these roads, but chances of seeing them are slim.

Sylvan Lake, at the upper end of the park, existed as a mink farm in the 1930s and 1940s, but the proprietor couldn't pay his taxes so it came to the government. The road beyond (Forest Road 400), to Crooked Creek Pass (9,995 feet), doesn't present new habitat although at the top of the pass you might find Pine Grosbeak. Therefore, turn around unless you want to make a round-trip on a rough road to Basalt and Glenwood Springs.

DeLorme grid: P. 36 C3, D3-4.
Elevation: 6,600 to 9,995 feet.
Nearest food, gas, lodging: Eagle.
Camping: Yes.
For more information: Sylvan Lake State Park, P.O. Box 1475, Eagle, CO 81631; (970) 328-2021; www.parks.state.co.us. U.S. Forest Service, 125 West 5th Street, Eagle, CO 81631; (970) 328-6388; www.fs.fed.us/r2/whiteriver.

Habitats: Pinyon/juniper, ponderosa, foothills riparian, aspen, spruce/fir, alpine.

Specialty birds: *Resident:* Lewis's Wood-

pecker, Pinyon Jay, Pine Grosbeak. *Summer:* Common Merganser.

Best times to bird: Spring, summer, fall.

About this site

Below the towering Sawatch Range, Buena Vista and Leadville habitats range from pinyon/juniper to alpine. Colorado's highest mountains, full of surveying and mining history, provide a striking backdrop for birding from valley to peak top. The Arkansas River rises northeast of Leadville on Fremont Pass (Highway 91). Roads penetrate most valleys between Buena Vista and Leadville; we recommend four valleys with better birding; all four roads close in winter.

Directions

US 24 runs from Leadville to Buena Vista, and US 285 south from there.

The birding

Pinyon/juniper: The northwest side of Buena Vista itself has, for the moment, P/J habitat that attracts the usual species including Pinyon Jay. Turn left a half mile north of the Main Street traffic light onto Crossman Avenue (look in tall cottonwoods for Lewis's Woodpecker) and right at a subdivision sign. If the pinyons have a good cone crop, Pinyon Jays will cruise in to feed. The road curves around to a promontory where you can look at *Ice Lake* and the ducks that stop here. Surrounded by subdivided lots, this lake probably has a less birdy future.

Two miles south of Buena Vista, US 24 joins US 285 and turns east; 1 mile after it crosses the Arkansas River, County Road 304, on the left, leads to *Collegiate Peaks Overlook*. Besides striking views of the peaks that rise across the valley, this overlook sits in pinyon/juniper habitat; Road 304 continues through similar habitat. In a mile, stop at the Fourmile Trailhead for more P/J birds.

Another road with good P/J, *County Road 321* starts off West Main Street, 0.8 mile west of US 24. Drive through grassland and one of the few accessible ponderosa pine woodlands in the area, to a productive P/J forest 7 miles from Buena Vista; the road drops down to County Road 162 at Mount Princeton Hot Springs.

Montane valleys: Several roads penetrate the steep-sided valleys of the Sawatch peaks; four offer good birding. County Road 162, reachable either from Road 321 (see above) or by driving south 4.5 miles on US 285 from its intersection with US 24 (2 miles south of Buena Vista), climbs up *Chalk Creek Valley*. The road has several turnoffs and trailheads. Up the road 2.4 miles from the hot springs, a trail winds through pinyon/juniper to the edge of the Chalk Cliffs. Two miles farther, the rough 1-mile trail to Agnes Vaille Falls passes through an open ponderosa woodland before it starts its rocky climb to the falls. The pavement ends in another 2.5 miles, and Forest Road 292, on the right, crosses Chalk Creek into mid-elevation willow carrs and aspen groves. In 5 miles the main road reaches picturesque St. Elmo, an old mining town amid a dense spruce/fir forest (Pine Grosbeak). Beyond there, it climbs to Hancock, just below timberline, where a trail heads to Hancock Lakes, above timberline at 11,700 feet.

Hook up to the Cottonwood Pass road, County Road 306, by going west on Buena Vista's West Main Street. As mentioned under Gunnison (Site 70), the 12,126-foot summit provides the most interesting birding, with a possibility of White-tailed Ptarmigan.

A third road, County Road 390 up *Clear Creek,* has less traffic and similar habitats to the others but a rougher road. The upper end of Clear Creek Reservoir (within the first mile) might have a few ducks (Common Merganser, Mallard) and gulls (California), and you can walk down to the willows for Wilson's Warbler and Lincoln's Sparrow. From there the road passes through aspen and spruce/fir to two

One of four highways that cross the Continental Divide from the Arkansas River to the Gunnison River Drainage, Independence Pass rises over 12,000 feet.

ghost towns, Vicksburg and Winfield, with summer museums, that reward the persistent driver.

Closed in winter, Highway 82, from Twin Lakes to Aspen, crosses the Continental Divide at *Independence Pass* (12,095 feet). It goes through a variety of habitats; diligent exploration at the top, a few hundred feet above timberline, might yield ptarmigan, pipits, and rosy-finches. This description covers the Twin Lakes side; see the section on Aspen for the west side.

Stop at any wide place. A trail on the left, 14.5 miles from the Twin Lakes turnoff, climbs up LaPlata Peak (14,336 feet); birders can follow it a short way to find aspen and spruce/fir birds. Nineteen miles from the turnoff to Twin Lakes, just as the highway makes its first hairpin turn, park on the right for the North Lake Fork Trailhead. Its first half mile parallels an extensive willow carr with breeding Wilson's Warblers and White-crowned and Lincoln's Sparrows. It climbs to montane meadows and spruce/fir, and the birds of those habitats (Mountain Bluebird, Red-breasted Nuthatch, Ruby-crowned Kinglet, Hermit Thrush, Yellow-rumped Warbler, and Pine Grosbeak).

The road climbs up from North Lake Fork 4.5 miles to the summit—a parking lot opens to a well-used trail on the left. Hike prudently up here: The high altitude causes shortness of breath even for high-country residents. The trail gently climbs a ridge to 12,812 feet. American Pipits constantly flutter up from the tundra, and farther on, ptarmigan and rosy-finches are possible. A trek across the highway to the north—a steeper climb—has a better potential for the latter species, both because fewer people use the trail and because it climbs near cliffs that rosy-finches favor. For even a chance of finding these species, plan on up to 5 miles of hiking and at least two to four hours.

DeLorme grid: Buena Vista, P. 60 B1; Collegiate Peaks Overlook, p. 60 B2; Chalk Creek, p. 60 C1, p. 59 C7; Cottonwood Pass, p. 60 B1, p. 59 B6-7; Clear Creek, p. 47 D7, p. 59 A6; Independence Pass, p. 47 D5-7.

Elevation: 8,000 to 12,812 feet.

Hazards: Altitude, weather.

Nearest food, gas, lodging: Leadville, Buena Vista, Salida; lodging and food at Twin Lakes and Chalk Creek.

Camping: Yes.

For more information: U.S. Forest Service, 2015 North Poplar, Leadville, CO 80461; (719) 486-0749. U.S. Forest Service, 325 West Rainbow Boulevard, Salida, CO 81201; (719) 539-3591; www.fs.fed.us/r2/psicc.

70 Gunnison

Habitats: Montane riparian, sagebrush, aspen, spruce/fir.

Specialty birds: *Resident:* Gunnison Sage-Grouse. *Migrant:* Warblers, swallows. *Winter:* Rosy-finches.

Best times to bird: Spring and summer.

About this site

Sagebrush hills surround Gunnison, the epicenter of the Gunnison Sage-Grouse. Riparian trails near the city provide riverside birding, and two mountain passes to the north (out of Crested Butte) lift you into aspen and conifer forests.

In winter, feeders around the city collect rosy-finches by the hundreds—all three species, though Brown-capped predominate.

The birding

Gunnison Sage-Grouse occur in many parts of the Gunnison Basin, especially the Gunnison Sage-Grouse lek, aka Waunita lek.

Riparian: On either side of U.S. Highway 50 on the east side of Gunnison, city parks welcome visitors. For one pleasant riparian walk, turn south on Teller, on the west side of Jorgensen Park; in 3 blocks turn left on San Juan and then quickly right on a dirt road with a sign for *W Mountain Trail.* Park at the gate and use the walk-through; when the road turns left, go straight ahead to another walk-through in the fence, into the field. Follow the trail over an irrigation ditch, through hay-fields, and along cottonwood and willow-lined Tomichi Creek for about a mile. Fall migrants include Mallard, Northern Pintail, Osprey, Swainson's Hawk, Logger-head Shrike, Marsh Wren, Orange-crowned, Virginia's, and Yellow-rumped Warblers, Green-tailed Towhee, and Brewer's and Lincoln's Sparrows.

To reach the most productive riparian site, *Neversink Trail,* measure 5.5 miles west on US 50 from its midtown intersection with Highway 135; park in the lot on the left. Tall cottonwoods, thick riparian shrubs including willows, dogwood, and alders, with adjacent wet fields and sagebrush, attract many montane riparian species.

A half mile farther west on US 50, a road on the right leads, in 0.5 mile, to *Gunnison SWA,* another riparian stream bottom. A colony of Gunnison prairie dogs lives just below an interpretive sign as you enter the SWA.

Neversink and Gunnison SWA have similar birds. Breeders in both include Cinnamon Teal, Common Merganser, Red-tailed and Swainson's Hawks, Common Nighthawk, Red-naped Sapsucker, Western Wood-Pewee, Violet-Green, Tree, and Cliff Swallows, Black-headed Grosbeak, Pine Siskin, Yellow-headed and Brewer's Blackbirds, and Bullock's Oriole. Neversink has Gray Catbird, Fox and Song

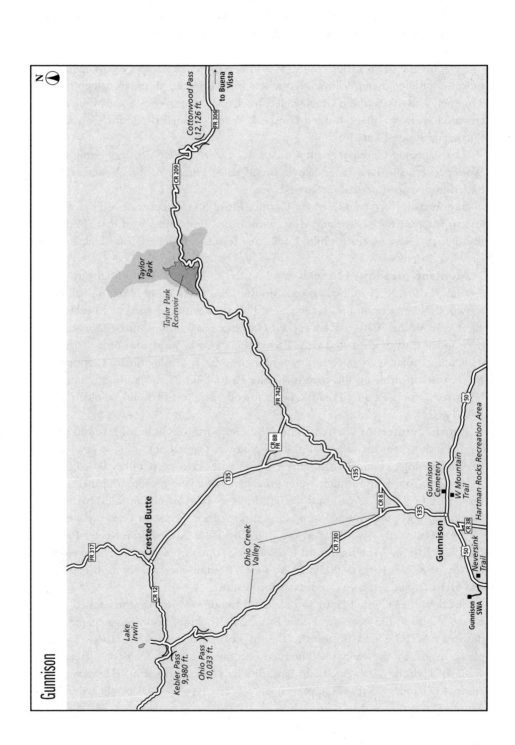

Sparrows, Lazuli Bunting, and even Bobolink (look in flooded fields before the turnoff). Migrants might include Rock Wren, Ruby-crowned Kinglet, Mac-Gillivray's and Wilson's Warblers, Northern Waterthrush, Western Tanager, and Cassin's Finch.

SWA breeders also include Wilson's Snipe, Wilson's Phalarope, Red-naped Sapsucker, Cordilleran and Willow Flycatchers, Say's Phoebe, Mountain Bluebird, Sage Thrasher, Wilson's Warbler, Green-tailed Towhee, Brewer's, Vesper, and White-crowned Sparrows, Black-headed Grosbeak, Yellow-headed Blackbird, Cassin's Finch, and Pine Siskin.

The *Gunnison Cemetery,* about a mile east of town on US 50, has nesting Lewis's Woodpeckers; also Red-tailed Hawk, Broad-tailed Hummingbird, Western Kingbird, and perhaps Eurasian Collared-Dove.

Sagebrush: Turn off US 50 on County Road 38, 2 miles west of Highway 135 to *Hartman Rocks Recreation Area,* with several trails and a road that climbs through extensive sagebrush hills. Look for Mountain Bluebird, Sage Thrasher, and Brewer's Sparrow.

Montane meadow: Hayfields grow north of Gunnison along Highway 135; County Road 730 (4 miles, left) goes up the *Ohio Creek valley,* alongside tall cottonwoods where Swainson's Hawks nest. This road achieved notoriety because, for eight years in the 1970s, a Red-backed Hawk (a *Buteo* of the Andes) summered here and at least twice mated with a Swainson's Hawk. Suspicious of its origin, state and national records committees refused to list it as a legitimate U.S. occurrence. You can drive up this road to Kebler Pass (about 25 miles) or return to Highway 135 on County Road 8. Look for other raptors including Golden and Bald Eagles.

Aspen/conifer: At Crested Butte (48 miles north of Gunnison), an old mining, new ski town that calls itself the "Wildflower Capital of Colorado," two roads head to the high country. Turn left on White Rock Avenue (County Road 12) to *Kebler Pass.* You drive through aspen groves and montane meadows up to spruce/fir. In 7 miles a road on the right leads to *Lake Irwin* (2.5 miles), with a picnic area and campground. Stop along this road for spruce/fir birds including Gray Jay, Ruby-crowned Kinglet, and Pine Grosbeak. Back on the Kebler Pass road, in a half mile, the road from Ohio Creek comes in (see above), just below the top of Kebler Pass (10,003 feet). You can continue over the top into Paonia and Delta (aspen, scrub oak, montane shrublands).

For the other Crested Butte ramble, go through town to Mount Crested Butte, where Highway 135 becomes Forest Road 317. It climbs up through splendid flower fields and willow bottoms to the spruce/fir forests of *Schofield Pass.* Don't plan a trip down the west side: The road becomes too rough for passenger cars.

Taylor Park and *Cottonwood Pass* have different habitats. Turn off Highway 135 at Almont (11 miles north of Gunnison) onto Forest Road 742. It parallels the Taylor

River (Steller's Jay and American Dipper likely) to Taylor Park, a huge sagebrush-filled mountain park with a large reservoir at one end. Forest Road 209, to Cottonwood Pass, goes right 3 miles after you climb over the dam. The road offers few incentives for birders until the top (12,126 feet), where you might possibly find American Pipit and White-tailed Ptarmigan.

DeLorme grid: P. 58 D1-2; Kebler Pass, p. 58 B1; Cottonwood Pass, p. 58 C3-4, p.59 B4-7.

Elevation: 7,700 to 12,500 feet.

Hazards: Altitude, sudden storms.

Nearest food, gas, lodging: Gunnison, Crested Butte.

Camping: Forest Service campgrounds.

For more information: Gunnison District Ranger, 216 North Colorado, Gunnison, CO 81230; (970) 641-0471; www.fs.fed.us/r2/gmug.

PHOTO © WENDY SHATTIL/BOB ROZINSKI

A Steller's Jay climbs a pine tree "as if it were a spiral staircase, starting down low and hopping upwards from branch to branch around the trunk."—Roger Tory Peterson, 1941

Habitats: Wet meadow, sagebrush.
Specialty bird: Gunnison Sage-Grouse.

Best times to bird: March 30 to May 15.

About this site

The newly discovered species, Gunnison Sage-Grouse, exists tenuously in south-western Colorado (a tiny contingent lives in southeastern Utah). Small and diminishing numbers make it a candidate for federal and state listing as a threatened species; even if not listed by either agency, its population remains sensitive, and we as birders must recognize the importance of protecting the species from disturbance by us.

A consortium of state, federal, and nonprofit organizations provides this viewing site for use by the birding public. Strict rules govern its use in order to protect the birds that use this lek. They include:

• **Arrive** a half hour before dawn.
• **Stay** until the birds leave the lek, usually three hours after sunrise.
• **Stay in your car,** and *do not* get out at all (no morning coffee).
• Keep **headlights off;** no camera flashes.

Following the special instructions will enhance the experience for all birders at the viewing blind for the Gunnison Sage-Grouse lek.

Please honor these strictures so that after you view the birds, others can also enjoy the performance.

Directions

From Gunnison, drive 16 miles east on US 50; turn north (left) on County Road 887 to a viewing blind and parking area in 0.5 mile. From the east, turn right on County Road 887 0.5 mile west of Doyleville. On US 50, look for the signs to "Waunita Hot Springs."

The birding

From year to year the grouse move their dancing grounds to different parts of this high mountain meadow. In 2005 they used an area about 0.25 mile long, a third of a mile distant over a fence that bisects the broad meadow in front of the blind. The grouse perform their extraordinary dance for a two-month stint during what the calendar calls spring. Males spread their banded tails in a fan, puff up air sacs contained in a big white-feathered beardlike pouch, and march back and forth. The presence of a female stirs them to more dramatic strutting. The birds seem oblivious to birders in the blind, as long as we don't move about. When they conclude the morning performance, many fly right over the blind.

Bring a scope to accommodate your distance from the birds. We also recommend that you skip morning coffee because of the strict stay-in-your-car or stay-in-the-blind rules. Please respect these standards; researchers and the Division of Wildlife generously share this location with the public—let's not jeopardize their trust. Despite the restraint of viewers so far (the viewing site opened in 2000), grouse numbers at this site have diminished over the years.

You can see other birds from the viewing site: In early May a list of fifteen included Mallard, Swainson's Hawk, Horned Lark, Common Raven, Ruby-crowned Kinglet, Western Meadowlark, Song Sparrow, and Brewer's and Red-winged Blackbirds. A Gunnison prairie dog crept up in front of the blind and began to munch the new leaves of a sagebrush 10 feet away. (This small prairie dog hibernates and emerges in April.)

Gunnison has one of the coldest winter (and spring) climates in Colorado. Besides your scope, bring all the warm clothes you can muster, including something to keep your feet toasty.

In July and August you can find family groups of Sage-Grouse on Gunnison-area roads. Try County Road 38 (Gunnison) 5 to 8 miles south of town.

DeLorme grid: p. 69 A5.

Elevation: 8,100 feet.

Hazards: Cold, cold, cold.

Nearest food, gas, lodging: Gunnison.

Camping: No.

For more information: Sisk-a-dee Environmental Organization, 323 North Wisconsin Street, Gunnison, CO 81230; www.siskadee.org, http://www.western.edu/bio/young/gunnsg/gunnsg.htm.

72 Aspen Area W⊕

Habitats: Wetlands, willow carr, aspen, montane grassland, spruce/fir.

Specialty birds: *Resident:* Gray Jay, Red-breasted Nuthatch, Brown Creeper, American Dipper, Red Crossbill. *Summer:* Williamson's Sapsucker, Olive-sided and Willow Flycatchers, Golden-crowned Kinglet, Orange-crowned and MacGillivray's Warblers, Fox Sparrow. *Winter:* Rosy-finches.

Best time to bird: Summer.

About this site

Aspen visitors have a wide choice of places to find western birds, from a nature center in town to spectacular scenic drives and hikes in White River National Forest. Skiers see typical ski-area birds on the downhill slopes (Snowmass has feeders at Coney Glade, with rosy-finches), and cross-country enthusiasts can find winter birds along backcountry trails. Recreational trails run the length of urban Aspen, from Woody Creek to Difficult Campground, generally following the Roaring Fork River. The following directions assume summer visitation unless otherwise indicated.

The birding

Willow-lined streamsides in all the sites mentioned below feature a suite of common species: Orange-crowned and MacGillivray's Warblers and Lincoln's, Fox, and Song Sparrows.

The *Aspen Center for Environmental Science (ACES)* owns thirty acres right in Aspen. Turn north on Mill Street (by the Jerome Hotel); in 1 block, at a three-way stop, turn left on Puppy Smith Street and drive into the center. ACES's trails, open to the public, wander through wetlands, a pond, and the Roaring Fork. The usual streamside species occur here, and sometimes birders find Sora and Virginia Rail. The pond, fed by a warm spring, stays open in winter so that it attracts ducks year-round, although heavy use by ACES classes tends to deter most ducks.

East from Aspen, Highway 82 goes through wetlands and riparian sites; so does a recreational trail that parallels the highway. From the four-way stop sign at the east end of Aspen, where the highway turns left, the *North Star Natural Area* (IBA) is 3.5 miles away. Well protected, with viewing only from the road and trail, this wet meadow and beaver-pond complex attracts such breeding species as Mallard, Cinnamon and Green-winged Teal, American Coot, and Spotted Sandpiper.

Two miles farther, enter the *Difficult Campground,* on the right. Walk the entrance road—it passes a productive wetland: Belted Kingfisher, Red-naped Sapsucker, and Evening Grosbeak are possible. Park in the day-use area, before the official campground entrance. Walk to the stream and cross the bridge. American Dippers use a nest box mounted on the bridge; they time their nesting with the

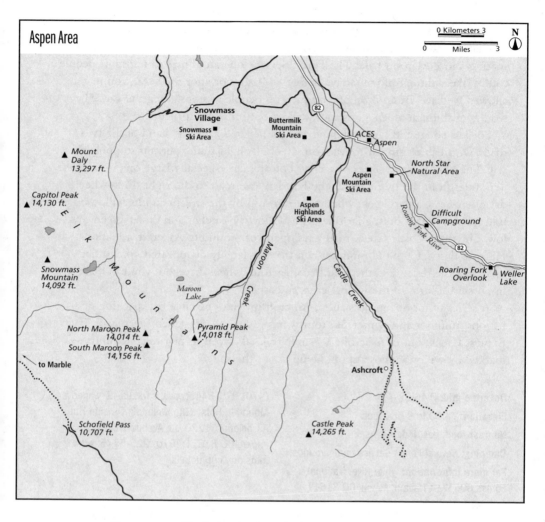

0 Kilometers 3

0   Miles   3

N

Snowmass Village

Snowmass ■
Ski Area

**Buttermilk
Mountain
Ski Area** ■

82

ACES
■ *Aspen*

▲ *Mount
Daly
13,297 ft.*

Aspen ■
Mountain
Ski Area

*North Star
Natural Area*

Capitol Peak
▲ *14,130 ft.*

Aspen ■
Highlands
Ski Area

Roaring Fork River

*Difficult
Campground*

E l k

▲
*Snowmass
Mountain
14,092 ft.*

*Maroon
Lake*

M o u n t a i n s

82

*Roaring Fork
Overlook* ▲ Weller
Lake

*North Maroon Peak
14,014 ft.* ▲

*Pyramid Peak
14,018 ft.* ▲

*South Maroon Peak
14,156 ft.* ▲

Castle Creek

Maroon Creek

→ **to Marble**

Ashcroft ○

*Schofield Pass
10,707 ft.*

*Castle Peak
14,265 ft.* ▲

snow runoff; young usually fledge in June. A short trail goes along the stream in both directions, with the common willow birds, plus Olive-sided Flycatcher. In winter cross-country skiers can look for the few birds that remain among the cottonwoods.

Continuing on Highway 82 for 3 miles, go right at a turnoff marked only by ONE-WAY signs (0.4 mile past Milepost 49). A trail drops to the Roaring Fork and across a bridge. The left fork leads to *Roaring Fork Overlook,* the right to *Weller Lake.* Along the overlook trail, through tall, tall firs and spruces, deep-woods birds breed: Three-toed Woodpecker (maybe), Olive-sided Flycatcher, Red-breasted Nuthatch, Brown Creeper, Ruby-crowned and Golden-crowned Kinglets, and Red Crossbill. The Weller Lake Trail, which climbs up 1 mile via switchbacks, takes you through less imposing trees that have similar birds (Williamson's Sapsucker possible), and Spotted Sandpiper at the lake.

West of Aspen, at the traffic circle, turn left for Castle Creek and *Maroon Creek.* The latter draws huge numbers of visitors to view the *Maroon Bells,* poster peaks soaring above Maroon Lake. The Forest Service operates buses to transport people to the lake, although if you arrive before 8:00 A.M. or after 5:00 P.M., you may be allowed to drive. Buses drop off and pick up people at stops along the way. The road goes through aspen, grasslands, willow bottoms, and spruce/fir.

For less congested bird-watching, try *Castle Creek,* the left-hand of the two roads, with habitat similar to Maroon Creek. Its light traffic permits stopping at will. The road passes a series of willow bottoms, an especially large one in 6 miles. Ten miles from the traffic circle, the Hayden Pass road to the right (four-wheel drive) crosses Castle Creek, where you can stop by the stream and its willows; a trail runs upstream on the far side, with Willow Flycatcher and Violet-green Swallow. The main Castle Creek road stays open year-round to Ashcroft, a National Historic District and old mining town that has largely disappeared. In another mile, past the restaurant, the road becomes four-wheel drive, but you can walk it in pursuit of birds of the willow carrs and aspen.

A series of mountain huts above Ashcroft provides possible backpacking destinations, summer and winter. Ski tours can produce White-tailed Ptarmigan. Try Express Creek, out of Ashcroft: A 5-mile trek takes you to ptarmigan country—marked by willows whose tips poke up above the snow.

DeLorme grid: P. 46 C2-4.

Elevation: 7,900 to 9,550 feet.

Nearest food, gas, lodging: Aspen.

Camping: Several Forest Service campgrounds.

For more information: White River National Forest, 806 West Hallam, Aspen, CO 81611; (970) 925-3445; www.fs.fed.us/r2/whiteriver. Mountain Huts: 10th Mountain Division Hut Association, 1280 Ute Avenue, Suite 21, Aspen, CO 81611; (970) 925-5775; www .huts.org/hut_details.

73 Glenwood Springs Area [W](symbol)

Habitats: Foothills riparian, canyon, wetlands, montane meadow, pinyon/juniper, aspen, spruce/fir.
Specialty birds: *Resident:* Lewis's Woodpecker, Brown Creeper, Pine Grosbeak, Red Crossbill. *Summer:* Band-tailed Pigeon, Black Swift, Purple Martin, Golden-crowned Kinglet, Mountain Bluebird, Virginia's and Orange-crowned Warblers, Western Tanager, Green-tailed Towhee, Brewer's and Lark Sparrows. *Winter:* Barrow's Goldeneye.

Best times to bird: Spring, summer, fall.

About this site

The Roaring Fork Valley south of Glenwood Springs provides convenient access to typical western Colorado habitats amid magnificent mountains. Mount Sopris dominates the valley, though only 12,953 feet high and despite much higher mountains (six 14,000-foot peaks) southwest of Aspen.

The birding

Fourmile Road (summer), past Sunlight Ski Area, rises into aspen and spruce/fir woodlands. From Highway 82 in south Glenwood Springs, turn west on 27th Street, cross the river, and in 1.5 miles, go right at the stop sign. You can stop in some places for foothills riparian species—occasional Band-tailed Pigeons use this area. Purple Martins swoop around the first lift tower at the ski area.

At the ski area (10 miles), bear right on Forest Road 300 through aspen and spruce. Cattle graze this forest and sprawling Fourmile Park, but the habitat improves farther along. Go as far as you can; you'll encounter good samples of Colorado montane habitats. The road crosses a divide in 7 miles and drops into the valley of North Thompson Creek. Look for Purple Martin in the aspen. Spruces have the typical species, including Brown Creeper, Golden-crowned Kinglet, Pine Grosbeak, and Red Crossbill. Along the road, look for dying spruce and pines; Hairy Woodpecker and, potentially, Three-toed Woodpecker pound on the trees. Another outside chance: Northern Pygmy-Owls nest in the spruce.

For P/J and low-altitude species, try **Thompson Creek Road** west of Carbondale. From Highway 82, go 1 mile on Highway 133; turn right on County Road 108 (briefly labeled County Road 106), but bear left across the bridge when Road 106 continues along the river. The road passes through open fields and, after a large ranch, starts, in 2 miles, to climb through excellent pinyon/juniper habitat. (You might try the road to the right [2.8 miles; County Road 125, which meets Fourmile Road—see above] for more P/J birds.) The road crosses sagebrush flats where you can find Mountain Bluebird, Brewer's, Chipping, Lark, and Vesper Sparrows, Green-tailed Towhee, and Western Meadowlark. A Golden Eagle may soar above. At 7.3 miles an unmarked road on the left goes through scrub oak to an

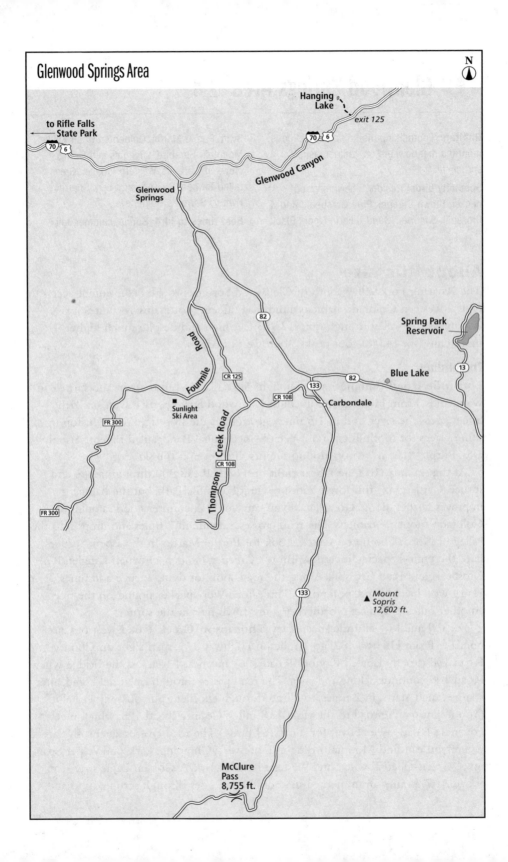

Hanging
Lake

exit 125

to Rifle Falls
State Park

70 6

70 6

Glenwood Canyon

Glenwood
Springs

82

Spring Park
Reservoir

CR 125

82

Blue Lake

13

FR 300

Sunlight
Ski Area

CR 108

133

Carbondale

Thompson
Creek Road

Foumile
Road

CR 108

FR 300

133

Mount
Sopris
12,602 ft.

McClure
Pass
8,755 ft.

informal campground surrounded by tall Douglas-fir trees. At dusk you might encounter Common Poorwill along this spur.

On County Road 108 past the left fork, the panorama features views of the Ragged Mountains. The road turns right, up the canyon of North Thompson Creek and at a cattle guard enters the White River National Forest. From here to a closed gate, 2.5 miles, it traverses deep woods—spruce, aspen, cottonwood—with a dense understory of dogwood, alder, maple, and oak. Foothills riparian birds abound: Olive-sided and Dusky Flycatchers, Steller's Jay, White-breasted Nuthatch, Virginia's and Orange-crowned Warblers, Western Tanager, Black-headed Grosbeak, and Pine Siskin.

Perched above the Roaring Fork Valley amid low hills, **Spring Park Reservoir (**IBA) attracts waterbirds that find few suitable sites among the high mountains all around. To reach it, turn north at El Jebel (County Road 13, off Highway 82 about 9 miles east of Highway 133 at Carbondale). Up the road 3.6 miles, you can stop at a small parking area and, with a scope, look at the birds close to the dam. You can view the water only from the road, which runs along the west side. Likely birds, mostly migrants, include Pied-billed, Eared, Western, and Clark's Grebes, dabbling and diving ducks including Ruddy and Bufflehead, and, in spring, Barrow's Goldeneye. Roadside birds include Mountain Bluebird, Orange-crowned and Yellow-rumped (in migration) Warblers, Spotted and Green-tailed Towhees, and Savannah and Song Sparrows.

Winter birders may find Barrow's Goldeneye and Hooded Merganser at **Blue Lake,** an artificial pond on Highway 82, a mile west of El Jebel.

A drive to **McClure Pass** presents striking views of the mountains that surround this stunning valley. Take Highway 133 through Carbondale; it follows the Crystal River for 22.5 miles, then cuts right. The valley road borders the Crystal up to Marble, an old quarry town that produced marble used on the Tomb of the Unknown Soldier and Lincoln Memorial.

Highway 133 climbs quickly up the pass; try stopping 2.1 miles from the bottom, at a hidden track on the left side of the road, immediately beyond a rock cut. Walk down through the tall aspens for aspen species (lots of Violet-green Swallows). At one time Purple Martins nested here, although recently only one observer has reported them. Over the pass at McClure Campground, 1.7 miles west of the summit (8,755 feet), you have a chance to find aspen and spruce species.

A well-used trail to **Hanging Lake** (IBA), from exit 125 on I-70 in Glenwood Canyon, provides a steep 1-mile hike to see Black Swifts. You can reach the trailhead and return to the interstate *only* in the direction of Glenwood Springs. Though short, the trail is steep: It gains 900 feet in a mile (6,387 to 7,323 feet). It receives heavy use, and during summer days the parking lot may fill up—in which case no more cars may park.

This shouldn't bother Black Swift hunters because you should get to the lake by sunup, before the birds leave to feed. In early morning swifts actively swoop

Exits from I–70 through Glenwood Canyon provide river views where, in winter, you can look for Barrow's Goldeneye.

over the lake and waterfall for terrific views. By the time you go back down for breakfast, you'll find the trail jammed with hikers. Along the trail you may also spot Black-headed Grosbeak and maybe a Peregrine Falcon.

In winter in **Glenwood Canyon,** you can potentially spot Barrow's Goldeneye at any rest stop. Safety requires you to exit to scan for these winter ducks. American Dippers also use the river—you might even see one by the dipper display board at Grizzly Gulch. In summer Band-tailed Pigeons often populate the Noname exit, just east of Glenwood Springs; try it at 9:00 A.M. after you return from Hanging Lake.

DeLorme grid: Fourmile Road, p. 45 A–B 6–7; Thompson Creek, p. 45 A–B7; Spring Park Reservoir and Blue Lake, p. 46 A1; McClure Pass, p. 45 B–C7; Hanging Lake and Glenwood Canyon, p. 35 D7, p. 36 D1.

Elevation: 5,150 to 9,200 feet.

Hazards: Traffic.

Nearest food, gas, lodging: Glenwood Springs, Carbondale.

Camping: Yes.

For more information: White River National Forest, 620 Main Street, Carbondale, CO 81623; (970) 963–2266; www.fs.fed.us/r2/whiteriver.

74 Rifle Falls State Park W◉ $ ♿

Habitats: Waterfall, foothills riparian.

Specialty birds: *Summer:* Black Swift,

Cordilleran Flycatcher, American Dipper.
Winter: Barrow's Goldeneye.

Best times to bird: Summer, dawn or dusk.

About this site

A dusk or dawn trip to Rifle Falls between early June and mid-September offers a good chance to see Black Swift, at probably one of the easiest Colorado sites to view this mysterious bird.

Directions

From exit 90 on I–70 at Rifle, go north on Highway 13 through town (not the truck route) 4 miles to Highway 325. It enters Rifle Gap State Park (a fishing hot spot) in 4 miles and goes up to and turns right on a dam. After County Road 226 (2.8 miles), the road divides two habitats: on the right, a lush riparian stream bottom and on the left, pinyon/juniper. As you enter Rifle Falls State Park, turn right.

The birding

Black Swifts nest behind the three-pronged falls—maybe a 300-yard walk—but the birds normally swoop in and out only at dawn and dusk. See the "Box Cañon" site for a description. During the rest of the day, Rough-winged Swallows swoop around the falls and Lazuli Buntings sing from the tall box-elders. A trail on the left goes to the top of the falls—three overlooks in one-third of a mile—and down via a different route. Signs describe how early settlers harnessed the water power of the falls.

Upstream from the park on Highway 325—about half a mile—a small parking lot on the right sits by a nice riparian area. From the catwalk, look for American Dippers that frequent the braided stream. Upstream on Highway 325 another quarter mile, a series of ponds in the Rifle Fish Hatchery lie on the right. These ponds may remain open in winter and host ten to twenty-five Barrow's Goldeneyes.

Another mile upstream on Highway 325 is Rifle Mountain Park, a delightful riparian area dominated by large blue spruces and sheer cliffs. Expect to hear lots of Cordilleran Flycatcher, Ruby-crowned Kinglet, and Townsend's Solitaire.

DeLorme grid: P. 34 C4.

Elevation: 6,525 feet.

Hazards: Slippery rocks.

Nearest food, gas, lodging: Rifle, Newcastle, Glenwood Springs.

Camping: Yes.

For more information: Rifle Gap State Park, 5775 Highway 325, Rifle, CO 81650; (970) 625-1607; www.parks.state.co.us.

San Luis Valley

The largest "mountain park" in Colorado, the San Luis Valley spans 100 miles north to south and 50 miles east to west. It has an outstanding collection of wetlands at three national wildlife refuges, several State Wildlife Areas, and one Nature Conservancy property. Great Sand Dunes National Park and Preserve and Rio Grande National Forest protect additional habitats, from pinyon/juniper to alpine tundra.

Scenic attributes stand out: The valley, like much of mountain Colorado, excels both in bird-watching and in scenery-watching. Bounded on the east by the towering peaks of the Sangre de Cristo Range (ten 14,000-foot peaks), on the north by Mount Ouray and the Cochetopa Divide, and on the west by the foothills of the San Juan Mountains, the mountain backdrop adds a spectacular dimension to splendid bird-watching. Covering the flat valley floor, greasewood and rabbitbrush provide a shrubby and often monotonous foreground to the mountain views. Scattered cottonwoods (remnants from old farms) host nesting Great Horned Owls. The valley has 230,000 acres of wetlands scattered over its vastness.

Migrating Sandhill Cranes (20,000 to 30,000) use the valley's refuges for month-long stopovers, spring and fall. With them large flocks of Canada and Cackling Geese, Northern Pintail, Mallard, and other ducks graze in grain fields maintained by the refuges and some private landowners. Big flocks of Red-winged Blackbirds stream back and forth among the refuge cattails.

The Monte Vista Crane Festival, usually the second weekend in March, offers roving biologists and a variety of tours, as well as a large craft and information fair. All federal and state agencies with landholdings in the valley have booths, as does a raptor group that displays live hawks and owls. For information about the Monte Vista Crane Festival, call (719) 852–3552 or visit www.cranefest.com.

Sandhill Cranes provide memorable visual and auditory encounters. Peaking in March and October, they stay mid-February to mid-April and mid-September to mid-November. Food sources dictate crane distribution in the valley; in recent years the bulk spend most of their time in or near Monte Vista NWR, especially in spring. They feed from sunrise to midmorning and again from midafternoon to sunset and loaf during the middle of the day. They persist in family groups (adult

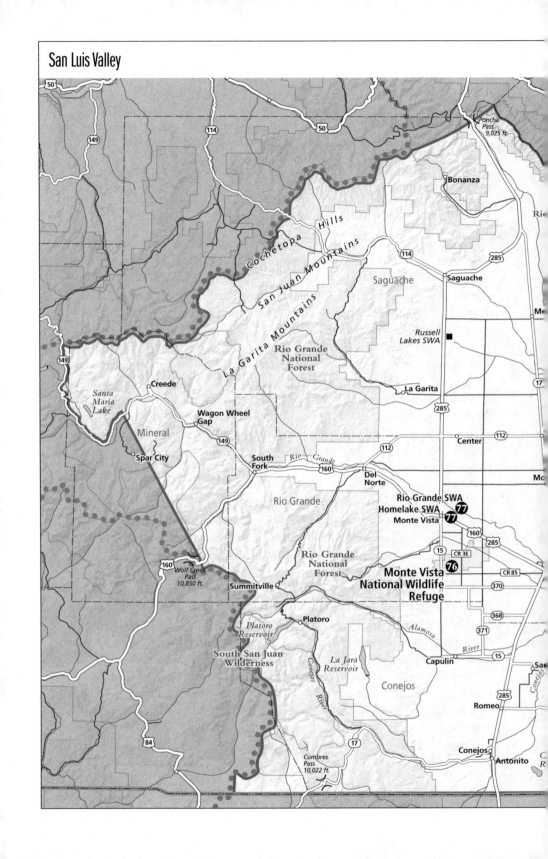

San Luis Valley

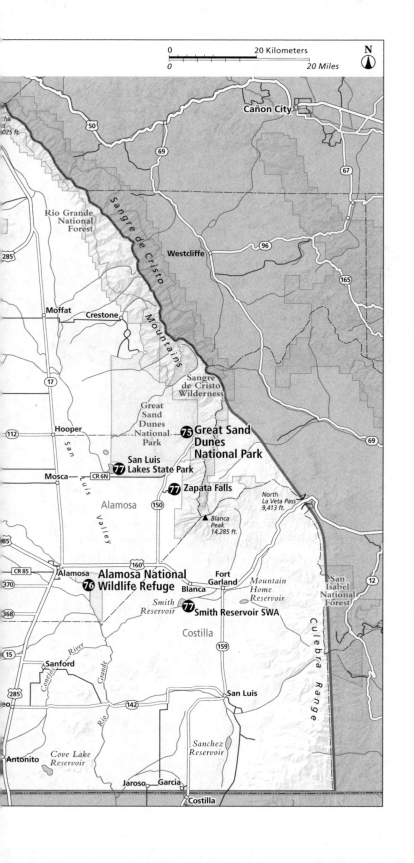

0   20 Kilometers

0   20 Miles

N

Cañon City

50

69

67

Rio Grande
National
Forest

285

96

165

Westcliffe

Sangre de Cristo

Moffat

Crestone

17

Mountains

*Sangre
de Cristo
Wilderness*

112

Hooper

*Great
Sand
Dunes
National
Park*

75 **Great Sand
Dunes
National Park**

69

77 **San Luis
Lakes State Park**

San

Mosca   CR 6N

77 **Zapata Falls**

*North
La Veta Pass
9,413 ft.*

Alamosa

150

Luis

▲ *Blanca
Peak
14,285 ft.*

85

Valley

160

Fort
Garland

*Mountain
Home
Reservoir*

San
Isabel
National
Forest

12

CR 85

Alamosa

76 **Alamosa National
Wildlife Refuge**

Blanca

370

*Smith
Reservoir*

77 **Smith Reservoir SWA**

368

Costilla

Culebra Range

15

159

Sanford

River

285

Conejos

Grande

San Luis

142

Rio

Cove Lake
Reservoir

*Sanchez
Reservoir*

Antonito

Jaroso   Garcia

Costilla

The snow-capped Sangre de Cristo Mountains provide an awe-inspiring backdrop for the awe-inspiring Sandhill Cranes during their spring and fall stopovers in the San Luis Valley.

pair and one [rarely, two] youngster) that travel together until they arrive on the breeding grounds. The refuge has an informative handout about Sandhill Cranes with information about their biology and favorite sites in the valley.

In winter a very cold climate limits bird variety, although fifty to one hundred Bald Eagles stay through the freeze and congregate in spring at sites where thawing ice heaves up fish for an eagle feast. Fickle spring weather can vary from very cold to warm and comfortable. During summer's pleasant climate, the valley attracts a variety of western breeding birds from Sage Thrasher to Brewer's Sparrow to Black Swift.

The summary of valley sites that follows includes only those easily accessible from the valley floor. Forays east, north, and west into the national forests will yield the typical mix of mountain birds.

75 Great Sand Dunes National Park

Habitats: Riparian, pinyon/juniper, ponderosa, aspen, spruce/fir.

Specialty birds: *Resident:* Red-tailed Hawk, Pinyon Jay, Juniper Titmouse. *Summer:* Common Nighthawk, White-throated Swift, Broad-tailed Hummingbird, Lewis's Woodpecker, Clark's Nutcracker. *Winter:* Dark-eyed Junco, Pine Grosbeak.

Best times to bird: Spring, summer, fall.

About this site

Extensive sand dunes, up to 750 feet tall, huddle below the soaring peaks of the Sangre de Cristos and draw most visitors to this park; the dunes provide fun but no birds. Dune wildlife listed in the park brochure consists of two grasses, two flowers, one mammal (kangaroo rat), and seven insects found nowhere else on earth—one with the impressive name of Giant Sand Treader Camel Cricket.

Great Sand Dunes National Preserve stretches from the edge of the park to the crest of the Sangre de Cristos. Alpine tundra, lakes, and 13,000-foot peaks top its 41,676 acres, which protect watersheds critical to the dunefield. Only trails and the four-wheel-drive Medano Pass Road penetrate the high country; in winter, only skis or snowshoes.

Directions

From Highway 17, 1 mile north of Mosca, go east on County Road 6N 16 miles to Highway 150, then north 5 miles to the park; or from U.S. Highway 160, 5 miles west of Blanca and 10.5 miles east of Alamosa (intersection of Highway 17 and US 160), go north 18.5 miles on Highway 150 to the entrance.

The birding

To sample the park's limited birding, drive the one, short, park road. It goes through a section of P/J with a few ponderosa pines; particularly large pinyons grow in the campground. A primitive road tracks through similar habitat another mile or so to the "Point of No Return." From here, the park allows only foot traffic or four-wheel-drive vehicles (drop your tire pressure to 15 psi). Beyond here, if your vehicle gets stuck, a sign announces a minimum towing fee of $100.

Look in P/J areas and stream courses for Broad-tailed Hummingbird, Dusky Flycatcher, Mountain Chickadee, Bushtit, Juniper Titmouse, Steller's Jay, MacGillivray's Warbler, Western Tanager, Spotted Towhee, and Black-headed Grosbeak. Walk through the campground or strike out in any direction from the road. Lewis's Woodpeckers favor old ponderosas and cottonwoods with holes for roosting and nesting.

Pinyon/juniper woodlands herald the approach to the Great Sand Dunes.

Trails up Medano and Music Passes lead through mountain habitats to spruce/fir. A branch trail goes around the north edge of the park, mainly across dunes and the sparse dune vegetation.

DeLorme grid: P. 80 B6–C6.
Elevation: 8,175 feet.
Nearest food, gas, lodging: April through October, at park boundary; Alamosa year-round.

Camping: Yes.
For more information: Great Sand Dunes National Park, 11999 Highway 150, Mosca, CO 81146-9798; (719) 378–6399; www.nps.gov/grsa.

76 Monte Vista and Alamosa National Wildlife Refuges

Habitats: Wetlands, desert shrublands, riparian (Alamosa).

Specialty birds: *Resident:* Northern Harrier, Great Horned Owl, Short-eared Owl. *Summer:* Snowy Egret, Black-crowned Night-Heron, White-faced Ibis, Black Tern, Marsh Wren,

Sage Thrasher, Savannah, Brewer's, and Vesper Sparrows. *Migrant:* Sandhill Crane, Peregrine and Prairie Falcons, Mountain Bluebird. *Winter:* Bald Eagle, Rough-legged Hawk.

Best times to bird: Spring, summer, fall.

Monte Vista National Wildlife Refuge

Of the two refuges, Monte Vista provides better viewing and a better auto tour route, and Sandhill Cranes use it more. Open from sunrise to sunset, it provides excellent views of cranes and ducks. Within its 23 square miles the refuge has numerous permanent and temporary ponds, wetlands, and managed grain fields.

Directions

From the intersection of U.S. Highways 285 and 160 in Monte Vista, take Highway 15 south 6.5 miles; turn left at the small refuge sign just beyond employee housing. Here a display board and, during the week, the office, provide information about the refuge and its birds.

The birding

Crane-watchers should visit the valley in March, April, October, or November.

A 1.5-mile *auto tour* starts by the display board. Spring and fall crane "fly-outs" at sunrise and "fly-ins" at sunset are fabulous: Get up before breakfast to see them lift off, and postpone supper to see them come in to roost. Equally impressive to seeing cranes, hearing them adds a memorable dimension. Cranes spend the night standing in shallow water, which presumably protects them from predators. (Now, mainly coyotes: Although coyotes can't take a healthy crane, they can down injured birds. Sometimes during the day, when cranes feed in the fields, a coyote wanders out and causes the flock to take wing.)

Besides cranes, the ponds teem with geese (mostly Canada, a few Snow, Ross's, and Greater White-fronted), ducks, Great Blue and Black-crowned Night-Herons, Snowy Egret, and a few shorebirds, especially American Avocet, Long-billed Dowitcher, and Wilson's Phalarope, and a few American Pipits. As you drive the tour at dusk, look for Short-eared Owls touring the cattails. The only accessible stand of trees, just south of the refuge headquarters on Highway 15, could have a few migrants (for example, Northern Parula and Golden-crowned Sparrow among White-crowned).

In the spring and fall, migrating Sandhill Cranes spend the night in the shallow ponds of Monte Vista National Wildlife Refuge.

In summer, refuge ponds teem with fledgling ducks, grebes, and coots, along with Marsh Wren, Yellow-headed and Red-winged Blackbirds, and Song Sparrow. Look especially for the bizarrely marked baby Pied-billed Grebe and American Coot. Wilson's Snipe hunker down in the cattails. Northern Harriers rock over the marshes searching for rodents and small birds, and a few Swainson's Hawks may soar overhead. White-faced Ibis nest away from the tour route but may visit roadside ponds to feed. Troops of mosquitoes help feed the abundant wildlife.

Drive south on Highway 15 from the refuge entrance. Pull-offs on the right and left provide views of ponds and grain fields used by flocks of cranes and waterfowl. Turn left on County Road 8S to a pull-off with tall cottonwoods. During the day, grain fields here often have thousands of cranes and many geese and ducks (Northern Pintails predominate). You can continue on CR 8S for 2 miles, then turn left on County Road 2E through greasewood and rabbitbrush, beyond the right turn to County Road 7E. Cranes, in some years, use these grain fields. Look carefully in any stands of cottonwoods for owl nests.

Alamosa National Wildlife Refuge

The Alamosa refuge provides good nesting habitat for waterfowl, and an extensive bottomland along the Rio Grande River where Bald Eagles often congregate in winter. Willow Flycatchers (southwestern race) breed along the Rio Grande River south of the Alamosa Visitor Center. Like other valley refuges, Alamosa has extensive desert shrublands.

Directions

Three miles east of the intersection of Highway 17 and US 160 (east side of Alamosa), turn right on El Rancho Lane; the visitor center and refuge office (open weekdays) is 2.5 miles south.

The birding

A mile-long **auto tour** starts near the refuge office. It traverses cattail marshes and shallow ponds. Likely birds include nesting Black Tern, Northern Harrier, and various ducks.

The *Rio Grande Nature Trail* starts at the Alamosa Visitor Center. On this 1.5-mile walk, likely birds include Swainson's Hawk, Willow Flycatcher, and Blue Grosbeak.

Starting 1.5 miles north of the visitor center, the *Bluff Overlook Drive* proceeds 8 miles east and south through greasewood and rabbitbrush—look for Sage Thrasher and Brewer's Sparrow—to a series of overlooks from which you can see the bottomlands of the Rio Grande. Watch carefully for tour road signs. Wetlands and ponds attract Northern Harrier, waterfowl, and elk. In February and March, Bald Eagles, seeking food and rest, perch along fences and in faraway cottonwoods. Try it in the morning because the views look west and the sun shines at you in the afternoon. A scope is essential.

DeLorme grid: Monte Vista, p. 90 A1-2; Alamosa, p. 91 A4.

Elevation: 7,500 to 7650 feet.

Nearest food, gas, lodging: Monte Vista, Alamosa.

Camping: No.

For more information: Alamosa/Monte Vista NWR, 9383 El Rancho Lane, Alamosa, CO 81101; (719) 589-4021; www.fws.gov/alamosa.

77 San Luis Valley Sites ⓌⒽ Ⓢ

Habitats: Pinyon/juniper, wetlands, shrubland, waterfall.

Best times to bird: Spring, summer, fall.

Specialty birds: *Summer:* White-faced Ibis, Snowy Plover, Common Poorwill, Black Swift. *Winter:* Bald Eagle.

About this site
Several places in the valley merit attention. They offer the full panoply of habitats, from lakes and wetlands to desert shrubland to pinyon/juniper to a waterfall with nesting Black Swifts.

The birding
San Luis Lakes State Park, a large reservoir surrounded by shrubland, has but one tree, at the far northwestern corner. Bald Eagles constitute the main users in

Vast stretches of desert shrubs cover the valley floor, framed with a backdrop of 14,000-foot peaks.

spring, fishermen in summer. During spring thaw, Bald Eagles throng to the lake seeking fish thrown up by heaving ice. (In March 2005 we counted 225 eagles scattered along the shoreline.) Ducks, particularly diving ducks, use the reservoir. Migration attracts gulls, terns, and a few shorebirds, such as Marbled Godwit and Long-billed Curlew.

North of the park, playa lakes at two State Wildlife Areas attract nesting ducks and shorebirds including White-faced Ibis, Snowy Plover, and American Avocet. San Luis Creek, as it crosses through these SWAs, is intermittently wet; when water does seep into the stream, its saline nature spurs lots of invertebrates to come to life, which in turn attract lots of birds to consume them. Trails provide access but the Division of Wildlife keeps these two areas closed during nesting season.

To reach the park from Highway 17, 1 mile north of Mosca, go east on County Road 6N, 7.5 miles to the park entrance. Or from US 160, take Highway 150, the road to the Great Sand Dunes, north 13.5 miles, then turn left on County Road 6N 8 miles to the park entrance.

A handy place to search for Black Swifts, **Zapata Falls** requires a half-mile hike to the waterfall. From US 160 and Highway 150 (see directions to San Luis Lakes), go north 10.8 miles on Highway 150, or from County Road 6N and Highway 150, drive south 2.8 miles to the BLM road, which hairpins up through P/J woodlands to a parking area and trailhead. A series of trails, with multiple trailheads along the road, winds through the pinyon/juniper and offers the chance to find P/J birds.

At the parking area a half-mile trail leads to Zapata Falls, where Black Swift and American Dipper nest. The secretive Black Swifts leave their nest/roost sites in early morning and return only late in the afternoon—to see them, go early or late; afternoon works well. At dawn or dusk, you may hear Common Poorwill calling. Once the trail reaches the creek, you must wade into the stream, climb a small ladder, and walk through a narrow gorge to view the falls. The trail continues 3.5 miles to South Zapata Lake, through the typical high-country habitats.

Migrant waterbirds of all kinds use **Smith Reservoir SWA** as a stopover. From US 160 on the west side of Blanca, drive south 3.5 miles on County Road 12 to the entrance, on the left. A primitive road skirts the south side of the reservoir to provide views into the lake. The stand of willows on the west side may snag interesting migrants, along with nesting blackbirds, warblers, and sparrows.

At the edge of Monte Vista, **Homelake SWA** (IBA) also offers its best birding during migration. From the intersection of US 285 and US 160 in Monte Vista, go east 1 mile; bear left on Sherman Avenue (signs point to Ski-Hi Stampede and Home Lake) for 2 miles to the lake and County Road 3E. A road circles the lake. Though managed principally for fishing, this small reservoir attracts ducks, and occasionally in the trees that surround the lake an unexpected passerine migrant may appear (for example, Northern Parula and Cerulean Warbler). Look also along the irrigation ditch on the north.

You can also drive north on County Road 3E to the **Rio Grande** (about half a mile). A State Wildlife Area stretches along the river from here east to the county line; it has limited access, both physically and seasonally. Winter and spring may show you Bald Eagle, Say's Phoebe, and Mountain Bluebird. Any roads that cross the river offer chances to find similar species and to locate Sandhill Cranes feeding during the day.

North of Monte Vista 25 miles on US 285, *Russell Lakes SWA* (IBA) collects nesting White-faced Ibis, Snowy Egret, American Bittern, and Wilson's Phalarope. Migrants include Black-necked Stilt, Long-billed Curlew, and Marbled Godwit.

During his unsuccessful attempt to climb his namesake mountain, Zebulon Pike first saw Common Ravens in Colorado when his climbing party ate (for the first time in forty-eight hours) meat on a deer's rib that the ravens hadn't scavenged.

DeLorme grid: San Luis Lakes State Park, p. 81 C5; Zapata Falls, p. 81 D6; Smith Reservoir SWA, p. 91 A6; Homelake SWA, p. 80 D2; Russell Lakes p. 80 A1-2.

Elevation: 7,525 to 7725 feet; Zapata Falls, 9,400 feet.

Hazards: Pesky biting insects.

Nearest food, gas, lodging: Alamosa, Monte Vista.

Camping: San Luis Lakes.

For more information: San Luis Lakes State Park, P.O. Box 175, Mosca, CO 81146; (719) 378-2020; www.parks.state.co.us. Colorado Division of Wildlife, 722 County Road 1 East, Monte Vista, CO 81144; (719) 852-4783; wildlife.state.co.us/landwater/statewildlife areas.

Western Plateau Country

Western Colorado's unique scenery of canyons, desert, mesas, and high peaks presents a different face to the Centennial State. The different topography generates a different subset of birds, at least below 8,000 feet. In habitats not found on the Eastern Slope, its birds buttress the state list with desert and canyon species: Black Phoebe, Scott's Oriole, and Gray Vireo breed here; Gambel's Quail and Chukar have their Colorado stronghold here. The Grand Junction area has the most Western Screech-Owls in the state. Brewer's, Black-throated, and Sage Sparrows breed commonly. Grace's Warblers hopped over the San Juan massif to find the ponderosas on the Uncompahgre Plateau.

The incomparable canyons of the Gunnison and San Miguel/Dolores Rivers feature White-throated Swift and Violet-green Swallow swooping around vertical cliffs. Sandhill Cranes stop in numbers at Fruitgrowers Reservoir, which brings in a varied collection of waterbirds. Pinyon/juniper woodlands grow where the mesas and mountains rise from the valleys. Black Swifts specialize in western waterfalls, and the best-studied population thrives in Ouray. Yet above 8,000 feet, habitats of the Central Rockies occur: aspen, ponderosa, and spruce/fir.

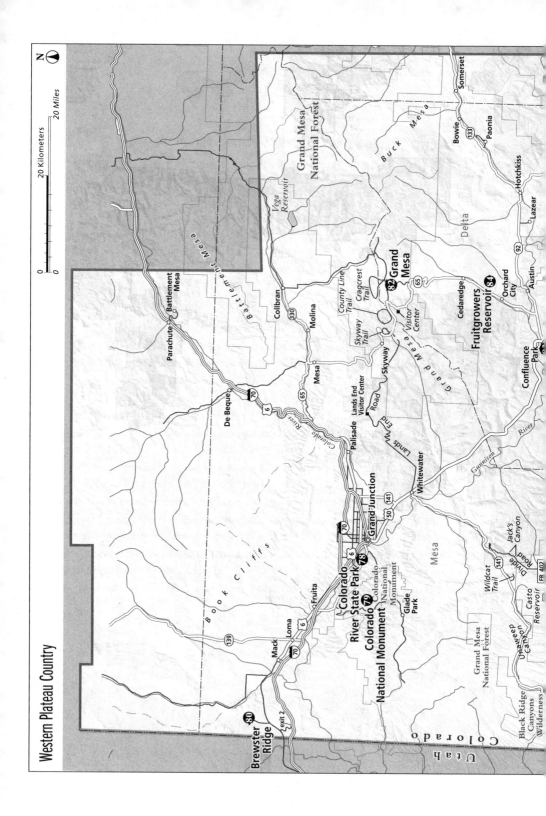

Western Plateau Country

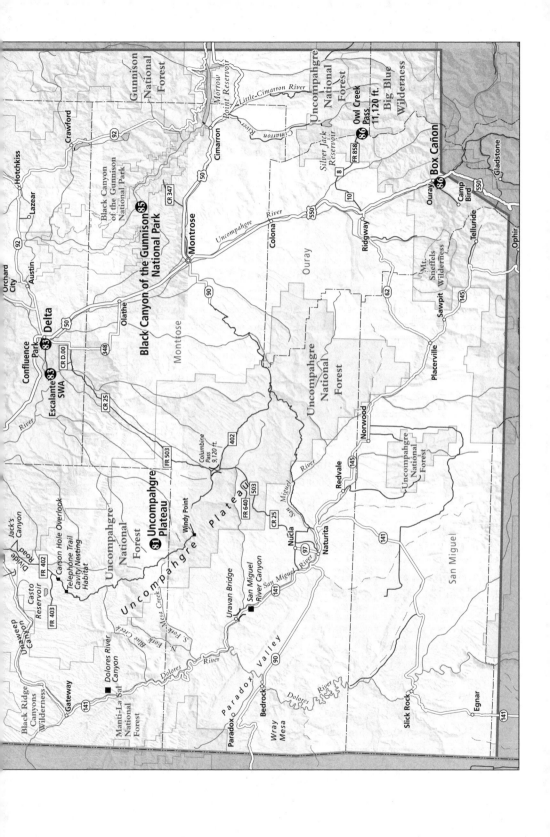

78 Colorado River State Park

Habitats: Riparian, wetlands.

Specialty birds: *Resident:* Gambel's Quail, Bewick's Wren. *Summer:* Lewis's Woodpecker (erratic), Bushtit, Black-headed and Blue Grosbeaks. *Migrant:* Three mergansers, Long-tailed Duck, grebes, Great, Snowy, and Cattle Egrets, Common Loon (fall).

Best times to bird: Spring and fall for land birds and waterfowl, winter for waterfowl.

About this site

The junction that is "Grand" forms just south of downtown Grand Junction where the Gunnison River joins the Colorado River, once named the Grand.

This park has four units. Of the four, Connected Lakes offers the best diversity of habitat, perhaps the richest lowland riparian habitat in western Colorado. (Other units cater principally to waterbirds.) Resident Gambel's Quail scurry around the trails, Bewick's Wrens (and, in winter, Winter Wrens) chatter from the shrubs, and land birds and their predators inhabit the cottonwoods, shrubs, and grasslands. Tamarisk, the scourge of western Colorado rivers, has spread like wildfire along the river to form impenetrable thickets. In some places native species persist and elsewhere land managers, with lots of hard work, have rooted out this pest. Nevertheless, some birds use tamarisk.

The park encompasses a number of gravel pits converted into wildlife ponds, a city-long riverside trail, and excellent lowland riparian habitat. A yearlong survey on a 1-mile segment tallied 237 species.

The birding

Directions use Interstate 70 as a reference. Starting on the west with the *Fruita unit* (best in winter), from exit 19 (Fruita) go south on Highway 340 half a mile and turn right into the park. The gravel pit on the left attracts waterfowl in winter, along with Bald Eagles, Red-tailed Hawks, elusive accipiters, and occasional Peregrine Falcons.

Connected Lakes: From First Street and Broadway, take Broadway (Highway 340) across the Colorado River to Power Road (immediately on the other side of the bridge). Take Power Road 1.7 miles to the park entrance. (The riverside trail has an entrance from the shopping center on the left.) To get to First and Broadway from exit 28, go south on 24 Road 1.5 miles, left on U.S. Highways 6 and 50 to First Street and Broadway.

On the right notice a shelter, the banding station operated by the Rocky Mountain Bird Observatory during migration months. From the parking lot beside the Colorado River, you can walk in several directions through excellent riparian

Colorado River State Park, Colorado National Monument

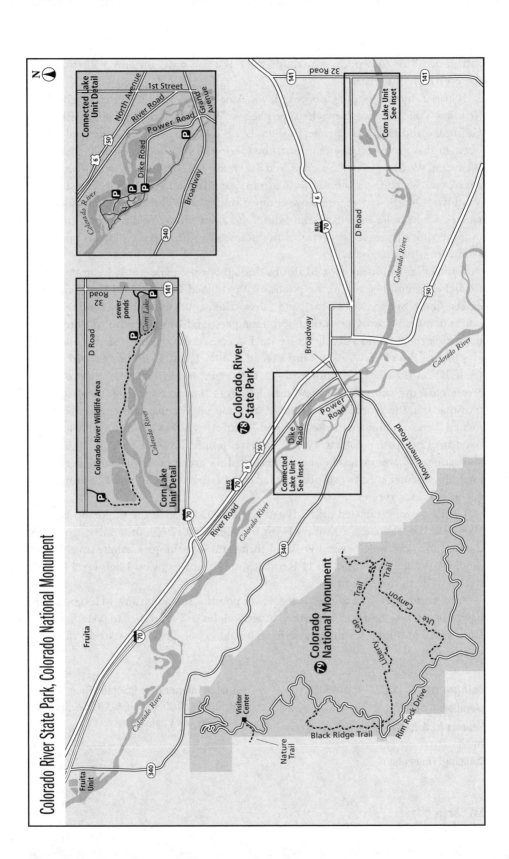

N

Connected Lake Unit Detail

North Avenue
1st Street
River Road
50
6
Colorado River
Power Road
Dike Road
Grand Avenue
P
P
P
P
Broadway
340

Corn Lake Unit Detail

D Road
32 Road
sewer ponds
Colorado River Wildlife Area
Colorado River
Corn Lake
P
P
P
141
70
BUS
River Road
Colorado River

Fruita
70
Colorado River
Fruita Unit
340

Visitor Center
Nature Trail

⑦ Colorado National Monument

Black Ridge Trail
CCC Trail
Liberty
Ute Canyon Trail
Rim Rock Drive
Monument Road

340
6
50
70
BUS
Dike Road
Power Road
Connected Lake Unit See Inset

⑱ Colorado River State Park

Broadway

6
70
BUS
D Road
50
Colorado River
Colorado River

141
32 Road
Corn Lake Unit See Inset
141

habitat of tall cottonwoods, skunkbush, thick Russian olive, shrubby willows, and the ever-present tamarisk.

Riparian birds abound: Cooper's Hawk, American Kestrel, Western Kingbird, Warbling Vireo, Bushtit, Bewick's Wren, Yellow Warbler, Black-headed and Blue Grosbeaks, and Bullock's Oriole; possibly Lewis's Woodpecker. In winter only the wren, of that group, remains, but in come Hermit Thrush (occasional), Cedar Waxwing, White-crowned Sparrow, and an occasional Merlin. Migrants include flycatchers, warblers—mainly Wilson's (most abundant bird at the banding station), Virginia's, Orange-crowned, Yellow-rumped, and MacGillivray's—but also such rarities as Magnolia and Black-and-white, and a few vireos (oddly, the area has more records of the far-western Cassin's [four to five] than the Colorado breeder, Plumbeous [two to three]).

Gambel's Quail sneak around shrubs throughout the park. Look along the river for Belted Kingfisher and in the ponds for Pied-billed Grebe, Wood Duck, herons, egrets (Great, Snowy, and Cattle), and Great-tailed Grackle. In fall and winter the ponds frequently host Common Loon, Trumpeter and Tundra Swans, all three merganser species, and virtually every duck species ever seen in western Colorado.

Colorado River Wildlife Area: On D Road at 30¼ Road. Continue toward town (easterly) on Broadway to Business I–70, turn right, and in 1.1 miles, right on 9th Street; cross the railroad tracks and turn left on D Road; at 3.8 miles turn right into this unit, the product of a habitat restoration project that mitigated environmental damage somewhere else. The ponds attract waterfowl, and the park has a good strip of riparian habitat. Typical of gravel ponds along the river, it has, in fall, a selection of waterfowl—the site has recorded six grebe species (Red-necked rare), three scoter species (unusual), Long-tailed Duck (rare), as well as common goose and duck species.

Corn Lake unit: Located off 32 Road, south of D Road at the Colorado River. From exit 37, take US 6 (Business I–70) to Highway 141 (about a mile); go south 2 miles, and 0.25 mile beyond D Road turn right into the park. Alternatively, from the State Wildlife Area, stay on D Road 1.5 miles; turn right on Highway 141 a quarter mile to the entrance.

After turning in, take a look at the sewer ponds across Highway 141; they often have a smattering of ducks and other waterfowl. From November to March, Corn Lake itself holds lots of winter waterfowl. It's also a good place to start on the river-walk trail.

DeLorme grid: P. 42 C3 and p. 43 D4.
Elevation: 4,500 feet.
Nearest food, gas, lodging: Grand Junction, Fruita.
Camping: Fruita unit.

For more information: Colorado River State Park, P.O. Box 700, Clifton, CO 81520; (970) 434-3388; www.parks.state.co.us.

79 Colorado National Monument

W/ⓈⓈ♿ IBA

Habitats: Pinyon/juniper, cliff.

Specialty birds: *Resident:* Peregrine Falcon. *Summer:* White-throated Swift, Gray Fly-catcher, Gray and Plumbeous Vireos.

Winter: Juncos, rosy-finches.

Best time to bird: Summer.

About this site

Colorado National Monument affords breathtaking views of cliffs and monoliths and the most reliable place in the Grand Valley area to find Gray Vireo. White-throated Swifts plunge through the sky; sometimes you hear their wings as they swoop close to your head. Peregrine Falcons, though seldom seen, nest in Monument Canyon. Curving among trees and rock layers as you drive the monument road, you feel an intimacy with cliffs and woodlands.

Like Rocky Mountain and Yosemite National Parks, this monument had its champion, John Otto, who tirelessly campaigned for local and national recognition; his efforts succeeded in 1911 when the government recognized this stunning place. He then served as caretaker of the park—at $1.00 a month for sixteen years.

Directions

The monument has two entrances, one from downtown Grand Junction and one from Fruita. From Grand Junction, take Broadway (Highway 340) 0.8 mile from its intersection with US 50; go left on Monument Road 3.5 miles to the entrance station. For the Fruita entrance, leave I–70 at exit 19, and in 2.4 miles turn right onto the monument road.

The birding

Roads climbing up to the monument have pull-outs where you can stop and seek the specialty birds. Gray Vireos populate the lower reaches, where junipers and pinyons grow only a head-and-a-half high; as they grow taller and bigger, Plumbeous Vireos take over. Look for Gray Vireo at any of the pull-offs between the Fruita entrance and the *visitor center*. At the center (4.5 miles from the Fruita entrance), a *nature trail* across the road is a good place to look for them.

Other P/J specialists occur throughout the monument, but a warning: This habitat supports only a limited density of birds, and you may have to walk a while to find its denizens. From sheer cliffs, Canyon Wrens sing their cascading bell-like song, White-throated Swifts swoop, and croaking Common Ravens lumber through the sky. Listen for the querulous cries issued by flocks of Pinyon Jays. Look for Broad-tailed and Black-chinned Hummingbirds, Ash-throated and Gray

Flycatchers, Say's Phoebe, Western Scrub-Jay, Clark's Nutcracker, Juniper Titmouse, Bushtit, Bewick's Wren, Black-throated Gray Warbler, and Brewer's and Black-throated Sparrows. Rosy-finches (all three species) and Dark-eyed Junco (all five or more forms) arrive in winter.

Six miles from the visitor center, you can test the Liberty Cap Trail, a fairly level trail that traverses a P/J woodland for several miles. The park brochure lists eight short and six long backcountry trails, more avenues into the canyons, mesas, and overlooks.

DeLorme grid: P. 42 D3.

Elevation: 4,700 to 6,479 feet.

Hazards: Cliffs, lightning, high winds, flash floods; carry water and sunscreen.

Nearest food, gas, lodging: Grand Junction, Fruita.

Camping: Yes.

For more information: Colorado National Monument, Fruita, CO 81521-9530; (970) 858-3617; www.nps.gov.

The poster bird for avian recovery from the pesticide DDT, Peregrine Falcons now breed in close to 100 aeries in Colorado.

PHOTO © WENDY SHATTIL/BOB ROZINSKI

80 Brewster Ridge ⓦ⊛ IBA

Habitats: Desert brush, sagebrush.

Specialty birds: *Resident:* Chukar, Eurasian Collared-Dove, Long-eared Owl. *Summer:* Log-gerhead Shrike, Ash-throated Flycatcher, Gray Vireo, Black-throated Sparrow, Scott's Oriole.

Best time to bird: Summer.

About this site

Brewster Ridge, your best chance to find Scott's Oriole in Colorado, also sports a few Gray Vireos among its scattered junipers. This dry landscape has its own small but unique suite of birdlife. *Caution:* The dirt roads become muddy quagmires in wet weather (admittedly an unusual event).

Directions

Go west from Grand Junction on I–70 to exit 2 and go right into the Rabbit Valley parking lot. You can scramble up the Rabbit Valley interpretive trail—mainly a fossil exhibit. The quarry has produced large specimens of several dinosaur species.

The birding

From the Rabbit Valley parking lot, take the dirt road on the left. It hairpins up a bluff; try one of the dirt tracks to the right—the first one leads to a rocky overlook of Rabbit Valley. Check the cliffs for a lucky glimpse of a Chukar. Continue on the dirt track another 2 miles to a paved road (old U.S. Highways 6 and 50, now M.50 Road). Go right on the paved road for 2 miles, then left on a gravel road; in 1.1 miles turn right at the fork. In the sagebrush for the first mile or two beyond M.50 Road, look for Sage Thrasher and Lark, Sage, and Brewer's Sparrows (also leopard lizards). Long-billed Curlews recently nested in the desert grasslands beyond this sagebrush stand.

As you proceed, junipers gradually crop up and become more prevalent; start looking for Gray Vireo, Scott's Oriole, and Black-throated Sparrow; also Common Raven, Loggerhead Shrike, Mountain Bluebird, and Northern Mockingbird. To return, you can take M.50 Road east to Mack (9 miles; Eurasian Collared-Doves have moved in here) and then right onto I–70.

DeLorme grid: P. 42 C1 and B1.

Elevation: 5,000 feet.

Hazards: Muddy roads, high temperatures.

Nearest food, gas, lodging: Fruita, Grand Junction.

Camping: Informal.

For more information: Bureau of Land Management, 2815 H Road, Grand Junction, CO 81506; (970) 240-5300; www.blm.gov/co/st/en.html.

81 Uncompahgre Plateau/ Dolores–San Miguel Canyon

Habitats: Shrubland, sagebrush, pinyon/ juniper, aspen, ponderosa, spruce/fir, riparian, canyon.

Specialty birds: *Resident:* Peregrine Falcon, American Dipper. *Summer:* Lewis's Wood-

pecker, Black Phoebe, Grace's Warbler, Fox Sparrow. *Migrant:* Nashville and Townsend's Warblers (early fall).

Best times to bird: Spring, summer, fall; the plateau road closes in winter.

About this site

The scenic nature of this route rivals the birdlife. Had a writer with the talent, passion, vigor, and proselytizing and political skills of John Muir or Enos Mills come here in 1900, he could have electrified the nation into designating it as a national park. The plateau, from Colorado National Monument south to the San Juan Mountains, plus the scenic blockbuster San Miguel/Dolores Canyon, presents a first-class visual spectacle and wildlife display. With varied habitats, this drive offers the chance to find a quarter of Colorado's breeding birds in one day. *Atlas* blocks on the Uncompahgre Plateau found fifty-six to eighty breeding species, and one in Dolores Canyon reported seventy-four species.

The plateau shares its name with the river that runs below on its east from Ouray to Delta, and with southwestern Colorado's tallest peak (14,309 feet). Uncompahgre (*oon*-cum-*pah*-gray) comes from a Ute Indian word that means hot water spring, possibly referring to those at Ouray.

Directions

Fill up with gas before tackling this stunning 180-mile drive, which starts at Whitewater, south of Grand Junction, climbs westerly and southerly to the Uncompahgre Plateau, straddles the divide between the Uncompahgre and Dolores Rivers, drops down to the San Miguel and Dolores Rivers to Gateway, then returns through Unaweep Canyon to the start. The varied habitats feature enough birds for an all-day drive.

You can vary the route described below by reversing it or approaching from Delta, Montrose, or Ridgway. Snow closes the plateau section of the route until May or June (depending on snowmelt). Highways 141 and 145 remain open year-round, so that you can drive from Whitewater to Gateway on 141, south to Placerville on 145, over Dallas Divide on Highway 62 to U.S. Highway 550 at Ridgway, then north to Montrose, Delta, and Grand Junction.

The birding

From the intersection of Highway 141 and US 50 south of Grand Junction, follow Highway 141 to Whitewater (2.5 miles), then turn right where Highway 141 leaves US 50. At the Gunnison River crossing, good riparian habitat has produced rarities such as Northern Parula and Rose-breasted Grosbeak.

Try for foothills riparian breeders 1.7 miles from US 50 (East Creek Day Use Area) and 7 miles on, a pull-off with narrow-leaf cottonwoods. They may produce Cooper's Hawk, Dusky and Cordilleran Flycatchers, Virginia's and Black-throated Gray Warblers, Yellow-breasted Chat, and Spotted Towhee. At East Creek, Canyon Wrens sing from the cliffs and a few P/J birds drift in such as Ash-throated Flycatcher and Plumbeous Vireo.

The road starts to climb through rough P/J habitat. In the lower reaches, where junipers predominate but grow far apart, Gray Vireos breed. At any pull-off listen for the two-note up-and-down conversation of vireos (*Note:* Gray and Plumbeous sound alike). Grays give way to Plumbeous as the pinyons and junipers grow taller. In the cottonwoods and irrigated fields, look for Western Kingbird, Rough-winged Swallow, Mountain Bluebird, Lark Sparrow, and Lesser Goldfinch. In the sagebrush flats around Cactus Park Road (6 miles from East Creek), Sage Thrasher and Brewer's, Vesper, and Sage Sparrows breed. A mile farther, in a rock formation on the left, Rock Wren, Cliff Swallow, and White-throated Swift must have nested for centuries—their guano has piled up a foot deep!

Fourteen miles from Whitewater, turn left on *Divide Road* (Forest Road 402) to reach the Uncompahgre Plateau. During its ascent the road passes through scrub oak and P/J habitat; look and listen for both riparian and P/J birds such as Dusky and Gray Flycatchers, Mountain Chickadee, Juniper Titmouse, Bushtit, Bewick's Wren, Virginia's and Black-throated Gray Warblers, and Black-headed Grosbeak. Golden Eagles often soar over the road. Stop at 2.2 miles for Unaweep View, an awesome panorama of the canyon 1,000 feet below.

At *Jack's Canyon,* 1.2 miles from Unaweep View, spend time in the unique ecotone, a mile-long mix of ponderosa and pinyon pines, scrub oak, aspen, serviceberry, narrow-leaf cottonwood, and a plethora of shrubs. Flammulated and Northern Saw-whet Owls nest here. In mid-May, Dusky Grouse perform their mating dance. Other breeders include Red-tailed Hawk (high on the cliff to the left), Red-naped Sapsucker, Blue-gray Gnatcatcher, Western Bluebird, Orange-crowned, Virginia's, Yellow, and Yellow-rumped Warblers, Spotted Towhee, and Cassin's Finch. In fall Clark's Nutcracker, Red-breasted Nuthatch, and Ruby-crowned Kinglet stop when dropping down from the high country.

Divide Road climbs via several hairpin turns through P/J that favors Plumbeous Vireo, into sagebrush flats with Green-tailed Towhee and Vesper Sparrow. Over the next 25 miles, the road crosses several sections of ponderosa pine woodland; breeders include Flammulated, Pygmy, and Northern Saw-whet Owls,

Williamson's Sapsucker, Dusky Flycatcher, Steller's Jay, Pygmy Nuthatch, House Wren, Western Bluebird, and Cassin's Finch.

Seven miles from Jack's Canyon, try a side road (Forest Road 403) that leads to *Casto Reservoir,* often good for waterbirds. In 3.5 miles turn right at a cattle guard for a view of the lake. Eared Grebes nest here, and possibly Sandhill Cranes as well as several species of dabbling ducks, Ring-necked Duck, Lesser Scaup, Sora, Mountain Bluebird, and Savannah Sparrow. (Don't bother to go on to Big Creek Reservoir.)

Back on Divide Road, stop at *Carson Hole Overlook,* 0.7 mile from the Casto turnoff, to look down on White-throated Swift and Violet-green Swallow and to hear from the conifers far below Olive-sided Flycatcher and Clark's Nutcracker. Across a cattle guard 1.8 miles farther, *Telephone Trail Cavity Nesting Habitat* recognizes the importance of dead trees to wildlife. Flickers, Hairy Woodpecker, and Williamson's Sapsucker drill nest holes used later by aspen cavity-nesters.

Just past Divide Forks Campground a creek crosses the road (prior to Milepost 16). Check the right side for MacGillivray's Warbler. Lewis's Woodpecker occurs on the plateau only between Divide Forks and Cold Springs Work Center (3.5 miles). The road passes through aspen and spruce/fir forests with the common birds of those habitats. Check patches of tall willows for Fox Sparrow (slate-colored race, *schistacea*), as well as Lincoln's Sparrow and Wilson's Warbler. In the 10 miles beyond Windy Point (19.5 miles from Cold Springs and 4.5 miles from the Montrose County line), a roadside survey found Flammulated Owls at ten of twenty stops. The road intersects Forest Road 503 (which comes up from Delta) 10.5 miles from Windy Point. Bear right on FR 402/503 over *Columbine Pass* (9,120 feet); then take the right fork, FR 503, to Nucla. (Left is also okay: It goes to Iron Springs, where the spruce/fir habitat improves and higher-elevation species such as Gray Jay and Pine Grosbeak occur.) FR 503 drops into Tabeguache Basin, full of scrub oak and Orange-crowned Warbler (and the Colorado Hairstreak butterfly), plus two colonies of Purple Martin.

In 9.5 miles a pine/oak woodland extends across both sides of *Glencoe Road* (Forest Road 640). Grace's Warblers sing from the treetops. Other nesting species include Williamson's Sapsucker, Dusky Flycatcher, White-breasted Nuthatch, Western Bluebird, Yellow-rumped Warbler, Dark-eyed Junco, and during good cone crop seasons, Red Crossbill. For the next 1.5 miles, expect those species as well as, in August and early September, migrating Nashville and Townsend's Warblers.

Forest Road 503 becomes County Road 25; in Nucla (12 miles from Glencoe Road) it turns south onto County Road 29. Turn right at the intersection of CR 29 and 10th Street (County Road CC), pass through rural fields and wetlands, and in 4.7 miles turn right on Highway 141. This highway follows the *San Miguel and Dolores Rivers* to Gateway through a spectacular canyon, little known because of its remoteness.

On the right, within 100 yards of the turn onto Highway 141, Black Phoebes nest on a big rock. A 20-mile float trip on the San Miguel in 1998 from Naturita to Uravan discovered nearly forty Black Phoebe nests—a dense population in a state where, until 1972, no one even knew they nested. A few American Dippers nest downstream on the Dolores drainage, but only where they find tributaries with clean water; a bridge on West Creek above Gateway supports the lowest-elevation nest in Colorado.

The Nature Conservancy (TNC) preserves tracts along the San Miguel to protect the Rio Grande cottonwood/skunkbush/sumac/coyote-willow riparian association. It launched a massive effort to exterminate exotic invaders: tamarisk, Russian olive, and Siberian elm. At *Tabeguache Preserve* (7 miles of river), stop at the visitor area (9 miles from the Nucla turnoff, at Milepost 74), which has a kiosk, outhouse, picnic tables, and short trail. You can inspect TNC's efforts while seeking riparian birds. Besides the usual riparian species, look for Black and Say's Phoebes, Rough-winged, Cliff, and Barn Swallows, Yellow-breasted Chat, Lazuli Bunting, Lark Sparrow, and Lesser Goldfinch. Peregrine Falcons use several aeries between here and Utah. Stop at the *Uravan bridge* for Black Phoebe. (Uravan, now razed as part of a Superfund cleanup, thrived on uranium mining in the 1950s and 1960s but left a toxic legacy.) The good habitat ends about 30 miles from the Nucla turnoff; from here on to Gateway, huge feathery tamarisks choke the side of the river as they crowd out native vegetation.

At Gateway the road goes right to climb up to *Unaweep Canyon*. From the highway check the wetland and two ponds on the right side, 20.5 miles from Gateway, for nesting Eared Grebe, Cinnamon Teal, Ring-necked Duck, Sandhill Crane, and maybe a Wilson's Snipe perched on a fence post. At Milepost 133, a mile beyond this wetland, *Wildcat Trail* (640) leaves from an unmarked parking area; it crosses the grassy valley to pinyon/juniper, sagebrush, and even aspen and conifers if you climb high enough.

The road meets the Divide Road, where you started the climb up Uncompahgre Plateau, 28.5 miles from Gateway, and reaches US 50 in another 14 miles.

DeLorme grid: P. 54–55 and 64–65.
Elevation: 4,800 to 9,130 feet.
Hazards: Biting and other annoying insects; bring sunscreen. Hot summer temperatures in Dolores Canyon.

Nearest food, gas, lodging: Grand Junction, Delta, Montrose, Ridgway, Ouray.
Camping: Yes.
For more information: U.S. Forest Service, 2250 Highway 50, Delta, CO 81416; (970) 874-6600; www.fs.fed.us/r2/gmug.

82 Grand Mesa W&

Habitats: Montane shrubland, willow carr, aspen, spruce/fir.

Specialty birds: *Resident:* Dusky Grouse, Boreal Owl, Three-toed Woodpecker, Red-breasted Nuthatch, Red Crossbill. *Summer:*

Golden-crowned Kinglet, Hermit Thrush, Swainson's Thrush, Fox Sparrow.

Best times to bird: Summer (but the winter can also be very interesting).

About this site

From a distance, massive Grand Mesa really looks flat—locals tout it as the world's largest flat-topped mountain. Dotting its landscape, over 300 lakes (some natural, some dammed) perch amid a dense spruce/fir forest. The lakes attract few ducks, but accessible conifer forests host all the spruce/fir birds, including Boreal Owl.

Directions

Grand Mesa has three access points, from the south, west, and north:

South road: Highway 65 spans the mesa from Cedaredge to Mesa (the town). From US 50 in Delta (1st and Main), go east 6 miles on Highway 92, turn left on Highway 65 (sign to Grand Mesa; the same directions as for Fruitgrowers Reservoir); continue past Eckert and Cedaredge toward the visitor center.

North road: From exit 49 on I–70, go east and south on Highway 65 for 23 miles to the visitor center.

Lands End road: From US 50 south of Grand Junction, turn left 5.5 miles south of Highway 141. The road climbs quickly up the mesa to the Lands End overlook, then 12 miles to Highway 65.

The birding

All three roads climb through juniper, scrub oak, and aspen to the spruce/fir of the mesa top. Stop at safe turnouts for roadside birding. In aspen groves in June, Tree and Violet-green Swallows, feeding their young, swoop in and out constantly, and babies of Red-naped Sapsucker and Hairy Woodpecker cry loudly from inside their cavities.

Coming from the south, 14.5 miles past Eckert, the Old Grand Mesa Road (Forest Road 123) goes right; 2.8 miles beyond (23.5 miles from Highway 92), at a wide hairpin around a creek, stop and park on the right just before the stream. Fox Sparrows nest in the tall willows, and a walk up the hillside or across the road leads to spruce/fir. Three miles farther, at the junction, turn right to the visitor center.

Gray Jays haunt the *visitor center,* although they don't beg obtrusively. A short nature trail (fifteen to thirty minutes) behind the center winds through a pleasant, dense spruce/fir forest with that habitat's typical birds. The road right from the visitor center goes past a campground, picnic area, and a collection of cabins nestled above two lakes to the junction with Forest Road 123 (Old Grand Mesa Road).

Continue past the junction 0.4 mile to a parking lot for the east trailhead of the *Cragcrest Trail,* the first trail in the United States designated as a National Recreation Trail. Hikers on this 10-mile loop might find Sharp-shinned Hawk, Three-toed Woodpecker, and Pine Grosbeak among other spruce/fir birds. They certainly find great views in all directions—Elk Mountains east, Flattops north, Uncompahgre Plateau and Utah west, and San Juan Mountains south. (The west trailhead is opposite Island Lake, half a mile past the visitor center on Highway 65.)

Back on Highway 65 at the visitor center, go westerly 3 miles to *County Line,* a parking area with a cross-country ski trail worth walking at least a short distance in non-snow seasons. Among scattered copses of spruce/fir and flower-filled meadows, try for Pine Grosbeak, Red and White-winged (rare) Crossbills, and an outside chance of finding Dusky Grouse.

Highway 65 meets the Lands End road in 1.5 miles; 12 miles on it takes you to *Lands End Visitor Center,* where one afternoon thrilled observers watched three California Condors, far from their Arizona home in Grand Canyon. You can drop down to US 50 from here (or come up from there to the mesa). If you stay on Highway 65, another mile takes you to *Skyway* and a second ski trail worth exploring. The road drops through spruce/fir and an extensive aspen forest before it leaves the national forest in 8 miles.

DeLorme grid: P. 43 D7, p. 44 D1-2, p. 56 A2.

Elevation: 10,000 to 10,839 feet; Cragcrest Trail, 11,183 feet.

Nearest food, gas, lodging: Grand Junction, Delta, and Mesa; food and lodging in Grand Mesa.

Camping: Yes.

For more information: U.S. Forest Service, 2250 Highway 50, Delta, CO 81416; (970) 874-6600; www.fs.fed.us/r2/gmug.

83 Delta

Habitats: Riparian, wetlands.

Specialty birds: *Resident:* Bewick's Wren, Western Screech-Owl. *Summer:* Willow Fly-catcher, Great-tailed Grackle. *Migrant:* Osprey, White-faced Ibis.

Best times to bird: Year-round.

About this site

Located at the north end of Delta, **Confluence Park** embraces the confluence of the Gunnison and Uncompahgre Rivers. Riparian trees and shrubs that string along the river's edge and a pond account for surprising migrants that are out of place on the Western Slope.

Confluence Park in Delta corrals a surprising variety of migrant birds.

Directions

Go north a block from the intersection of US 50 and Highway 92 (1st and Main) in Delta, and turn left between KFC and McDonalds; drive past the Recreation Center to a T intersection. The pond sits to the left; to the right you'll find a parking area in 200 yards, a picnic area, the Gunnison River, and the best riparian habitat.

The birding

The pond sometimes picks up migrating waterfowl; the site has records of four goose and three scoter species, Osprey, White-faced Ibis, Least Tern, and Black Swift. Double-crested Cormorants loaf on the islands.

On the right, scan the picnic area for migrants and the river for waterbirds. A wide trail parallels the riparian section along the Gunnison; try any of several branches on the right. Patches of shrubs and tall trees often harbor a variety of birds. Bewick's Wrens (residents) chatter from shrubby patches and Lewis's Woodpeckers may stop in October. In the small ponds on the left, look for nesting Great-tailed Grackle and Common Yellowthroat. At the confluence you can cross a swinging bridge to prowl in more thickets, although the trail soon peters out. An evening foray might yield a calling Western Screech-Owl. Winter visitants include Bushtit, Mountain Bluebird, and Yellow-rumped Warbler. Eurasian Collared-Doves hang around the adjacent industrial areas.

Nearby, **Escalante SWA** (IBA) offers a different habitat mix. This large wildlife area has extensive sites for nesting waterbirds, most of it protected by restricted access. Trails into the Hamilton section give a flavor of riverine species. The Division of Wildlife has under way a project to rid the site of tamarisk.

To get there, go west on 5th Street in Delta 2 miles and bear right at the intersection with Sawmill Mesa Road; in 1 mile note a pond on the right, which sometimes collects White-faced Ibis, herons, geese, and other waterfowl. Just beyond, go into the parking lot on the left, the Hamilton Tract.

From trails here, study the shelterbelts of junipers and berry bushes and listen carefully to songs emanating from the willows on the left of the entry trail. Willow Flycatchers nest here (formerly thought to belong to the threatened southwestern race). The SWA hosts lowland riparian species including Black-chinned Hummingbird, Blue Grosbeak, Bullock's Oriole, and Lesser and American Goldfinches. Great Blue Herons nest across the river, and feeding herons scatter over much of the SWA. Escalante once hosted nesting Yellow-billed Cuckoos, one of the last Western Slope nesting spots for this declining species that may no longer nest on the west side of the Continental Divide.

DeLorme grid: Confluence Park, p. 56 C1; Escalante, p. 55 C7.

Elevation: 4,920 feet.

Nearest food, gas, lodging: Delta.

Camping: No.

For more information: Colorado Division of Wildlife, 2300 South Townsend Avenue, Montrose, CO 81401; (970) 252-6000.

84 Fruitgrowers Reservoir IBA

Habitats: Wetlands, riparian, shrubland.

Specialty birds: *Summer:* Western and Clark's Grebes, Black-crowned Night-Heron, American White Pelican, Burrowing Owl, Willow Fly-catcher, Marsh Wren, Yellow-headed Blackbird. *Migrant:* Sandhill Crane, White-faced Ibis, shorebirds. *Winter:* Bald Eagle.

Best times to bird: Spring, summer, fall.

About this site

This midsize irrigation reservoir with abundant waterbirds, shorebirds, and marsh birds serves as an important migratory stopover for Sandhill Cranes—20,000 stop by in the spring. It's the best shorebird migrant stop in western Colorado. Western and Clark's Grebes nest here, along with a wide selection of ducks, herons, American Bittern, both Sora and Virginia Rail, Willet (rare breeder in Colorado), and a few land birds including Willow Flycatcher and Marsh Wren.

Directions

Go east on Highway 92 from US 50 in Delta (1st and Main) for 6 miles and turn left on Highway 65 (sign to Grand Mesa). At 5 miles make a sharp right on 21

Sandhill Cranes migrate in numbers to Fruitgrowers Reservoir, and Western Grebes nest here regularly.

Road and an immediate left on Fruitgrowers (M.00) Road. In a mile the road bears right, up across the dam to a parking lot on the other side.

The birding

From the dam parking, use a scope to view waterbirds near and far—ducks, grebes, pelicans, and cormorants. Western Grebes (ferrying young on their backs by late May and still feeding their begging but swimming juveniles in September) scatter all over the lake. Great Blue Heron and Double-crested Cormorant—and sometimes Red-tailed Hawk and Great Horned Owl—nest in the cottonwoods across the lake. A second parking lot, in another 0.1 mile, perches closer to the lake amid some tall shrubs. The first lot, 20 feet above water level, provides better lake views; at the second lot you might find land birds in tall shrubs and cottonwoods. A dirt road runs along the edge of the reservoir—better to walk it than drive it, and a caution: When muddy it can swallow your car (as it did ours).

Go back to Highway 65, north a half mile, and right on Myers (M.50) Road. Lewis's Woodpeckers nest in the tall cottonwoods, and you might see them hawking insects. Follow as the road swings left (and becomes 21.90 Road) and turn right in half a mile onto N.00 (North) Road. Just beyond the HARTS BASIN sign the road flattens out and crosses the marshes that line the upper side of the reservoir.

On the North Road, drive slowly—and cautiously: Passing pickup trucks drive very fast. Pull off way to the side. Water, shoreline, and bushes line both sides of the road. On the water you'll usually see groups of American White Pelican, ducks, Western Grebe, and other waterbirds. The shoreline attracts migrant shorebirds—the list includes Black-bellied, American Golden-, and Semipalmated Plovers, Marbled Godwit, Pectoral and Stilt Sandpipers, and Red-necked and Red Phalaropes.

An irrigation ditch pours water in from the left, and from the lush growth of small trees, Willow Flycatchers sing, along with more pedestrian Song Sparrows. Just beyond, from the extensive cattails, Marsh Wrens sing and call their higgledy-piggledy sounds and Yellow-headed Blackbirds make cacophonous calls. In spring thousands of Sandhill Cranes and substantial numbers of White-faced Ibis use the marsh, and Western Grebes perform their spectacular mating dance on the open water. Look for other marsh species such as Black-crowned Night-Heron and Green Heron.

The Sandhill Cranes light down mostly in the fields and wetlands at the north end of the reservoir. N Road, the road across the causeway, provides the best viewing.

DeLorme grid: P. 56 B2.
Elevation: 5,600 feet.
Hazards: Fast pickup trucks, muddy roads.
Nearest food, gas, lodging: Delta, Cedaredge.

Camping: No.
For more information: www.audubon.org/chapter/co/co/IBA/IBA%20sites/6.htm.

85 Black Canyon National Park

Habitats: Cliff, montane shrubland, pinyon/juniper.

Specialty birds: *Resident:* Western Scrub-Jay, Steller's Jay, Canyon Wren. *Summer:* White-throated Swift, Dusky Flycatcher, Violet-green Swallow, Rock and Canyon Wrens, Virginia's, Orange-crowned, and MacGillivray's Warblers, Spotted and Green-tailed Towhees. *Winter:* Townsend's Solitaire.

Best time to bird: Summer.

About this site

Another of western Colorado's magnificent geological features, Black Canyon of the Gunnison National Park displays a 2,772-foot-deep gorge carved in gray-black schist: Its vertical cliffs drop precipitously to the Gunnison River. Through its 48-mile chasm, the river loses more elevation than the Mississippi River does in 1,500 miles from Minnesota to Louisiana. One spectacular overlook after another offers awesome views of the canyon and superb views of soaring and feeding swifts and swallows.

Directions

Go east on US 50 from its intersection with US 550 in downtown Montrose for 7.5 miles and turn left on Highway 347. The road rises to the park entrance through greasewood into hillsides clad with P/J and scrub oak.

The birding

Overlooks along the park road cater to canyon-viewers and canyon birds. Observers can look down on White-throated Swift and Violet-green Swallow plying the canyon air for insects. One overlook precedes the South Rim Visitor Center, and the South Rim Road passes ten more, each with breathtaking glimpses of the canyon and river below. Check any or all for canyon birds; Common Ravens soar high above or down below, and Canyon Wrens sing at every stop. Each overlook trail has a few land birds—Rock Point has the most—such as Western Scrub-Jay, Steller's Jay, and Pine Siskin. Though rarely seen, at least one pair of Peregrine Falcons breeds here. At the end of the rim road, you can park at High Point and walk through a P/J woodland to the last promontory, Warner Point. In early spring you might chance onto Dusky Grouse, known to display on top of picnic tables.

After you sate your interest in views of the canyon and canyon birds, you can check the montane shrubland on Oak Flats Trail. Although it starts at the visitor center (parking always available), its upper terminus gets you into better shrubs sooner. Go back to the campground, just inside the park entrance, and park in the lot by the campground kiosk. (This sometimes fills with large RVs, so that parking

From the cliff rims of Black Canyon National Park, you can look down on zooming swifts and swallows.

becomes iffy in midsummer.) Walk straight down the campground road to the last turn, where the trail begins. In a few hundred yards, take the left fork, labeled OAK FLATS, VISITOR CENTER, which takes you through an excellent shrubby ecosystem of scrub oak, serviceberry, squaw currant, sagebrush, and snowberry. (The trail crosses the entrance road; cross it for more of the montane shrub system.) Birds include Dusky Flycatcher, Black-capped Chickadee, Blue-gray Gnatcatcher, Mountain Bluebird, Virginia's, Orange-crowned, and MacGillivray's Warblers, Spotted and Green-tailed Towhees, and Black-headed Grosbeak.

DeLorme grid: P. 56 D4.

Elevation: 8,200 feet.

Hazards: Hazardous footing, weathered rock.

Nearest food, gas, lodging: Montrose.

Camping: Yes.

For more information: Black Canyon of the Gunnison National Park, 102 Elk Creek, Gunnison, CO 81230; (970) 641-2337; www.nps.gov/blca.

86 Box Cañon

Habitats: Waterfall, scrub oak/conifer

Specialty birds: *Summer:* Black Swift, Cassin's Finch, Evening Grosbeak

Best times to bird: June 20 to September 15.

About this site

Box Cañon Falls provides the premier place to observe Black Swifts nesting. Long a tourist mecca for Ouray, this spectacular booming waterfall is only a 500-foot walk from the gate. Park brochures, the visitor guide, and local signage use a swift head as a logo. The desk clerk will gladly tell you about the swifts and where to find them. To reinforce your quest, an informative sign sits on the railing opposite the nests. The canyon trail arrives at the falls on a metal catwalk (with railing), but first, stop at the sign about the swifts.

Directions

From downtown Ouray, go up (south) on US 550 half a mile to the well-signed entrance (sign on the left, turn on the right); follow the signs 0.4 mile to the park. (A left fork, Forest Road 853—quite rough—turns into a four-wheel-drive road—ascends steeply into Yankee Boy Basin, a spectacular high-altitude flower extravaganza in July and August.)

The birding

Black Swifts nest in a dark and damp cleft in the sheer rock face across the chasm from the catwalk. Opposite the sign that discusses the swifts, look for incubating birds on small ledges—black birds perched in matching shade; they just sit there. Your eyes take time to adjust to the dim light—you may have to wait a while to spot the black birds roosting in niches on the gray-black walls. The cleft holds as many as a dozen nests, though you have to look carefully to spot any.

Black Swifts have a unique biology. They incubate for three to four weeks, and young fledge after a prodigious forty-five-day nestling period. During the incubation and nestling phases, adults search the skies for clouds of flying ants. On daytime feeding trips swifts range 25 miles or more, from low-elevation stream bottoms up to 14,000-foot peaks. They store their catch in throat sacs to regurgitate to the nestling. By late July the one egg hatches. During the day nestlings fast (go into torpor), waiting for their parents to return at dusk with an all-night supply of ants. The youngsters' maiden flight supposedly jump-starts their migration to winter quarters in South America.

To see swifts on the wing, visit the park at dusk or wait outside the park at daybreak. During summer the park stays open from 8:00 A.M. to dusk. Sometimes,

At Box Cañon birders can get rare views of nesting Black Swift.

during the day, swifts feed in the US 550 canyon that drops down into Ouray from Silverton. You can stop at a pull-off and scan the skies for the soaring acrobats—or look for them high in the sky above the town.

Box Cañon also attracts other birds. In the parking lot, watch for soaring White-throated Swifts—they chatter incessantly. By the office, bird feeders attract Cassin's Finch, Pine Siskin, and Evening Grosbeak. Other park birds include Broad-tailed and Rufous Hummingbirds, Cordilleran Flycatcher, Violet-green Swallow, American Dipper, Townsend's Solitaire, Cedar Waxwing, and Yellow-rumped, Yellow, MacGillivray's, and Wilson's Warblers.

Ouray offers hot springs and spectacular mountain drives. Besides the Million Dollar Highway, try **Owl Creek Pass.** From US 550, turn right 11 miles north of Ouray (1 mile north of Ridgway) on County Road 10. It traverses scrub oak, aspen, and spruce/fir as it climbs toward Chimney Peak and Courthouse Mountain. Across the pass you can go right into more spruce/fir and willow carrs, or left to US 50 east of Montrose.

DeLorme grid: P. 66 D4.

Elevation: 7,800 feet.

Hazards: Slippery rungs on the stairs; bring a sweater—it's 20 degrees cooler in the canyon.

Nearest food, gas, lodging: Ouray.

Camping: Ouray.

For more information: Box Cañon Park, City of Ouray, Ouray, CO 81427; (970) 325-7080.

San Juan Basin

The 12,000-square-mile mass of the San Juan Mountains bounds the San Juan Basin on the north and east. Brilliantly colored rocks and extensive mineralization occur throughout the range, carved from volcanic ash and breccias. The mountains form a bright palette and stunning skyline of precipitous crests and narrow arêtes. At Molas Pass a sign quotes W. H. Holmes, an 1876 surveyor, describing these mountains: "If you should, in your imagination, put together in one small group, perhaps 12 miles square, all the heights and depths, the rugged precipices and polished faces of rock, and all the sharp pinnacles and deeply-indented crests, and twenty times the inaccessible summits that both of us have ever seen, you would not have a picture equal to this."

Heavy winter snowfall (465 inches at Wolf Creek Pass) generates lush high-country forests and flower fields—Yankee Boy Basin above Ouray excels. High-country meadows and carpets of tundra above timberline harbor bright wildflower islands (except where sheep graze them down). The San Juan River rises on Wolf Creek Pass and drains the basins below the high peaks. It and smaller rivers (Piedra, Animas) drop precipitously from the peaks through dense spruce/fir, spread out in montane meadows, and course through cottonwood copses as they flow south. Over the divide west of Durango, the Dolores River flows north, and its white-water rapids tempt river runners.

Ponderosa woodlands extend from Pagosa Springs to Dove Creek; pinyon/juniper forests clothe the low hills across the center of the basin, over Mesa Verde, to Hovenweep National Monument. Desert grassland and shrubs extend south of Cortez to the Four Corners.

The basin's ponderosas specialize in Lewis's Woodpecker and Grace's Warbler, its canyons and cliffs in White-throated Swift. The P/J, particularly from Mesa Verde west, features Cooper's Hawk and Gray Vireo. Waterfalls in the high country, some available conveniently by car, host Black Swift. Wolf Creek Pass and the Million Dollar Highway wind through high-country aspen and conifer forests.

Cortez offers a spring birding festival—generally the second weekend in May. For information, contact the Cortez Cultural Center, 25 North Market Street, Cortez, CO 81321; (970) 565–1151; www.cortezculturalcenter.org.

San Juan Basin

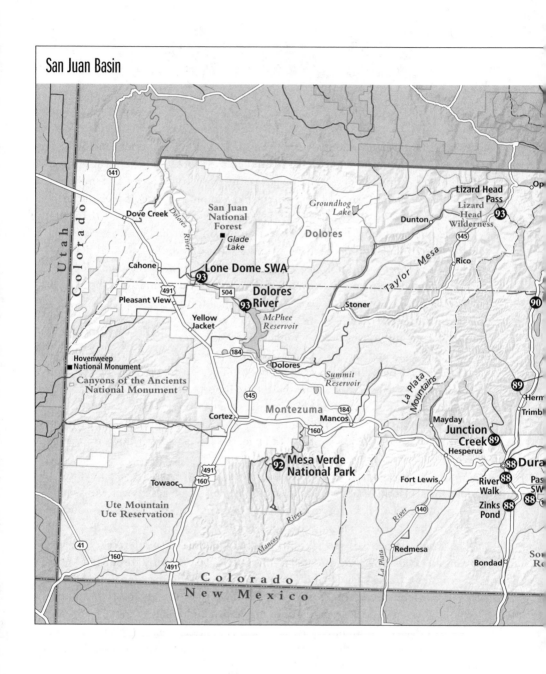

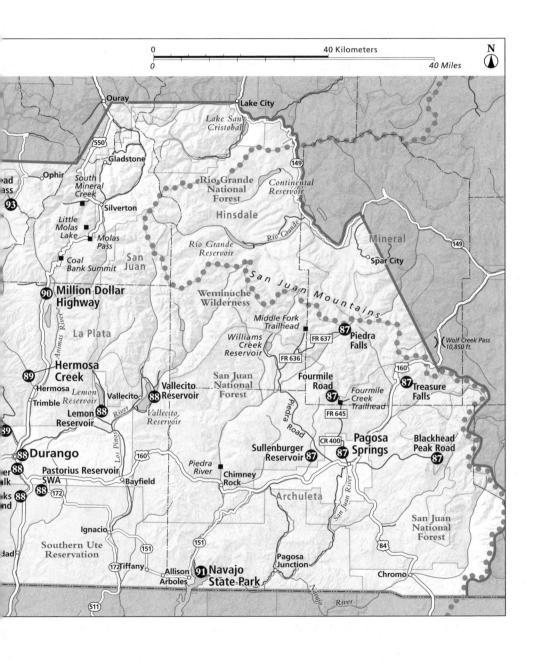

87 Pagosa Springs ⓦ🐚

Habitats: Ponderosa, mixed conifer/aspen, spruce/fir, foothills riparian, grassland.

Specialty birds: *Resident:* Lewis's Woodpecker, Gray Jay, three species of nuthatch, Evening Grosbeak. *Summer:* Black Swift, Olive-sided, Hammond's, and Cordilleran Flycatchers, Plumbeous Vireo, Hermit Thrush, Western Bluebird, MacGillivray's Warbler.

Best time to bird: Summer.

About this site

Pagosa Springs could claim the title of headquarters for Lewis's Woodpeckers. You see them in cottonwoods along the river in town, in the cemetery on the north side of U.S. Highway 160, and in parklike ponderosa woodlands west of town.

Radiating north and east of town, forest roads lead through stunning mountain backdrops into superb habitat for mountain birds. Roads and appealing trails deliver a generous supply and diversity of birds. Black Swifts nest at Treasure Falls, Piedra Falls, and up Fourmile Trail.

Winter birders can stay in Pagosa Springs and ski on Wolf Creek Pass, which has the usual ski-area birds (refer to Summit County).

The birding

Ponderosas grow tall and straight around Pagosa, often with an understory of scrub oak. This rich habitat harbors a rewarding variety of breeding birds: not only Lewis's Woodpecker, but Broad-tailed Hummingbird, Cordilleran Flycatcher, Plumbeous and Warbling (where aspens pop into view) Vireos, Steller's Jay, Violet-green and Tree Swallows, Pygmy, Red-breasted and White-breasted Nuthatches, Western Bluebird, Virginia's Warbler, Western Tanager, Green-tailed Towhee, Lazuli Bunting, and Brewer's Blackbird.

Of the Pagosa roads, **Fourmile Road** traverses the most attractive habitat mix. From US 160 just west of the arcaded Archuleta County courthouse, turn north at the traffic light at Fifth Street and cut left, then up right away, staying on Fifth Street. Fifth turns into County Road 411, which turns into County Road 400, then into Forest Road 634. In 5 miles you enter ponderosa woodlands; stop along the road at promising spots, but because of private property, stay on the road. At a junction 1.2 miles past the forest boundary, turn right on Forest Road 645.

Starting with the ponderosas, an interesting mix of mountain birds populates the roadside. The habitat changes from pure ponderosa to a mixture of ponderosa, aspen, white fir, and higher up, Engelmann spruce, that combine in a multilayered forest. Depending on habitat mix, you can encounter ponderosa birds plus others such as Broad-tailed, Rufous, and maybe Calliope Hummingbirds, Hairy and Downy Woodpeckers, Red-naped and Williamson's Sapsuckers, Olive-sided and

Hammond's Flycatchers, Common Raven, Ruby-crowned Kinglet (noisy in June, quiet by mid-July), Hermit Thrush, MacGillivray's Warbler, Lincoln's and White-crowned Sparrows, Red Crossbill, Pine Grosbeak, Cassin's Finch, Pine Siskin, and Evening Grosbeak.

From the junction, Road 645 continues 4.5 miles to the *Fourmile Creek Trailhead*. Black Swifts nest 4 to 5 miles up Fourmile Trail, at both Fourmile and Falls Creek Falls. Sometimes they feed over the woodlands along Forest Roads 634 and 645.

Another attractive forest road starts at the top of the long hill on the west side of Pagosa Springs; turn north (right if you're coming from town) on Piedra Road (County Road 600). At **Sullenburger Reservoir** (north of US 160 1.7 miles; just beyond Cloud Cap Avenue, look for an informal road on the left that leads 100 yards to the edge of the water), breeding Western Grebes carry babies on their backs by mid-July. County Road 600 turns into Forest Road 631. North of US 160 about 15.5 miles, try the turnoff to Piedra Picnic Area, two parking areas immediately on the right. The willow bottom here hosts Willow Flycatcher, Yellow Warbler, Song Sparrow, and Bullock's Oriole.

Pagosa Springs' Blackhead Peak Road leads into splendid forests of ponderosa, aspen, and spruce/fir.

Continue on County Road 600, which, 17.5 miles from US 160, turns into Forest Road 631; in 2.5 miles bear right on Forest Road 636 (to Middle Fork Trailhead), and in 1.8 miles, turn right on Forest Road 637 to **Piedra Falls.** At a parking lot 7.5 miles from the fork, a short half-mile trail leads through a spruce forest to this cascading waterfall. Birds along the trail include Northern Flicker, Hammond's Flycatcher, Warbling Vireo, Steller's Jay, Violet-green Swallow (swooping around the cliffs above the trail and over the stream), Western Tanager, Pine Siskin, and Evening Grosbeak. American Dippers fly up and down the stream below the falls. The falls themselves plunge over pot-holed lava rocks, a cool destination on a hot day. A dusk or dawn hike may yield Black Swifts.

When you return to Forest Road 636, you can turn right and drive over a rough road to the *Middle Fork Trailhead*. The road winds through spruce and aspen to the trailhead, where the Middle Fork of the Piedra River flows through foothills riparian shrubs and trees and attracts a different collection of birds: Belted Kingfisher, Broad-tailed (and maybe Rufous) Hummingbirds, Red-naped Sapsucker, Downy Woodpecker, Western Wood-Pewee, Olive-sided and Hammond's Flycatchers, Virginia's Warbler, Western Tanager, Chipping and Lincoln's Sparrows, and Dark-eyed Junco.

Forest Road 631 goes on to *Williams Creek Reservoir* (go right on Forest Road 640, 2 miles from the Middle Fork turnoff). Drive through Teal Campground to the State Wildlife Area. An Osprey may cruise along the reservoir, and a small pond on the right may have Mallard and American Coot.

East of Pagosa Springs, **Blackhead Peak Road** offers some of the same and some different habitats. From US 160 on the east side of town, go south 0.3 mile on U.S. Highway 84 and turn left on County Road 302 (Mill Creek Road). It crosses fields and drops down to follow Mill Creek, featuring foothills riparian trees and shrubs. Possible riparian birds include Red-tailed Hawk, Olive-sided, Dusky, and Cordilleran Flycatchers, Cliff Swallow, Plumbeous Vireo, Western Bluebird, MacGillivray's Warbler, Green-tailed Towhee, and Lesser Goldfinch. In 6 miles it becomes Forest Road 662. A half mile farther, bear right up an unnumbered road (actually Forest Road 665). You'll come into ponderosa pines; in 2005 the Forest Service started grubbing out underbrush by using huge mulching machines that grind up scrub oak on-site as the machines lumber through the woodland. As a result, the pines will recover more normal woodland spacing that tends to resist devastating crown fires—and favors ponderosa birds.

In these woodlands expect ponderosa and oak species such as Hammond's Flycatcher, Plumbeous Vireo, both chickadees, all three nuthatches (especially Pygmy), Steller's Jay, Mountain and Western Bluebirds, Hermit Thrush, Western Tanager, Green-tailed Towhee, Chipping Sparrow, Black-headed Grosbeak, and Cassin's Finch. Interspersed among the ponderosas, patches of scrub oak grow; look for little gray butterflies—the Colorado Gray Hairstreak, Colorado's state insect. They have orange spots on their hind wings that look like eyes—presumably to fool predators into nabbing their wings instead of their bodies.

Stay left on Forest Road 665 at forks 11.1 and 11.9 miles from US 84. The road rises through aspen and then spruce, and in the open spaces you can look toward Nipple Mountain (identify it by its shape, Blackhead Peak to its right). Keep left at Aspen Spur Road (it crosses a stream and takes you through aspen to a closed gate about 3 miles in; similar to the main road, but denser forest with no views). At 18.5 miles (from US 84) park at *Little Blanco Trailhead*. Although the road continues on from here, it's better to park and walk: The road narrows and cars bottom out on rocky stream crossings—only high-clearance vehicles can proceed.

Along the road expect Red-tailed Hawk, Downy Woodpecker, Steller's Jay, Clark's Nutcracker, Common Raven, Tree and Violet-green Swallows, Brown Creeper, Ruby-crowned Kinglet, MacGillivray's Warbler (fairly common), and Evening Grosbeak. Beyond Little Blanco Trailhead, flower fields and willows feature Broad-tailed and Rufous Hummingbirds and Lincoln's and White-crowned Sparrows. Gray Jay and Pine Grosbeak are possible, and Western Tanagers also range up this high. You can also try the *Blanco Basin road,* which leaves US 84 about 6 miles south of Blackhead Peak Road. Turn left on 326, which turns into Forest Roads 325 and 660.

Wolf Creek Pass, which US 160 ascends east of Pagosa Springs, has a stop for Black Swift seekers—a short trail to **Treasure Falls.** At the foot of the west side (if coming from the west, on the right about 9 miles from Pagosa Springs; if coming from Del Norte, about 4 miles from the top of the pass, just after the second hairpin turn, and on the left). The conifers hold the usual birds, but keep on track to the falls to see swifts. As in all Black Swift colonies, the most likely viewing time is dawn and dusk. See the Box Cañon site about Black Swift breeding habits.

West of Pagosa Springs 22 miles on US 160, Forest Road 622 on the right goes up the *Piedra River.* Ponderosas tower along the valley floor and hillsides. There and in the campground (another tenth of a mile on US 160, across the river), look for Grace's Warbler. Along the river in the campground look for Gray Catbird. In 2004 a Hooded Warbler spent a month here.

DeLorme grid: P. 88 A and B 1–3.

Elevation: Pagosa Springs, 7,105 feet; Four-mile Trail, 9,125 feet; Piedra Falls, 8,400 feet; Little Blanco Trailhead, 10,000 feet; Treasure Falls, 9,200 feet.

Hazards: Rough roads.

Nearest food, gas, lodging: Pagosa Springs.

Camping: Yes.

For more information: San Juan National Forest, 180 Pagosa Street, P.O. Box 310, Pagosa Springs, CO 81147; (970) 264–2268; www.fs.fed.us/r2/sanjuan.

88 Durango [W⊕]

Habitats: Ponderosa, wetlands, riparian.

Specialty birds: *Resident:* Acorn and Lewis's Woodpeckers. *Summer:* Common Poorwill, Ash-throated, Hammond's, and Gray Flycatchers, Juniper Titmouse, Bushtit, Blue-gray Gnat-catcher, Grace's and Black-throated Gray Warblers. *Winter:* Barrow's Goldeneye.

Best times to bird: Acorn Woodpecker site, year-round; River Walk, Pastorius, and Zinks Pond, spring and fall; Lemon and Vallecito, spring, summer, and fall.

About this site

Durango serves as a gateway to the rugged San Juan Mountains. Its specialty bird, Grace's Warbler, breeds in woodlands of tall ponderosa pines with scrub oak understory. Durango also boasts Colorado's only consistent site to find Acorn Woodpecker. It has a paucity of waterbird sites but a surfeit of splendid, scenic mountain habitats. The *Atlas* block that included the city recorded eighty-three breeding species; nearby mountain blocks tallied fifty-five species at midelevation and thirty-two species in the high country.

Directions

A short guide to Durango directions: At the south end of downtown, near the railroad depot, U.S. Highway 550 from the north joins US 160 (from the west). US 550 and 160 run together, going downstream along the Animas River, for 5 miles until 550 goes right, south to New Mexico. The directions below refer to West 550/160 and East 550/160 (where the highways separate on the west and east, respectively).

The birding

Acorn Woodpeckers, first discovered in 1992, inhabit a ridge covered with scrub oak and scattered ponderosa pines next to a sprawling subdivision. To see these birds, go west along US 160 from West 550/160 for 2 miles; turn left on Wildcat Canyon Road (County Road 141); continue 2 to 3 miles and turn right into the Rafter J subdivision (Meadow Road, County Road 142). Continue as it turns to gravel and starts downhill. Across the ravine, clown-faced Acorn Woodpeckers perch in the three tall ponderosas, each with many snags. They vault up and down the individual pines and fly back and forth among them. Sometimes they fly over to the road to stash acorns in holes in the power poles. Lewis's Woodpeckers also cruise over this hillside, and the Acorn Woodpeckers vigorously defend their acorn caches from the Lewis's. (Please stay on the road, as the land is private property.)

Two sites provide most of the water- and marsh-bird sightings in the Durango area. They attract a surprising variety, though not great numbers. **Pastorius SWA,**

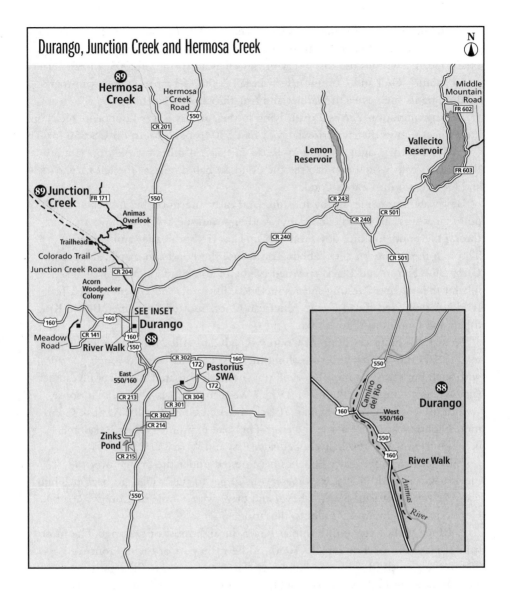

Durango, Junction Creek and Hermosa Creek

89 Hermosa Creek

Hermosa Creek Road

550

CR 201

Middle Mountain Road

FR 602

Lemon Reservoir

Vallecito Reservoir

FR 603

89 Junction Creek

FR 171

550

Animas Overlook

CR 243

CR 501

CR 240

CR 240

CR 501

Trailhead

Colorado Trail

Junction Creek Road

CR 204

Acorn Woodpecker Colony

SEE INSET

Durango

160

160

88

Meadow Road

CR 141

160

River Walk

550

East 550/160

CR 302

172

Pastorius SWA

160

172

CR 213

CR 301

CR 304

CR 302

CR 214

Zinks Pond

CR 215

550

550

160

Camino del Rio

West 550/160

88 Durango

550

160

River Walk

Animas River

an oasis amid pastureland, has a surprisingly large list of species for a small pond, probably due to its isolation. To get there from East 550/160, go 3 miles east on US 160 to Highway 172; turn right and, at 2.1 miles, as the highway curves left, go straight onto County Road 302; at 0.8 mile bear right on County Road 304 and at 0.3 mile turn into the wildlife area.

An alternative (or to get there on your way to or from Zinks Pond): From East 550/160, take US 550 south 4.8 miles and turn left onto County Road 302; in 2 miles turn left on County Road 301 and in 2 more miles turn right on the afore-mentioned County Road 304, then left into the SWA.

Shorebird migration brings in White-faced and Glossy (rare) Ibis, Semipalmated Plover, Solitary Sandpiper, Marbled Godwit, Long-billed Dowitcher, and Wilson's Phalarope. A few gulls use this reservoir as well as, in spring of 2005, a Least Tern, and a Sabine's Gull and Common Tern in fall 2006. The riparian areas can trap tired migrants such as Palm Warbler and Ash-throated Flycatcher.

During migration **Zinks Pond,** lying in the Animas River floodplain, picks up ducks, geese, and other waterfowl. From East 550/160, go south on US 550 for 5.3 miles and turn right on County Road 214; at 1.4 miles turn left on County Road 215, from which you can see the pond. In half a mile, at the left turn, park and look down into Zinks Pond.

Best watching comes in the morning and early afternoon because the view point faces west. In cloudy and rainy weather, seven species of swallows may throng the pond; looking down on them makes ID both easier and harder. Through the summer a few dabbling ducks use the pond and marsh, along with Great Blue Heron and Black-crowned Night-Heron. Sora and Virginia Rail inhabit the marshes. Nesting species include Cinnamon and Green-winged Teal, Ruddy Duck, Pied-billed Grebe, American Coot, Spotted Sandpiper, Belted King-fisher, and Common Yellowthroat.

Return to the intersection of County Roads 214 and 215, and go left as the road crosses the Animas and runs along the west bank. It passes through good P/J, with such birds as Common Poorwill (maybe), Ash-throated and Gray Flycatchers (also Western Kingbird), Plumbeous Vireo, Western Scrub Jay, Juniper Titmouse, Bushtit, Blue-gray Gnatcatcher, and Black-throated Gray Warbler. At dusk Common Nighthawks cruise along the river. The road turns into River Road and comes out onto US 160 halfway between East and West 550/160.

Another diversion: Black Phoebes have nested under the bridge over the Florida River south of Pastorius Reservoir. To get to the bridge, go back to Highway 172 (see "Pastorius SWA," above) and drive west 1 mile to County Road 307. Continue south about 4.5 miles to the bridge.

A **River Walk** follows the Animas River through most of Durango. The most fruitful place for local birders lies south of the main part of town. From West 550/160 go south (downstream) and turn left at the *second* traffic light (the one after Santa Rita; a bit over a half mile). Park in the corner of the parking lot next to the buildings. From this corner, a concrete trail leads down to the River Walk. Turn right and follow the path through the arch of towering cottonwoods interspersed with box-elders and shrubs. Here Durangoans have found a number of eastern rarities, including Chestnut-sided and Black-and-white Warblers, American Redstart, and Northern Waterthrush. Summer birds include Western Wood-Pewee, Rough-winged Swallow, Yellow Warbler, Song Sparrow, and Lesser Goldfinch.

North and east of Durango, two reservoirs have camping and birds. To reach **Lemon Reservoir,** turn east from Main Street onto 32nd Avenue; at 1.3 miles go right at the T intersection and left at the next T (1 block) onto Florida Road

(County Road 240). (In Durango you pronounce this "Flow-*reed*-a," accent on the "reed.") In 8.5 miles you enter the Missionary Ridge fire area; look at the tree skeletons high on the ridge. In 2002 this huge fire burned 70,485 acres between the Animas River and Vallecito Reservoir. In 11.7 miles take the left fork (i.e., go straight), onto County Road 243 to the reservoir. The road goes through fir/spruce/aspen woodlands; on the north you can see the burn, and the green that marks the forest's recovery. Skip Florida Campground, 7.3 miles up the road after you turn onto Road 243, and follow the road another mile as it climbs to Transfer Campground (with tall aspen and spruce), a good place to look for the conifer/aspen mix of birds.

Back on County Road 240, you can reach **Vallecito Reservoir** by continuing easterly another 2.7 miles, then left on County Road 501. (Alternatively, go north from US 160 at Bayfield 9 miles on County Road 501 to this point.) In 4.5 miles you come to the reservoir. Stay on the left side of the lake and at the end, in 5.2 miles, turn left on County Road 500; this takes you to Vallecito Campground and trailhead. The trail leads up Vallecito Creek through mixed pine/aspen/spruce habitat into the Weminuche Wilderness.

Returning to County Road 501, go left to continue on around the reservoir (and to more campgrounds). The county road turns into Forest Road 602, which in another 3.6 miles starts to climb up Pine Creek. To continue on the perimeter road, turn right at the ELK POINT LODGE sign; although the road looks primitive and private, you're welcome to drive through, past the private campground and restaurant, on your way around the lake. The road re-enters the national forest as Forest Road 603 and takes you through a section of the burn where you can marvel at the forest renaissance—sun-loving plants such as grasses, shrubs, and aspen have sprouted up to redeem the dead timber—and the birds that have populated it. From Middle Mountain, the road passes five public campgrounds and finally crosses the dam to rejoin County Road 501 at the south end of the lake.

As you drive along the roads ringing both reservoirs, look for Osprey (especially on Vallecito) as well as more common birds such as Mallard, Great Blue Heron, and Belted Kingfisher. From roads, campgrounds, and trails, you can find Olive-sided and Hammond's Flycatchers, Steller's Jay, Common Raven, Violet-green Swallow, the three nuthatches, Western Bluebird, Grace's Warbler, Western Tanager, Green-tailed Towhee (in brushy areas), Lincoln's Sparrow, and Black-headed and Evening Grosbeaks. In the streams listen for the noisy rattle of American Dipper.

In November, before it freezes, Vallecito attracts a few Barrow's Goldeneyes.

DeLorme grid: P. 86 B2-3, A4 and p. 87 A5.

Elevation: Durango, 6,400 feet; Pastorius, 6,860 feet; Zinks Pond, 6,200 feet; Lemon Reservoir, 8,200 feet, Vallecito Reservoir 7,600 feet.

Hazards: Fast bicyclists on the River Walk.

Nearest food, gas, lodging: Durango.

Camping: Durango, national forests.

For more information: San Juan Public Lands Center, 15 Burnett Court, Durango, CO 81301; (970) 247-4874; www.fs.fed.us/r2/sanjuan.

Habitats: Ponderosa pine.
Specialty birds: *Resident:* Red Crossbill.
Summer: Band-tailed Pigeon, Hammond's and

Cordilleran Flycatchers, Orange-crowned and Grace's Warblers.
Best time to bird: Summer.

About this site

These two sites, close to Durango, feature Grace's Warbler.

The birding

The road to **Junction Creek** leaves from Durango itself: From US 550 (Durango's Main Street), turn west (left if coming from the south) on 25th Street (turns into Junction Street and equals County Road 204). Stay left (straight) at the first junction in 2.8 miles. In another half mile you'll cross into the San Juan National Forest; you can park here to follow a trail along the cottonwoods of Junction Creek or drive another mile to parking for the south terminus of the 470-mile Colorado Trail (Durango to Denver).

Grace's Warblers nest at the beginning of the Colorado Trail. They prefer woodlands with tall ponderosas and a scrub oak understory. Typical ponderosa birds inhabit the woodlands—Mountain Chickadee, Pygmy Nuthatch, and Red Crossbill. Along the riparian trail (where you first enter the national forest), expect Broad-tailed Hummingbird, Red-naped Sapsucker, Cordilleran Flycatcher, Western Tanager, and Blue and Black-headed Grosbeaks. If you continue up the road another 1.5 miles, at the Log Chute trails you can find similar species (and Virginia's Warbler) with fewer hikers, and past Animas Overlook (6 miles), if you're really lucky, a Northern Goshawk.

For **Hermosa Creek,** drive north on US 550 to Hermosa, 8 miles from Durango; turn left, not at the store onto County Road 202 but on the next road, County Road 201, just before the railroad tracks; a sign directs you to "Lower Hermosa Road."

The road winds up the side of the hill; look above you for Band-tailed Pigeons that come into feeders above the road. (Careful: The narrow road has no space for parking.) It passes through scrub oak and lush pinyon/juniper and then into ponderosa habitat. At 3.2 miles, near Milepost 2 (for the Forest Service road), a particularly productive stand of ponderosa hosts a great collection of birds: conspicuous among them, Grace's, Orange-crowned, and Yellow-rumped Warblers; also, Hairy Woodpecker, Warbling Vireo, Mountain Chickadee, Pygmy and White-breasted Nuthatches, Western Tanager, and Red Crossbill.

Grace's Warblers nest in these pines on Junction Creek.

The road reaches Lower Hermosa Campground (4 miles from US 550) and a trailhead, still dominated by ponderosa pine. A trail from the campground joins one from the road's end to trek up the Hermosa Creek valley, 10 miles to Purgatory ski area.

DeLorme grid: Junction Creek, p. 86 B2; Hermosa Creek, p. 86 A3.

Elevation: Junction Creek, 7,500 to 8,000 feet; Hermosa Creek, 6,800 to 7,800 feet.

Nearest food, gas, lodging: Durango.

Camping: Yes.

For more information: San Juan Public Lands Center, 15 Burnett Court, Durango, CO 81301; (970) 247–4874; www.fs.fed.us/r2/sanjuan.

90 Million Dollar Highway [W]

Habitats: Aspen, spruce/fir, montane meadow, willow carr.

Specialty birds: *Resident:* Gray Jay, Pine Grosbeak. *Summer:* Ring-necked Duck, Black Swift, Hermit Thrush.

Best time to bird: Summer.

About this site

Coloradans call the incomparable US 550, from Durango to Silverton to Ouray, the "Million Dollar Highway" because its first constructed section, from Ouray to Red Mountain, cost a million dollars to build—a huge sum for a 1924 highway segment. It crosses three mountain passes between Durango and Ouray, where it bottoms out into the comparatively flat Uncompahgre Valley. It keeps you looking: Rugged peaks range from gray granite to bright red sedimentary rocks, their colors punctuated by snowfields, aspens, and conifers.

Little Molas Lake presents a stunning setting in which to see spruce/fir and subalpine wetland species.

The birding

Don't get distracted by stopping at lower-elevation sites such as Haviland Lake SWA and Chris Park or, higher up, Old Lime Creek Road (extremely rough and unsuitable for cars).

At *Coal Bank Summit* (10,640 feet) you can stop and walk into a handsome spruce/fir woodland, although an electronic installation across the highway from the restrooms disturbs the habitat some. Andrews Lake has nice facilities but limited bird-watching. It does have nesting Ring-necked Duck, Mallard, and Spotted Sandpiper. Better to push on to *Molas Pass* (10,910 feet)—worth a stop simply to look at the Needle Mountains—and then head to Little Molas Lake (turnoff 0.4 mile beyond the top of the pass).

A prime site, *Little Molas Lake* combines a stunning high-mountain setting with interesting high-mountain birds and a high-mountain section of the Colorado Trail. Drive in about a mile, keeping to the right as best you can until you can swing around to the west side of the lake. It's an up-and-down dirt road, not graveled and therefore rutted. Campers nestle their tents among the spruce thickets and spruce birds. Carpets of flowers light up the landscape: blue larkspur, monkshood, Jacob's ladder, and chiming bells; red and cream paintbrush; white ramshorn, wand lily (death camas), and yarrow; yellow arnica and parsley; purple penstemon.

On the lake and its edge, you should encounter Ring-necked Duck, Mallard, Spotted Sandpiper, and American Coot. In the swampy willows look for Wilson's Warbler and Lincoln's and White-crowned Sparrows (the flamboyant White-crowneds will almost seek you out). In spruce copses, Pine Grosbeak, Gray Jay, Hermit Thrush, and Pine Siskin nest.

Beyond Little Molas Lake, the highway drops into *Silverton,* an old mining town and the terminus of the narrow-gauge railway that runs from Durango. Designated a National Historic District, the town has a nineteenth-century ambience, but also service stations, restaurants, lodging, souvenir shops, and House Sparrows. Beyond Silverton, contrasting colors rivet your attention: Bright red and orange rock slopes contrast with lines of light green aspen and dark green spruces.

Two miles from Silverton, turn left onto County Road 7, to *South Mineral Creek.* (A sign announces NATIONAL FOREST ACCESS.) Immediately the road runs beside tall willows where Wilson's Warbler and Lincoln's and Fox Sparrows nest. About 3 miles along, look across South Mineral Creek at the waterfalls that drop precipitously into the valley. In some years Black Swifts nest behind the falls, but only at dawn and dusk do they fly in and out, as at the Box Cañon site. South Mineral Creek Campground, 4.4 miles from US 550, sits among tall spruces. A trail climbs up through high-altitude aspen and spruce/fir, up above timberline into alpine meadows carpeted with wildflowers on the way to Ice Lakes Basin (about 4 miles).

Back on the pavement, US 550 climbs up again, to Red Mountain Pass (11,018 feet), and follows the course of an old toll road. Old mines line the highway, with a historic site at the Idarado mine. Although paved, the highway evokes the ruggedness of that original pathway—perched several hundred feet above the canyon, a white line at the edge of the road instead of a guardrail. Some folks find this section quite scary. The highway traverses steep aspen- and conifer-covered hillsides and broad willow-covered valleys. From Silverton to Ouray (also a National Historic District), the road covers 23.5 miles, but even without stopping for birds, mines, and scenery, plan on an hour for this part of the trip.

Occasionally, at some parking spots on the way down to Ouray, you can see Black Swifts feeding at or above eye level, but only sometimes. Just before the road drops into Ouray, a turnoff leads to Yankee Boy Basin (jeep road with fabulous wildflowers) and Box Cañon—where you're guaranteed to see Black Swifts.

DeLorme grid: P. 86, 76, and 66 A–D 3–4.
Elevation: 7,500 to 11,018 feet.
Hazards: Narrow road with drop-offs and no guardrail—drive with care.
Nearest food, gas, lodging: Durango, Silverton, Ouray.
Camping: Yes.

For more information: U.S. Forest Service, 110 West 11th Street, Durango, CO 81301 (970) 247-4874; www.fs.fed.us/r2/sanjuan. U.S. Forest Service, 101 North Uncompahgre, Montrose, CO 81402 (970) 249-3711; www.fs.fed.us/r2/gmug.

The raspy "chick-a-dee-dee-dee" of the Mountain Chickadee can erupt from any Colorado conifer forest.

91 Navajo State Park Ⓦ🧭 Ⓢ ♿ 🐾

Habitats: Wetlands, riparian, pinyon/juniper, sagebrush.

Specialty birds: *Summer:* Common Poorwill,

Western Bluebird, Yellow-breasted Chat, Lesser Goldfinch.

Best times to bird: Spring, summer, fall.

About this site

Few bird-watchers explore Navajo Reservoir, so we know little of its birdlife. It may attract an interesting mix of waterfowl during migration. From the state park, this reservoir—3 to 5 miles in extent—looks large for Colorado; however, it extends south into New Mexico another 20 miles, with tentacles reaching up a surprising number of side canyons. Park trails cover the gamut of southwestern Colorado habitats. Three *Atlas* blocks that included the reservoir or the San Juan River recorded sixty-five to sixty-seven breeding species.

In summer, temperatures hit the 90s; early morning birding produces more birds, more comfortably. Extensive use by boaters (in everything from personal watercraft to 80-foot houseboats) makes waterbirds scarce in summer.

Directions

From Durango, go east 8 miles on US 160 from East 550/160 and right on Highway 172. The road passes through low hills and farm fields, probably once covered by sagebrush and P/J. At Ignacio go left on Highway 151. In 18 miles at County Road 982, turn right 1.5 miles to the visitor center.

From Pagosa Springs, go west 17 miles on US 160, then turn left on Highway 151 and proceed 15.5 miles to the Watchable Wildlife site (see below), or 18 miles to Road 982. You can also drive south from Pagosa Springs on County Road 500 (Trujillo Road, 3 blocks west of the courthouse) takes you to the first day-use area on the San Juan River.

The birding

Opposite the visitor center, *Lakeview Trail* (actually two parallel trails 50 feet apart) penetrates dense shrubs. Cross the road toward the lake and go left for the best habitat. Walk a short distance or 1.5 miles to Wind Surf Beach. (You can drive to Wind Surf Beach on a side road 0.7 mile before the park entrance.) Along the trail expect common migrant swallows, warblers, and sparrows, Common Nighthawk, Olive-sided Flycatcher, goldfinches, and Pine Siskin.

From the visitor center, go south on the park road, keeping right, and at *Mooring Cove* turn left into a parking lot. Look here for P/J birds including Common Poorwill (if you're lucky, at dusk), Black-chinned Hummingbird, Ash-throated and Gray Flycatchers, Pinyon Jay, Bewick's Wren, Western Bluebird, and Black-throated

Gray Warbler. If you walk far enough out the point, you can start listing birds in New Mexico—the state line crosses the south third of this peninsula. (The park has several other P/J sites along Highway 151 and County Road 500.)

Return to Highway 151, go right 2.3 miles; an unmarked road on the right turns into the *Watchable Wildlife Area*. A short trail leads to a reconstructed railroad bridge (augmented by a shady, roofed shelter) that spans the Piedra River. Cliff and Barn Swallows nest under the bridge. Across the bridge, check the cottonwood groves on both sides of the railroad grade, and between the bridge and parking lot, sample the willow thickets. Likely birds in the trees include Cooper's Hawk, Lewis's Woodpecker, Red-naped Sapsucker, Cassin's Kingbird, Warbling Vireo and Yellow-breasted Chat; in the shrubs, Dusky Flycatcher, Northern Mockingbird, Indigo as well as Lazuli Buntings, Vesper and Lark Sparrows, and Blue Grosbeak.

Highway 151 crosses the Piedra River; 0.2 mile from the Watchable Wildlife Area, try the Piedra River Picnic Area (left), shaded by cottonwoods. One mile from the Watchable Wildlife Area, turn right on County Road 500 to the east arm of the reservoir. Several day-use areas have limited appeal to bird-watchers (Arboles Point, 3.5 miles from Highway 151, has okay P/J). In 8 miles, just beyond Milepost 35, you can turn right to walk the half-mile grove of tall cottonwoods bordering the San Juan River. In farmyards you might spot a Say's Phoebe.

In spring and fall look for waterbirds. You might find a few grebes, Double-crested Cormorant, Common Merganser, and Ruddy Duck.

If from County Road 982 (the road to park headquarters) you go left on Highway 151 (west toward Ignacio), in 3 miles County Road 988 on the left leads to *Sambrito Wetlands* (1.75 miles to the parking lot). The picnic shelter shields several dozen Cliff Swallow nests. A 0.75-mile nature trail leads past two cattail marshes to Sambrito Bay. The marshes harbor Virginia Rail, Sora, American Coot, Common Snipe, dabbling ducks, herons, and Common Yellowthroat. The bay attracts waterfowl and possibly grebes and loons.

DeLorme grid: P. 87 D6-7.
Elevation: 6,100 feet.
Hazards: Heat.
Nearest food, gas, lodging: Durango, Pagosa Springs, and Ignacio; food and gas at Arboles.

Camping: Yes.
For more information: Navajo State Park, P.O. Box 1697, Arboles, CO 81121; (970) 883-2208; www.parks.state.co.us.

92 Mesa Verde National Park

Habitats: Pinyon/juniper, scrub oak, cliffs.
Specialty birds: *Resident:* Common Raven.
Summer: White-throated Swift. *Winter:* Rosy-finches.

Best times to bird: May to September.

About this site

Mesa Verde, of course, offers the premier suite of ancestral Puebloans' cliff dwellings that everybody should sample. The park has 4,000 archaeological sites including 600 cliff dwellings. Roads and trails lead to such gems as Cliff Palace, Balcony House, Spruce Tower, and Far View. Park programs, naturally, orient toward its human history, but birders can find many places to seek P/J, scrub-oak, and cliff-dwelling birds. Naturalists at the visitor centers can help with your birding.

Directions

From Cortez, drive 10 miles east on US 160 to the park entrance, on the right. From Durango, take US 160 west 36 miles to the entrance, on the right (to an overpass).

The birding

White-throated Swifts swoop through the skies at practically every stop, performing their in-air gymnastics throughout the park. The splendid *Far View Visitor Center,* 15 miles from US 160, has exhibits and manages reservations for tours of Cliff Palace, Balcony House, and Long House. Chapin Mesa, 10 miles farther, operates year-round, while Wetherill Mesa (turn off a mile from Far View Visitor Center) opens only in summer.

Before you arrive at Far View, the road climbs rapidly. *Mancos Valley Overlook* offers views of the ranching valley below Mesa Verde and the La Plata Mountains behind it; to the north the pinyon/juniper woodland stretches all the way to the San Miguel Mountains' three 14,000-foot peaks. The road takes you through what looks like a devastated landscape—marked by the extensive Bircher fire that burned 22,405 acres in 2000 and left few live trees. Yet underneath, a green carpet forms in the spring, scrub oaks sprout, and cover and birds will return. Ecosystems adjust to these periodic incidents.

Between Far View and Chapin Mesa the Long Meadow fire of 2002 burned 2,601 acres. An exhibit at Far View shows the extent of fires in the past fifty years—fires that together covered almost the entire park. You won't find many birds in the burned areas, but you can find typical P/J species in recovered, older burn areas.

Drive the 6-mile *Mesa Top Loop,* at the end of the Chapin Mesa section of the park, and stop at the overlooks. Extra fine, large, pinyon pines and junipers here host a plentiful collection of P/J birds. White-throated Swifts twitter and twinkle at each canyon overlook. Every 50 yards a Black-throated Gray Warbler sings its distinctive *Don't you just love P/J?* song. You might ferret out a Bewick's Wren, a roving band of Bushtits, a slow-singing Plumbeous Vireo, or a pair of Juniper Titmice. Listen for noisy flocks of Pinyon Jays. Other likely species include Black-chinned Hummingbird, Ash-throated Flycatcher, and Spotted Towhee. Habitat generalists in the P/J include Wild Turkey, Broad-tailed Hummingbird, Steller's and Western Scrub Jays, Mountain Chickadee, White-breasted Nuthatch, and Chipping Sparrow. At night you can hear Common Poorwill and possibly a Northern Saw-whet Owl. Spotted Owls nest in some remote canyons.

Other walks in P/J habitat yield the same collection of birds. In unburned stretches of scrub oak, you can also find Sharp-shinned Hawk, American Kestrel, Western Scrub-Jay, Mountain Bluebird, Townsend's Solitaire, Blue-gray Gnatcatcher, Virginia's Warbler, Spotted Towhee, and Black-headed Grosbeak.

At canyon overlooks, soaring birds include not only the zooming swifts, but also Violet-green Swallow, Common Raven, Turkey Vulture, and perhaps a Red-tailed Hawk, Golden Eagle, or Peregrine Falcon (especially near the park entrance at the towering Knife Edge). Listen for a singing Canyon Wren.

Its elevation a little higher than Mesa Top Loop, *Far View Community,* lacking the comparatively lush woodland of the Loop, has fewer birds. Still, you may find here species such as chickadees, titmice, and jays.

Because of constant people traffic, most birds avoid the Ruin Trails. However, you can sample P/J habitat on several 1- to 2-mile hikes on Chapin Mesa (the main section, open all year): Soda Canyon Overlook, Petroglyph Point, and Spruce Canyon. On Wetherill Mesa (open May to September), two trails run through P/J.

DeLorme grid: P. 85 B and C 4.

Elevation: 7,000 to 8,000 feet.

Hazards: Rattlesnakes, gnats, mosquitoes, and other biting critters.

Nearest food, gas, lodging: Cortez, Dolores, and Mancos; food and lodging in the park in season.

Camping: Yes.

For more information: Mesa Verde National Park, P.O. Box 8, Mesa Verde National Park, CO 81330; (970) 529-4465; www.nps.gov/meve.

Dolores River/Lone Dome SWA

Habitats: Riparian, pinyon/juniper, ponderosa, Douglas-fir.

Specialty birds: *Summer:* White-throated Swift, Black Phoebe, Cordilleran Flycatcher.

Best times to bird: May to October.

About this site

Especially striking in spring when snow covers their higher reaches, Utah's LaSal Mountains, on the west as you drive along US 491, rise above the landscape like an island in the sky. Along the Dolores River the floodplain offers the typical western riparian species. The road crosses through pinyon/juniper and ponderosa woodlands where you can stop, look, and listen for the birds of those habitats and admire the beautiful sandstone cliffs and domes.

Directions

From Cortez, drive north on US 491 for 22 miles (2 miles past Pleasant View); turn right on County Road EE 1.5 miles to a T intersection, then left 1.5 miles on County Road 16, then right on County Road S to Bradfield Bridge. After checking out the cottonwoods along the stream, drive across the bridge and go right on Forest Road 504 along the river. You can drive 12 miles along the Dolores River to the McPhee dam, 7 miles of it through Lone Dome SWA.

The birding

The bird of the county, White-throated Swift, swoops over the river and around the cliffs. Fellow swoopers include Violet-green, Rough-winged, and Cliff Swallows. Nighthawks and Common Poorwills break the silence of dusk. Along the river look for Great Blue Heron, Spotted Sandpiper, Belted Kingfisher, American Dipper, and migrating Osprey. An occasional Black Phoebe nests here. Riparian groves attract Cordilleran Flycatcher, Orange-crowned and MacGillivray's Warblers, Yellow-breasted Chat, Gray Catbird, Savannah, Vesper, and Lark Sparrows, Lazuli Bunting, and Yellow-headed and Brewer's Blackbirds. Migration brings Wilson's Warbler and White-crowned Sparrow.

Farther upstream, among the conifers (ponderosa pine and Douglas-fir), look for Plumbeous Vireo, Brown Creeper, Western and Mountain Bluebirds, Steller's and Western Scrub-Jays, Clark's Nutcracker (more likely in winter), and Western Tanager.

If you're in a pioneering mood, try Forest Road 504 (straight instead of right from Bradfield Bridge), which rises into conifers and aspen to *Glade Lake,* where Eared Grebes nest in a pocket surrounded by spruce and aspen. Take a map to negotiate the maze of forest roads to Highway 145: Forest Roads 514, 532, and 535 go generally easterly.

Highway 145 goes northeasterly from Cortez through Rico (aspen) and over **Lizard Head Pass** (alpine meadows). The views of Lizard Head Peak make you understand why the first climbers of this strange spire found it so scary that chewing gum dried in their mouths. The highway traverses spruce/fir down to Telluride and foothills riparian along the San Miguel River to Placerville.

DeLorme grid: P. 74 C3.

Elevation: 6,500 to 6,700 feet.

Hazards: Rattlesnakes, biting insects.

Nearest food, gas, lodging: Cortez, Dove Creek.

Camping: Yes.

For more information: Colorado Division of Wildlife, 151 East 16th Street, Durango, CO 81301; (970) 247-0855; www.wildlife.state .co.us.

The cryptic Common Poorwill favors dry, rocky, and shrubby hillsides.

PHOTO © GLENN WALBEK

Appendix A: Specialty Birds by Habitat

Many birders visit Colorado hoping to find western species or birds that are hard to find in other parts of the country. The following two appendices provide information about how to use this book to find western birds (and other birds on the state list).

Each habitat (described in the introduction) has a particular set of birds. Under Habitats, each account lists habitats at the site. This appendix catalogs likely birds by habitat. By cross-referencing a site habitat to appendix A, you can figure out the birds to expect at a particular site in addition to the season-specific ones in the site account.

Typical Breeding Species by Habitat

Data from *Colorado Breeding Bird Atlas*.
Asterisks denote the most common species in each habitat.
Boldface indicates western specialties.

RIPARIAN

LOWLAND RIPARIAN

American Kestrel	* **Western Kingbird**	House Wren
Mourning Dove	Eastern Kingbird	* Yellow Warbler
Great Horned Owl	Blue Jay (east)	Blue Grosbeak
Northern Flicker	**Black-billed Magpie**	* **Bullock's Oriole**
Western Wood-Pewee	Black-capped Chickadee	

FOOTHILLS RIPARIAN (DECIDUOUS)

Broad-tailed Hummingbird	Warbling Vireo	* Yellow Warbler
* Northern Flicker	House Wren	Song Sparrow
Western Wood-Pewee	* American Robin	

FOOTHILLS RIPARIAN (CONIFEROUS)

* **Broad-tailed Hummingbird**	Golden-crowned Kinglet	American Robin
* **Cordilleran Flycatcher**	* **Ruby-crowned Kinglet**	**Yellow-rumped Warbler**
Mountain Chickadee	**Swainson's Thrush**	**Western Tanager**

WILLOW CARR

Broad-tailed Hummingbird	Black-capped Chickadee	Fox Sparrow
Rufous Hummingbird (migr.)	**Swainson's Thrush**	Song Sparrow
Red-naped Sapsucker	Yellow Warbler	* **Lincoln's Sparrow**
Willow Flycatcher	**MacGillivray's Warbler**	* White-crowned Sparrow
Dusky Flycatcher	* **Wilson's Warbler**	

WETLANDS BREEDERS

Waterbirds

* Mallard	Green-winged Teal	American Coot
Blue-winged Teal	* American White Pelican	**California Gull**
Cinnamon Teal	Double-crested Cormorant	* Ring-billed Gull

WETLANDS BREEDERS (continued)

Waders and Shorebirds

Great Blue Heron
Virginia Rail
* Sora

* Killdeer
American Avocet
Spotted Sandpiper

* Wilson's Snipe
Wilson's Phalarope

Landbirds

Northern Harrier
* Common Yellowthroat
Belted Kingfisher

Savannah Sparrow
Song Sparrow
* Red-winged Blackbird

Brewer's Blackbird
Yellow-headed Blackbird

WETLANDS MIGRANTS

Waterbirds

* Canada Goose
Cackling Goose
Gadwall
American Wigeon
Northern Shoveler
Northern Pintail
Canvasback
* Redhead

Lesser Scaup
Bufflehead
Common Goldeneye
* Common Merganser
Hooded Merganser
Common Loon
Pacific Loon (rare)
Pied-billed Grebe

* **Western Grebe**
Clark's Grebe
Horned Grebe
Eared Grebe
* Franklin's Gull
Bonaparte's Gull
Herring Gull

Waders and Shorebirds

White-faced Ibis
Osprey
* Lesser Yellowlegs
* Greater Yellowlegs
Willet

Semipalmated Sandpiper
Western Sandpiper
Least Sandpiper
White-rumped Sandpiper
* **Baird's Sandpiper**

Pectoral Sandpiper
Stilt Sandpiper
Long-billed Dowitcher
American Pipit

GRASSLANDS

SHORT-GRASS PRAIRIE

Swainson's Hawk
Ferruginous Hawk
Killdeer
Mourning Dove

Burrowing Owl
Common Nighthawk
* Horned Lark
Cassin's Sparrow

Lark Sparrow
* **Lark Bunting**
Grasshopper Sparrow
* **Western Meadowlark**

Specialists: Mountain Plover, Long-billed Curlew, McCown's and **Chestnut-collared Longspurs**

PLAINS (WINTER)

Red-tailed Hawk
* Rough-legged Hawk
Golden Eagle

Merlin
Northern Shrike
* Horned Lark

American Tree Sparrow
Dark-eyed Junco
* Lapland Longspur

MONTANE GRASSLAND

Horned Lark
* **Mountain Bluebird**

* Vesper Sparrow
* **Western Meadowlark**

Brewer's Blackbird

ALPINE TUNDRA

Prairie Falcon
* **White-tailed Ptarmigan**

* Horned Lark
Rock Wren

* **American Pipit**
* **Brown-capped Rosy-Finch**

SHRUBLAND

DESERT SHRUB

Mourning Dove
Loggerhead Shrike
* Horned Lark

Sage Thrasher
* Brewer's Sparrow
Vesper Sparrow

Lark Sparrow
* Western Meadowlark

SCRUB OAK

Dusky Flycatcher
Western Scrub-Jay
Orange-crowned Warbler

* Virginia's Warbler
Blue-gray Gnatcatcher
* Green-tailed Towhee

* Spotted Towhee
Black-headed Grosbeak

SAGEBRUSH

Mourning Dove
Sage Thrasher
* Green-tailed Towhee

* Brewer's Sparrow
* Vesper Sparrow

Lark Sparrow
Western Meadowlark

FOOTHILLS SHRUB

* Broad-tailed Hummingbird
Dusky Flycatcher
Blue-gray Gnatcatcher

Virginia's Warbler
MacGillivray's Warbler

* Spotted Towhee
* Green-tailed Towhee
(Western Slope)

MOUNTAIN FORESTS

PONDEROSA PINE

Northern Flicker
Western Wood-Pewee
* Steller's Jay
Mountain Chickadee

White-breasted Nuthatch
* Pygmy Nuthatch
Western Bluebird

Chipping Sparrow
* Western Tanager
Red Crossbill

PINYON/JUNIPER (P/J)

Red-tailed Hawk
* Mourning Dove
Common Nighthawk
Northern Flicker
Gray Flycatcher
Ash-throated Flycatcher

Gray Vireo
Plumbeous Vireo
Western Scrub-Jay
* Pinyon Jay
Mountain Chickadee
Juniper Titmouse
Bushtit

Bewick's Wren
Blue-gray Gnatcatcher
Mountain Bluebird
Black-throated Gray Warbler
Spotted Towhee
* Chipping Sparrow

LODGEPOLE PINE

Mountain Chickadee
* Ruby-crowned Kinglet

Hermit Thrush
* Yellow-rumped Warbler

* Red Crossbill
Pine Siskin

SPRUCE/FIR

Olive-sided Flycatcher
Hammond's Flycatcher
Gray Jay
* Mountain Chickadee

Red-breasted Nuthatch
* Ruby-crowned Kinglet
* Hermit Thrush
Yellow-rumped Warbler

Dark-eyed Junco
Pine Grosbeak
Pine Siskin

ASPEN

* **Red-naped Sapsucker**
  Northern Flicker
  Western Wood-Pewee
* Warbling Vireo
  Purple Martin (west)

Violet-green Swallow
Tree Swallow
Black-capped Chickadee
* House Wren

Mountain Bluebird
American Robin
Yellow-rumped Warbler
Dark-eyed Junco

Appendix B: Colorado Checklist

This appendix lists 482 species in three sections.

List A

Species that an observer *who goes to the right place at the right time* has a reasonable chance of seeing during the year (324 species).

An abbreviated chart such as this one condenses its information, so interpret with care. For instance, a duck that occurs statewide obviously won't winter at an ice-covered lake in the mountains or plains, and usually migrating warblers stay only briefly on their journey to or from the breeding grounds.

Refer to specific site accounts for more definite information on time of year, location, and other bird-watching information.

Guide to the columns:

Season: Most likely time(s) of year for the species.

Region: General location(s) within the state where the species occurs.

Habitat: Likely habitats.

Likelihood: Your chances of finding the species. In order of frequency: High, Good, Fair, or Low.

Specialty Sites: Lists likely places described in this guide to find some species. For visitors from the East, it locates western specialties, and for Coloradans and westerners, it offers sites for some eastern species. Most species occur in other places as well.

This column also qualifies some information in the preceding columns (for example, for a species present year-round, if the status changes between summer and winter). A few sites mentioned don't appear in the guide; for example, the Flattops Wilderness and the Park Range host the only breeding sites for Barrow's Goldeneye and Bufflehead, respectively, but you can't visit them easily—they require long hikes (or backpacks) to reach the remote breeding sites.

List B

Species that observers have only a slight chance of finding. To see these birds, one must visit a particular site within the window of opportunity. Observers who follow Cobirds by e-mail or Internet can keep abreast of occurrences (eighty-three species).

List C

Birds on the Colorado checklist with fewer than ten occurrences (seventy-five species).

Explanation of terms

Season

Migration: Fall and spring, during the normal migration season for the species (for example, March and April for ducks, mid-April through May for warblers).

Summer: Includes migration—many mountain breeders appear on the plains and western valleys in migration. However, in the Specialty Sites column, an entry labeled "Summer" usually refers only to the breeding season.

Winter: Includes migration—many species appear in various habitats during migration and then winter in the same or other parts of the state (for example, Ruby-crowned Kinglets that breed in the high country migrate in the valleys and winter, sparingly, in riparian zones, especially in southern Colorado).

Abbreviated Geographical Terms

Arkansas Valley: Arkansas Valley from Pueblo to the state line east of Lamar; "Lower Arkansas" refers to the eastern section, from Rocky Ford east.

Front Range: Urban/rural corridor along the edge of the mountains from Fort Collins south through Denver, Colorado Springs, and Pueblo to Trinidad.

Local: Within the particular geographical area, the species occurs in only a few sites.

Mountains: High country from 7,500 to 12,500 feet (few birds occur above 12,500 feet).

Plains: From the eastern border up to the edge of the mountains, including the Front Range.

Plains Rivers: South Platte, Arkansas, and Republican (Bonny State Park) River valleys.

Transition: Elevations 5,500 to 8,500 feet, mainly foothills along the Front Range and mesas, hills, and plateaus in southeastern and western Colorado.

Western Slope: The western third of the state, the part west of the Continental Divide.

Western Plateau: Mesas, hills, and plateaus in western Colorado.

Space-saving Abbreviations

Ag: Agricultural lands, croplands, farm and ranch shelterbelts
SLV: San Luis Valley
SP: State park
NWR: National Wildlife Refuge
RMNP: Rocky Mountain National Park

Tony Leukering applied his vast knowledge of the distribution of Colorado birds to review this list. My thanks and appreciation to him.

List A: Birds apt to be seen during the year

SPECIES	SEASON	REGION	HABITAT	LIKELI-HOOD	SPECIALTY SITES
☐ Greater White-fronted Goose	Fall, winter	East of mountains	Lakes	Fair	John Martin, Great Plains Res., Jumbo, Poudre, Barr
☐ Snow Goose	Fall, winter	Plains, esp. SE	Lakes	High	John Martin, Great Plains Res., Jumbo, Poudre, Barr
☐ Ross' Goose	Fall, winter	East of mountains	Lakes	Fair	John Martin, Great Plains Res., Jumbo, Poudre, Barr
☐ Cackling Goose	Fall, winter	East of mountains	Lakes	Fair	
☐ Canada Goose	Year-long	Statewide	Urban, lakes	High	
Ducks	Winter	Statewide	Lakes, streams		With freeze-up, move down-mountain and south
☐ Wood Duck	Year-long	Front Range	Riparian	Fair	Scarce in winter
☐ Gadwall	Year-long	Statewide	Lakes, streams	Good	
☐ American Wigeon	Year-long	Statewide	Lakes	Good	*Summer:* scarce except North Park
☐ Mallard	Year-long	Statewide	Lakes, streams	High	
☐ Blue-winged Teal	Summer	Statewide	Lakes	Good	
☐ Cinnamon Teal	Summer	Statewide	Lakes	Good	Front Range and west
☐ Northern Shoveler	Year-long	Statewide	Lakes, streams	Good	
☐ Northern Pintail	Year-long	Statewide	Lakes	Good	*Summer:* scarce
☐ Green-winged Teal	Year-long	Statewide	Lakes	Good	
☐ Canvasback	Year-long	Statewide	Lakes	Fair	*Summer:* very scarce, only in west
☐ Redhead	Year-long	Statewide	Lakes	Good	*Summer:* scarce
☐ Ring-necked Duck	Summer	Mountains	Lakes	Good	*Migration, Winter:* statewide
☐ Greater Scaup	Fall, winter	Statewide	Lakes	Low	
☐ Lesser Scaup	Year-long	Statewide	Lakes	Good	*Summer:* scarce
☐ Surf Scoter	Fall	Statewide	Lakes	Low	Spinney & Eleven-Mile, Boulder Res., Fossil Cr., Pueblo Res., Colorado R. SP
☐ White-winged Scoter	Fall	Statewide	Lakes	Low	Spinney & Eleven-Mile, Boulder Res., Fossil Cr., Pueblo Res., Colorado R. SP
☐ Black Scoter	Fall	Statewide	Lakes	Low	Spinney & Eleven-Mile, Boulder Res., Fossil Cr., Pueblo Res., Colorado R. SP
☐ Long-tailed Duck	Winter	Statewide	Rivers, lakes	Low	Denver South Platte
☐ Bufflehead	Summer	NW - Park Range	Ponds in conifer forests	Low	
	Winter	Statewide	Lakes	Good	
☐ Common Goldeneye	Winter	Statewide	Lakes	Good	

SPECIES	SEASON	REGION	HABITAT	LIKELI-HOOD	SPECIALTY SITES
☐Barrow's Goldeneye	Year-long	Mountains	Lakes	Fair	*Summer:* Flattops Wilderness; *Winter:* Denver South Platte, Silverthorne Sewage Pond, Blue R, Rifle Fish Hatchery, Glenwood Canyon
☐Hooded Merganser	Year-long	Statewide	Lakes, streams; more in winter	Good	Denver South Platte, Wheat Ridge Greenbelt, Fountain Cr., Lathrop; very scarce in summer
☐Common Merganser	Year-long	Statewide	Rivers, lakes	Good	*Summer:* mountains and west
☐Red-breasted Merganser	Migration	Statewide	Lakes	Fair	
☐Ruddy Duck	Summer	Statewide	Lakes	Fair	Scarce during breeding season
☐Chukar	Year-long	West edge of state	Dry, rocky desert shrubland	Fair	Brewster Ridge
☐Ring-necked Pheasant	Year-long	Plains	Ag	Good	
☐Greater Sage-Grouse	Year-long	Western Plateau, NW	Sagebrush	Fair	Road 80, North Park
☐Gunnison Sage-Grouse	Year-long	Gunnison, SW	Sagebrush	Good	Gunnison lek
☐White-tailed Ptarmigan	Year-long	Mountains	Alpine	Fair	RMNP, Guanella Pass
☐Dusky (formerly Blue) Grouse	Year-long	Mountains	Aspen, conifers	Fair	RMNP, White Ranch, Black Canyon, Grand Mesa, Uncompahgre Plat.
☐Sharp-tailed Grouse	Year-long	NW	Shrubland, grassland	Fair	20-mile Road
☐Greater Prairie-Chicken	Year-long	Sandhills, NE corner	Sandsage, grassland	Fair	Wray
☐Lesser Prairie-Chicken	Year-long	SE	Grassland, sandsage	Fair	Campo lek
☐Wild Turkey	Year-long	Statewide	Pine/oak woodlands, lowland riparian	Fair	
☐Northern Bobwhite	Year-long	Plains	Riparian	Good	
☐Scaled Quail	Year-long	SE	Sandsage, grassland	Good	Two Buttes, Cottonwood Canyon, Pueblo Res., Cañon City
☐Gambel's Quail	Year-long	Western Plateau, San Juan Basin	Riparian	Fair	Connected Lakes
☐Pacific Loon	Fall	Front Range	Lakes	Low	
☐Common Loon	Fall	Statewide	Lakes	Good	
☐Pied-billed Grebe	Year-long	Statewide	Wetlands, lakes	Good	
☐Horned Grebe	Migration	Plains	Lakes	Fair	

SPECIES	SEASON	REGION	HABITAT	LIKELI-HOOD	SPECIALTY SITES
☐Eared Grebe	Summer	SE, North Park	Lakes	Good	*Summer:* North Park, Holbrook
	Migration	Statewide	Lakes	Good	
☐Western Grebe	Summer	Plains, mountain parks (local)	Lakes	Good	Barr, Fruitgrowers, Sullenburger
	Migration	Statewide	Lakes	Good	Mainly east of mountains
☐Clark's Grebe	Summer	Plains	Lakes	Good	Front Range, Rocky Ford SWAs, SLV
	Migration	Statewide	Lakes	Fair	Mainly east of mountains
☐American White Pelican	Summer	Plains, mountain parks (local)	Lakes	High	
☐Double-crested Cormorant	Summer	Plains, West Slope	Lakes	High	Plains, North Park, Fruitgrowers
☐American Bittern	Summer	Plains, SLV	Wetlands	Low	
☐Great Blue Heron	Year-long	Statewide	Wetlands, riparian	High	
☐Great Egret	Summer	Plains, SLV	Wetlands, riparian	Low	Walden/Sawhill, Barr, SLV
☐Snowy Egret	Summer	N. Front Range, SLV	Wetlands	Fair	Barr, SLV
☐Cattle Egret	Summer	N. Front Range, SLV	Pastures, riparian	Low	Lower Latham
☐Green Heron	Summer	Front Range, plains rivers	Riparian	Low	Rocky Ford SWA, Poudre, Denver South Platte
☐Black-crowned Night-Heron	Year-long	Statewide	Wetlands, riparian	Good	*Winter:* scarce except Denver S. Platte
☐White-faced Ibis	Migration	Statewide	Wetlands	Good	*Summer:* SLV
☐Turkey Vulture	Summer	Statewide	Canyon/cliffs	High	SE, Fruitgrowers, SLV, Pastorius, mountain parks
☐Osprey	Summer	Statewide	Lakes, rivers	Good	Breeding: west of I-25
☐Mississippi Kite	Summer	SE	Riparian, urban	Good	Arkansas Valley, Pueblo to state line; Cottonwood/Carrizo
☐Bald Eagle	Year-long	Statewide	Riparian, lakes	Good	
☐Northern Harrier	Year-long	Statewide	Wetlands, grassland	High	
☐Sharp-shinned Hawk	Year-long	Statewide	Conifers, aspen	Fair	Arkansas Valley, lower Colorado R. valley
	Winter	Statewide	Woodlands, urban	Fair	
☐Cooper's Hawk	Year-long	Statewide	Woodlands	Fair	
	Winter	South half	Woodlands, urban	Fair	
☐Northern Goshawk	Year-long	Mountains	Conifers, aspen	Low	RMNP, Central Rockies, NW, San Juan Basin
☐Broad-winged Hawk	Migration	Plains	Riparian	Fair	Dinosaur Ridge, Chatfield/Waterton, Boulder Cr., Poudre R., Fountain Cr., Cañon City Riverwalk, Valco Ponds

SPECIES	SEASON	REGION	HABITAT	LIKELI-HOOD	SPECIALTY SITES
☐ Swainson's Hawk	Summer	Statewide	Riparian, grassland	High	Pawnee, Bonny, Fossil Cr., Barr, Fountain Cr., Two Buttes, Steamboat Lake, Gunnison, SLV
☐ Red-tailed Hawk	Year-long	Statewide	Plains to timberline	High	
☐ Ferruginous Hawk	Year-long	Plains, NW	Grassland, semi-desert shrubland	Fair	Pawnee, Rocky Mtn. Arsenal NWR, Dinosaur Ridge, Big Johnson, SLV
☐ Rough-legged Hawk	Winter	Plains, West Slope	Grassland	Good	Pawnee, Fossil Cr., SLV
☐ Golden Eagle	Summer	Statewide	Cliffs in any habitat	Fair	Pawnee, Raven Lane, Roxborough, Aiken Canyon, North Park, Yampa R. Preserve, Browns Park, Ute Pass, Uncompahgre Plat.
☐ American Kestrel	Year-long	Statewide	Plains to 8,000 ft.	High	
☐ Merlin	Winter	Statewide	Grassland, riparian edge	Fair	Pawnee, Bonny, Tamarack, Raven Lane, Pueblo Res., Colorado R. SP
☐ Peregrine Falcon	Summer	Mountains and west	Cliffs in any habitat	Low	
	Migration	Statewide	Various, esp. lakes	Low	
☐ Prairie Falcon	Summer	Statewide	Cliffs in various habitats	Fair	Mesa Trail, Castlewood, Garden of the Gods, Sheep Mtn.
	Winter	Plains	Open habitats	Good	Jumbo, Pawnee, Raven Lane
☐ Virginia Rail	Year-long	Statewide	Wetlands	Fair	
☐ Sora	Summer	Statewide	Wetlands	Fair	Mainly Front Range and west in spring and summer; fall migrant on plains.
☐ American Coot	Year-long	Statewide	Lakes, wetlands	High	
☐ Sandhill Crane	Migration, summer	SLV, western mountains	Wetlands, ag	High	*Migration:* Monte Vista NWR, Fruitgrowers; *Summer:* Steamboat Lake
☐ Black-bellied Plover	Migration	Plains	Shorelines	Low	
☐ Snowy Plover	Summer	SE, SLV	Shorelines	Low	Adobe Cr., Cheraw, Great Plains Res., San Luis L.
☐ Semipalmated Plover	Migration	Plains, West Slope	Shorelines	Low	
☐ Piping Plover	Summer	SE	Shorelines	Fair	John Martin, Great Plains Res., Adobe Cr.
☐ Killdeer	Year-long	Statewide	Shorelines, wetlands, grassland	High	
☐ Mountain Plover	Summer	Plains, south	Short-grass prairie	Fair	Pawnee, Adobe Cr., Raven Lane

SPECIES	SEASON	REGION	HABITAT	LIKELI-HOOD	SPECIALTY SITES
☐Black-necked Stilt	Summer	Plains, mountain parks	Wetlands, shorelines	Fair	Meredith, Cheraw, Lower Latham
☐American Avocet	Summer	Statewide	Wetlands, shorelines	Good	
☐Greater Yellowlegs	Migration	Statewide	Shorelines	Good	
☐Lesser Yellowlegs	Migration	Statewide	Shorelines	Good	
☐Solitary Sandpiper	Migration	Plains	Shorelines	Good	
☐Willet	Summer	North Park, Fruitgrowers	Shorelines	Fair	*Migrant:* widespread though scarce, statewide; *Summer:* Walden Res., Arapaho NWR, Lake John
☐Spotted Sandpiper	Summer	Statewide	Wetlands, shorelines	Good	
☐Upland Sandpiper	Summer	NE corner	Tall grass-land, wet meadows	Fair	Highway 138 north of Tamarack
☐Long-billed Curlew	Summer	Plains	Short-grass prairie	Fair	Cottonwood/Carrizo, Adobe Cr., Great Plains Res., E Unit Comanche Natl Grass-land, Walden Res.
☐Marbled Godwit	Migration	Plains	Shorelines	Fair	
☐Sanderling	Migration	Plains	Shorelines	Low	
☐Semipalmated Sandpiper	Migration	Plains	Shorelines	Fair	
☐Western Sandpiper	Migration	Statewide	Shorelines	Fair	
☐Least Sandpiper	Migration	Statewide	Shorelines	Good	
☐White-rumped Sandpiper	Spring	Plains	Shorelines	Fair	Mid-May to early June
☐Baird's Sandpiper	Migration	Statewide	Shorelines	Good	
☐Pectoral Sandpiper	Migration (esp. fall)	Plains	Shorelines	Fair	Prewitt, Jackson, John Martin, Great Plains Res.
☐Stilt Sandpiper	Migration	Plains	Shorelines	Fair	
☐Long-billed Dowitcher	Migration	Statewide	Shorelines	Good	
☐Wilson's Snipe	Year-long	Statewide	Wetlands	Fair	
☐Wilson's Phalarope	Summer	Statewide	Wetlands, shorelines	Good	*Summer:* North Park, SLV
☐Red-necked Phalarope	Migration	Statewide	Shorelines	Fair	
☐Franklin's Gull	Summer	North Park	Lakes	Good	North Park
	Migration	Statewide	Lakes, rural/urban, ag	High	More in fall, many more on plains
☐Bonaparte's Gull	Fall	Front Range	Lakes	Fair	
☐Ring-billed Gull	Year-long	Statewide	Lakes	High	
☐California Gull	Summer	Statewide	Lakes	High	
☐Herring Gull	Winter	Plains (esp. east)	Lakes	Good	
☐Thayer's Gull	Winter	Front Range, NE	Lakes	Low	

SPECIES	SEASON	REGION	HABITAT	LIKELI-HOOD	SPECIALTY SITES
☐Lesser Black-backed Gull	Fall, winter	Front Range	Lakes	Low	Larimer County, Cherry Cr. Res., Pueblo Res.
☐Glaucous Gull	Winter	Edge of mountains, NE	Lakes	Low	Larimer County, Cherry Cr. Res., Pueblo Res.
☐Great Black-backed Gull	Fall, winter	Front Range	Lakes	Low	Pueblo Res., Larimer County
☐Sabine's Gull	Fall	Front Range	Lakes	Low	
☐Caspian Tern	Summer	Front Range	Riparian, lakes	Low	Poudre, Denver South Platte
☐Common Tern	Migration	Plains	Lakes	Low	
☐Forster's Tern	Summer	Statewide	Wetlands	Fair	
☐Least Tern	Summer	Lower Arkansas	Lakes	Fair	John Martin, Great Plains Res., Adobe Cr.
☐Black Tern	Summer	Statewide	Lakes	Fair	Jumbo, Prewitt, Ramah, Holbrook, Cheraw, Adobe Cr., Monte Vista and Alamosa NWRs
☐Rock Pigeon	Year-long	Statewide	Urban/rural, ag, cliffs	High	
☐Band-tailed Pigeon	Summer	Transition	Ponderosa, scrub oak	Low	Junction Cr., Hermosa Cr., Durango, Glenwood Canyon
☐Eurasian Collared-Dove	Year-long	Statewide	Urban/rural	Good	Spreading
☐White-winged Dove	Year-long	Statewide	Urban/rural	Low	SW corner, town of Rocky Ford; spreading
☐Mourning Dove	Summer	Statewide	Urban/rural, riparian	High	
	Winter	SE, Western Slope	Urban/rural, riparian	Good	
☐Black-billed Cuckoo	Summer	NE corner	Riparian	Low	Tamarack
☐Yellow-billed Cuckoo	Summer	Plains	Riparian	Low	Tamarack, Bonny, Cotton-wood/Carrizo, Two Buttes
☐Greater Road-runner	Year-long	SE	P/J, cactus grassland	Fair	John Martin, Two Buttes, Cottonwood/Carrizo, Cañon City
☐Barn Owl	Year-long	Plains, western valleys	Cliffs, riparian, rural	Low	
☐Flammulated Owl	Summer	Mountains	Ponderosa, aspen	Low	Rist, Mesa Trail, RMNP, Golden Gate, Uncompahgre Plat.
☐Western Screech-Owl	Year-long	Western and SE riparian corridors	Riparian, urban/rural	Low	Cottonwood/Carrizo, lower Arkansas Valley, Pueblo, Colorado R. SP, Delta
☐Eastern Screech-Owl	Year-long	NE, N. Front Range	Riparian, urban/rural	Low	Bonny, Tamarack, Messex, Wheat Ridge
☐Great Horned Owl	Year-long	Statewide	Ubiquitous	Good	
☐Northern Pygmy-Owl	Year-long	Mountains	Conifers, aspen	Low	

SPECIES	SEASON	REGION	HABITAT	LIKELI-HOOD	SPECIALTY SITES
☐Burrowing Owl	Summer	Plains, Colorado R. valley	Short-grass prairie with prairie dog towns	Good	Tamarack, Pawnee, Bonny, Cottonwood/Carrizo, Larimer County Res., Rocky Mtn. Arsenal NWR, Arapaho NWR
☐Long-eared Owl	Year-long	Plains, mountains	Dense shrub-land and riparian	Low	
☐Short-eared Owl	Year-long	Statewide	Grassland, wetlands	Low	Monte Vista NWR, Larimer County Res.
☐Boreal Owl	Year-long	Mountains	Spruce/fir	Low	Cameron Pass, RMNP, Rabbit Ears Pass, Grand Mesa
☐Northern Saw-whet Owl	Year-long	Transition	Conifers	Low	Rist, Mesa Trail, RMNP, Castlewood, Uncompahgre Plat., Mesa Verde
☐Common Nighthawk	Summer	Statewide	Grassland and shrub-land up to 8,000 ft.	Good	
☐Common Poorwill	Summer	Transition	Scrub oak, ponderosa, P/J	Fair	Mesa Trail, Castlewood, Cottonwood/Carrizo, Thompson Cr., Zapata Falls, Navajo SP, Mesa Verde, Lone Dome
☐Black Swift	Summer	Mountains	Waterfalls	Good	Box Cañon, Hanging Lake, Treasure Falls, Zapata Falls
☐Chimney Swift	Summer	Plains	Urban	Good	
☐White-throated Swift	Summer	Canyons, transition	Cliffs	High	Red Rocks Park, Roxborough, Castlewood, Garden of the Gods, Dinosaur Natl Mon., Colorado Natl Mon., Uncompahgre Plat., Black Canyon, Box Cañon, Mesa Verde, Lone Dome
☐Black-chinned Hummingbird	Summer	Transition	P/J, riparian	Good	Cottonwood/Carrizo, Pueblo City Park, Cañon City, Colorado Natl Mon., Durango, Navajo SP, Mesa Verde
☐Calliope Hummingbird	Summer	Front Range, mountains	Riparian, moist meadows	Fair	Fawnbrook Inn, Steamboat Springs, Durango
☐Broad-tailed Hummingbird	Summer	Mountains	Aspen, riparian, montane meadows, conifers	High	
☐Rufous Hummingbird	July to Sept.	Mountains	Montane meadows, riparian, conifers	High	
☐Belted Kingfisher	Year-long	Plains, transition	Streams, lakes	High	

SPECIES	SEASON	REGION	HABITAT	LIKELI-HOOD	SPECIALTY SITES
☐Lewis's Woodpecker	Year-long	Front Range, southern tier	Ponderosa, riparian	Good	Cottonwood/Carrizo, Turkey Cr. Ranch, Buena Vista, Delta Confluence Park, Pagosa Springs, Navajo SP
☐Red-headed Woodpecker	Summer	Plains	Riparian, rural	High	Tamarack, Messex, Flagler, Bonny, John Martin
☐Acorn Woodpecker	Year-long	Durango	Ponderosa/ scrub oak	Fair	Durango
☐Red-bellied Woodpecker	Year-long	East edge of plains	Riparian	Good	Tamarack, Bonny, L. Hasty, Lamar (winter)
☐Williamson's Sapsucker	Summer	Mountains	Ponderosa, aspen	Fair	Golden Gate, Genesee, RMNP, Aspen, Uncompahgre Plat., Pagosa Springs
☐Red-naped Sapsucker	Summer	Mountains	Aspen, willow carrs	High	
☐Ladder-backed Woodpecker	Year-long	SE	P/J, riparian, shrubland	Fair	Two Buttes, Cottonwood/ Carrizo
☐Downy Woodpecker	Year-long	Plains, transition	Riparian, aspen	High	
☐Hairy Woodpecker	Year-long	Mountains	Conifers, aspen	High	
☐American Three-toed Woodpecker	Year-long	Mountains	Dying conifers, esp. spruce/fir	Fair	RMNP, Red Sandstone Road, Ute Pass, Grand Mesa
☐Northern Flicker	Year-long	Statewide	Any place with trees	High	
☐Olive-sided Flycatcher	Summer	Mountains	Spruce/fir	Good	
☐Western Wood-Pewee	Summer	Statewide	Forests, riparian	High	Barr, Chatfield/Waterton, mountains
☐Willow Flycatcher	Summer	Mountains, western plateau	Willow carrs	Fair	Steamboat Lake, Cata-mount, Red Sandstone Road, E. Brush Cr., Castle Cr., Alamosa, Escalante, Piedra Picnic Area
☐Least Flycatcher	Summer	Plains	Riparian	Low	Chatfield/Waterton
	Migration	Plains	Riparian	Fair	Tamarack, Bonny, Fountain Creek, Lamar, Two Buttes
☐Hammond's Flycatcher	Summer	Mountains	Conifers	Good	RMNP, Golden Gate, Manitou L., Rabbit Ears, Steamboat L., Shrine Pass, Pagosa Fourmile Road, Vallecito
☐Gray Flycatcher	Summer	West Slope, upper Arkansas Valley	P/J	Good	Colorado Natl Mon., Red Canyon Park, Lathrop, Buena Vista, Durango, Mesa Verde
☐Dusky Flycatcher	Summer	Mountains	Shrubs, deciduous riparian	Good	RMNP, Golden Gate, Steam-boat L., Black Canyon

SPECIES	SEASON	REGION	HABITAT	LIKELI-HOOD	SPECIALTY SITES
☐ Cordilleran Flycatcher	Summer	Mountains	Rocky out-crops in conifer and deciduous woodlands	Good	Mesa Trail, Castlewood, Golden Gate, Bear Cr., Fish Cr. Falls, Yampa Preserve, Red Sandstone Road, Rifle Falls, Box Cañon, Lone Dome
☐ Black Phoebe	Summer	San Miguel R.	Riparian	Fair	Uncompahgre Plat. (San Miguel R.)
☐ Eastern Phoebe	Summer	SE	Moist rocky ravines	Fair	Cottonwood/Carrizo
☐ Say's Phoebe	Summer	Plains, tran-sition	Dry shrub-land, rural	Good	
☐ Ash-throated Flycatcher	Summer	West Slope, SE	P/J	Good	Cottonwood/Carrizo, Cañon City, Pueblo, Colorado Natl Mon., Brewster Ridge, Navajo SP, Mesa Verde
☐ Great Crested Flycatcher	Summer	East edge of plains	Riparian	Low	Tamarack, Bonny
☐ Cassin's Kingbird	Summer	SE, SW, Mesa Co.	P/J, riparian	Fair	SE; Highway 10 (La Junta-Walsenburg)
☐ Western Kingbird	Summer	Statewide	Riparian, shelter belts	High	
☐ Eastern Kingbird	Summer	Plains (scarce on Western Slope)	Riparian, shelter belts	High	
☐ Loggerhead Shrike	Summer	Plains, West Slope	Plains tree copses, desert shrubland	Fair	Plains, Brewster Ridge
	Winter	SE, western valleys	Riparian, shrubland	Fair	
☐ Northern Shrike	Winter	Statewide	Riparian, shrubland	Good	
☐ Bell's Vireo	Summer	NE (east edge)	Shrubby thickets	Good	Tamarack, Bonny
☐ Gray Vireo	Summer	SE, West Slope	Juniper sec-tions of P/J	Good	Colorado Natl Mon., Brewster Ridge
☐ Plumbeous Vireo	Summer	Transition	P/J, ponder-osa, riparian	Good	Rist, Mesa Trail, RMNP, Castlewood, Aiken Canyon, Colorado Natl Mon., Uncompahgre Plat.
☐ Warbling Vireo	Summer	Statewide	Aspen, riparian	High	
☐ Warbling Vireo (eastern race)	Summer	East edge of plains	Riparian	Fair	Two Buttes, Tamarack
☐ Red-eyed Vireo	Summer	Plains	Riparian	Fair	Bonny, Two Buttes, Boulder Cr., Chatfield/Waterton; more seen in migration
☐ Gray Jay	Year-long	Mountains	High-country conifers	High	Ski areas

SPECIES	SEASON	REGION	HABITAT	LIKELI-HOOD	SPECIALTY SITES
☐Steller's Jay	Year-long	Mountains	Midelevation conifers, esp. ponderosas	High	
☐Blue Jay	Year-long	Plains	Urban/rural, riparian	High	
☐Western Scrub-Jay	Year-long	Transition	P/J, scrub oak	High	
☐Pinyon Jay	Year-long	Transition	P/J	Good	Buena Vista, Colorado Natl Mon.
☐Clark's Nutcracker	Year-long	Mountains	Conifers	Good	RMNP (Many Parks, Rainbow Curves)
☐Black-billed Magpie	Year-long	Statewide	Rural/urban, riparian	High	
☐American Crow	Year-long	Statewide	Rural/urban, agricultural	High	
☐Chihuahuan Raven	Year-long	SE	Grassland	Fair	Raven Lane, Cottonwood/Carrizo
☐Common Raven	Year-long	Statewide except plains	Canyons, mountains	High	
☐Horned Lark	Year-long	Plains	Prairie	High	
	Summer	Mountain parks, alpine, West Slope	Short-grass prairie	Good	
☐Purple Martin	Summer	West Slope	Aspen	Fair	McClure Pass, Road 80, Steamboat Lake, Uncompahgre Plat.
Swallows (6 species)	Migration	Statewide	Lowland riparian	High	Mixed flocks; feed over lakes in bad weather
☐Tree Swallow	Summer	Mountains and west edge of plains	Aspen	High	
☐Violet-green Swallow	Summer	Mountains	Cliffs, aspen	High	
☐Northern Rough-winged Swallow	Summer	Statewide	Riparian	Good	
☐Bank Swallow	Summer	Statewide	Riparian	Fair	
☐Cliff Swallow	Summer	Statewide	Cliff, bridges in any habitat	High	Intersection bird in metro Denver
☐Barn Swallow	Summer	Statewide	Rural/urban, bridges	High	Intersection bird in metro Denver
☐Black-capped Chickadee	Year-long	Statewide	Riparian, aspen	High	
☐Mountain Chickadee	Year-long	Mountains	Conifers	High	
☐Juniper Titmouse	Year-long	SE, West Slope	P/J	Good	Cottonwood/Carrizo, Red Canyon, Great Sand Dunes, Colorado Natl Mon., Mesa Verde
☐Bushtit	Year-long	Transition	P/J, shrub-land	Good	

SPECIES	SEASON	REGION	HABITAT	LIKELI-HOOD	SPECIALTY SITES
☐Red-breasted Nuthatch	Year-long	Mountains	Conifers	Good	
☐White-breasted Nuthatch	Year-long	Statewide	Conifers, aspen, riparian	High	
☐White-breasted Nuthatch (eastern race)	Year-long	East edge of plains	Riparian	Fair	Bonny, Tamarack, Lamar
☐Pygmy Nuthatch	Year-long	Mountains	Ponderosa	High	Rist, Genesee, RMNP, Mesa Trail, Manitou
☐Brown Creeper	Year-long	Mountains	Conifers	Good	*Winter:* also plains riparian
☐Rock Wren	Summer	Statewide	Rocky outcrops, rock dams and dirt arroyos on plains	Good	
☐Canyon Wren	Year-long	Transition	Cliffs	Good	Castlewood, Dinosaur, Colorado Natl Mon., Black Canyon, Mesa Verde
☐Bewick's Wren	Year-long	SE, West Slope	P/J	Good	Rocky Ford, Cottonwood/Carrizo, Connected Lakes, Delta, Navajo SP, Mesa Verde
☐House Wren	Summer	Statewide	Riparian, aspen	High	
☐Winter Wren	Winter	Front Range, plains	Streamside thickets	Low	Boulder Cr., Chatfield, Connected Lakes
☐Marsh Wren	Year-long	Statewide (local)	Wetlands	Fair	
☐American Dipper	Year-long	Mountains	Fast-flowing streams	High	Nests on streamside rocks and bridges
☐Golden-crowned Kinglet	Year-long	Mountains	Spruce/fir	Fair	Lower in winter
☐Ruby-crowned Kinglet	Summer	Mountains	High-country conifers	High	
	Winter	Western valleys	Riparian	Fair	
☐Blue-gray Gnatcatcher	Summer	Transition	Scrub oak, P/J	Good	
☐Eastern Bluebird	Year-long	East half of plains (mainly)	Riparian	Fair	Tamarack, Prewitt, Bonny, Lake Hasty
☐Western Bluebird	Summer	Transition	Ponderosa, P/J	Good	RMNP, Genesee, Castlewood, Golden Gate, Manitou Lake, Uncompahgre Plat., Pagosa Springs, Vallecito and Lemon Res., Navajo SP
☐Mountain Bluebird	Summer	Mountains	Grassland/aspen	High	
	Winter	South half	Riparian, desert	Good	Pueblo Res., Brewster Ridge

SPECIES	SEASON	REGION	HABITAT	LIKELI-HOOD	SPECIALTY SITES
☐ Townsend's Solitaire	Summer	Mountains	Conifers	Fair	
	Winter	Transition	Hillsides with junipers	Good	Castlewood Canyon, Genesee Mtn., Mt. Falcon, Lathrop, Pueblo Res., Colorado Natl Mon., Mesa Verde
☐ Veery	Summer	Mountains	Tall willow carrs	Fair	Mesa Trail, Arapaho NWR, Yampa R. Preserve, Catamount
☐ Swainson's Thrush	Summer	Mountains	Tall willow carrs with trees (spruce, cottonwood)	Fair	RMNP, Golden Gate, Steamboat Springs, Yampa R. Preserve, Summit County
	Migration	Plains	Riparian, rural	High	Mid- to late May
☐ Hermit Thrush	Summer	Mountains	Conifers, aspen	High	
☐ American Robin	Year-long	Statewide	Ubiquitous	High	
☐ Gray Catbird	Summer	Statewide	Dense riparian thickets	Fair	Dixon, Mesa Trail, Chatfield/Waterton, Turkey Cr., Yampa R. Preserve, Neversink, Lone Dome
☐ Northern Mockingbird	Summer	Plains, West Slope	P/J, rural/ urban, riparian	Good	Bonny, Holbrook, Cheraw, John Martin, Two Buttes, Brewster Ridge, Navajo SP
☐ Sage Thrasher	Summer	SLV, West Slope	Sagebrush	Good	North Park, SLV, Gunnison, Brewster Ridge, Lone Dome
☐ Brown Thrasher	Summer	Plains	Shrubby riparian, shelterbelts	Good	Bonny, Tamarack
☐ Curve-billed Thrasher	Year-long	SE	Cactus grassland	Fair	Two Buttes, Cottonwood/ Carrizo
☐ European Starling	Year-long	Statewide	Urban/rural, riparian	High	
☐ American Pipit	Summer	Alpine	Alpine grassland	High	RMNP, Mt. Evans, Guanella Pass, Loveland Pass, Shrine Ridge, Independence Pass
	Migration	Statewide	Streamside, lakes	Low	
☐ Bohemian Waxwing	Winter	Statewide	Urban/rural, riparian	Fair	Irregular; only present some years
☐ Cedar Waxwing	Summer	Transition	Riparian	Fair	
☐ Orange-crowned Warbler	Summer	West Slope mountains	Tall shrubland, aspen	Good	Fish Cr. Falls, Aspen, Glenwood Springs, Uncompahgre Plat., Black Canyon, Hermosa Cr., Lone Dome
	Migration	Plains, West Slope	Riparian, shrubland	Good	Plains and western plateau riparian
☐ Nashville Warbler	Migration	Plains, West Slope	Riparian	Low	

SPECIES	SEASON	REGION	HABITAT	LIKELI-HOOD	SPECIALTY SITES
☐Virginia's Warbler	Summer	Transition	P/J, low shrubland, scrub oak	Good	Roxborough, Castlewood, Golden Gate, Red Rocks Park, Deer Cr. Canyon, Aiken, Red Canyon, Thompson Cr., Uncompahgre Plat., Black Canyon, Pagosa Springs, Junction Cr., Mesa Verde
☐Northern Parula	Migration	Plains rivers	Riparian	Low	
☐Yellow Warbler	Summer	Plains, transition	Riparian, suburban	High	
☐Chestnut-sided Warbler	Migration	Plains rivers	Riparian	Low	A few breed in the Front Range foothills
☐Yellow-rumped Warbler	Summer	Mountains	Conifers, riparian	High	Audubon's form
	Migration	Plains, western valleys	Riparian	High	Both Audubon's and Myrtle
☐Black-throated Gray Warbler	Summer	West Slope, Arkansas Val. (Cañon City to Buena Vista)	P/J	High	Mesa Verde, Colorado Natl Mon., Black Canyon
☐Townsend's Warbler	Migration	Transition, plains	Ponderosa, riparian	Fair	Barr, Golden Gate, RMNP, Aspen, Uncompahgre Plat., Pagosa Springs
☐Grace's Warbler	Summer	San Juan Basin, Uncompahgre Plat.	Ponderosa/oak	Fair	Junction Cr., Hermosa Cr., Durango, Uncompahgre Plat.
☐Blackpoll Warbler	Migration	Plains rivers	Riparian	Low	
☐Black-and-white Warbler	Migration	Plains rivers	Riparian	Low	
☐American Redstart	Summer	Front Range, NW	Riparian	Fair	Chatfield/Waterton, Yampa R. Preserve
	Migration	Plains rivers	Riparian	Fair	
☐Ovenbird	Summer	Front Range foothills	Ponderosa/scrub oak	Fair	Deer Cr. Canyon, Bear Cr. Canyon, Rist
	Migration	Plains rivers	Riparian	Low	
☐Northern Waterthrush	Migration	Plains rivers	Riparian	Low	
☐MacGillivray's Warbler	Summer	Transition	Shrubland, aspen with shrubs	Fair	Usually moist shrubland within forest matrix or with nearby trees
☐Common Yellowthroat	Summer	Statewide	Wetlands	High	
☐Wilson's Warbler	Summer	Mountains	High-elevation willow carrs	High	
	Migration	Plains, western valleys	Riparian, shrubland, conifers	High	In spring, less common on plains

SPECIES	SEASON	REGION	HABITAT	LIKELI-HOOD	SPECIALTY SITES
☐Yellow-breasted Chat	Summer	Plains, West Slope	Riparian, shrubland	Good	Rocky Ford, Mesa Trail, Chatfield/Waterton, Fountain Cr., Tabeguache Preserve, Navajo SP, Lone Dome
☐Hepatic Tanager	Summer	SE	P/J, ponderosa	Low	Private land west of Cottonwood/Carrizo to Trinidad
☐Western Tanager	Summer	Mountains	Ponderosa, Douglas-fir	High	
☐Green-tailed Towhee	Summer	West Slope, transition	Shrubland	High	
	Migration	Plains	Riparian, shrubland	Fair	
☐Spotted Towhee	Year-long	Transition	Scrub oak, shrubland, P/J	High	Dixon, Mesa Trail, Roxborough, Red Rocks, Castlewood, Sonderman, Aiken, Great Sand Dunes, Mesa Verde
☐Canyon Towhee	Year-long	SE	P/J, dry scrubby hillsides	Good	Two Buttes, Cottonwood/Carrizo, Pueblo Res., Cañon City
☐Cassin's Sparrow	Summer	Plains	Sandsage, short-grass prairie	Good	Bonny, John Martin, Raven Lane, Two Buttes
☐Rufous-crowned Sparrow	Year-long	SE	Scrubby canyons	Good	Picture Canyon, Cottonwood/Carrizo, Tunnel Drive
☐American Tree Sparrow	Winter	Statewide (especially east)	Riparian with shrubby components, shrubland	High	
☐Chipping Sparrow	Summer	Mountains	Conifers	High	
	Migration	Plains, Transition	Riparian, shrubland, conifers	High	
☐Clay-colored Sparrow	Migration	Plains (esp. east)	Grassland	Good	Tamarack, Bonny, Great Plains Res., Two Buttes, Cottonwood/Carrizo
☐Brewer's Sparrow	Summer	Statewide (scarce in east)	Shrubland, sagebrush	High	Pawnee, North Park, NW, Gunnison, Brewster Ridge, SLV
☐Field Sparrow	Migration	Plains	Riparian, grassland	Low	
☐Vesper Sparrow	Summer	Transition	Shrubland, montane meadows	High	
☐Lark Sparrow	Summer	Plains, West Slope	Grassland with shrubby components	High	
☐Black-throated Sparrow	Summer	West Slope	Desert with scattered tall shrubs	Low	Colorado Natl Mon., Brewster Ridge
☐Sage Sparrow	Summer	West Slope, SLV	Sagebrush	Fair	

SPECIES	SEASON	REGION	HABITAT	LIKELI-HOOD	SPECIALTY SITES
☐Lark Bunting	Summer	Plains	Grassland	High	Pawnee, Bonny, Raven Lane, Two Buttes
☐Savannah Sparrow	Summer	Statewide	Grassland, wet meadows, lakeshores	Fair	
☐Grasshopper Sparrow	Summer	Plains	Grassland with tall forbs	Fair	Pawnee, Raven Lane, Mesa Trail
☐Fox Sparrow	Summer	Mountains	Tall willow carrs	Fair	RMNP, Blue R., Bailey Nest Area, Sarvis Cr., Yampa R. Preserve, E. Brush Cr., Neversink, Aspen, Uncompahgre Plat., Grand Mesa, Million Dollar Highway
☐Song Sparrow	Year-long	Statewide	Riparian, shrubland, wetlands	High	Mountains, summer only
☐Lincoln's Sparrow	Summer	Mountains	Willow carrs	High	
	Migration	Plains	Riparian, shrubland	Fair	
☐Swamp Sparrow	Winter	Plains	Wetlands	Low	
☐White-throated Sparrow	Winter	Plains	Riparian	Low	
☐Harris's Sparrow	Winter	East edge of plains	Shrubland	Low	Tamarack, Bonny
☐White-crowned Sparrow	Summer	Mountains	Willow carrs	High	
☐White-crowned (Gambel's) Sparrow	Winter	Plains	Shrubland	High	Especially southern tier
☐Dark-eyed (Gray-headed) Junco	Summer	Mountains	Conifers, aspen	High	
☐White-winged Junco	Winter	Front Range foothills	Ponderosa	Fair	
☐Other Junco forms	Winter	Statewide	Riparian, urban, shrubland	High	(Including Gray-headed)
☐McCown's Longspur	Summer	Pawnee	Short-grass prairie	Good	Pawnee
☐Lapland Longspur	Winter	Plains	Grassland, ag	Good	Plains, in flocks of Horned Larks
☐Chestnut-collared Longspur	Summer	Pawnee	Short-grass prairie	Good	Pawnee
☐Snow Bunting	Winter	NE, NW	Grassland, ag	Low	
☐Northern Cardinal	Year-long	East edge of plains	Riparian, wooded urban	Low	Tamarack, Wray
☐Rose-breasted Grosbeak	Migration	Plains	Riparian	Low	

SPECIES	SEASON	REGION	HABITAT	LIKELI-HOOD	SPECIALTY SITES
☐Black-headed Grosbeak	Summer	Transition	Riparian, conifers, montane, shrubland, scrub oak	High	
	Migration	Plains	Riparian	Fair	
☐Blue Grosbeak	Summer	Plains, West Slope	Riparian, shelterbelts	Good	Rocky Ford, Cottonwood/Carrizo, Dixon, Connected Lakes, Delta, Navajo SP
☐Lazuli Bunting	Summer	Transition	Shrubland	Good	Front Range foothills, Central Rockies, NW, San Juan Basin, Uncompahgre Plat.
☐Indigo Bunting	Summer	Plains, West Slope	Riparian, shrubland	Low	Front Range foothills, Cottonwood/Carrizo
☐Dickcissel	Summer	Plains (esp. east)	Weedy fields	Fair	
☐Bobolink	Summer	Front Range, Yampa R., White R.	Moist hay fields	Fair	Castlewood (Winkler Ranch), Carpenter Ranch
☐Red-winged Blackbird	Year-long	Statewide	Wetlands, ag	High	
☐Western Meadowlark	Year-long	Statewide	Grassland, ag	High	Fewer in winter
☐Yellow-headed Blackbird	Summer	Statewide	Wetlands	Good	Lower Latham, SLV, Fruitgrowers, Browns Park
☐Brewer's Blackbird	Summer	Mountains and west, mainly	Ag with scattered trees, meadows	High	
☐Common Grackle	Summer	Statewide	Urban/rural, riparian	High	
☐Great-tailed Grackle	Year-long	Statewide	Wetlands, rural	Fair	Fewer in winter; local and rare in winter
☐Brown-headed Cowbird	Summer	Statewide	Ubiquitous	High	
☐Orchard Oriole	Summer	Plains (esp. east)	Riparian	Good	Bonny, Rocky Ford, John Martin, Great Plains Res., Dixon
☐Baltimore Oriole	Migration	East edge of plains	Riparian	Fair	Tamarack, Bonny
☐Bullock's Oriole	Summer	Statewide	Lowland riparian	High	
☐Scott's Oriole	Summer	West edge	Edges of desert, grassland with junipers	Fair	Brewster Ridge
☐Gray-crowned Rosy-Finch	Winter	Mountains	Feeders, open hillsides	Fair	Gunnison, Fawnbrook Inn, Snowmass ski area
☐Black Rosy-Finch	Winter	Mountains	Feeders, open hillsides	Fair	Gunnison, Fawnbrook Inn, Snowmass ski area

SPECIES	SEASON	REGION	HABITAT	LIKELI-HOOD	SPECIALTY SITES
☐Brown-capped Rosy-Finch	Year-long	Mountains	*Summer:* Alpine cliffs and snow-fields; *Winter:* feeders and open hillsides	Fair	*Summer:* RMNP, Mt. Evans, Guanella Pass, *Winter:* Gunnison, Fawnbrook Inn, Snowmass ski area
☐Pine Grosbeak	Year-long	Mountains	Spruce/fir	Good	
☐Cassin's Finch	Year-long	Mountains	Conifers	Good	
☐House Finch	Year-long	Statewide	Riparian, urban/rural	High	
☐Red Crossbill	Year-long	Mountains	Conifers with good cone crops	Fair	
☐White-winged Crossbill	Year-long	Mountains	Conifers with good cone crops	Low	
☐Common Redpoll	Winter	NE (irregular)	Riparian, ag, grassland	Low	
☐Pine Siskin	Year-long	Transition, mountains	Montane meadows, conifers, shrubland	High	
	Winter	Plains	Riparian, shelterbelts	Fair	
☐Lesser Goldfinch	Summer	Transition	P/J, riparian, scrub oak	Good	Front Range foothills, Cottonwood/Carrizo, Durango, Cortez, Colorado R. SP
☐American Goldfinch	Year-long	Plains, transition	Riparian	High	
☐Evening Grosbeak	Year-long	Mountains, transition	Conifers, aspen	Fair	
☐House Sparrow	Year-long	Statewide	Urban/rural	High	

List B: A slight chance to find these birds

SPECIES	SEASON	REGION	HABITAT
☐ Brant	Migration	Front Range	Lakes
☐ Trumpeter Swan	Migration	Statewide	Lakes
☐ Tundra Swan	Migration	Statewide	Lakes
☐ Eurasian Wigeon	Winter	Statewide	Lakes
☐ Ruffed Grouse	Year-long	Private land west of Dinosaur	Shrubland
☐ Red-throated Loon	Migration	Front Range	Lakes
☐ Yellow-billed Loon	Migration	Statewide	Lakes
☐ Red-necked Grebe	Migration	Plains	Lakes
☐ Least Bittern	Summer	Plains	Cattail marshes
☐ Little Blue Heron	Migration	Plains	Shorelines
☐ Tricolored Heron	Migration	Front Range	Shorelines
☐ Glossy Ibis	Migration	Plains	Marshes, shorelines
☐ Red-shouldered Hawk	Migration	Plains	Riparian
☐ Black Rail	Summer	Lower Arkansas	Cattail marshes
☐ American Golden-Plover	Migration	Plains	Shorelines
☐ Whimbrel	Spring	·Plains	Shorelines
☐ Hudsonian Godwit	Migration	Plains	Shorelines
☐ Ruddy Turnstone	Migration	Plains	Shorelines
☐ Red Knot	Migration	Plains	Shorelines
☐ Dunlin	Migration	Plains	Shorelines
☐ Buff-breasted Sandpiper	Migration	Plains	Shorelines
☐ Short-billed Dowitcher	Migration	Plains	Shorelines
☐ Red Phalarope	Migration	Plains	Shorelines
☐ Pomarine Jaeger	Migration	Plains	Lakes, shorelines
☐ Parasitic Jaeger	Migration	Plains	Lakes, shorelines
☐ Long-tailed Jaeger	Migration	Plains	Lakes, shorelines
☐ Laughing Gull	Migration	Front Range	Lakes, shorelines
☐ Little Gull	Migration	Plains	Lakes, shorelines
☐ Mew Gull	Winter	Front Range	Lakes, shorelines
☐ Glaucous-winged Gull	Migration	Front Range	Lakes, shorelines
☐ Black-legged Kittiwake	Migration	Front Range	Lakes, shorelines
☐ Arctic Tern	Migration	SE	Lakes, shorelines
☐ Inca Dove	Year-long	Lamar, Rocky Ford	Riparian
☐ Snowy Owl	Winter	Plains	Grassland
☐ Spotted Owl	Year-long	Transition	Wooded canyon
☐ Lesser Nighthawk	Summer	SE	Grassland
☐ Yellow-bellied Sapsucker	Winter	Front Range	Urban
☐ Eastern Wood-Pewee	Migration	Plains	Riparian
☐ Alder Flycatcher	Migration	Plains	Riparian
☐ Vermilion Flycatcher	Summer	Plains	Riparian
☐ Scissor-tailed Flycatcher	Summer	SE	Riparian
☐ White-eyed Vireo	Migration	Plains	Riparian
☐ Yellow-throated Vireo	Migration	Plains	Riparian
☐ Cassin's Vireo	Migration	Statewide	Riparian
☐ Blue-headed Vireo	Migration	Plains	Riparian

SPECIES	SEASON	REGION	HABITAT
☐ Philadelphia Vireo	Migration	Plains	Riparian
☐ Carolina Wren	Year-long	Plains	Riparian shrubland
☐ Sedge Wren	Migration	Plains	Cattail marshes
☐ Gray-cheeked Thrush	Migration	Plains	Riparian
☐ Wood Thrush	Migration	Plains	Riparian
☐ Varied Thrush	Winter	Statewide	Riparian
☐ Sprague's Pipit	Migration	NE	Grassland
☐ Blue-winged Warbler	Migration	Plains	Riparian
☐ Golden-winged Warbler	Migration	Plains	Riparian
☐ Tennessee Warbler	Migration	Plains	Riparian
☐ Lucy's Warbler	Summer	SW - Montezuma County	Riparian
☐ Magnolia Warbler	Migration	Plains	Riparian
☐ Cape May Warbler	Migration	Plains	Riparian
☐ Black-throated Blue Warbler	Migration	Plains	Riparian
☐ Black-throated Green Warbler	Migration	Plains	Riparian
☐ Hermit Warbler	Migration	Plains	Riparian
☐ Blackburnian Warbler	Migration	Plains	Riparian
☐ Yellow-throated Warbler	Migration	Plains	Riparian
☐ Pine Warbler	Winter	Front Range	Conifers
☐ Prairie Warbler	Migration	Plains	Riparian
☐ Palm Warbler	Migration	Plains	Riparian
☐ Bay-breasted Warbler	Migration	Plains	Riparian
☐ Prothonotary Warbler	Migration	Plains	Riparian
☐ Worm-eating Warbler	Migration	Plains	Riparian
☐ Louisiana Waterthrush	Migration	Plains	Riparian
☐ Kentucky Warbler	Migration	Front Range	Riparian
☐ Mourning Warbler	Migration	Plains	Riparian
☐ Hooded Warbler	Migration	Statewide	Riparian
☐ Canada Warbler	Migration	Plains	Riparian
☐ Summer Tanager	Migration	Plains	Riparian
☐ Scarlet Tanager	Migration	Plains	Riparian
☐ Eastern Towhee	Year-long	Plains	Riparian shrubland
☐ Baird's Sparrow	Migration	Plains	Grassland
☐ Golden-crowned Sparrow	Migration	Transition	Shrubland
☐ Painted Bunting	Summer	SE	Shrubland
☐ Eastern Meadowlark	Summer	Plains	Grassland
☐ Rusty Blackbird	Winter	Statewide	Riparian
☐ Purple Finch	Winter	Statewide	Woodland

List C: Fewer than 20 state records

- ☐ Black-bellied Whistling-Duck
- ☐ Fulvous Whistling-Duck
- ☐ American Black Duck
- ☐ Garganey
- ☐ Tufted Duck
- ☐ Harlequin Duck
- ☐ Arctic Loon
- ☐ Brown Pelican
- ☐ Neotropic Cormorant
- ☐ Anhinga
- ☐ Magnificent Frigatebird
- ☐ Reddish Egret
- ☐ Yellow-crowned Night-Heron
- ☐ White Ibis
- ☐ Roseate Spoonbill
- ☐ Wood Stork
- ☐ Black Vulture
- ☐ Swallow-tailed Kite
- ☐ Common Black-Hawk
- ☐ Zone-tailed Hawk
- ☐ Harris's Hawk
- ☐ Crested Caracara
- ☐ Gyrfalcon
- ☐ Yellow Rail
- ☐ King Rail
- ☐ Purple Gallinule
- ☐ Common Moorhen
- ☐ Whooping Crane
- ☐ Eskimo Curlew
- ☐ Sharp-tailed Sandpiper
- ☐ Curlew Sandpiper
- ☐ Ruff
- ☐ American Woodcock
- ☐ Black-headed Gull
- ☐ Iceland Gull
- ☐ Slaty-backed Gull
- ☐ Kelp Gull

- ☐ Ross's Gull
- ☐ Ivory Gull
- ☐ Royal Tern
- ☐ Black Skimmer
- ☐ Long-tailed Murrelet
- ☐ Ancient Murrelet
- ☐ Common Ground-Dove
- ☐ Groove-billed Ani
- ☐ Barred Owl
- ☐ Whip-poor-will
- ☐ Green Violet-ear
- ☐ Broad-billed Hummingbird
- ☐ White-eared Hummingbird
- ☐ Blue-throated Hummingbird
- ☐ Magnificent Hummingbird
- ☐ Ruby-throated Hummingbird
- ☐ Anna's Hummingbird
- ☐ Costa's Hummingbird
- ☐ Buff-breasted Flycatcher
- ☐ Dusky-capped Flycatcher
- ☐ Sulphur-bellied Flycatcher
- ☐ Thick-billed Kingbird
- ☐ Long-billed Thrasher
- ☐ Bendire's Thrasher
- ☐ Phainopepla
- ☐ Tropical Parula
- ☐ Cerulean Warbler
- ☐ Swainson's Warbler
- ☐ Connecticut Warbler
- ☐ Red-faced Warbler
- ☐ Painted Redstart
- ☐ Henslow's Sparrow
- ☐ Le Conte's Sparrow
- ☐ Nelson's Sharp-tailed Sparrow
- ☐ Pyrrhuloxia
- ☐ Bronzed Cowbird
- ☐ Hooded Oriole*
- ☐ Brambling

*Subject to review by the Colorado Records Committee.

Appendix C: Birding Resources

Road Conditions
Colorado Department of Transportation
(303) 639–1111 (in-state toll-free: 877–315–ROAD)
www.cotrip.org

Bird-finding resources
Cobirds, an e-mail listserv for the discussion of Colorado birds managed by
Colorado Field Ornithologists: http://cfo-link.org. To read the archives go to
http://lists.cfo-link.org/read/?forum=cobirds.

Colorado Birding Trail. Go to this Web site to find birding sites in southeastern
Colorado, sites listed in this guide as well as many others, including some private
ranches: www.coloradobirdingtrail.com.

Western Slope birds, an e-mail listserv for discussion of birds in western Colorado. To subscribe, send a blank e-mail to: wsbn-subscribe@yahoogroups.com.

Rare-bird alert: (720) 274–BIRD (720–274–2473).

Reference Books and Web Sites
Birds of Colorado. Bailey and Niedrach. Denver: Denver Museum of Natural His-
tory, 1965. (Out of print.)
Birds of Western Colorado Plateau and Mesa Country. Righter, Levad, Dexter, and
Potter. Grand Junction: Grand Valley Audubon Society, 2004.
Colorado Birding Society. Web site with recent observations, birding locations,
and a calendar of trips: http://home.att.net/~birdertoo.
Colorado Birds. Andrews and Righter. Denver: Denver Museum of Natural His-
tory, 1992.
Colorado Breeding Bird Atlas. Kingery, ed. Denver: Colorado Bird Atlas Partner-
ship and Colorado Division of Wildlife, 1998. (Out of print.)
Colorado County Birding. Pieplow and Spencer. This Web site lists over 900
bird-watching sites: www.coloradocountybirding.com.
Colorado Wildlife Viewing Guide. Young. Helena, Mont.: Falcon Press, 1999.

Colorado Bird Clubs and Organizations
Aiken Audubon Society
6660 Delmonico Drive
Suite D-195
Colorado Springs, CO 80919-1856
aikenaudubonsociety@aikenaudubonsociety.org
www.aikenaudubonsociety.org

Arkansas Valley Audubon Society
P.O. Box 11187
Pueblo, CO 81001
www.socobirds.org

Audubon Colorado (National Audubon Society)
1966 13th Street
Suite 230
Boulder, CO 80302
(303) 415–0130
www.auduboncolorado.org

Audubon Society of Greater Denver
9308 South Wadsworth Boulevard
Littleton, CO 80128
(303) 973–9530
info@denveraudubon.org
www.denveraudubon.org

Black Canyon Audubon Society
P.O. Box 1371
Paonia, CO 81428-1371
www.western.edu/audubon

Boulder County Audubon Society
P.O. Box 2081
Boulder, CO 80306
info@boulderaudubon.org
www.boulderaudubon.org

Colorado Field Ornithologists
P.O. Box 481
Lyons, CO 80540
www.cfo-link.org

Denver Field Ornithologists
Zoology Department
Denver Museum of Natural History
2001 Colorado Boulevard
Denver, CO 80205
www.dfobirders.org

Evergreen Naturalists Audubon Society
P.O. Box 523
Evergreen, CO 80437
(303) 679–0661
info@evergreen-naturalists.org
www.dipper.org

Fort Collins Audubon Society
P.O. Box 271968
Fort Collins, CO 80527-1968
www.fortnet.org/Audubon

Grand Valley Audubon Society
P.O. Box 1211
Grand Junction, CO 81502
(970) 241–4670
question@audubongv.org
www.audubongv.org

Platte & Prairie Audubon Society
30 South Fremont Avenue
Johnstown, CO 80534

Roaring Fork Audubon Society
P.O. Box 1192
Carbondale, CO 81623

San Juan Audubon Society
P.O. Box 2716
Durango, CO 81302

Regional and National Bird Organizations
American Birding Association
P.O. Box 6599
Colorado Springs, CO 80934-6599
(719) 578–9703, (800) 850–2473
member@aba.org
www.americanbirding.org

Rocky Mountain Bird Observatory
14500 Lark Bunting Lane
Brighton, CO 80603-8311
(303) 659–4348
www.rmbo.org

Appendix D: Bibliography

Gould, Patrick J., Jeff J. Jones, and David M. Elwonger. *Birds of Trout Creek*. http://troutcreekstudy.jonestc.com/Birds-of-Trout-Creek.pdf, 2005.

Griffiths, Thomas M. *San Juan Country*. Boulder: Pruett Publishing, 1984.

Jones, Stephen R., and Ruth Carol Cushman. *Colorado Nature Almanac*. Boulder: Pruett Publishing, 1998.

Kingery, Hugh E., ed. *Colorado Breeding Bird Atlas*. Denver: Colorado Bird Atlas Partnership and Colorado Division of Wildlife, 1998.

Mutel, Cornelia Fleischer, and John C. Emerick. *From Grassland to Glacier*. Boulder: Johnson Books, 1992.

Parsons, Eugene. *A Guidebook to Colorado*. Boston: Little Brown, 1911.

Taylor, Ralph C. *Colorado South of the Border*. Denver: Sage Books, 1963.

Whittle, C. L. Miscellaneous bird notes from Montana. Condor 24:73–76, 1922.

Index

Bird names are in **boldface** type.

A

Adobe Creek Reservoir SWA, 58–59
Aiken Canyon, 146–47
Alamosa National Wildlife Refuge, 227–29
Alfred M. Bailey Nesting Area, 195
alpine habitat, 131, 132, 192, 197, 203
alpine tundra habitat, 14–15, 280
Antero Reservoir, 141
Arapaho National Wildlife Refuge, 104, 170–71
Arkansas River Trail, 156–58
Aspen area, 212–14
Aspen Center for Environmental Science (ACES), 212
aspen habitat, 12–13, 98, 125, 176, 185, 192, 199, 201, 203, 206, 212, 215, 225, 242, 246, 260, 270, 282
Atwood SWA, 31
Audubon Nature Center, 116
Avocet, American, 62, 85, 115, 120, 149, 171, 173, 227, 231, 280

B

Barr Lake State Park, 107–9
Baseline Reservoir, 94
Bear Creek Greenbelt, 115
Bear Creek Regional Park, 140
Bear Lake, 102
Bee Lake, 81
Belmar Park, 115
Bent's Old Fort National Historic Site, 57
Big Creek Lakes, 173
Big Johnson Reservoir, 148–49
Birds: apt to be seen in Colorado, 285–301; rarely seen in Colorado, 303–4; resources, 305–7; slight chance of finding in Colorado, 301–3; and their habitats, 279–83
Bittern: American, 42, 73, 85, 90, 91, 111, 164, 187, 232, 250; **Least,** 42, 91
Black Canyon National Park, 252–53
Black Hole, 66
Blackbird: Brewer's, 56, 74, 85, 124, 125, 184, 206, 211, 260, 277, 280;

Great-tailed, 85; **Red-winged,** 42, 55, 57, 73, 74, 85, 108, 119, 125, 173, 181, 211, 228, 280; **Yellow-headed,** 57, 73, 74, 78, 85, 107, 108, 173, 181, 206, 208, 228, 250, 251, 277, 280
blackbirds, 117, 164, 231
Black-Hawk, Common, 119, 164
Blackhead Peak Road, 262
Blue Lake, 58–59, 217
Blue River Campground, 193
Bluebird: Eastern, 8, 28, 29, 31, 39, 40, 41, 43, 45, 55, 62, 155, 164; **Mountain,** 15, 16, 62, 111, 122, 124, 126, 128, 145, 147, 153, 155, 161, 164, 180, 185, 195, 197, 205, 208, 215, 217, 227, 232, 241, 243, 244, 249, 253, 262, 276, 277, 280, 281, 282; **Western,** 12, 102, 103, 122, 124, 125, 127, 128, 145, 147, 161, 163, 164, 243, 244, 260, 262, 267, 273, 277, 281
bluebirds, 13, 98, 146, 147
Bluff Overlook Drive, 229
Bobolink, 91, 124, 178, 183, 184, 208
Bobwhite, Northern, 8, 30, 31, 43
Bonny Lake State Park, 39–43
Bootleg Bottom, 125
Boulder Area, 87–89
Boulder Creek, 87
Boulder Reservoirs, 94–96
Box Cañon, 254–55
Boyd Lake, 82
Brewster Ridge, 241
Bridge Creek, 125
Browns Park NWR, 187
Buena Vista, 203–5
Buffalo Park Road, 174
Buffalo Pass, 176
Bufflehead, 177, 217, 280
Bunting: Indigo, 29, 64, 92, 123, 146, 274; **Lark,** 7, 9, 34, 35, 58, 60, 65, 66, 67, 280; **Lazuli,** 45, 62, 92, 116, 117, 120, 121, 122, 123, 128, 138, 141, 146, 162, 181, 182, 183, 184, 202, 208, 219, 245, 260, 274, 277; **Painted,** 55, 56, 66, 67, 69, 152; **Snow,** 39
Bushtit, 77, 147, 156, 159, 162, 164, 225, 236, 238, 240, 243, 249, 264, 266, 276, 281

Roxborough State Park, 121
Russell Lakes, 232

Lark, 8, 9, 39, 42, 46, 60, 66, 67, 69, 117, 141, 146, 161, 180, 215, 241, 243, 245, 274, 277, 280, 281; **Lincoln's,** 15, 45, 46, 77, 102, 117, 125, 147, 171, 174, 175, 177, 180, 182, 196, 198, 200, 204, 205, 206, 212, 244, 261, 262, 263, 267, 271, 279; **Rufous-crowned,** 9, 66, 67, 68, 69, 159; **Sage,** 17, 241, 243; **Savannah,** 45, 85, 170, 171, 173, 180, 181, 184, 193, 201, 202, 217, 227, 244, 277, 280; **Song,** 15, 73, 108, 119, 120, 125, 175, 180, 182, 193, 202, 206, 211, 212, 217, 228, 251, 261, 266, 279, 280; **Spizella,** 42; **Swamp,** 118, 145, 158; **Vesper,** 9, 16, 17, 42, 45, 66, 67, 117, 147, 161, 173, 184, 185, 208, 215, 227, 243, 274, 277, 280, 281; **White-crowned,** 9, 15, 40, 45, 77, 87, 108, 114, 117, 162, 164, 174, 175, 180, 196, 198, 200, 205, 208, 227, 238, 261, 263, 271, 277, 279; **White-throated,** 9, 29, 40, 46, 155, 164

sparrows, 9, 31, 36, 67, 73, 76, 91, 107, 108, 117, 119, 147, 150, 152, 179, 231

Spinney Mountain Reservoir, 141

Spring Park Reservoir, 217

spruce/fir habitat, 13, 83, 98, 131, 132, 140, 174, 176, 179, 185, 192, 197, 199, 201, 203, 206, 212, 215, 225, 242, 246, 260, 270, 281

Stagecoach State Park, 181–82

Standley Lake, 115

Starling, European, 108

starlings, 74

Steamboat Lake State Park, 179–80

Steamboat Springs, 176–78

Stilt, 108; **Black-necked,** 59, 85, 232

stream habitat, 176

Sullenburger Reservoir, 261

Summit County, 192–96

Swallow: Bank, 114, 146; **Barn,** 8, 57, 125, 173, 245, 274; **Cliff,** 41, 43, 65, 66, 68, 115, 124, 125, 147, 176, 182, 184, 200, 206, 243, 245, 262, 274, 277; **Northern Rough-winged,** 114, 146, 150, 151; **Rough-winged,** 43, 219, 243, 245, 266, 277; **Tree,** 108, 124, 125, 126, 147, 173, 176, 177, 200, 206, 246, 260, 263, 282; **Violet-green,** 121, 124, 125, 126, 127, 138, 177, 200, 206, 214, 217, 244, 246, 252, 255, 260, 262, 263, 267, 276, 277, 282

swallows, 13, 77, 98, 116, 117, 200, 206, 266, 273

Swan: Trumpeter, 55, 80, 141, 238; **Tundra,** 55, 141, 238

Sweetwater State Wildlife Trust Area, 63

Swift: Black, 14, 104, 215, 217, 219, 230, 231, 249, 254, 260, 262, 263, 270, 271, 272; **Chimney,** 8; **White-throated,** 36, 121, 122, 124, 128, 138, 146, 159, 188, 225, 239, 243, 244, 252, 255, 275, 276, 277

Sylvan Lake State Park, 202

T

Tabeguache Preserve, 245

Tamarack SWA, 28–29

Tanager: Hepatic, 152; **Scarlet,** 46, 119; **Summer,** 66, 119, 158; **Western,** 12, 64, 91, 98, 114, 116, 117, 118, 122, 124, 125, 138, 141, 147, 162, 176, 177, 200, 201, 202, 208, 215, 217, 225, 260, 262, 263, 267, 268, 277, 279, 281

Taylor Park, 208

Teal: Blue-winged, 85, 279; **Cinnamon,** 85, 120, 171, 172, 173, 180, 181, 182, 185, 206, 212, 245, 266, 279; **Green-winged,** 171, 180, 196, 200, 212, 266, 279

teals, 39, 40, 42, 187

Telephone Trail Cavity Nesting Habitat, 244

Tern: Arctic, 59, 63, 80; **Black,** 27, 31, 45, 59, 109, 227, 229; **Caspian,** 59, 63, 73; **Common,** 31, 59, 80, 94, 111, 266; **Forster's,** 27, 31, 59, 111, 172, 173; **Least,** 11, 45, 55, 56, 58, 59, 249, 266; **Royal,** 63

terns, 58, 63, 172, 231

Thompson Creek Road, 215

Thrasher: Brown, 8, 31, 39, 40, 42, 45, 55, 63, 64, 66, 77, 147, 150; **Curve-billed,** 9–10, 66, 67, 69; **Long-billed,** 152; **Sage,** 17, 31, 93, 153, 155, 172, 173, 208, 227, 229, 241, 243, 281

thrashers, 108

Thrush: Gray-cheeked, 55; **Hermit,** 13, 29, 45, 64, 66, 74, 77, 87, 92, 98, 126, 147, 150, 174, 175, 177, 180, 186, 192, 197, 200, 205, 238, 246, 260, 261, 262, 270, 271, 281; **Swainson's,** 9, 15, 45, 74, 77, 87, 91, 102, 104, 108, 147, 150, 176, 177, 183, 184, 192, 193,

About the Author

Author Hugh Kingery has watched birds since age thirteen and participated in myriad activities connected with his avocation. He directed the compilation of the *Colorado Breeding Bird Atlas* and edited its publication in 1998. He has served as president of the Denver Audubon Society, Denver Field Ornithologists, and The Colorado Mountain Club. He edited the *C.F.O. Journal*, published by the Colorado Field Ornithologists, for four years, and *Trail*

Hugh and Urling Kingery

and *Timberline*, the monthly magazine of the mountain club, for six years.

In 1993 one of the editors of the prestigious Birds of North America series sponsored by the American Ornithologists asked him, "What are your favorite birds?" The result: Hugh researched and wrote two monographs for the series, on Pygmy Nuthatch and American Dipper. When Colorado's first coordinator for the Breeding Bird Survey (sponsored by the U.S. Fish and Wildlife Service) wanted to retire, Hugh took on this task; within ten years the state quintupled its number of routes. The Denver Audubon Society, Boulder Audubon Society, Denver Field Ornithologists, and Colorado Field Ornithologists presented service awards to him. He conducted a twelve-year census of breeding birds in a cottonwood stand in Chatfield State Park, which led to the U.S. Army Corps of Engineers (builder of Chatfield Dam) awarding him a Civilian Service Medal—for bird-watching!

Through the Denver Audubon Society, he and his wife, Urling, who helped prepare this book, teach a class for beginning bird-watchers (twice each year since 1979) and lead a monthly bird walk for Audubon. For twelve years, he has written a column for the bimonthly Audubon newsletter called *Backyard Birds*.

Besides the *Colorado Breeding Bird Atlas*, Hugh wrote the book *The Colorado Mountain Club: 75 years of a Highly Individual Corporation* and helped his mother and Louisa Ward Arps write their lively book, *High Country Names*, an account of the names of all the geographic features in Rocky Mountain National Park.